MW00354030

The THEOLOGICAL WORDBOOK

The 200 Most Important Theological Terms
and Their Relevance for Today

OTHER BOOKS BY DONALD K. CAMPBELL

A Case for Premillennialism (coeditor)
Chafer's Systematic Theology: Abridged Edition, 2 vols. (consulting editor)
Daniel: God's Man in a Secular Society
Judges: Leaders in Crisis Times
Nehemiah: Man in Charge
Walvoord: A Tribute (editor)

OTHER BOOKS BY JOHN F. WALVOORD

Armageddon, Oil, and the Middle East Crisis
The Bible Knowledge Commentary, 2 vols. (coeditor)
The Bib Sac Reader (coeditor)
The Blessed Hope and the Tribulation
Chafer's Systematic Theology: Abridged Edition, 2 vols. (editor)
The Church in Prophecy
Daniel
End Times
The Final Drama
The Holy Spirit at Work Today
The Holy Spirit
Inspiration and Interpretation (editor)
Israel in Prophecy
Jesus Christ Our Lord
The Life of Christ Commentary (coeditor)
Major Bible Prophecies
Major Bible Themes
Matthew: Thy Kingdom Come
The Millennial Kingdom
The Nations in Prophecy
Philippians: Triumph in Christ
Prophecy Knowledge Handbook
The Rapture Question
The Return of the Lord
The Revelation of Jesus Christ
The Thessalonian Epistles
To Live Is Christ
Truth for Today
What We Believe
World Events and Prophecy

OTHER BOOKS BY JOHN A. WITMER

Immanuel

SWINDOLL
LEADERSHIP
LIBRARY

The
THEOLOGICAL
WORDBOOK

The 200 Most Important Theological Terms
and Their Relevance for Today

DON CAMPBELL · WENDELL JOHNSTON
JOHN WALVOORD · JOHN WITMER

CHARLES R. SWINDOLL, *General Editor*
ROY B. ZUCK, *Managing Editor*

WORD PUBLISHING
NASHVILLE
A Thomas Nelson Company

THE THEOLOGICAL WORDBOOK
Swindoll Leadership Library

Published in association with Dallas Theological Seminary (DTS):
General Editor: Charles Swindoll
Managing Editor: Roy B. Zuck
The theological opinions expressed by the author are not necessarily the
official position of Dallas Theological Seminary.

Library of Congress Cataloging-in-Publication Data

The Theological wordbook: 200 most important theological terms and their relevance
for today / Donald K. Campbell . . . [et al.]; Charles R. Swindoll, general editor;
Roy B. Zuck, managing editor
p.   cm.—(Swindoll leadership library)
Includes bibliographical references.
ISBN 0-8499-1381-0
1. Theology—Terminology.   2. Bible—Theology.
I. Campbell, Donald K.   II. Swindoll, Charles R.   III. Zuck, Roy B.   IV. Series
BR96.5 .T442000
00-026807
CIP

Printed in the United States of America
98 99 00 01 02 03 04 05 BVG 9 8 7 6 5 4 3 2 1

Contents

—T—

—U—

—V—

—W—

Foreword

IN THIS TREMENDOUS REFERENCE TOOL, *The Theological Wordbook,* four Dallas Theological Seminary stalwarts and theological statesmen— Donald K. Campbell, Wendell G. Johnston, John F. Walvoord, and John A. Witmer—discuss numerous terms that you will encounter as you read and study the Scriptures. These men have devoted their lives to theological education—studying and teaching the Bible and theology, and each one has served for many years as adminstrators at Dallas Seminary. You will realize the seasoned years of study these men have invested as soon as you scan the first few entries.

One of the distinctives of Dallas Theological Seminary has been our strong emphasis on theology. After all, it's our middle name! From the beginning, our theological curriculum has been based on the Scriptures. The school's founder and first president, Lewis Sperry Chafer, placed strong emphasis on a biblical theology derived from a thorough study of God's inerrant Word. This legacy has been passed down to our current authors with its appropriate subtitle, *What the Bible Says on 200 Theological Terms and Their Relevance for Today.*

Each of the two hundred terms discussed in this volume focus on what the Scriptures say on that topic. And at the end of each topic is a brief, one-sentence application, suggesting one way that doctrinal truth should impact our thoughts, attitudes, or actions. These short admonitions demonstrate that every aspect of theology is relevant to our lives.

The two hundred terms discussed in *The Theological Wordbook* cover the gamut of the Scriptures, ranging from Angels to Antichrist, from Depravity to Demons, Babylon to Baptism, and Suffering to Worship— words pertaining to all the major doctrines in God's precious Word.

Our authors have done the body of Christ an outstanding service by highlighting an emphasis on precision in theological thinking. Those of us who minister to others are indebted to them for their diligent and discerning labor.

I suggest you do what I have done. Place this volume in a special, easy-to-find spot in your personal library. You and I will be reaching for it often!

—CHARLES R. SWINDOLL
General Editor

Preface

YOU ARE READING THE BIBLE IN YOUR DEVOTIONS, and you run across a word or phrase in the Scriptures that puzzles you. For example, you read of apostasy, the laying on of hands, the Transfiguration, or firstfruits.

Or you are preparing a sermon, and you want to know what the rest of Scripture says about a certain subject, such as fasting, hope, prayer, rewards, or temptations.

Perhaps you are preparing a Bible lesson on a topic such as angels, assurance, forgiveness, the Trinity, or wisdom.

Where can you find a succinct yet thorough discussion of these and many other doctrinal topics that are mentioned in Scripture and elsewhere? *The Theological Wordbook* is the answer!

This volume gives you a concise summary of what the Bible teaches on exactly two hundred theological and biblical topics. And every essay is packed with an abundance of Bible references so that you can check the Scriptures themselves.

The Bible's doctrinal themes are far from irrelevant. And that's why each article in *The Theological Wordbook* concludes with a one-sentence application, a pithy exhortation or statement to help drive home the relevance of that theological subject to life.

The initials at the end of each article designate the person who wrote the article.

DKC—Donald K. Campbell
WGJ—Wendell G. Johnston
JAW—John A. Witmer
JFW—John F. Walvoord

These men, each one a skilled Bible expositor and theologian, are retired faculty members of Dallas Theological Seminary. Each author has contributed fifty topics in this compilation of two hundred topics.

We trust you will find this book helpful as you study—and share— God's precious Word.

—ROY B. ZUCK
Managing Editor

Aa

Abiding

IN HIS TEACHING ON ABIDING Jesus took a well-known word meaning "to dwell" or "to remain" and gave it a significance that transcends its normal use. The Greek word for abide (*menō*) occurs over one hundred times in the New Testament, with more than half of these occurrences in John's Gospel and 1 John. This word describes the unique relationship to Christ of all those who belong to Him.

Some Old Testament verses use the word *abide* or *dwell* to express a believer's relationship with God the Father. These suggest safety, rest, and a nearness to God, but they lack the dimension of the New Testament teaching on abiding in Christ. Examples include Psalms 15:1 ("LORD, who may *dwell* in your sanctuary?") and 91:1 ("He who *dwells* in the shelter of the Most High will rest in the shadow of the Almighty"; italics added).

In John 6:56 Christ first alluded to the relationship He desired for His disciples. "Whoever eats my flesh and drinks my blood remains [*menō*] in me, and I in him." The disciples found these words difficult to comprehend. Jesus explained their meaning in His Upper Room Discourse the night before He was crucified. He told them He was leaving to go back to God the Father, but that they would not understand this until He was resurrected. "On that day you will realize that I am in my Father, and you are in me, and I am in you" (14:20). Thus the relationship between the Father and the Son was both the model and the basis of the relationship believers would have with Christ (17:20–23).

Since the disciples enjoyed the physical presence of Christ during His days on the earth, the concept of abiding in Him seemed strange. How could they abide in Him when He would be leaving them? He explained that after His ascension He would abide in them through His word (15:7). The Holy Spirit, whom He would send to guide them into all truth (16:13), would teach them, reminding them of everything Jesus had taught them (14:26). They in turn could abide in Him by being obedient to His word. "If you obey my commands, you will remain [abide] in my love" (15:10). He compared this close relationship to the connection between a grapevine and its branches, an analogy they could readily understand.

Abiding in fellowship with Christ, like branches "abiding" in a vine, results in a vital prayer life. Another result from abiding in Christ is a productive spiritual life; the disciples would bear fruit just as a branch bears fruit when it is part of the vine. Although He did not identify the nature of the fruit, apparently whatever they would do while depending on Him would qualify as "fruit." In fact, because of this unique relationship they would bear "much fruit" (15:8) and do greater works than He had done (14:12).

In 1 John 2–4 the apostle John expanded on Jesus' teaching about abiding. The twenty-six references to abiding in these three chapters give evidence that this is a major theme in the epistle. Abiding in Christ affects one's conduct, for as John wrote, "Whoever claims to live [menō] in him must walk as Jesus did" (2:6). Abiding "in the light" is associated with love of other believers (2:9–11). Abiding or remaining in God's Word enables believers to overcome the evil one (2:14), and it guards them from being deceived by false teachers (2:26–27; see also 4:6). Abiding in fellowship with Christ gives confidence about the future (2:28; 4:17). Those who abide are characterized by righteous living (3:6), and the Holy Spirit's indwelling assures them that they are abiding in Christ (4:13).

There is one other possible New Testament reference to abiding in Christ. It was written by one who had also been in the Upper Room with John and Christ. Although Peter did not use the term *abiding*, there are several similarities between 2 Peter 1:1–11 and John 15:1–11. Jesus explained to His disciples that fruitfulness would result from abiding in Him (15:5), and according to Peter fruitfulness depends on possessing the qualities that characterize Christ (1 Pet. 1:8). Then Jesus told them He would abide in them through His Word (John 15:7). Peter wrote that the Lord has given us "his very great and precious promises" (that is, in His Word) so that through these promises we may share in His divine nature (2 Pet. 1:4). Jesus said obedience to His Word was the way for the disciples to abide in Him (John 15:10), and Peter said, "If you *do* these things, you will never fall" (2 Pet. 1:10, italics added). When a believer is abiding, the fruit produced will last (John 15:16), and Peter wrote that believers will receive a rich welcome into the eternal kingdom of the Lord (2 Pet. 1:11).

Conscious abiding in Christ should be the desire of every believer, and the way to abide is clearly delineated in Scripture. **—WGJ**

Nothing can be compared to the joy of abiding
in an intimate loving relationship with Jesus Christ.

Abomination

IN THE OLD TESTAMENT four Hebrew words are translated "abomination(s)," describing what is detestable, hateful, or unethical. Heathen rites of worship in Old Testament times were especially detestable to God. In the New Testament the Greek word *bdelygma* is translated "abomination" (Matt. 24:15; Mark 13:14; Rev. 17:4–5), "detestable" (Luke 16:15), and "shameful" (Rev. 21:27). It is clear that God abhors sins of all kinds, and this is a basis for divine judgment.

From a prophetic standpoint the most important expression is that of "the abomination that causes desolation," spoken of by Daniel. The first occurrence of this phrase is in Daniel 8:13, in which Daniel asked, "How long will it take for the vision to be fulfilled—the vision concerning the daily sacrifice, the rebellion that causes desolation, and the surrender of the sanctuary and of the host that will be trampled underfoot?" The phrase also occurs in Daniel 9:27; 11:31; and 12:11. The references in Daniel 8:13 and 11:31 are to the desecration of the sanctuary carried out by Antiochus Epiphanes IV, ruler of Syria from 175 to 164 B.C. He attempted to stamp out the Jewish religion and replace it with pagan worship. To that end, he built a pagan altar in 168 B.C. as a place for burnt sacrifices. Sacrifices were offered, including a sow, which was an abomination to the Jews.

The altar Antiochus IV erected was in honor of Zeus, the supreme Greek god. First and 2 Maccabees record that thousands of Jewish men, women, and children were killed in his attempt to stamp out the Jewish religion. But even before Antiochus's death by natural causes in

164 B.C., the Jewish temple had been cleansed and the Jewish sacrificial system restored. This sequence of events is described in Daniel 11:21–33, which specifically mentions the desecration of the temple and the temporary abolishing of the daily sacrifices.

Daniel 12:11 predicts, "From the time that the daily sacrifice is abolished and the abomination that causes desolation is set up, there will be 1,290 days." Most amillenarians say this was fulfilled by Antiochus Epiphanes. Premillenarians say this abomination is the same as that spoken of by Christ in Matthew 24:15. It will occur in the seven-year period of Tribulation immediately preceding the Second Coming, and will follow the pattern of Antiochus Epiphanes in the second century B.C. The abomination of Matthew 24:15 refers to the setting up of an image of the Antichrist in the Jerusalem temple, an image that the false prophet will miraculously cause to speak (Rev. 13:14–15; see also 2 Thess. 2:9). This will occur for three and a half years or forty-two months, the second half of the seven-year period indicated in Daniel 9:27 (see Rev. 13:5). —JFW

In a world of confusing and competing values believers should call detestable and abominable what God calls detestable and abominable, and love what God loves and hate what He hates.

Adam

GOD GAVE THE NAME "ADAM" to the first human being He created. The word most likely derives from the Hebrew verb "to be red" and is also related to the noun for "earth" or "ground." Besides being a proper name, the Hebrew word also means "man," "human being," or "humankind" (see Gen. 1:26–27; 2:7; 3:8). Adam is significant as the father of all humanity. Because we are all descendants of Adam, differences of skin color, culture, customs, and language are of no ultimate importance. No one race is intrinsically better than any other.

God created Adam "in his own image" (Gen. 1:27), but on a finite level. As a result people have intellect, since God is omniscient, that is, infinitely knowledgeable and wise (Ps. 139:1–6); sensibilities or emotions, because "God is love" (1 John 4:8, 16), and He feels anger (Pss. 30:5; 103:8–9) and delight (Prov. 11:1, 20); and will, since God is the sovereign Creator and Ruler of the universe (Dan. 4:34–35). Human beings also share imperfectly and finitely in other attributes such as life, love, wisdom, justice. In addition people have responsibility to "rule over" the earth (Gen. 1:26).

The biblical account suggests that God created Adam physically full grown and mentally mature. This is borne out by the fact that God placed Adam in the Garden of Eden to work it and take care of it and then brought to him all the birds and animals to name them (2:19–20). Since "no suitable helper was found" for Adam among the animals, God created the woman out of a rib taken from Adam (2:21–25).

Although innocent when created by God, Adam—and also Eve when she was created for him—was spiritually alive. This conclusion is drawn from the fact that Adam and Eve were created "in the image of God" (1:27) and the fact that God talked with Adam (2:16–17) and fellowshipped with Adam and Eve in the Garden of Eden. Furthermore God warned Adam not to eat "from the tree of the knowledge of good and evil, for when you eat of it you will surely die" (2:17), indicating that they possessed life. When Adam and Eve ate of that tree, spiritual death was instantaneous (3:7–8), and the process of physical death began immediately and was consummated for Adam after 930 years (5:5).

When Eve was approached by the serpent, she succumbed to the temptation and ate of the fruit and gave some to Adam and he ate (3:6). God spoke to Adam, however, as the responsible head of the first couple (3:9–11, 17–19). Romans 5:12 identifies Adam as the head of the human race.

How did God's judgment of physical and spiritual death pass from Adam to all humanity? Two major views seek to answer this question. One is called the federal theory, or the covenant view, which considers Adam as the representative of the human race with whom God had established a covenant of works for all humanity. When Adam sinned, God's judgment of both physical and spiritual death was imputed not only to him but also to the entire human race that sprang from him.

The second view is called the natural or seminal headship view or the Augustinian view. This theory considers Adam as the seminal head of the human race, viewing every human being as residing seminally in Adam and thus participating in his sin and judgment of physical and spiritual death. A biblical example of this is the statement that "Levi, who collects the tenth, paid the tenth through Abraham, because when Melchizedek met Abraham, Levi was still in the body of his ancestor" (Heb. 7:9–10). Similarly Paul's statement that "just as sin entered the world through one man, and death through sin, and in this way death came to all men, because all sinned" (Rom. 5:12) seems to present this view. It appears to be confirmed by Paul's words that "the many died by the trespass of the one man" (5:15) and "the result of one trespass was condemnation for all men" (5:18) and "through the disobedience of the one man the many were made sinners" (5:19).

The biblical account of the creation of Adam and Eve "in the image of God" contradicts the theory of modern science that mankind evolved from primates. In addition, even though there may be gaps in the genealogical records of Genesis 5 and 11 prior to Abram, the elapsed time since the creation of Adam and Eve according to the Bible is much less than the seven hundred thousand years suggested by many anthropologists for human evolution. Genesis presents Adam as a historical person whom God created comparatively recently.

The New Testament supports the fact that Adam was the first human being and head of the human race. Luke traced the Lord Jesus' physical ancestry back to "Adam, the son of God" (Luke 3:23–38). And Jude wrote of "Enoch, the seventh from Adam" (Jude 14). Even Jesus testified to the truthfulness of the Genesis account of the creation of Adam and Eve (Matt. 19:4–5; Mark 10:6–8, quoting Gen. 1:27 and 2:24). Paul also accepted the historicity of Adam, speaking of him more frequently than any other Old Testament person (see, for example, 1 Cor. 15:22, 45; 1 Tim. 2:13–14).

As the first human being and the head of the entire human family responsible for the introduction of sin and death, both physical and spiritual, Adam, Paul said, is a type of Christ, the antitype. This relationship between Adam and Christ is seen in the antithesis between the introduction of death through Adam and the conquest of death by Christ (1 Cor. 15:21–22). This relationship between Adam and Christ continues in Paul's discussion of the nature of the resurrection body given by Christ, "the last Adam" (15:45), in contrast to the physical body acquired through the first Adam, who is also called "the first man" (15:45, 47).   —JAW

Since we are all related in some way to every living human being,
we should hold no prejudice in our hearts against others.

Adoption

WHEN THE APOSTLE PAUL used the phrase "the riches of God's grace" (Eph. 1:7), he spoke of the magnitude of God's redemption made possible through the death of Christ. Among the many concepts related to grace is adoption (1:5). When a person believes in the Lord Jesus Christ for salvation, that individual is placed at that moment into the family of God with all the rights and privileges of an adult (Rom. 8:15). The Christian becomes an heir of everything God has made available for those who are His children (8:17). The believers' inheritance is not limited to this life; complete fulfillment will be theirs in heaven (8:23).

Adoption is a practice well known among many cultures. In biblical times couples who had no son could adopt one, and that son would function in the home as one of the family and would become an heir of the family estate. Adoption was usually certified legally according to the custom of the society. Even though there is no Hebrew equivalent to the Greek term for adoption, the Scriptures record some possible examples. Abraham was willing to consider his servant Eliezer as an heir (Gen. 15:3). Archeological evidence from the time of the patriarchs throws light on this relationship between Abraham and his servant. Pharaoh's daughter adopted Moses, and he grew up in her home (Exod. 2:10).

The theological significance of adoption is developed exclusively by Paul. Chronologically the first mention of this concept is in the Book of Galatians. The apostle affirmed that faith in Jesus Christ, not obedience to the Law, brings justification (Gal. 2:16). Christ redeems those who were under the Law (4:5), and one of the results of that gracious act of God is adoption. In Galatians 4:5 the New American Standard Bible has "adoption as sons," and the New International Version has "the full rights of sons." Evidence of this adoption is the indwelling Spirit of God, who helps believers understand and enjoy the privileges of sonship (4:6).

Paul expanded the concept of adoption in the Book of Romans. He stated that those who are in Christ have been placed under the control of the Holy Spirit (8:9) and have received "a spirit of adoption" (8:15, NASB). This means that adopted sons are heirs of God and coheirs with Christ (8:17). While they are heirs of spiritual privileges now, they also wait in anticipation for the day when all the promises of God will be brought to fruition (8:23).

Paul's statement in Ephesians 1:5 adds another dimension. He declared that this marvelous and gracious privilege of adoption was in the heart and plans of God before the creation of the world. His children were chosen by Him so He could lavish His love on them. This results in praise and adoration to God and enhances His glory (1:6). Being adopted as a child of God is a great spiritual privilege, stemming from the riches of His grace.　　　　　　　　　　　　　**—WGJ**

Count the specific blessings you have because
you have been graciously received into the family of God.

Adultery

VOLUNTARY SEXUAL RELATIONS by either a man or a woman in violation of the marriage bond constitutes adultery, a specific form of fornication forbidden by the seventh commandment in the Mosaic Law (Exod. 20:14; Deut. 5:18; Luke 18:20). Adultery was punishable by death by stoning (Lev. 20:10–12; Deut. 22:20–27).

The seriousness of the sin of adultery and the severity of its punishment spring from the sanctity of the marital relationship established by God with His creation of Eve as a "helper suitable" for Adam (Gen. 2:18, 20–23), and also from the intimacy of this union (2:23–24; Matt. 19:4–6; 1 Cor. 6:16). The sanctity and intimacy of the marital relationship also explain the seriousness of any form of illicit relations in God's sight, because in sexual union a man and a woman "become one flesh"

(Gen. 2:24; Matt. 19:5; 1 Cor. 6:16). For this reason Jesus listed adultery as a sin as serious as murder, theft, or slander (Matt. 15:19).

The unfaithfulness to the marriage vow displayed in adultery illustrates the spiritual unfaithfulness of Israel to God. Israel's covenantal relationship to God (Exod. 19:3–8; 24:3–8) is described as a marriage between God as the "husband" (Isa. 54:5; Jer. 31:32) and Israel as the "wife" (Isa. 54:6). Israel's unfaithfulness in forsaking the Lord to worship false gods was called adultery (Jer. 3:6, 8–9, 20), and Israel was called an "adulterous wife" (Ezek. 16:32). Because of Israel's spiritual adultery God will forsake and punish her (16:38), but only temporarily (Isa. 54:6–7; Ezek. 16:59–60). God's dealings with Israel in her spiritual adultery are illustrated by the prophet Hosea and his unfaithful wife Gomer (Hos. 1:2; 2:2; 3:1). Any forsaking of the Lord God is spiritual adultery (James 4:4). **—JAW**

Christ calls us all not only to physical faithfulness
but also to faithfulness in every passing thought and glance.

Advocate

JOB, A SERVANT OF THE LORD, whose life was the epitome of righteous living, was tested by Satan. The experience was severe and caused him great loss. In his struggles he sought an advocate, someone to stand in his defense (Job 16:19–21). This is the only place where the New International Version uses the word *advocate*. In 1 John 2:1 the New International Version translates *paraklētos* as "one who speaks to the Father in our defense," whereas *advocate* is the term used in both the New American Standard Bible and the New King James Version.

An advocate is someone who argues for a cause or pleads on behalf of another person. In Job's case he needed someone who could defend him before God, since what had happened to him seemed so unjust. Job desperately sought an advocate, while the apostle John declared that believers do have an advocate.

When a person places his or her faith in Christ, the penalty of sin is removed. Yet Christians still have the capacity to sin (1 John 1:8).

Though a believer is not characterized by a life of sin (3:9), he or she still occasionally commits sin (1:9). However, when a Christian sins, he is not condemned, because he has an Advocate, Jesus Christ, who pleads his case before the Father.

In His Upper Room Discourse Jesus used the word *paraklētos* four times in referring to the Holy Spirit (John 14:16, 26; 15:26; 16:7). The New International Version translates this word as "Counselor." Since Christ would no longer be with them as He had in the past, He was asking the Father to give them someone like Himself to be in them (14:17). As the indwelling Counselor (literally, "one called alongside to help"), the Holy Spirit, Jesus said, would be the disciples' Teacher (14:26) and a witness to the character of Christ (15:26). The Holy Spirit would also convict the world of guilt (16:7–8). Yet in relation to sin in believers' lives, the Lord has retained the responsibility of being their Advocate Himself. **—WGJ**

Knowing that the risen Christ defends you before God the Father, don't allow Satan to intimidate you because of your sins.

Age

THE PRINCIPAL OLD TESTAMENT WORD for "age" is *'ôlam,* which may designate an indefinite period. Sometimes it is used in the sense of everlasting, either in the past or future. For instance, God is said to be "from all eternity" (Ps. 93:2). In Micah 5:2 the future messianic Ruler is described as "one who will be ruler over Israel, whose origins are from of old, from ancient times." The expression "ancient times" can be translated "as from days of eternity [*'ôlam*]." This points to the Messiah's existence from eternity past.

Besides being used frequently to refer to past time, *'ôlam* is also used of an indefinite future time. In this sense the word may refer to the unknown length of a person's life (Deut. 15:17; Ps. 61:7). Also the earth is said to exist for an indefinite time. It is in this sense that Genesis 13:15 used *'ôlam* in His promise to Abraham: "All the land that you see I will give to you and your offspring forever" (Gen. 13:15). Since the earth will ultimately be destroyed, including the Promised Land (Rev. 20:11; 21:1), Genesis 13:15 refers to the land existing not into eternity but rather for an indefinite period of time into the future.

In Isaiah 45:17 the word "ages" (*ôlam* in the plural) is used of Israel's ongoing future: "You [Israel] will never be put to shame or disgraced to ages everlasting."

Frequently in Scripture the word *'ôlam* ascribes eternity to God. "The LORD is the everlasting God" (Isa. 40:28). "I live forever" (Deut. 32:40). "From everlasting to everlasting you are God" (Ps. 90:2). "The God of Israel, [is] from everlasting to everlasting" (106:48; see also Neh. 9:5). God "lives forever" (Dan. 12:7). Also God's love is "from everlasting to everlasting" (Ps. 103:17).

In the New Testament the Greek word *aiōn* is similar in meaning to *'ôlam*. *Aiōn* indicates an indefinite period of time, either of the past or the future. God's promises were made in the past ("long ago," Luke 1:70; Acts 3:21) and His saving of Gentiles has been known in the past ("known for ages," Acts 15:18). The plural "ages" is a comprehensive expression of all past ages, as in 1 Corinthians 2:7 ("before time began"), Ephesians 3:9 ("for ages past"), and Colossians 1:26 ("the mystery that has been kept hidden for ages and generations"). Also Ephesians 3:11 refers to God's "eternal purpose" (literally, "the purpose of the ages").

The future ages are in view in the angel's promise to Mary that her son "will reign over the house of Jacob forever ['unto the ages,' *aiōnas*]" (Luke 1:33). Age (singular) is often used in the sense of forever, that is, eternity, as in John 6:51, 58; 1 Peter 1:25; 1 John 2:17; and 2 John 2. The plural *ages* also means eternity, as in, for example, Romans 1:25; 9:5; 11:36; and 2 Corinthians 11:31. The unusual expression "unto the age of the age" in Hebrews 1:8 means "for ever and ever." The phrase "unto the ages of ages," meaning "for ever," occurs a dozen times, often in doxologies (for example, Rom. 16:27; Rev. 7:12). This phrase is also used of God's eternal existence (Rev. 4:9–10; 10:6; 15:7).

An important use of *aiōn* is in reference to a long period of time in the present or the future. Jesus distinguished these two when He said that the blasphemy of the Holy Spirit "will not be forgiven, either in this age or in the age to come" (Matt. 12:32).

Often the return of Christ is described as beginning a new age and consummating the present age. The disciples asked Him, "What will be the sign of your coming and of the end of the age?" (Matt. 24:3).

It is important to note that the present age contrasts with both the past Old Testament era and the future yet-to-come age. In the present age Christians enjoy many spiritual blessings, blessings that will continue on for eternity. Believers now have eternal life (John 3:16, 36; 5:24; 6:47), spiritual life that will continue after death for all eternity. Believers who sacrifice possessions and family for Christ "in this present age" will be richly rewarded, receiving "a hundred times as much . . . in the age to come" (Mark 10:30). The present age is a time of burdens; the phrase "the worries of this life" (Matt. 13:22; Mark 4:19) is literally "the cares of this age." Believers are not to be conformed to or to love the sinful ways of the present age ("world," Rom. 12:2; 2 Tim. 4:10; cf. Titus 2:12).

In contrast to the present age, which is a time of satanic power (Satan is the ruler of "this age," 2 Cor. 4:4) and evil (Gal. 1:4), the future Millennium, when Satan will be bound, will introduce a totally new age in which Christ will rule from Jerusalem. Following the millennial kingdom, God will usher in the eternal age in which all things will be brought to their consummation. God's redemptive program, enjoyed now by believers, will be fully displayed in the Millennium and in the eternal state. "In the coming ages [God will] show the incomparable riches of his grace, expressed in his kindness to us in Christ Jesus" (Eph. 2:7).   —JFW

Do not be conformed to or love the sinful ways of this present age.

Angels

AT LEAST THIRTY-THREE BOOKS OF THE BIBLE mention angels, with more than one hundred references in the Old Testament and more than 160 in the New Testament. Angels are also called "sons of God" (Job 1:6, NASB; 38:7, NASB); "holy ones" (Ps. 89:7); and "host" (1 Sam. 17:45; Ps. 89:8, NASB). Several times Christ affirmed the existence of angels (Matt. 18:10; 22:29–30; 25:31–32, 41). Those who deny the reality of angels argue that Christ referred to angels (and demons) for pedagogical purposes and/or that He shared the superstitions of His contemporaries. But the former view implies that Christ was intellectually dishonest, and the latter makes Him subject to error. It is clear that Christ truly believed in and testified to the existence of angels. To deny their reality is therefore to impugn His reliability.

God created angels by His Word (Ps. 148:5). Though the time of their creation is not known, they were present when the earth was created and sang praises to the Lord (Job 38:7). Specifically, we are told that angels were created by and for Christ (Col. 1:16). The angels were created holy (Mark 8:38; Acts 10:22) and are innumerable (Dan. 7:10; Matt. 26:53; Heb. 12:22; Rev. 5:11). Their numbers neither increase nor decrease, for they do not have children (Matt. 22:30) nor do they die (Luke 20:36).

On occasion angels appeared to men in the form of human bodies (Gen. 18:2; Matt. 28:3). Yet they are called spirits (Heb. 1:14). As spirit beings they may perhaps possess bodies of a spiritual order (1 Cor. 15:44).

Angels are personal beings, for they possess the essential elements of personality—intelligence (1 Pet. 1:12), emotions (Luke 2:13; 15:10), and will (Jude 6). Their knowledge, while greater than that of humans, is limited. They are not omniscient. Angels have greater power than humans, but they are not omnipotent. They can appear and disappear, but they are not omnipresent. Angels were not created in God's image and do not share redemption in Christ. In the age to come, redeemed humanity will be exalted above the angels and will judge the fallen among them (1 Cor. 6:3).

Of the fallen angels, called demons, some are bound (2 Pet. 2:4; Jude 6) and others are free. Demons are referred to as Satan's "angels" (Rev. 12:7, 9). The unfallen angels, called "elect angels" (1 Tim. 5:21), may be distinguished as follows: (1) Michael, the only angel called the archangel, is the defender of Israel (Dan. 10:13, 21; 12:1; Jude 9; Rev. 12:7). (2) Gabriel, an angel of high rank, was entrusted with delivering important messages from God to individuals such as Daniel (Dan. 8:16; 9:21), Zechariah (Luke 1:19), and Mary (Luke 1:26). (3) "Rulers," "principalities," "authorities," and "powers," referred to frequently in the Scriptures, seem to be good and evil angels who engage in an unending struggle to control human beings and governments (Dan. 10:13; Eph. 1:21; 3:10; 6:12; Col. 2:15). (4) Cherubim are the guardians of the holiness and presence of God (Gen. 3:24; Exod. 25:17–22; Pss. 80:1; 99:1; Isa.

37:16; Ezek. 10:4–5). (5) Seraphim are mentioned only in Isaiah 6:2–6, where they are described as praising God and extolling His holiness. (6) The Angel of the Lord, a term found frequently in the Old Testament often seems to refer to the preincarnate Christ (Gen. 16:7, 9, 11; 22:11, 15; Exod. 3:2; Judg. 2:1, 4; 6:11–12, 21–22; 13:3, 13, 15–17, 20–21; 2 Sam. 24:16; Zech. 1:11–12; 3:1, 5–6; 12:8).

As God's messengers or ambassadors, unfallen angels have ministered in a variety of ways. They were involved when God created the world, when He gave the Mosaic Law (Acts 7:38, 53; Gal. 3:19; Heb. 2:2), during Christ's first advent (Matt. 2:13–15, 19–20; 4:11; 28:2, 5; Luke 2:13; 22:43; Acts 1:10), and during the early days of the church (Acts 8:26; 12:7; 27:23–24; 1 Cor. 4:9). And they will be involved in announcing judgments in the Tribulation (Rev. 8–10; 14–16), they will accompany Christ at His second coming (Matt. 24:31; 25:31), and they will be engaged in events following His return (Matt. 13:39; Rev. 19:17–18; 20:1–3).

Angels appear before God (Job 1:6; 2:1), worship God (Pss. 103:20; 148:20; Luke 2:13; Heb. 1:6; Rev. 5:11–12; 7:11–12), and obey God (Ps. 103:20–21).

Some verses suggest that one of the ministries of angels is to protect and guard believers (Exod. 23:20; Pss. 34:7; 91:11–12; Matt. 4:6; 18:10). Angels minister to Christians (Heb. 1:14); and they deliver believers from harm, as in the case of Lot (Gen. 19:15–17), Joseph (48:16), the Israelites (Num. 20:16), Daniel's three friends (Dan. 3:28), Daniel himself (6:22), the apostles (Acts 5:19), and Peter (12:7). Apparently angels know what happens on the earth (Luke 15:10; 1 Cor. 4:9; 11:10). Angels can guide (Acts 8:26), give strength (1 Kings 19:5, 7; Dan. 10:18–19; Luke 22:43), and comfort (Luke 1:30; 2:10; Matt. 28:5; Acts 27:23–24).

Popular interest in angels is sometimes carried to an unbalanced extreme. When heretics at Colossae worshiped angels as divine intermediaries, Paul sent a strong warning (Col. 2:18) and affirmed that angels are under Jesus, "who is the Head over all power and authority" (2:10). The object of the believers' faith is Jesus, not angels.   **—DKC**

Thank God for the protective care of angels.

Anointing

THE PRACTICE OF ANOINTING with oil was widespread in Bible times. Olive oil in particular was applied after bathing (Ruth 3:3), on wounds (Luke 10:34), dead bodies (John 19:39), or released prisoners (2 Chron. 28:15). The head and feet of honored individuals were sometimes anointed with special oils or perfumes (Ps. 23:5; John 12:3).

The first reference to anointing in Scripture (Gen. 31:13) is when Jacob anointed a pillar he had set up as a memorial of his encounter with God at Bethel. In Old Testament times anointing often had a religious significance, setting objects and persons apart for God's service. Specially prepared oils were used to anoint the tabernacle, its furniture, and Aaron and his sons (Exod. 28:40–42; 29:1–46; 30:22–33; 40:10–11). These persons and objects were thus sanctified or set apart for religious purposes.

While the Old Testament occasionally mentions the anointing of prophets (1 Kings 19:16), references to the anointing of kings are more frequent, dating from the beginning of the monarchy. Samuel, sometimes called "the king-maker," anointed both Saul and David (1 Sam. 10:1; 16:13). Of special significance is the fact that when David was anointed, the Spirit of the Lord came on him and departed from Saul. Thus the anointing not only set rulers aside to serve God, but it also symbolized the coming of the Holy Spirit to enable God's servants to do their work for Him. In this connection the Messiah declared, "The Spirit of the Sovereign LORD is on me, because the LORD has anointed me to preach good news to the poor" (Isa. 61:1).

The Hebrew word for anointed, *mašîaḥ* (transliterated "messiah," and which means the "anointed one"), refers to a range of individuals who were appointed to special tasks, even the Persian king Cyrus (Isa. 45:1). The term came to be applied to the coming King from the line of David, the Messiah, who will one day rule over the restored Davidic kingdom. Messianic prophecies abound in the Old Testament, and the New Testament identified Jesus as the ultimate Anointed One, *the* Messiah (John 1:41; 4:25).

The practice of anointing continued in New Testament times but not for induction into leadership. Literal anointing with oil or perfume is mentioned (Mark 14:8; Luke 7:46; John 12:3), but some passages use the term in a figurative sense in affirming that God anoints believers (2 Cor. 1:21; 1 John 2:20, 27). This anointing at the moment one believes in Christ refers to the impartation of the gift of the Holy Spirit. It brings to mind the anointing of the Old Testament priests with oil.

The Roman Catholic Church uses James 5:14 to support their sacrament of extreme unction. But, as verses 14–15 show, the elders, not priests, were to pray for the sick person and anoint him with the oil. The anointing was not to prepare the individual for death but to anticipate his restoration to health. The Greek word here translated "anoint" means "to rub with oil," not "to anoint ceremonially." Much as a modern nurse would rub a patient's body with lotion, so in the ancient world, in similar fashion, olive oil would be used. It was not a ritual or ceremonial anointing but a means of refreshment, comfort, and grooming in anticipation of the patient being healed and able to leave the sickbed and face the world.   **—DKC**

Consider the fact that every true believer has been anointed by God for His service.

Antichrist

THE WORD *antichrist* refers to anyone who is against Christ, for the prefix "anti" means "against." But since the prefix can also mean "instead of," the word also refers to *the* one who in the future Tribulation will seek to be a substitute for Christ, that is, a pseudo-Christ.

Only four verses (1 John 2:18, 22; 4:3; 2 John 7) include the word *antichrist*, but the idea of an antichrist pervades the Old and New Testaments. The key to the doctrine is found in 1 John 2:18. "Dear children, this is the last hour; and as you have heard that the antichrist is coming, even now many antichrists have come. This is how we know it is the last hour." In contrast to the many antichrists mentioned, there is a specific antichrist who was still future at the time John wrote this epistle.

In defining the antichrist as one who "denies the Father and the Son" (2:22), John had in view the presence of antichrists in the church age. However, the antichrist idea is much broader, covering any person or movement that is contrary to God, whether in the Old or New Testaments.

Thus the concept of antichrist in the Old Testament includes those who were guilty of idolatry (Deut. 13:13), rape or sexual sins (Judg. 19:22–25; 20:53), disregard or disrespect of God (1 Sam. 2:12), and lying or evil expressions (1 Kings 21:10, 13; Prov. 6:12; 16:27).

The concept of a specific antichrist is seen in the prophecies related to Antiochus Epiphanes IV, a king of Syria (175–164 B.C.), who, according to Daniel 11:21–36, would prove to be an antichrist in his persecution of Israel, his desecration of the temple, and his abolishing of Israel's daily sacrifices. In this he prefigured the future Antichrist of the end times.

Daniel 7:7–8 anticipates a revival of the Roman Empire in the end times in the form of ten kingdoms. The little horn mentioned in 7:8 depicts a ruler who will uproot three of the ten horns, that is, he will subdue three kingdoms (7:24) and then rule over all ten countries of the revived Roman Empire. He will become a world ruler (Rev. 13:8). Called "Antichrist" in 1 John 2:18, he will be against Christ and will be His principal opponent in the end times. He will attempt to be a substitute for Christ, the King of kings, for Satan will enable the Antichrist to have a world government in the last three and a half years before the Second Coming.

The Antichrist will sit in the future temple (which Israel will build to restore the Mosaic system of sacrifices) to be worshiped (Dan. 11:36–37; Matt. 24:15; 2 Thess. 2:4). Daniel called him "the ruler who will come" (Dan. 9:26) and "the king who will do as he pleases" (11:36), and Paul dubbed him "the man of lawlessness" and "the lawless one" (2 Thess. 2:3, 9). This will cause an abomination in that Jewish sacrifices will be stopped and sacrifices of a pagan character will be substituted (Dan. 9:27; 12:11).

The revived Roman Empire will be like a beast out of the sea, having seven heads and ten horns (Rev. 13:1; see also Dan. 7:7). Besides being presented as an eleventh horn, the Antichrist is depicted as the eighth head on the beast (Rev. 17:11), which points to his leadership of the revived Roman Empire.

He will recover from what is called "a fatal wound" (13:3, 12). Some interpreters say this wound suggests that someone from the past will be resurrected to fulfill this role. Many individuals have been suggested, including Nero. But no one from the past has fulfilled the function of the future Antichrist. The view that the Antichrist will die from the wound and be resurrected is supported by the fact that the word "slain" (13:3, literal translation) is also used of Christ (5:6; 13:1–8). However, it may be preferable to say that Satan will heal the Antichrist from a serious wound, because one of his heads, not his entire body, will have a mortal wound. In any case he will come on the scene as a supernatural person empowered by Satan, and he will gain worldwide acceptance, exercising authority over the entire world for forty-two months (13:5–8).

The Antichrist's number 666 (Rev. 13:18) has been interpreted in many various ways. Perhaps the number simply means that just as six is one less than seven, often considered a "perfect" number, so 666 is less than 777 and thus suggests that the Antichrist, while pretending to be divine, will fall short of that pretension.

At the second coming of Christ the Antichrist will be captured and "thrown alive into the fiery lake of burning sulfur" (19:20). Paul referred to this event when he called the Antichrist "the man doomed to destruction" (2 Thess. 2:3), and Daniel wrote that this future world ruler "will come to his end" (Dan. 11:45).

In the Reformation the church identified the Roman Catholic Church as the Antichrist, and in more recent times prominent individuals who have opposed the church and Christ have been said to be the Antichrist. The Roman Church retaliated by saying Protestants were antichrists. However, those who believe in a future fulfillment of many of the prophecies in Daniel and Revelation believe a personal Antichrist will dominate the world for three and a half years of terrible tribulation and then, as stated, will be destroyed by Christ at His second coming.

—JFW

Always be on guard for the spirit of antichrist that is prevalent in today's world.

Apostasy

THOUGH THE GREEK WORD *apostasia* is found only twice in the New Testament (Acts 21:21; 2 Thess. 2:3), the concept is found many times in Scripture. The word means "a falling away from," a deserting or turning from a position or view formerly held. In a political sense the concept of apostasy is sometimes seen as a defection from authority (Acts 5:37), or in a religious sense it is a defection from truth (Acts 21:21; 1 Tim. 4:1).

Spiritual apostasy occurs when a person who once claimed to be a believer departs from what he or she formerly professed to believe. An apostate is not one who was saved and then lost his or her salvation. An apostate, though having claimed to be a believer, never was saved in the first place. Relatively minor differences in doctrine are not referred to as apostasy; instead apostasy is a departure from major components of Christian truth.

Major characteristics of those who apostatize include embracing doctrines of demons, having a seared conscience, lying, forbidding marriage, and prohibiting the eating of certain foods (1 Tim. 4:1–3). Apostates may have a form of godliness but not know experientially its power or reality (2 Tim. 3:5). Apostasy is denounced in Hebrews 10:26–29; 2 Peter 2:15–21; and Jude 3–4.

Apostasy is a departure from truth not simply because of ignorance; it is deliberate and therefore merits divine judgment. The only cure for apostasy is for the individual to come to Christ for salvation, to become a true believer in Christ. The New International Version does not use the word *apostasy* but renders *apostasia* as "to turn away" from Moses (Acts 21:21) or as "rebellion" (2 Thess. 2:3). The latter reference speaks of the extensive apostasy that will occur in the seven-year period immediately preceding the second coming of Christ. **—JFW**

Avoid those who have departed from the truth of God and reject their teaching.

Apostleship

EARLY IN THE HIS MINISTRY Jesus chose twelve men from among His followers and named them apostles (Luke 6:13). He gave them authority to represent Him in His mission (Matt. 10:2; Mark 3:16). Interestingly Jesus Himself is called "the apostle" by the author of the

Book of Hebrews (Heb. 3:1), and in a true sense the pattern of apostle-ship was established by God's sending His Son to this earth on a stated mission (John 17:23).

Immediately after Jesus' ascension Peter declared it was necessary to choose someone to take the place of Judas, to maintain the number of twelve apostles. The qualifications were restrictive because whoever was chosen had to have been with Jesus and the disciples from the time of John's baptism and a witness of the resurrection (Acts 1:21–22). At least two men were qualified, but the final decision rested with the Lord and was accomplished by drawing lots (1:24–26). Because this was the first decision made after the Ascension, it may be assumed that this need was communicated by Christ during the forty days before He left them (1:3). Peter also had the authority of the Old Testament Scriptures which he quoted (1:16, 20). The uniqueness of the twelve apostles will continue for eternity, for in the New Jerusalem the names of the twelve apostles will be inscribed on the city's twelve foundations (Rev. 21:14).

Glimpses of the ministry of the Twelve can be seen in the Book of Acts, since these men were part of the foundation of the church (Eph. 2:20; 4:11). They provided leadership for the early believers and explained the work of the Spirit in their midst (Acts 2:14–36; 3:11–26). These men were in the forefront of the proclamation of the gospel, focusing on the ministry of evangelism (4:2, 8–12; 5:42). Worship was emphasized by the apostles as they led the church in prayer and praise (5:23–31). The overall care of the believers was entrusted to them, which included physical (4:35, 37) as well as spiritual needs (6:4). In protecting the purity of the church, the apostles were also responsible for discernment and discipline (5:1–11). Miraculous signs and wonders were performed by these men, as the work of the Lord was authenticated among the people and unbelievers were brought to Christ (5:12; 9:32–35). Miracles validated the work of the Spirit especially as the gospel spread beyond Jerusalem (8:14–17; 2 Cor. 12:12). Important doctrinal teachings were approved or rejected in the early church based on the testimony of the apostles (Acts 15:6–11).

Apostleship extended beyond the Twelve but was distinct from that group. Paul was an example of an apostle who was not one of the Twelve. His apostleship is well attested in Scripture. In his introductions to nine of his letters he referred to himself as an apostle (see, for example, 1 Cor.

1:1; Gal. 1:1). He was the apostle to the Gentiles just as Peter was to the Jews (Gal. 2:8–9). Paul himself recognized the uniqueness of his apostleship (1 Cor. 15:8–10). A few others were referred to as apostles, including Barnabas (Acts 14:14) and Andronicus and Junias (Rom. 16:7). How and when they received this designation is not stated, but like the Twelve, they were sent with delegated authority to minister for the Lord. They were sent on their missions by local churches. No biblical evidence exists to suggest that there are apostles today, as the gift of apostleship is defined in the New Testament.

—WGJ

Give thanks to the Lord for the faithful work of the apostles and especially the apostles' letters of instruction recorded in the Bible.

Ark of the Covenant

THE ARK OF THE COVENANT was the only piece of furniture in the Most Holy Place of the tabernacle and later the temple. The ark was made of acacia wood and was overlaid with gold, inside and out. Measuring three and a half feet in length and two and a half feet in both width and height, this chest had a lid of solid gold which is called in some English versions "the mercy seat" (Exod. 25:17, 21–22, NASB; 1 Chron. 28:11, NASB), and which the New International Version sometimes calls "an atonement cover" (Exod. 25:17). Once a year on the Day of Atonement the high priest sprinkled blood on the mercy seat to make atonement for the sins of the people of Israel (Lev. 16). This ceremony made the ark of the covenant with its "atonement cover" the most important piece of furniture in the tabernacle proper.

In addition to providing for atonement, the mercy seat was the place where the presence of God was "localized" and revealed (Exod. 25:22; Lev. 16:2). Since the Israelites were not permitted to make any material likeness of God, the mercy seat seems to have been the clearest reminder of God's presence among His people, particularly with the pillar of cloud by day and the pillar of fire by night hovering over it.

The ark of the covenant was assembled and placed within the sanctuary at Mount Sinai (Exod. 40:21–22). It accompanied the Israelites on their journey from Sinai to Canaan and served as a constant reminder of God's presence with His people. At the entrance into Canaan (Josh. 3–4), the conquest of Jericho (6:6–11), and the covenant renewal at Mount Ebal (8:33), the ark played a significant role.

In the period of the judges, religious life in Israel sank to a low level, and the ark came to be looked on as a fetish. At the Battle of Aphek the Israelites rushed the ark into the conflict as they were being defeated by the Philistines (1 Sam. 4:1–10). But such misuse of the ark was not to be tolerated and God allowed it to be captured by the Philistines (4:11) while imposing defeat on Israel and death on Eli the high priest and his house (4:13–22). Samuel, the last and best of the judges, did not attempt to restore the ark to the tabernacle but allowed it to remain in Kiriath Jearim, near Jerusalem (6:21–7:2). The godly prophet and judge stressed Israel's need for direct repentance toward God.

In the monarchial period David brought the ark to his newly established capital, Jerusalem (2 Sam. 6). Though he wanted to build a permanent temple for the ark and the Lord, that privilege was granted to Solomon, his son. When that magnificent structure was completed, the ark was installed behind the curtain in the Most Holy Place and the glory cloud filled the temple (1 Kings 8:1–11). Throughout the remainder of the kingdom period to the fall of Jerusalem in 586 B.C. the ark remained in the temple except for its temporary removal during the reign of the apostate King Manasseh (2 Chron. 35:3). What happened to the ark when Nebuchadnezzar destroyed Jerusalem remains a mystery. Various theories have been propounded. Some say the ark was destroyed along with the temple in 586 B.C. Others suggest Jeremiah hid the ark in a cave on Mount Nebo (2 Maccabees 2:4–8). Still others say the ark remains concealed under Jerusalem's temple mount, and some suggest that the ark was taken to heaven where it will eventually be seen by all worshipers (Rev. 11:19).

The departure of God's glorious presence at the time of the exile from above the mercy seat was graphically described by Ezekiel the prophet (Ezek. 10:4, 18; 11:23). Isaiah declared that because of Israel's sin God no longer accepted their sacrifices at the temple (Isa. 1:11–14). Most importantly, the coming of Jesus Christ eliminated the need for the Old Testament worship system. The ark of the covenant, and particularly the mercy seat, pointed forward to Jesus Christ whom God presented as a "sacrifice of atonement" (Rom. 3:25). The Greek word *hilastērion,* rendered "propitiation" in some Bible versions, translates the Hebrew word for mercy seat or atonement cover. Placed in the ark of the covenant were Aaron's rod, a pot of manna, and the stone tablets on which were written the Ten Commandments, which Israel repeatedly violated. Israel thus stood condemned by the Law, but the blood of sacrifice sprinkled on the mercy seat changed what must otherwise have been a place of judgment into a place of mercy. The blood came between the violated Law and the people who were the violators. In fulfillment of this crucial Old Testament type the blood of Jesus fully satisfied the just requirements of God's Law, which humankind had broken. The guilt and penalty of sin was removed, and God's wrath is thereby averted for those who believe (3:23–26).　　　**—DKC**

Thank God that the purpose and function of the ark of the covenant were fulfilled in the person and work of Jesus Christ.

Ascension

THE ASCENSION OF CHRIST was prophesied in the Old Testament (Pss. 68:18; 110:1) and was referred to frequently in the New Testament. On numerous occasions Jesus spoke of returning to His Father, and He specifically predicted His ascension (John 6:62; 20:17). Luke reported the event in Luke 24:51 and more completely in Acts 1:6–11. Paul wrote of Christ ascending "higher than all the heavens" (Eph. 4:10) and as having been "taken up in glory" (1 Tim. 3:16). Other passages state that the Lord "has gone into heaven" (1 Pet. 3:22) and "through the heavens" (Heb. 4:14). The numerous verses referring to Christ's present session at the right hand of the Father presuppose the Ascension.

Acts 1:9–11 describes the actual event witnessed by many of His disciples. It occurred on the Mount of Olives where now a church (converted into a mosque) marks the supposed site. As Jesus went up before the astonished eyes of the disciples, a cloud hid Him from their sight. They continued to be transfixed by what they had seen until two angels appeared, uttering the remarkable promise that "this same Jesus" would one day "come back in the same way you have seen Him go into heaven."

Some theologians have taught, based on John 20:17, that Christ ascended privately to heaven before His public ascension to fulfill certain Old Testament types. But Jesus' words to Mary Magdalene, "I ascend" (NASB), should no doubt be considered a futuristic present tense verb referring to the yet-future public ascension as a certain event. Christ did not therefore ascend to heaven immediately after His resurrection to present His blood as an emblem of His finished work on the cross, even though the Old Testament high priest presented the blood of the animal sacrifice in the earthly Most Holy Place on the Day of Atonement. The Hebrews passage which declares, "he entered the Most Holy Place once for all by his own blood" (Heb. 9:12), is better rendered "through his blood" or "by virtue of his blood."

The Ascension brought to an end the earthly ministry of our Lord with its self-limitations, its humiliations and sufferings, and the veiling of His glory. The triumphant entrance into heaven brought a wonderful answer to Jesus' prayer, "And now, Father, glorify me in your presence with the glory I had with you before the world began" (John 17:5). The ascension also marks the first appearance of resurrected and glorified humanity in heaven. Christ's presence in glory made possible the descent of the Holy Spirit (16:7). In heaven Christ is seated at the Father's right hand and ministers to believers as their High Priest (Heb. 7:23–8:2). He also serves as the all-powerful "head over everything for the church" (Eph. 1:22).

Along with Jesus' incarnation, atoning death, and resurrection, His ascension forms a vital part of the foundation of our Christian faith.

—DKC

Focus on the ascended Christ who intercedes for us and who will come for us.

Assurance

THE WEALTHY YOUNG RULER who talked with Jesus seemingly had everything except the assurance of eternal life. This lack of assurance was reflected in the question he asked Jesus: "What must I do to inherit eternal life?" (Mark 10:17; Luke 18:18). The text gives no indication that the man was insincere or seeking to trap Jesus. In fact Mark recorded the Lord's favorable response to him: "Jesus looked at him and loved him" (Mark 10:21). The man had done what he thought was required to obtain eternal life, but he wanted to be sure he hadn't overlooked something. The Lord's words were not reassuring. They revealed that the young man had a deeper problem: His trust was in his money and thus his faith was defective. Heeding the invitation to follow Christ would have been the step of faith needed for salvation and the assurance of eternal life he sought.

Salvation is a gift of God and cannot be earned or acquired by human effort. It must be received by faith. Assurance is one's understanding and conviction of the supernatural work of God through the death and resurrection of Christ that declares a believing sinner righteous and imparts eternal life, which transaction can never be rescinded.

Since assurance has a strong subjective element, lack of assurance can cause uncertainty, emotional anguish, or despair. The basis of assurance is objective; however, it is possible for a person to be a genuine believer and yet lack a sense of assurance. Sometimes a specific sin may cause a believer to doubt his salvation. Often lack of assurance stems from the failure to take into account what the Bible teaches about salvation and to accept what God has said in His Word about sin and forgiveness.

Assurance of salvation is based on the character of God and His Word. He can be trusted regardless of the circumstances or issues involved. Jesus said that anyone who believes on Him has eternal life (John 3:16, 36; 5:24; 6:47). Thus the moment a person places his or her faith in Jesus Christ, that individual can be assured right then that he or she possesses eternal life. Since Jesus' words are the basis of this assurance, a person doesn't need to wait till a later time to base assurance of salvation on his or her works.

The apostle Paul wrote that God remains true and His Word certain even if people are false and unfaithful (Rom. 3:3–4). Salvation is of the Lord, available only through the supernatural work of Jesus Christ on the cross. Because God does the saving, the forgiving, and the imparting of eternal life, salvation is much more objective than subjective. God is faithful, His Word is true, His ways are perfect, and His salvation is sure.

The entire Godhead is involved in assurance, since God, who gave His Son to die for us, sent His Spirit to dwell in our lives, and the Spirit testifies to the truth that we are His children (Rom. 8:16; Gal. 4:6).

The ministry of the risen Lord Jesus as our Great High Priest is one of the major themes in the Book of Hebrews. The writer declared that Jesus by His once-for-all sacrifice for our sins "has made perfect forever those who are being made holy" (Heb. 10:14). This objective truth has subjective implications. Believers are encouraged to draw near to God with sincere hearts with complete or full assurance because God has provided relief from their guilty consciences (10:22).

Assurance is one of the themes in 1 John. The apostle John explained the objective reality of this assurance with the words, "God has given us eternal life, and this life is in his Son. He who has the Son has life; he who does not have the Son of God does not have life" (1 John 5:11–12). John then declared that these things were written so that those who believe in Christ may know that they have eternal life (5:13). This objective fact has subjective and practical ramifications. Our prayer life is a daily reminder of our relationship with God and adds to the assurance that we belong to Him (5:14–15).

The love believers have for each other witnesses to the reality that they belong to the truth and it "sets our hearts at rest in his presence whenever our hearts condemn us" (3:18–19). John allowed for the fact that Christians do not always know the motive of their hearts, and so he wrote that "God is greater than our hearts, and he knows everything" (3:20). This combination of subjective and practical assurance finds its ultimate reality in the character of God who knows the inner depths of our hearts.

—WGJ

Live each day with the reality that your sins have been forgiven
and that nothing can separate you from the love of God.

Atonement

ETYMOLOGICALLY the English verb "to atone" and the noun "atonement" signify the process and/or result of two estranged persons becoming "at one," that is, in agreement or reconciled. Biblically the word is used mainly in the Old Testament to describe the result of various Levitical animal sacrifices. "To atone" is a translation of the Hebrew word *kāpar*, "to cover," and signifies God's temporary dealing with the sins of His people Israel corporately or individually. The sacrifices Israel offered anticipated God's final and permanent dealing with human sin in the death of Jesus Christ on the cross.

The Day of Atonement was instituted at God's directions by Moses as an annual observance. On that day the high priest was to sacrifice a young bull as a "sin offering to make atonement for himself and his household" (Lev. 16:6) and then sacrifice a goat as a "sin offering for the people" (16:15). Then he was to "lay both hands on the head of [another] goat and confess over it all the wickedness and rebellion of the Israelites—all their sins—and put them on the goat's head." Then the goat was sent "away into the desert" (16:21), symbolically carrying "on itself all their sins to a solitary place" (16:22). The atonement (literally, "covering") of the priest's and congregation's sins was a temporary provision, because it was repeated annually (16:29, 34).

In the Old Testament the word *atonement* occurs almost eighty times, beginning in Exodus 29:33. There it is used in relation to the sacrifice of the ram for the atonement and consecration of Aaron and his sons as priests of God. Also a bull was sacrificed each day for seven days to achieve the atonement and consecration of the altar of sacrifice (29:36–37). Later, instructions were given for the sacrifices of burnt offerings to be offered on the altar "to make atonement" (Lev. 1:4–5). The offerer identified himself with the offering by laying his hands on its head. The same ritual was followed with the animals sacrificed as sin offerings for the entire community of Israel (4:13–20), a leader of Israel (4:22–26), or any member of the community (4:27–35).

Since the sacrifices of the Day of Atonement were repeated each year and the burnt offerings and sin offerings were repeated countless times, the atonement (covering) achieved by them secured only a temporary, not a permanent, dealing with sin and satisfaction of God's righteous demands. Hebrews declares that "it is impossible for the blood of bulls and goats to take away sins" (Heb. 10:4), for "again and again" the priests offered "the same sacrifices, which can never take away sins" (10:11). Earlier the writer reasoned that if "the same sacrifices repeated endlessly year after year" could "make perfect those who draw near to worship . . . would they not have stopped being offered?" (10:1–2).

By way of contrast to the temporary value of the Old Testament animal sacrifices, the Lord Jesus is "the Lamb of God, who takes away the sin of the world" (John 1:29). As the complete, final sacrifice for sin, Christ has now "appeared once for all at the end of the ages to do away with sin by the sacrifice of himself" (Heb. 9:26). Because He "was sacrificed once to take away the sins of many people" (9:28), believers in Jesus Christ "have been made holy through the sacrifice of the body of Jesus Christ once for all" (10:10; see also 10:12, 14, 17–18).

God could and did righteously cover and forgive the sins of people in past ages on the basis of animal sacrifices offered in faith and obedience to His commands (9:13, 22), in anticipation of Christ's death "as a ransom to set them free from the sins committed under the first covenant" (9:15). This was valid because in God's eternal plan Jesus was "the Lamb that was slain from the creation of the world" (Rev. 13:8; see also 1 Pet. 1:20). God's sole requirement in any age to receive His gracious forgiveness is faith (Gen. 15:6; Rom. 3:3), now expressed toward Jesus Christ and His redemptive death (3:22–24; 4:23–25; Eph. 2:8).

Since the word *atonement* is used to describe the temporary covering of sins in the Old Testament, it is inappropriate to use it in the New Testament to refer to Christ's finished work of redemption. "Atonement" (Greek, *katallagē*) in Romans 5:11 in the King James Version is a mistranslation and should be rendered "reconciliation." Similarly "atonement" in the New International Version's translation of *hilastērios* in Romans 3:25 should read "propitiation." And "to make atonement" (which translates the verb *hilaskomai*; Heb. 2:17) should read "to propitiate."

In understanding the significance of Christ's death on the cross, the foundational, repeated emphasis of Scripture is that He died a substitutionary death in the place of sinners. This idea of substitution is illustrated in the Old Testament by the priests and individuals laying hands on the heads of the sacrificial animals (Lev. 1:4; 4:4, 15, 24, 29, 33) and on the head of the goat sent into the desert on the Day of Atonement (16:21–22). The idea that Christ's death was a substitutionary sacrifice is stated frequently in the New Testament, perhaps nowhere more clearly than in 1 Peter 2:24: "He himself bore our sins in his body on the tree."

Other verses that state this truth are Romans 4:25; 2 Corinthians 5:21; Galatians 1:4; 3:13; Colossians 2:14; 1 Thessalonians 5:10; 1 Timothy 2:6; and Titus 2:14. The clearest and most extensive statement of Christ's vicarious death, however, is in Isaiah 53:4–6. In His death Jesus took the place of the sinner (Heb. 2:9) and bore the curse of God's judgment (Gal. 3:13; 2 Cor. 5:21), thereby satisfying God's just demands (Rom. 3:25-26) and providing forgiveness (Matt. 26:28; Luke 24:47), peace, and reconciliation with God (Rom. 5:11; Col. 1:20), and eternal life (Rom. 6:23; 1 John 5:11–12) to everyone who believes in the Lord Jesus.

Another interpretation of the Atonement was held by Origen (around 185–254 B.C.), who taught that Jesus' death was a ransom paid to Satan. The Bible says nothing about God paying anything to Satan. However, Jesus' death was like a ransom that releases believing sinners from the grip of sin. Jesus said that He came "to give his life as a ransom for many" (Matt. 20:28; Mark 10:45). The word translated "ransom" is *lytron,* which signifies the purchase-money paid to release slaves. Paul used the compound noun *antilytron* when he wrote that Jesus "gave himself as a ransom for all men" (1 Tim. 2:6), and he used the compound verb *antilytroō* when he wrote that Jesus "gave himself for us to redeem us from all wickedness" (Titus 2:14; see also 1 Pet. 1:18).

A later view of the Atonement was the moral influence theory, first advanced by Abelard (1079–1142) and promoted among liberal theologians. This view teaches that Jesus' death demonstrated His faithful commitment to His message and ministry that God loves everyone and desires their loving response to Him and each other. This theory ignores the biblical emphasis on Christ's death as a sacrifice and expiation for sin, satisfying God's just and righteous demands and providing redemption and salvation to all who believe.

Of course, the eternal, infinite love of God for His creation and for humankind was the motivation for both the incarnation and the redemptive death of His eternal Son (John 3:16; Rom. 5:8; Eph. 2:4–5; Titus 3:4–5). The fact that "God is love" (1 John 4:8, 16), however, cannot dismiss or override His holiness and righteousness and the satisfaction of their just requirements.

Anselm, archbishop of Canterbury (1033–1109), developed a fuller view of the Atonement in *Cur Deus Homo?* ("Why Did God Become Man?"). He taught that God's majesty had been dishonored by sin to such an extent that only God Himself could render appropriate satisfaction. This He did by becoming man and dying. Anselm's view is called the satisfaction theory.

The Reformers returned to the biblical view in emphasizing sin as the breaking of God's Law and Christ's death as a substitutionary atonement.

A final question in discussing the Atonement theologically is "For whom did Christ die?" That Jesus' sacrificial death did not provide redemption for Satan and his host of fallen angels is seen in the fact that "the eternal fire" was "prepared for the devil and his angels" (Matt. 25:41; see also 2 Pet. 2:4; Jude 6; Rev. 19:20; 20:10). That it did include the cosmic creation is seen in the fact that "the creation waits in eager expectation for the sons of God to be revealed" (Rom. 8:19; see also Isa. 65:17; 66:22; Acts 3:21; Rom. 8:20–22; 2 Pet. 3:13; Rev. 21:1). The debate centers on whether Christ died for all humanity or only for the elect, those chosen by God.

The view that Christ died only for the elect focuses on the fact that believers were chosen by God "before the creation of the world" (Eph. 1:4) and were predestined "to be adopted as his sons through Jesus Christ" (1:5). The other view believes that the infinite value of the death of Christ paid the price for all human sin and provided remission sufficient for everyone and is applied to those who believe. Advocates of this view refer to John 3:16 ("God so loved the world that he gave his one and only Son, that whoever believes in him shall not perish but have eternal life") and also to John 1:29; 3:15, 17; 4:42; 2 Corinthians 5:19; 1 Timothy 4:10; Hebrews 2:9; 1 John 2:2; 4:14. In this view Christ died for the sake of all people. As the Synod of Dort (1618–1619) put it, His death is "sufficient for all but efficient for the elect." "Everyone who calls on the name of the LORD will be saved" (Joel 2:32; Acts 2:21; Rom. 10:13), but only those chosen by God, the elect, will respond. Jesus said, "All that the Father gives me will come to me, and whoever comes to me I will never drive away" (John 6:37). The gospel message is "whoever will may come," but only those chosen by God the Father and given to Christ will come to Him.

—JAW

In the power of the indwelling Holy Spirit live as a person
freed from the slave market of sin by Christ's atoning death.

Bb

Babylon

BABYLON IS A PROMINENT FEATURE of Scripture, referred to in the Bible more than three hundred times. In general three distinctions need to be observed. First, Babylon refers to an ancient, literal city, about fifty miles south of Baghdad in present-day Iraq. Second, Babylon suggests the Babylonian religion with its numerous gods. A third aspect of Babylon was the Babylonian Empire known as Babylonia, which existed for many centuries in one form or another, with Neo-Babylonia being prominent in the seventh and sixth centuries B.C. Though the empire was conquered in 539 B.C., the city of Babylon has continued to the present time. While much of the city lies in ruins, a small settlement has continued there under other names. The history of Babylon is long and detailed and the subject of extensive archaeological investigations. From the viewpoint of Christian doctrine, Babylon is significant in that it is frequently mentioned in the prophetic Scriptures.

Daniel predicted in Daniel 2 and 7 that the Babylonian Empire would be conquered by another empire; this empire is identified in Daniel 8:20 as that of the Medes and the Persians. The downfall of the city of Babylon, recorded in Daniel 5, took place on October 12, 539 B.C. While Babylon the empire is no longer in existence, Babylon the city is the subject of extensive biblical prophecies. Beginning in Isaiah 13, the Book of Isaiah includes a number of prophecies concerning the fall of and God's judgment on Babylon. More than one hundred sixty references to Babylon are in the Book of Jeremiah. Particular details of judgment on Babylon are described in Jeremiah 51–52, including the statement that Babylon will be completely destroyed and uninhabited. For example, "Babylon will be a heap of ruins, a haunt of jackals, an object of horror and scorn, a place where no one lives" (Jer. 51:37). Her total destruction is also mentioned in 51:43–44. "Her towns will be desolate, a dry and desert land, a land where no one lives, through which no man travels. I will punish Bel in Babylon and make him spew out what he has swallowed. The nations will no longer stream to him. And the wall of Babylon will fall." Interpreters dispute whether these prophecies have already been fulfilled or are subject to future fulfillment. Babylon, though partially in ruins through the centuries, has always had some inhabitants and has never been totally destroyed. So its final destruction is yet to be fulfilled. Also Zechariah's vision recorded in Zechariah 5:5–11 points to a yet-future Babylon.

The religious aspect of Babylon is depicted in Revelation 17 as a harlot astride a scarlet-colored beast. The woman will represent false religions, and the beast she will ride, with its seven heads and ten horns, is representative of a revived Roman Empire. This foreshadows a world church movement in which the influence of Babylon on Christianity will be worldwide (17:15, 18). The ten nations of the revived Roman Empire will destroy the woman. "They will bring her to ruin and leave her naked; they will eat her flesh and burn her with fire" (17:16). This apparently will be fulfilled three and a half years before the second coming of Christ in order to allow the world religion of the end time to be entirely a religion of the Antichrist in which he will demand that he be worshiped (Dan. 11:36–37; 2 Thess. 2:4).

Revelation 18 records a further prophecy about Babylon. She is described as a gigantic commercial city, which will be destroyed by earthquake and fire at the Second Coming. Scholars differ as to whether this should be taken literally or symbolically. It is possible, however, that the city of Babylon will become the capital of the world empire of the last three and a half years before Christ's return, in which case it will probably be extensively rebuilt and will become a leading economic center of the world under the Antichrist. An alternative view is that the Babylon of Revelation 17 and 18 refers to Rome. This is supported by Revelation 17:9, where the woman bearing the title "Babylon the Great" (17:5) is said to sit on seven hills. The city of Rome was built on seven hills. Also according to this view, in John's day Rome was "the great city that rules over the kings of the earth" (17:18). Yet a third view is that the Babylon/Rome imagery represents all earthly political power structures.

Apparently the city of Babylon will be destroyed as part of God's judgment at the time of Jesus' second coming. This dramatically violent destruction (18:21–24) will cause all activity to cease, destroying the city completely. Care must be taken to distinguish prophecies that relate to the Babylonian Empire, prophecies that relate to the city of Babylon, and prophecies that relate to the Babylonian religion. A number of prophecies about Babylon have been fulfilled, but much remains to be fulfilled in connection with the Second Coming.　　　—JFW

Rejoice that God will bring judgment on every stronghold of Satan.

Baptism

THEOLOGICAL CONTROVERSY about the doctrine and practice of baptism has persisted throughout the Christian era. Almost every fact relating to baptism is variously interpreted. A large portion of the church regards baptism as a sacrament or an ordinance, that is, a sacred recognition of God's provision of salvation.

According to the Baptist view, water baptism requires immersion, and it is administered in the name of the Father, the Son, and the Holy Spirit (Matt. 28:19). The act of baptism is a recognition that one's sins have been forgiven (Acts 2:38; 22:16). It also represents union with Christ (Gal. 3:26–28) and the indwelling of the Holy Spirit (1 Cor. 6:19). The act of baptism recognizes that the church is the body of Christ, formed by the baptism of the Spirit (1 Cor. 12:13). The Baptist view is that baptism is only for children, youth, and adults who are believers and that there is no validity to infant baptism.

In contrast, the Reformed view is that baptism may be administered by sprinkling or pouring, and that infants as well as adults may be baptized. Various views are held within the Reformed interpretation, some regarding baptism as little more than a dedication of infants, others as an impartation of grace short of salvation. The concept of the recipient being introduced into a covenant of grace similar to the rite of circumcision in the Old Testament is frequently mentioned. Though variously defined, the Reformed view regards baptism as representing union with Christ, a concept also present in the Baptist view. Both the Baptist and Reformed traditions say baptism pictures washing from sin.

Immersionists base their view of the mode of baptism on the statement that when Jesus was baptized, "He went up out of the water"

(Matt. 3:16). Though not stated, the implication is that He was immersed. Those who do not practice immersion, however, point to the fact that the word *baptō*, meaning "to dip," is never used in the New Testament and that *baptizō* means "to wash or to purify with water." In other words, in this view the main idea in baptism is cleansing, not immersion. Baptists, however, respond that *rantizō*, "to sprinkle," is never used of this Christian ordinance.

Baptismal regeneration is the idea that the new birth occurs at the moment of water baptism. Some Lutheran theologians hold that when a child is baptized he is regenerated, but they say this means that grace is imparted but that confirmation by faith as an adult is required for salvation. While many churches practice infant baptism, the Bible does not clearly record any such instance (though some argue that the baptism of the Philippian jailer's household would have included small children).

The rite of water baptism also pictures the baptism of the Holy Spirit. Eleven references to spiritual baptism are found in the New Testament (Matt. 3:11; Mark 1:8; Luke 3:16; John 1:30–33; Acts 1:5; 11:16; Rom. 6:1–4; 1 Cor. 12:13; Gal. 3:27; Eph. 4:5; Col. 2:12). Predictions of baptism by the Spirit were not fulfilled until the Day of Pentecost. The baptism of the Spirit, by which He places the believer into the body of Christ, is distinct from regeneration, indwelling, and sealing. The Pentecostal and Holiness traditions assert that it takes place at a time subsequent to conversion, but other evangelicals believe that it takes place at the same time.

In 1 Corinthians 15:29 Paul referred to the custom some people followed in being "baptized for the dead." Of the dozens of explanations of this phrase, one possible view is that new converts were being baptized to replace the ranks of those who died ("for" meaning "in place of"). The Mormon practice of "proxy baptism" (the living being baptized on behalf of dead ones to bring them into the fold of Mormonism) conflicts with the rest of Scripture. After death, there is no hope of salvation for the unsaved. (Heb. 9:27)

—JFW

Realize that being baptized is a testimony of your faith in Christ.

Blasphemy

ANY REMARK THAT MOCKS GOD or is contemptuous of Him can be defined as blasphemy. The Old Testament penalty for blasphemy is described in Leviticus 24:10–16. When the son of an Israelite woman and an Egyptian father "blasphemed the Name with a curse" (v. 11), God declared, "Anyone who blasphemes the name of the LORD must be put to death" (v. 16). It was likely Ezra who accused Israel of "awful blasphemies" (Neh. 9:18) when at Sinai the nation referred to the golden calf as "the god who brought you up out of Egypt." On Israel's journey to the plains of Moab, Moses delivered God's words to the people, declaring that a deliberate, defiant sin is blasphemous because it arrogantly challenges Yahweh's lordship. The guilty were to be "cut off," that is, they were to be excommunicated and executed (Num. 15:30–31). Because Israel was a theocracy, civil penalties were properly applied against religious offenses.

The Old Testament also describes how unbelieving nations blasphemed Israel's God. Nathan rebuked David for his sin with Bathsheba and declared that that sinful act had "given occasion to the enemies of the LORD to blaspheme" (2 Sam. 12:14, NASB). When the Assyrians likened the Lord to the gods of other countries, Isaiah, as God's spokesman, called that blasphemy (2 Kings 19:4, 6, 22). During Israel's captivity the Babylonians blasphemed God (Isa. 52:5). Other enemies of Israel, including Edom, mocked God because of the miserable condition of His people (Pss. 44:14; 74:10; Ezek. 35:12, NKJV).

Subsequently the Jews, out of dread of being inadvertently guilty of blasphemy, took the position that the name of God was too sacred to pronounce. So they substituted *'ădōnāy* ("Lord") for *Yahweh*. Some think the expression "kingdom of heaven" in Matthew in place of "kingdom of God" in Mark and Luke reflects this practice of Jewish avoidance of God's name.

In the New Testament, blasphemy is a hostile, contemptuous attitude toward God. Again, Gentiles are said to blaspheme God's name because of the hypocrisy of the Jews (Rom. 2:24). The Jews also were guilty of blasphemy in their response to Paul's message that Jesus is the Messiah. Luke recorded that the Jews "resisted and blasphemed" (Acts 18:6, NASB). The form their blasphemy took is not revealed, but it was possibly a direct cursing of Christ whom Paul proclaimed as God manifest in the flesh.

The Synoptic Gospel writers unite in charging that the Jews blasphemed when they insulted, reviled, and mocked Christ (Matt. 27:39; Mark 15:29; Luke 23:39).

It is startling that the religious leaders accused Christ of blasphemy on more than one occasion (Matt. 26:65; Mark 2:7; 14:64; Luke 5:21; John 10:33). As these passages show, the identity of Christ was the key issue. The leaders would not acknowledge that Jesus was the God-Man, the true and only Son of God, and so they charged Him with blasphemy when He claimed to be God and to have the authority to forgive sins.

Christ's words regarding blasphemy against the Holy Spirit have been much discussed. When the Pharisees perversely charged that the works Christ performed were accomplished by Satan's power rather than by God's power, that is, in the power of the Holy Spirit, Jesus responded with strong words. "I tell you the truth, all the sins and blasphemies of men will be forgiven them. But whoever blasphemes against the Holy Spirit will never be forgiven; he is guilty of an eternal sin" (Mark 3:28–29). This is usually called "the unpardonable sin."

Since the death of Christ makes possible the forgiveness of *every* sin, a person who blasphemed against the Holy Spirit would be forgiven *if* he subsequently came to faith in Christ. Jesus, however, affirmed that such a person, so hardened against Christ, will never come to faith and therefore he will never be forgiven. This heinous sin may therefore be described as "the unpardoned sin" rather than the "unpardonable sin."

While Bible scholars do not all agree, it would seem that because this grievous sin had a unique historical context which no longer exists, the unpardoned sin cannot be committed today. With the departure of Jesus from the earth, it is no longer possible for this particular offense to be performed. Blasphemy itself, however, has not passed away. False teachers practice it (2 Pet. 2:12), and it will be the abominable habit of the Antichrist during the Tribulation (Rev. 13:1, 5–6).   **—DKC**

Realize the seriousness of mocking or insulting God,
and be sensitive to the holiness of His name and person.

Blessing

WHEN GOD CREATED THE HEAVENS and the earth, He saw that it was good. After creating the creatures of the sea and the birds, He blessed them (Gen. 1:22). He made a man and a woman in His own image and blessed them (1:28), and after the six days of creation He set apart the seventh day and blessed it (2:2–3). Blessing is enrichment of something beyond its normal quality (Allen P. Ross, *Creation and Blessing* [Grand Rapids: Baker, 1988], 66). Enrichment can relate to material things such as land and food (Gen. 28:4; Deut. 12:15; 16:15), or it can be spiritual (Num. 6:24–27; Isa. 19:25). Blessing finds its ultimate source in God, for He has the power to bring enrichment to fruition.

God blessed individuals like Noah (Gen. 9:1), Abraham (24:1), and Isaac (26:3). On occasions God was the recipient of blessing from believers in the form of praise and worship (Gen. 24:48, NASB; Ps. 103:1, NASB). In this sense, to bless God was to desire that He be enriched or glorified by praise. An individual could evoke blessing on another person: Jacob blessed Joseph (Gen. 48:15), and Rebekah's family blessed her (24:60). David ascribed praise to God for sending Abigail and then bestowed a blessing on her for restraining him (1 Sam. 25:32–33). Jacob blessed his sons and foretold their future (Gen. 49:28). A blessing had great significance and was not to be treated lightly, as demonstrated by Esau's desire for a blessing (27:38; Heb. 12:17). Christian parents today may follow the patriarchs' example by affirming their children's worth, encouraging their spiritual growth, making provisions for their success, and challenging them to excel.

Since God is the source of blessing or enrichment, no legitimate blessing can be attributed to God or taken away unless He permits. The story of Balak and Balaam illustrates this. Balak hired Balaam to curse the Israelites, but Balaam could not curse them because God had blessed them (Num. 22:12).

Worship by godly Israelites, as reflected in the psalms, centered on the subject of blessing, often translated by the word *praise*. The blessing frequently came from an individual in extolling the greatness of God (Ps. 103), and some psalms express God's promises to bless (Ps. 115). Often the reason for God's blessings is stated (1:1–3; 5:12).

The prophets spoke freely of blessings from the Lord. The one who trusted in God would prosper and have no fears (Jer. 17:7–9). God desires to bless all those who wait for Him (Isa. 30:18) and are obedient to Him (56:1–2). God withheld blessing from the disobedient (Jer. 18:10, NASB). In the Millennium, when God will restore Israel to her land, He will bless her with security and an abundant harvest (Isa. 32:18–20; Ezek. 34:25–29). Though Israel has been an object of cursing among the nations, she will be blessed when God delivers her (Zech. 8:13).

In the New Testament there is a shift in the meaning of the term *blessing*, perhaps because there is no Greek word similar to the Hebrew term. The New Testament does not emphasize the promises relating to material prosperity so closely associated with Israel's blessings. The Greek word used to translate the Hebrew is *eulogia*, which means to speak well of someone or to praise and extol that person. Another New Testament term is *makarios*, which means "happy" or "fortunate."

In Jesus' Beatitudes (Matt. 5:3–11) He used the word *makarios* to emphasize inner qualities of immediate benefit to those whose hearts were turned to the Lord. The sermon also anticipated a future time when the meek will truly inherit the earth (5:5), as spoken of by the prophets. The Pharisees were not blessed by God, for while they emphasized an outward display of piety they lacked inner reality (5:20).

The New Testament epistles speak of the believers' blessing as the inner delight that stems from a personal, intimate relationship with the risen Christ. Paul described the blessedness of being justified by faith (Rom. 4), and he emphasized that believers in Christ are recipients of all spiritual blessings (Eph. 1:3). The blessing given to Abraham (salvation by faith) is also available to the Gentiles (Gal. 3:13–14). James called the man blessed who is able to stand up under trials and testing, because he will receive a reward from the Lord (James 1:12). Peter admonished people who follow Christ to seek a blessing by behaving in a way that reflects the graciousness of Christ, even when pressured or insulted (1 Pet. 3:9).

How fitting that the New Testament closes with majestic scenes of Christ in heaven seated next to the Father and receiving blessing (praise) from angels and every creature in heaven and earth (Rev. 5:11–14). For truly He is worthy! The apostle John wrote that those who trust Christ are called "blessed and holy" and will reign with Him for a thousand years (20:6). —WGJ

*Write down all the blessings that come from your being
in the body of Christ, and regularly give thanks for them.*

Blindness

JESUS HEALED MANY BLIND PEOPLE, as seen, for example, in Matthew 9:27–30; 11:5; 12:22; 15:31–32; 20:29–34; 21:14; Luke 4:18; and John 5:3; 9:1–12. His ability to heal blindness (as well as many other serious illnesses) helped demonstrate that He is the Son of God.

Another form of blindness is spiritual. This blindness results from sin (Zeph. 1:17). Isaiah announced that Israel's sinful leaders were blind (Isa. 43:8; 56:10). Several times Jesus told the Pharisees they were blind, that is, they lacked spiritual insight; they were unable and unwilling to receive divine revelation about who He is (Matt. 23:16–17, 19, 24, 26; John 9:39–41). Many people who heard Jesus' parables did not comprehend their meaning because they were spiritually blind; like the people to whom Isaiah ministered, they saw with their physical eyes but they did not perceive spiritually (Isa. 6:9–10; Matt. 13:14–15). In fact they could not believe because of their blindness to God's ways (John 12:39–40).

Those who are blind (*typhlos*) to spiritual things are also said to have heart-hardness or dullness (*pōrōsis*). The New International Version renders this word "stubborn" (Mark 3:5), "darkened" in understanding (Eph. 4:18), and "hardening" (Rom. 11:25). The verb *pōroō* is rendered "deadened" (John 12:40), "hardened" (Rom. 11:7), and "dull" (2 Cor. 3:14). To harden one's heart toward God leads to lack of theological discernment.

Because unsaved people do not have the indwelling Holy Spirit to teach them the truth of God, they are spiritually blind. As Paul wrote, "The man without the Spirit does not accept the things that come from the Spirit of God, for they are foolishness to him, and he cannot understand them, because they are spiritually discerned" (1 Cor. 2:14). "The minds of unbelievers" are blinded by Satan, "the god of this age" (2 Cor. 4:4). Though theology is typically a rational science built on facts organized in doctrinal form, the Scriptures make plain that even highly intelligent people may understand theology and yet be spiritually imperceptive because they are not saved.

Even sin in the life of a Christian can blind him or her to the truth (2 Pet. 1:9; 1 John 2:11; Rev. 3:17). The remedy to the spiritual blindness of the unsaved is regeneration, and for Christians who are blinded by sin the answer is yieldedness to the Holy Spirit. The "spiritual man" (1 Cor. 2:15) is able to understand the things of God. A Christian walking in the light of God's revelation (1 John 1:7) has his blindness lifted and is able to comprehend the truth of God.

In the present age Israel as a whole is hardened to the truth of the gospel (Rom. 11:7, 25). In God's judicial blinding of the nation they are unable to see (11:8); their spiritual eyes are darkened (11:10). But this is limited in time; it is "a hardening in part" (11:25) until the church age (in which many Gentiles are coming to Christ) is complete. Many Jews in the Tribulation will come to Christ. And after Christ, Israel's Messiah-Deliverer, comes at the Rapture, many Israelites will have their spiritual eyes opened and will recognize Jesus as their Messiah and Savior (11:26–27). —JFW

Pray daily that the Holy Spirit will open your eyes
to comprehend what God has revealed in His Word.

Blood

CIRCULATING THROUGHOUT THE BODY OF PERSONS and vertebrate animals, blood carries oxygen and nourishment to bodily tissues and removes poisonous matter like carbon dioxide. Scripture often uses the term *blood* in this normal sense of both animals and humans. Because it is essential for human existence, it is also employed as a synonym for life itself. The loss of blood thus often suggests violence, death of humans, or the death of animals in religious sacrifices.

While the word *blood* was thus connected closely with death, several Old Testament passages show how blood is also associated with life. Genesis 9:4 states, "Only you shall not eat flesh with its life, that is, its blood" (NASB). Leviticus 17:11 declares, "For the life of a creature is in the blood, and I have given it to you to make atonement for yourselves on the altar; it is the blood that makes atonement for one's life."

Deuteronomy 12:23 exhorts, "But be sure you do not eat the blood, because the blood is the life, and you must not eat the life with the meat."

These passages have provoked a theological debate as to whether the scriptural use of "blood" refers primarily to life or to death. Some, emphasizing the passages cited above, claim that in the offering of bloody sacrifices the life of the animal was released from the body and presented to God. The death of the animal is considered incidental. It is also contended that the New Testament references to the blood of Christ should be understood to mean Christ's life was set free to provide salvation.

Based on biblical evidence this view is to be rejected. The predominant association of "blood" is with death in the Old Testament, and such expressions as "the life of the creature" can be explained as meaning life yielded up in death in place of the sinner. Sin was considered so serious that it was to be punished by death: "The person who sins will die" (Ezek. 18:20, NASB). The sacrificial death of an animal was accepted as a substitutionary atonement for the human sinner. This truth is carried over into the New Testament, where it is clearly seen that salvation is provided, not by the life of Christ set free from His body, but by the death of Christ (for example, Col. 1:20, "by making peace through his blood, shed on the cross").

In the New Testament the word *haima*, "blood," occurs ninety-nine times. Sometimes it refers to death by violence, other times to animal sacrifices, and more than three dozen times to the blood of Christ.

The majority of the New Testament references to the blood of Christ are associated with His death on the cross. The blood He shed there is called by Paul "a sacrifice of atonement" (Rom. 3:25; see Lev. 17:11). In addition, many passages emphasize the benefits provided for us by Jesus' blood. Paul wrote that by the blood of Christ we are justified (Rom. 5:9), reconciled to God (5:10), redeemed (Eph. 1:7), brought near to God (2:13), forgiven (1:7), and given peace with God (Col. 1:20). Peter affirmed that we have been redeemed from our old and empty way of life "with the precious blood of Christ" (1 Pet. 1:18–19). John declared that Christ's blood provides continual cleansing for sin in the life of the believer (1 John 1:7). The writer of Hebrews emphasized that the Old Testament system of sacrifices and offerings found its final fulfillment in the blood of Christ, that is, in His sacrificial death (Heb. 9:7–28; 13:11–12).

As recorded in the Synoptic Gospels, Jesus at the Last Supper spoke of the cup as "the new covenant in my blood, which is poured out for you" (Luke 22:20). This is a clear reference to the redemptive significance of His death. We are exhorted to remember and proclaim His death by participating in the Lord's Supper, that is, by eating the bread and drinking the cup (1 Cor. 11:25–27).

John's Gospel records Jesus' discourse on the Bread of Life, in which He urged His listeners to "eat" His flesh and "drink" His blood (John 6:53–56). Jesus' cryptic expressions caused a violent argument among His listeners. The Jews should have understood that a literal meaning was not possible, because the Torah declared, "You must not eat . . . any blood" (Lev. 3:17; see also 17:10–14; Deut. 12:23). Further, as Tenney explained, "The metaphor of eating and drinking is the best possible figure that can be employed to express the assimilation of one body by another, the method whereby life is transferred from the eaten to the eater. The literal eating of Jesus' flesh and the drinking of His blood were not demanded. Jesus carefully explained that the process was analogous to His living by the Father, and certainly eating and drinking could not be literally applied there" (Merrill C. Tenney, *John: The Gospel of Belief* [Grand Rapids: Eerdmans, 1948], 122). We must appropriate by faith the sacrifice by which God grants forgiveness and eternal life. The blood of Christ is the "once for all" means of redemption. **—DKC**

In His love for us Christ did not hold back His own lifeblood,
thus calling us to a sacrificial pouring out of ourselves in service to others.

Body

WHEN GOD CREATED ADAM, He formed him from the dust of the ground and gave him a human body (Gen. 2:7). To this body God imparted life, and man "became a living being." Thus it is proper to conclude that every person has both a physical aspect and an immaterial aspect. In the beginning nothing sinful was associated with the human body because it was fashioned by God, and He said it was "very good" (1:31). The fact that Jesus possessed a physical body, which He said was prepared for Him (Heb. 10:5), is additional proof that the body in and of itself is not evil, because Jesus was perfect and without sin. Yet throughout church history some Christians have tended to think of the human body as intrinsically bad, leading to asceticism and certain monastic practices, denial of marriage, and excessive fasting. Viewing the body this way even led some in the early church to deny that Christ actually had a human body. Such views, of course, do not match with what the Bible teaches about the physical body.

When sin entered the world, it affected both the material and immaterial part of Adam, his entire being. Spiritually there was an immediate separation from God, and from that time on, his body would suffer pain and ultimately return to the ground (Gen. 3:17–19). Most of the Old Testament references to the term *body* relate to the physical body.

Jesus referred to the body numerous times in His teaching. He used two words to describe the material part of humankind: *sōma* ("body") and *sarx* ("flesh"). Though not identical, these two words are similar in some ways. Both denote the entire person (Matt. 6:23; 19:5). In referring to marriage Jesus used the term *flesh* (19:5; Mark 10:8). Jesus used *flesh* in a figurative way when explaining that a person must eat of His flesh, that is, believe in Him, to have eternal life (John 6:51–56). Jesus also used the term *flesh* to distinguish natural birth from spiritual birth (3:6). After His resurrection Jesus declared He had flesh and was not a ghost, thus affirming that He had a tangible body (Luke 24:39). When He instituted the Lord's Supper, He used the term *body* rather than *flesh* in referring to Himself (Matt. 26:26). Normally the term *body*, not *flesh*, was used of His crucified body (27:58; Mark 15:45; Luke 24:3).

The theological distinction between *sōma* and *sarx* is more clearly seen in Paul's epistles. The body (*sōma*) of the believer is to be an instrument of righteousness by which to glorify God as the temple of the Holy Spirit (Rom. 6:13; 8:11; 1 Cor. 6:19–20). Living for Christ in a sinful world demands that the bodies of believers be committed to Christ (Rom. 12:1–2). Exercising control of one's body is necessary for living a meaningful Christian life (1 Cor. 9:27). The body of every believer will be resurrected and changed and will endure forever (Rom. 8:23; 1 Cor. 15:52–53).

The flesh, Paul wrote, is hostile to God (Rom. 8:7), for those who live according to the flesh have their minds set on the things of the world and the ultimate result is death (8:5–6, NASB). Nothing about the flesh is pleasing to God (8:7–8, NASB). Even though the believer is in a struggle with the flesh, he cannot overcome it by human effort, for it takes the power of God (2 Cor. 10:3–4).

The church is said to be Christ's body, with Christ as its Head (Col. 1:18). Like parts of a human body, believers are to work together in unity (1 Cor. 12:12–26). As the head of the church, Christ enables it to grow spiritually (Eph. 4:15–16).

Paul also distinguished between the natural and the spiritual body (1 Cor. 15:42–49). The natural body is the physical body which will die and decay and then be raised when the Lord returns. The spiritual body is the body that is imperishable and will exist for eternity (15:53–54). The wording of 2 Corinthians 5:1–4 has led some scholars to suggest the possibility of an intermediate body, a body given to believers in heaven before their earthly bodies are resurrected. Since the evidence in this passage is inconclusive, it seems best simply to observe the distinction between our earthly and our heavenly bodies, one mortal and the other immortal.   —WGJ

Our physical bodies are a gift from God, to be accepted from Him as His creation. One day every believer will receive a new resurrected body in which he or she will serve Him.

Bride

MARRIAGE, INSTITUTED BY GOD in the Garden of Eden, was intended to provide a love relationship between husband and wife. Deepest intimacy was to be reserved for this relationship alone.

In Scripture, marriage is often used as an illustration of the relationship of God to believers. In the Old Testament Israel is described as one who started out as a bride and is now the wife of Yahweh, but who has been unfaithful to her marriage vows. Gomer, the unfaithful wife of the prophet Hosea, illustrates spiritual adultery. Though she was unfaithful,

Hosea loved her and took her back (Hos. 1:2–3; 3:1–3). Similarly after God chastises Israel for her unfaithfulness (2:1–13), He will restore her to Himself in the millennial kingdom (2:14–23; see also 3:5; 14:4).

In the New Testament, marriage illustrates the relationship of Christ and the church. Though the Scriptures predict that the church will be unfaithful, the ideal is described in 2 Corinthians 11:2, which speaks of the church as a pure virgin to be presented to Christ. This relationship is expounded in Ephesians 5:22–33. In New Testament times Jewish marriages had three stages: (a) the payment of a dowry by the parents of the bridegroom (which confirmed the couple's commitment to each other), (b) the bridegroom's claiming of the bride, sometimes up to a year later, and (c) the wedding feast. The parable of the ten virgins in Matthew 25:1–13 depicts a bridegroom with his friends parading through the streets at midnight to the home of the bride. When they arrive, she joins the procession with her girlfriends and goes to the home of the bridegroom, where there is a wedding banquet. This illustration is fulfilled in Christ's relationship to the church, for at the Rapture, Christ, like the bridegroom claiming his bride for himself, will take her to the Father's house.

At the second coming of Christ guests will be invited to Christ's wedding to His "bride," the church (Rev. 19:7). The word "wedding" means a wedding feast or banquet (see also 19:9; Matt. 22:2; 25:10); in New Testament times there was no marriage ceremony as such in Jewish weddings. The fact that the feast follows the bride's being claimed by the bridegroom tends to confirm that the Rapture will have already taken place before the Second Coming.

The church is already married to Christ because the price, like a dowry, has been paid by Christ on the cross. So the church should not be unfaithful to her "marriage vows" by loving the world or the things of the world (1 John 2:15). She is to have her affections centered on Christ (Col. 3:1–3).

The distinction between Israel as the unfaithful wife and the church as a virgin bride waiting for Christ is part of the contrast between God's purposes for Israel and His purposes for the church. While the church will be raptured at the beginning of the end-time events and taken to heaven, Israel will be restored after the second coming of Christ at the beginning of the millennial kingdom. At that time unbelieving Israelites will be purged out, and the righteous will enter into the millennial kingdom properly related to Christ (Ezek. 20:32–38). While the church will share with Christ in His reign over the earth, believing Israelites who will survive the Great Tribulation will move into the land promised to Abraham. Believing Israelites who have died through the centuries will be resurrected at Christ's second coming and will share in His reign on earth.

The figure of the bride emphasizes the central importance of believers loving the Lord, as Christ Himself declared in Matthew 22:37–38: "'Love the Lord your God with all your heart and with all your soul and with all your mind.' This is the first and greatest commandment."

In addition, the New Jerusalem, which will be the habitat of all saints in the eternal state, is called a bride. This imagery does not mean, as some suggest, that the New Jerusalem is to be inhabited only by church-age saints. Instead John was depicting the city as a beautiful place, as beautiful as a bride. —JFW

In heaven we will experience the sweet joy of being claimed
as His own by the One for whom we have been watching.

Building

TWO NOTEWORTHY BUILDINGS in biblical times were the tabernacle and the temple. The tabernacle was an elaborate tent built according to the instructions God gave Moses, a place where God dwelt among His people (Exod. 25:8). It was Israel's first place of worship and its importance can be seen by the number of references to it in Exodus and Leviticus.

The temple was equally significant. David spent many years preparing for this building, as it was his desire to build a house for God (2 Sam. 7:1–2; 1 Chron. 17:1). But God had different plans, for He told Solomon, David's son, to build the "house" (28:6). This temple was a magnificent building; yet it was God's presence that set it apart from all other structures. In contrast to the material building Solomon erected, the Lord promised David He would build a "house" for him (17:10). Metaphorically the term "house" referred to the family or dynasty God would build through David and his descendants. Even though, because of Israel's unfaithfulness, the temple was destroyed by the Babylonians in 586 B.C., the prophet Amos predicted God would rebuild it (Amos 9:11–12).

Zechariah described a "house" that was to be built in opposition to the house of God (Zech. 5:11), a place where wickedness will reside (5:8). The angel who revealed this to the prophet identified the location of this place as Babylonia (5:11; see also Rev. 17–18).

In the New Testament the concept of a physical building for worship was not significant. Jesus taught that a true understanding of God was far more important than any place of worship (John 4:21–24). Just as God promised to build a "house" for David, so Jesus said He would build a church that would be invincible (Matt. 16:18). The church He established was built on the apostles and prophets with Himself as the cornerstone (Eph. 2:20). It would be made up of believers from every national and ethnic group, all who have professed faith in Jesus Christ as their Savior (1:11–13; 2:22). Paul also described this unique group as the temple of the Holy Spirit (1 Cor. 3:9, 16). This church has taken on universal proportions, because visible expressions are on every continent of the world as believers meet together for worship and ministry. Peter used a similar figure to describe this building. Christ, he wrote, is the living Stone, and believers are living stones who are built into a spiritual house (1 Pet. 2:4–5).

The term *building* also refers figuratively to the spiritual growth of believers. God gave gifted people to the church so that Christians could be "built up" and reach spiritual maturity and be more like Christ (Eph. 4:11–13). People are built up as they apply the truth they have been taught (Col. 2:6–7). One way believers build each other up is by encouraging each other (1 Thess. 5:11).

Paul made an interesting comparison between the "tent" (body) Christians now live in and our bodies of the future. When the tent of a believer's present abode collapses in death, he or she will receive a new body, an eternal house in heaven, called a "building from God" (2 Cor. 5:1).

—WGJ

Be careful how you build your life, and make sure the quality of your deeds reflects your yieldedness to the Spirit.

Cc

Calling

IN THE OLD TESTAMENT God's calling related principally to His choosing Israel "out of all the peoples on the face of the earth to be his people, his treasured possession" (Deut. 7:6; 14:2; see also Pss. 132:13; 135:4). Israel is the nation God called (Isa. 48:12) and chose (44:1; see 45:4; Amos 3:2; Hag. 2:23) to be a channel of blessing to the world. He also called individuals to be sources of blessing, including Abraham (Gen. 18:19) and David (1 Chron. 28:10).

In the New Testament, divine calling relates to four aspects. The first of these is salvation (Rom. 8:28, 30; 1 Cor. 1:9, 24; Gal. 1:6, 15; 2 Thess. 2:13–15; Heb. 3:1; 9:15; 1 Pet. 1:15; 2:9; 5:10; 2 Pet. 1:3–6; Jude 1). A second form of calling is to special service, such as being an apostle (Rom. 1:1; 1 Cor. 1:1; 15:9; Gal. 1:15), missionary (Acts 13:2; 16:10), or priest (Heb. 5:4). A third form of calling is to any occupation, such as being a slave (1 Cor. 7:20–24). A fourth is God's calling to believers to lead holy and peaceful lives (1 Cor. 1:2; 7:15; Eph. 4:1; Col. 3:15; 2 Tim. 1:9; 1 Pet. 3:9).

Of significance in God's calling is the contrast between a general call or announcement of the gospel and God's effectual call which results in salvation (Rom. 8:28–30; 9:23–26). In Calvinistic theology this effectual calling to salvation is referred to as "irresistible" (see 8:29). This means that when this call comes it is part of God's program for salvation. It is obvious, however, that when the gospel is presented, the invitation to believe in Christ is not always followed by a favorable response on the part of those who hear. Arminians say this call means that God's common grace extends to all, so that everyone has sufficient grace by which to believe. While the Bible often speaks of grace (for example, Rom. 5:2; Eph. 2:5, 8), the terms "irresistible grace" and "sufficient grace" are not used. Christ's words in John 16:8–11, in which He spoke of the convicting work of the Holy Spirit, show that a person can be under conviction, fully aware of his or her need to receive Christ as Savior and still fall short of faith in Christ. Conviction, then, is related to God's general calling but is antecedent to an effectual calling to salvation. The call of God for salvation is initiated by God the Father, is made effective by the Holy Spirit, and results in a proper relationship with Jesus Christ as the Savior.

—JFW

Each believer is a "called" one,
summoned to escape the darkness and live in the light.

Canonicity

THIS WORD REFERS TO the Bible's quality of being canonical—that is, of possessing inherent authority as the God-breathed, infallible Word of God written by divinely chosen messengers. It also refers to the acknowledgment of this quality by the people of God throughout the centuries in accepting the books of the Bible as the sole rule of faith and practice—the canon of Scripture. This acknowledgment does not bestow canonicity on the books of the Bible; it recognizes and accepts their canonicity.

The word *canonicity* builds on the Greek word *kanōn*, which means "a rod," and then "a measuring rod," and "a rule" or "standard" (Gal. 6:16). The word *canon* is also used by various church groups to identify their authoritative rules for worship and government.

Since the Old Testament books were written largely by divinely appointed leaders in Israel—Moses, Joshua, David, Solomon, the judges, the prophets—they seem to have been accepted as canonical almost immediately. God Himself authenticated Moses' writings to Joshua (Josh. 1:7–8), who passed it on to Israel (23:6), as did David to Solomon (1 Kings 2:3). Their authority was stated numerous times later in the Old Testament (2 Kings 14:6; 23:25; Ezra 6:18; Neh. 8; Dan. 9:11–14; Mal. 4:4).

The acceptance of the Old Testament in New Testament times is seen in the fact that it is quoted approximately 250 times in every book except Esther, Ecclesiastes, and the Song of Solomon. The phrase "the Law or the Prophets" (Matt. 5:17) is an accepted designation for the entire Old Testament. For Jews the Council of Jamnia (A.D. 90) discussed some books that had been questioned and then confirmed the already recognized Old Testament books. Then in A.D. 170 Melito of Sardis produced the first list of thirty-nine books which constitute the Old Testament.

The New Testament books were written by apostles appointed by the Lord Jesus, by individuals associated with the apostles, or by half-brothers of Jesus who were leaders in the first-generation church. As a result, the authoritative character of those books was often quickly recognized, and sometimes was even stated in the books (see Col. 4:16; 1 Thess. 5:20; 1 Tim. 5:18; 2 Pet. 3:16). Various lists and discussions in the writings of the early church fathers show, however, that there was some debate over a few books for several hundred years. During the time up to A.D. 397 apocryphal and pseudepigraphical books were eliminated from inclusion in the canon, at which point the Council of Carthage designated the New Testament as the twenty-seven books we now have.

Although liberal theologians have denied the traditional authorship of numerous Old Testament and New Testament books, they have not removed any from the canon of Scripture. Conversely, none of the cults has established the canonicity of any of their so-called sacred writings.

—JAW

Receive and obey the words of the Bible,
whether spoken or written, as God's authoritative message.

Carnality

THIS WORD IS RELATED TO the Greek noun translated "flesh" (*sarx*) and its compounds (*sarkikos*, "carnal, fleshly," and *sarkinos*, "of flesh, fleshy"), and is derived from the Latin *carnalis*. It can simply refer to the fact that humans, as well as animals, birds, and fish, possess a body of flesh (Luke 24:39; 1 Cor. 15:39, 50; 2 Cor. 12:7). It can also refer to the finite condition of human beings with the normal appetites, desires, and sensations of the physical body (Rom. 7:14–15, NASB; 1 Cor. 3:1, NASB; 2 Cor. 3:3–5, NASB).

In theological usage, however, *carnality* normally has ethical, moral, and spiritual significance. Paul's confession, "I am carnal, sold under sin" (Rom. 7:14, NKJV), is true of every human being, "for all have sinned and fall short of the glory of God" (3:23; see also 5:12). Paul said unregenerate people follow "the ways of this world and of the ruler of the kingdom of the air" (Eph. 2:2) and seek to gratify "the cravings of [the] sinful nature [*sarx*] and following its desires and thoughts" (2:3). Even individuals who live highly ethical and moral lives are spiritually "dead in . . . transgressions and sins" (2:1) and therefore are in the basic state of carnality.

Carnality is also possible for the Christian, the "new creation" in Christ (2 Cor. 5:17; Gal. 6:15). Since the old sin nature is not eradicated by trusting Christ as Savior, it seeks to express itself in the Christian's actions whenever possible. Paul rebuked the Corinthian Christians, writing that he "could not speak to you as to spiritual people but as to carnal" (1 Cor. 3:1, NKJV). His complaint was that when, by reason of time, they should be more spiritually mature, "you are still carnal," evidenced by "envy [and] strife," and "behaving like [unregenerate] men" (3:3, NKJV).

This struggle between the residual sin nature and the new nature and indwelling Holy Spirit within the Christian continues throughout life. Paul wrote, "For the sinful nature desires what is contrary to the Spirit, and the Spirit what is contrary to the sinful nature. They are in conflict with each other, so that you do not do what you want" (Gal. 5:17). John also encouraged Christians not to "claim to be without sin" (1 John 1:8), but to "confess our sins" because God will forgive us (1:9). Furthermore, "if anybody does sin, we have one who speaks to the Father in our defense—Jesus Christ, the Righteous One" (2:1).

The secret to victory over the innate sin nature and carnality is "to offer your bodies as living sacrifices, holy and pleasing to God" (Rom. 12:1) and to "live by the Spirit" (Gal. 5:16; see also Rom. 8:5). "Since we live by the Spirit, let us keep in step with the Spirit" (Gal. 5:25), "because those who are led by the Spirit of God are sons of God" (Rom. 8:14).

—JAW

Though you cannot eradicate or outgrow carnality in this life,
you can control it by being submissive to the indwelling Holy Spirit.

Chastisement

THE HEBREW WORD *mûsār* and the Greek word *paideia* are translated "chastisement" by the King James Version, whereas other versions (for example, NASB, NIV) prefer the rendering "discipline." The basic meaning is that of education, guidance, correction, and sometimes punishment.

Discipline differs from condemnation. Paul declared, "Therefore, there is now no condemnation for those who are in Christ Jesus" (Rom. 8:1). But if a Christian willfully persists in sin there may be chastisement from God the Father, who is a perfect disciplinarian. Such chastisement can be avoided by following the counsel found in 1 Corinthians 11:31–32, "For if we would judge ourselves, we would not be judged. But when we are judged, we are chastened by the Lord, that we may not be condemned with the world" (NKJV). Thus the believer who has sinned should judge himself and make full confession to God. Such confession guarantees God's forgiveness and restoration to fellowship with Him (1 John 1:9). If a believer refuses to confess daily sin in this way, God may bring him or her under divine discipline.

The basic idea involved in the biblical treatment of chastisement is that God treats His people (the nation Israel in the Old Testament and individual believers in the New Testament) as a father treats his children. This involves training, guidance, correction, and punishment.

The central passage in the New Testament dealing with chastisement (discipline) is Hebrews 12:5–11, where the meaning of *paideia* carries the added sense of correction through suffering. The initial readers, Hebrew Christians, were suffering persecution and needed to be reminded that affliction is overruled by God and used for our instruction or training. The writer chided the believers for forgetting the encouragement found in Proverbs 3:11–12, where divine discipline is shown to be one evidence of divine love. This is a much-needed reminder in times of suffering. Further, divine discipline is an evidence of sonship. In fact, every child of God experiences the Father's chastening hand. The writer to the Hebrews drew on the analogy of earthly fathers, who have the responsibility of chastening or disciplining their children. Even though we were disciplined or chastened by our earthly fathers, we respected and obeyed them; how much more we should be submissive to the discipline of our heavenly Father. God's goal is that by means of His chastening we may "share in his holiness" (12:10), that is, reflect His holiness in our lives. Thus God chastens His people for their own spiritual benefit.

Other passages using the word *paideia* include Acts 7:22, where the emphasis is on the mental training or education of Moses; 1 Timothy 1:20, where Paul insisted that even through Satan beneficial discipline can be brought about; and Ephesians 6:4, where Christian fathers are exhorted by Paul to bring up their children in the "training [*paideia*] and instruction of the Lord."

—DKC

Thank God for His hand of discipline in our lives
because it proves that we are His children and that He loves us.

Children

SCRIPTURE MAKES IT CLEAR that children are a blessing and a gift from God (Pss. 127:3–5; 113:9; Gen. 33:5; 48:4). Sexual relations between Adam and Eve, conception, and the birth of a child are not mentioned until after the Fall and expulsion from the Garden of Eden (Gen. 4:1). However, as part of the marital union created and ordained by God, sexual relations and childbirth are not sinful but are natural and normal in the development of the human family and race.

Although conception of a child is considered a natural physical process, Scripture states that ultimately God is in control. Eve said, "With the help of the LORD I have brought forth a man" (4:1). Numerous times in Scripture God gave children to barren women—Sarah (18:10; 21:1–2), Rebekah (25:21), Rachel (30:22–23), Hannah (1 Sam. 1:19–20), and Elizabeth (Luke 1:7, 13, 24, 36–37)—and He withheld children from others, including Leah (Gen. 30:9). As a result, a husband and wife should prayerfully commit to the Lord their desire for a family.

Both parents are responsible to God for the physical, mental, and spiritual development of their children (Prov. 22:6), but Scripture places the primary responsibility on the father, both in the Old Testament (Deut. 6:7; 4:9; 11:19) and the New Testament (Eph. 6:4; Col. 3:21). To qualify as an elder or a deacon in a local church, a man must demonstrate control of his children and management of his household (1 Tim. 3:4–5, 12; Titus 1:6). In the control and discipline of their children, however, fathers are not to "exasperate" them (Eph. 6:4) nor "embitter" them so that they "become discouraged" (Col. 3:21). Constant criticism and correction of a child without corresponding approval and praise tends to produce either rebellion or low self-esteem.

In one sense all human beings are God's children by creation and providential control. At Athens the apostle Paul quoted with approval the Greek poet Aratus's statement that we are God's "offspring" (Acts 17:28–29). But in a special spiritual sense, people become children of God through faith in the Lord Jesus Christ (John 1:12–13) and are thus born "again" (Rom. 8:16–17, 19, 21, 23; Eph. 5:8; Phil. 2:15). Since believers in Christ are "dearly loved children," Paul commanded believers to "be imitators of God" (Eph. 5:1). As the heavenly Father of believers, God sets the example of human fathers in the discipline and training of children (Heb. 12:5–11).

While some people question whether young children need to be converted, the Scriptures point to the fact that everyone is born with a sinful nature (Pss. 51:5; 58:3; Rom. 3:9–12, 23). And the possibility of early childhood conversion is confirmed by Jesus' words that "little ones . . . believe in me" (Matt. 18:6) and "of such is the kingdom of heaven" (19:14, NKJV).

The Bible does not state specifically whether children who die as infants or toddlers go to heaven, but David's statement about going to be where his deceased one-week-old son was does suggest that they enter God's presence at the moment of death (2 Sam. 12:23). This would be fitting as an act of God's gracious love in providing heaven for very young children.   —JAW

Each day be a model of Christlike living to both your children and other young persons you contact.

Christ

THE ENGLISH WORD *Christ* transliterates the Greek *christos*, meaning "anointed one," which translates the Old Testament word *māšîaḥ*. Just as priests (Exod. 28:41; Lev. 8:12), the tabernacle and its furniture (Lev. 8:10–11; Num. 7:1), and kings (1 Sam. 9:15–16; 10:1; 15:1; 16:12–13; 2 Sam. 2:4; 1 Kings 1:39; Ps. 89:20) were anointed with oil in an act of consecration, setting them apart to spiritual service, so Christ was God's

"Anointed One" (Ps. 2:2; Acts 4:26). Even Daniel referred to Him as the "Anointed One" (Dan. 9:25–26).

Andrew told his brother Simon, "'We have found the Messiah' (that is, the Christ)" (John 1:41). And the Samaritan woman told Jesus, "'I know that Messiah' (called Christ) 'is coming'" (4:25).

Christ is one of many titles given to Jesus Christ in the New Testament, such as Lord (Mark 7:28), Son of God (Matt. 14:33), Son of Man (20:28), the Word (John 1:1; Rev. 19:13), Savior (John 4:42; 1 John 4:14), high priest (Heb. 2:17), and Prophet (Luke 24:19). He is referred to as Jesus, Jesus Christ, Christ Jesus, and the Lord Jesus Christ. He was also called Jesus Christ our Lord (Rom. 7:25), the Christ of God (Luke 23:35), and our Lord and Savior Jesus Christ (2 Pet. 3:18).

Christ's messiahship is related to His being the Son (descendant) of David. Christ did not use the term "Messiah" (or "Christ") of Himself, but He accepted it from His disciples. For example, Peter said, "You are the Christ, the Son of the living God" (Matt. 16:16; see also 16:20). When the high priest Caiaphas asked Jesus at His trial whether He was the Messiah, He answered, "It is as you say" (26:64).

On the Day of Pentecost Peter affirmed the messiahship of Jesus by proclaiming to the Jews "the resurrection of the Christ" and the fact that God "made this Jesus . . . both Lord and Christ" (Acts 2:31, 36). When Paul preached in the synagogue in Thessalonica, he reasoned with the Jews from the Scriptures that Jesus "is the Christ" (17:3). He did the same in Corinth (18:5), as did Apollos (18:27–28).

The Jews viewed the Messiah as a deliverer, whereas Christ Himself related His messiahship to His sacrifice on the cross (Matt. 16:21; Luke 24:26, 46), which would become a stumbling block to Jews (1 Cor. 1:23). The concept of a crucified Messiah, though difficult for the Jews to comprehend, was foundational in the teaching of the early church. Both Peter and Paul emphasized this truth that the Messiah would suffer (Acts 3:18; 17:3; 26:23).

At His return to earth, Jesus will reign over Israel as her promised Messiah, her Deliverer and King. **—JFW**

Honor the Lord Jesus Christ and worship Him wholeheartedly.

Church

THE ENGLISH WORD *church* derives from the Greek *kyriakon*, "belonging to the Lord." In the New Testament, however, *church* translates *ekklēsia*, "an assembly."

In the democratic city-states of Greece the citizens were called out to a local assembly to vote. This assembly was a group "called out," the basic idea in *ekklēsia*. In Acts 19:39 it is translated "a legal assembly."

Christ used the term only twice. In Matthew 16:18 He said to Peter, "And I tell you that you are Peter, and on this rock I will build my church, and the gates of Hades will not overcome it." In Matthew 18:17, in connection with disputes between brothers, Christ said, "If he refuses to listen to them, tell it to the church; and if he refuses to listen even to the church, treat him as you would a pagan or a tax collector." The assembly or church referred to in this verse is probably a Jewish assembly, rather than the universal church (the body of Christ) or a local church.

Elsewhere in the New Testament the word *ekklēsia* occurs many times, referring sometimes to a local church (for example, Antioch, Acts 13:1), sometimes to local churches in an area (for example, "to the churches in Galatia," Gal. 1:2), and other times to the church as the body of Christ (for example, Eph. 1:23 refers to true believers united spiritually to Christ similar to the way parts of a physical body are united to its head). This body of Christ is called the temple of the Holy Spirit (2:21) and "a spiritual house" (1 Pet. 2:5).

These references show that the word *church* is used (a) of the professing church, that is, those gathered geographically in a certain location, whether they are all actually saved or not, and (b) of the body of Christ composed of true believers who are not necessarily all assembled in one locality. Christ referred to the unity of believers in the body of Christ in John 17:1–26. The word *church* is used in a universal sense in reference to all true believers whether they are on earth or in heaven.

Why do we need local churches? It seems that God ordained them because He knew our needs: fellowship, worshiping with others, joint prayer, the teaching and study of scriptural truth, and service to each other's needs. The ordinances of the church, as outlined in Scripture, consist of water baptism and the Lord's Supper (Matt. 28:19; 1 Cor.

11:23–26). Ministers of the church are called elders or overseers (Acts 11:30; 20:17). Qualifications of elders are stated in 1 Timothy 3:2–7 and Titus 1:6–9.

According to Acts 6:1–6 deacons were appointed to care for various ministries such as the distribution of food, care for the widows, and similar matters. Qualifications for deacons are mentioned in 1 Timothy 3:8–12. Some leaders were distinguished as prophets by spiritual gifts (1 Cor. 12:28), but like teachers and those who have other gifts they were not considered officers with formal appointments. The gift of evangelism is recognized in Acts 21:8, but it too is not a formal classification.

Three forms of church government are followed today: (a) episcopal, in which a bishop is the governing authority over a group of churches; (b) presbyterian, in which elders govern the local church; and (c) congregational, in which the congregation acts as a whole on various matters.

For centuries some theologians have given the church the title "the new Israel," implying that Israel has forfeited its right to be called the people of God. This usage is much debated. The Reformed view tends to see more continuity between the Old and New Testaments and to emphasize the unity of the people of God in the one covenant, while the dispensationalist view is that there is more discontinuity, with Israel having its separate promises and destiny, so that the church should not be referred to as "the new Israel." In this view the church, the body of Christ, began on the Day of Pentecost and will maintain a distinctive identity throughout eternity.　　　　　　　　　　　—JFW

*Become involved in a local church for the purpose of
fellowship, worship, prayer, study, and service.*

Circumcision

CIRCUMCISION IS THE PROCESS of cutting off all or part of the foreskin of the male genital organ. Circumcision is performed as a religious rite by Jews on the eighth day of life (Lev. 12:3; Luke 1:59; 2:21; Phil. 3:5). It was practiced in ancient Egypt, Herodotus said, for hygienic reasons, and anthropologists have found it was performed by certain tribes in Africa, America, Malaysia, and Polynesia. Today it is frequently performed as a hygienic measure, usually shortly after birth. Both in the past and currently, some tribal peoples perform circumcision as a rite of passage from childhood to adulthood, usually at puberty.

God told Abraham that circumcision was "the sign of the covenant" between God and Abraham and his descendants (Gen. 17:11–14). "Abraham was ninety-nine years old when he was circumcised" (17:24). The fact that Ishmael was thirteen when he was circumcised (17:25) explains its practice in Islam when boys are thirteen. Since circumcision involves the shedding of blood, it may have signified the ratification of the covenant relationship. Commanded in conjunction with the change of Abram's name to Abraham and God's promise to make him "very fruitful" (17:6) and "the father of many nations" (17:4) and His promise of a son by Sarah (17:16, 19), circumcision can signify dependence on God, dedication to Him, and separation to Him from the world and its practices.

Despite God's command to Abraham concerning circumcision, its observance apparently was not always maintained in Israel's history (Exod. 4:25–26; Josh. 5:2–5). Circumcision eventually became a routine external religious rite. By New Testament times it had become a mark of Jewish ethnic and religious pride, and Jews looked on the uncircumcised with contempt. The apostle Paul confronted a form of this when the Jewish Christians from Judea came to Antioch and claimed that gentile believers must be circumcised to be saved (Acts 15:1). The same demand for gentile circumcision was made and rejected at the Council of Jerusalem (15:5–29). But the conflict with "the circumcision group" continued (Gal. 2:11–13; Titus 1:10).

The spiritual foundation for circumcision and its true significance was underscored by Moses in his farewell to Israel on the east side of the Jordan River: "Circumcise your hearts, therefore, and do not be stiffnecked any longer" (Deut. 10:16). Similarly just before the Babylonian captivity Jeremiah told the people of Judah and Jerusalem, "Circumcise yourselves to the LORD, circumcise your hearts" (Jer. 4:4). These were calls to separation from self and the world and to dedication to God as His covenant people.

As a Jew "circumcised the eighth day" (Phil. 3:5), the apostle Paul recognized circumcision's spiritual significance. He wrote, "Circumcision has value if you observe the law" (Rom. 2:25), and "A man is not a Jew if he is only one outwardly, nor is circumcision merely outward and physical. No, a man is a Jew if he is one inwardly; and circumcision is circumcision of the heart, by the Spirit" (2:28–29). Paul recognized, however, that the advantage "in being a Jew" and the value "in circumcision" was that circumcised Jews "have been entrusted with the very words of God" (3:1–2).

The time will come when God will redeem and restore His chosen people, Israel, and fulfill His covenantal promises to Abraham. Then, as Moses said, "The LORD your God will circumcise your hearts and the hearts of your descendants, so that you may love him with all your heart and with all your soul, and live" (Deut. 30:6). In this present church age, however, "Neither circumcision nor uncircumcision means anything; what counts is a new creation" (Gal. 6:15). "For in Christ Jesus neither circumcision nor uncircumcision has any value. The only thing that counts is faith expressing itself through love" (5:6). As a result of our faith in Jesus Christ and our position in Him we are "circumcised, in the putting off of the sinful nature, not with a circumcision done by the hands of men but with the circumcision done by Christ" (Col. 2:11).

—JAW

Acknowledge the Holy Spirit's spiritual surgery of circumcising your heart to separate you from the world to Christ.

Citizenship

WHEN THE APOSTLE PAUL wrote to the Christians in Philippi, a Roman colony whose residents held Roman citizenship, he reminded them that "our citizenship is in heaven. And we eagerly await a Savior from there, the Lord Jesus Christ" (Phil. 3:20). Earlier he urged them to "conduct yourselves in a manner worthy of the gospel of Christ" (1:27). The verb translated "conduct yourselves" literally means "live as citizens." Paul used the same verb of himself when he told the Sanhedrin, "I have fulfilled my duty [literally, 'lived as a citizen'] to God in all good conscience to this day" (Acts 23:1).

At the same time Paul recognized the importance of the rights and responsibilities of citizenship in this world. When he was arrested in Jerusalem, he told the commander, "I am a Jew, from Tarsus in Cilicia, a citizen of no ordinary city" (21:39). Later, when he was about to be flogged, he asked the centurion, "Is it legal for you to flog a Roman citizen who hasn't even been found guilty?" (22:25). When Paul, in response to the commander's question, confirmed that he was a Roman citizen, the commander said, "I had to pay a big price for my citizenship" (22:28), to which Paul responded, "I was born a citizen." Still later, when Festus would have sent Paul to Jerusalem from Caesarea to be tried, Paul appealed to Caesar (25:11), which was his right as a Roman citizen.

Earlier, when Paul and Silas were flogged and imprisoned in Philippi without a trial, the magistrates ordered them released the next morning and directed Paul and Silas to leave quietly in peace. Paul demanded that the magistrates come and escort them from the prison because their rights as Roman citizens had been violated by the public beating and imprisonment (16:37). When the magistrates "heard that Paul and Silas were Roman citizens, they were alarmed [and] came to appease them and escorted them from the prison" (16:38–39). Paul knew his rights as a Roman citizen and demanded that they be properly recognized.

Paul also acknowledged and proclaimed the Christian's responsibilities as a citizen. He wrote, "Everyone must submit himself to the governing authorities" because they have been established by God (Rom. 13:1). Submission is necessary "not only because of possible punishment but also because of conscience" (13:5). Paul directed Titus to "remind the people to be subject to rulers and authorities" (Titus 3:1), and Peter likewise wrote, "Submit yourselves for the Lord's sake to every authority instituted among men" (1 Pet. 2:13). Paul directed that "requests, prayers, intercession and thanksgiving be made for everyone—for kings and all those in authority" (1 Tim. 2:1–2; see also Ezra 6:10).

Identification as a Jew also involved a spiritual citizenship by virtue of the covenants and promises of God with Abraham, David, and the people of Israel. Before receiving Jesus Christ as their Savior, Gentiles were "excluded from citizenship in Israel" (Eph. 2:12), but when they place their faith in Christ they are "no longer foreigners and aliens, but fellow citizens with God's people" (2:19). Although Christians recognize their earthly citizenship and exercise their rights as citizens and fulfill their responsibilities, they, together with Abraham and other patriarchs, "are looking for a country of their own" (Heb. 11:14) and "longing for a better country-a heavenly one" (11:16). Christians recognize that "here we do not have an enduring city, but we are looking for the city that is to come" (13:14).   —JAW

Remember that believers are aliens in a foreign land, living here as ambassadors of our heavenly King and Lord.

Cleanness

IN THE LEVITICAL SYSTEM cleanness or uncleanness was either cere-monial or moral. Ceremonial cleanness or lack of it qualified or disqualified a person from participating in worship ceremonies. The moral aspect reflected the presence or absence of sin. That the two forms of cleanness were not to be severely divided is shown in Psalm 24:3–4: "Who may ascend the hill of the LORD? Who may stand in his holy place? He who has clean hands and a pure heart, who does not lift up his soul to an idol or swear by what is false."

Thus only a people both morally and ceremonially clean could approach the holy God and then only in the way He prescribed. God pointedly called Israel to cleanness or holiness because, in contrast to the capricious and vicious gods of the surrounding pagan cultures, He is holy. He said, "I am the LORD your God; consecrate yourselves and be holy, because I am holy" (Lev. 11:44).

The Mosaic Law stated a number of factors that rendered a person ritually or ceremonially unclean: (1) sexual matters—childbirth (Lev. 12), menstruation (15:19–24), unlawful intercourse (20:10–21), seminal emission (15:16–18; Deut. 23:10), an unnatural discharge (Lev. 15:1–15); (2) food—animals and food were classified as clean or unclean, and the clean could be eaten but not the unclean (Lev. 11); (3) disease—leprosy caused an unclean condition extending to anything the diseased person touched (Lev. 13–14); and (4) death—touching the dead brought uncleanness (Num. 19).

Various theories have been offered to explain the above laws. The principal ones are these: (1) Adherence to these laws would demonstrate to Israel and surrounding nations Israel's distinctiveness as the people of God. (2) Hygienic and dietary considerations, though sometimes depreciated, are supported by ongoing studies in the field of preventive medicine. Clean animals are seen to be safe for food, whereas unclean ones are to be avoided because they frequently transmit diseases and parasites. (3) The use of blood for atonement made it off limits for use as a food (Lev. 17:10–14). (4) Animals associated with pagan religions or with witchcraft were prohibited, such as swine, dogs, snakes, and others.

A complicated system of purification rites made provision for every form of uncleanness so that public worship of God could be resumed. (1) The lapse of time canceled secondary contaminations from a dead body (Num. 19:11), menstruation (Lev. 15:19), or childbirth (Lev. 12). (2) Water played a significant part in cleansing after contact with unclean things such as bodily discharges (15:5–11; see also Num. 8:7–19:9, 13; 19:17). (3) In certain situations defilement could be purged only by fire, as in the cases of contaminated pots (31:22–23), incest (Lev. 20:14), and idolatry (Exod. 32:20). (4) Sacrificial blood was the supreme source of purification for both ceremonial and moral defilements (Lev. 12:8; 14:21–32; 15:14–15, 29–30; 17:11). The uncleanness of sin or disease was viewed as transferred to the victim, thus illustrating the doctrine of substitutionary atonement.

In the New Testament, cleanness and uncleanness are discussed in relation to inward purity, although there are references to cleansing in the Levitical sense in connection with Judaism's rites and practices. Thus Jesus as an infant was brought to the temple for the rites of purification (Luke 2:22; see Lev. 12:2–8); the disciples of John the Baptist and some Jews discussed issues relating to purification (John 3:25); and there were jars for ceremonial washing at the wedding in Cana (2:6). Also, when Jesus healed some lepers, He sent them to the priests in Jerusalem to "offer the sacrifices that Moses commanded" (Luke 5:14; Lev. 14:2–32).

The question of ceremonial cleanness was an important concern in Jesus' controversy with the Pharisees. He rebuked ceremonial externalism; they were concerned with the outside of cups and plates while ignoring their own inner corruption (Matt. 23:25–26). True defilement,

Jesus taught, comes from the heart of the sinner and not from exterior pollution (Mark 7:14–23).

The Book of Acts and the Epistles continue the emphasis on inward purity. Acts 10 records how God taught Peter that Gentiles were not unclean and that Peter should receive them. The outcome was the conversion of the gentile centurion, Cornelius. In Romans 14:14 Paul wrote that "no food is unclean in itself." Yet a believer should not violate his own conscience by eating something he believes is unclean. Neither should he offend another Christian with a tender conscience by partaking without brotherly concern. The statements that "all food is clean" (14:20) and that "everything is permissible" (1 Cor. 6:12) were a rejection of ceremonialism. The Book of Hebrews was written to explain to Hebrew Christians that the rites and ceremonies of the Old Testament only foreshadowed the realities under Jesus' New Covenant. The Old Testament system provided for outward cleansing, whereas the blood of Christ cleanses the conscience (Heb. 9:10–14; 10:22). Thus ceremonial cleanness or uncleanness plays no part in the Christian era because "the blood of Jesus, his Son, purifies us from all sin" (1 John 1:7). **—DKC**

Pray with David, "Wash away all my iniquity and cleanse me from my sin" (Ps. 51:2).

Commandments

THIS WORD EXPRESSES AUTHORITY, whether divine or human, that expects obedience by the one who hears or reads. The term represents an important part of both the Mosaic and Christian systems. Various words in the Hebrew Old Testament and the Greek New Testament are translated "commandments," and these words occur about nine hundred times in Scripture.

In the Old Testament God's commandments clearly reveal His moral character. They were given to Israel, Moses said, for a specific purpose. "Keep his decrees and commands, which I am giving you today, so that it may go well with you and your children after you and that you may live long in the land the LORD your God gives you for all time" (Deut. 4:40). God's commandments in the Mosaic Law were thus given to the

Israelites to regulate their way of life, not to impart salvation, which came only by grace through faith in what God had revealed to them. Scripture makes it clear that the law(s) justified no one (Rom. 3:20); could not convey righteousness or life (Gal. 3:21); proved the innate sinfulness of man's nature (Rom. 7:11–13); shut sinful man up to faith as the only way of deliverance (Gal. 3:23); and served the Jews as a tutor (child-discipliner) until Christ would come (3:24).

Love alone would be able to motivate Israel to keep God's commandments. Moses charged, "Hear O Israel: the LORD our God, the LORD is one. Love the LORD your God with all your heart and with all your soul and with all your strength. These commandments that I give you today are to be upon your hearts" (Deut. 6:4–6). The Ten Commandments are usually divided into two groups, the first four pointing Godward and the last six pointing manward. Jesus thus summed up the Law by saying, "'Love the Lord your God with all your heart and with all your soul and with all your mind.' This is the first and greatest commandment. And the second is like it: 'Love your neighbor as yourself.' All the Law and the Prophets hang on these two commandments" (Matt. 22:37–40).

The Ten Commandments, one small section of the Mosaic Law, expressed God's righteous will and governed the moral life of Israel (Exod. 20:1–26). Following the Ten Commandments are the judgments that governed the social life of the nation (21:1–24:11). Then, the laws or ordinances regulating Israel's worship are given, beginning in Exodus 25:1. These divisions of the Law should not distract from the fact that Scripture views the Mosaic Law as a unit. Penalties, for example, for offenses cited in various parts of the Law were the same (see Lev. 10:1–7; Num. 15:32–36). James considered the Law as a unit when he declared that a single violation made the offender guilty of violating the entire Law (James 2:10).

The New Testament emphasizes that the Law has ended. Paul stated, "Christ is the end of the law so that there may be righteousness for everyone who believes" (Rom. 10:4). The leader of the Jerusalem Council gave an emphatic no in answer to the question of whether circumcision was required for salvation (Acts 15:1–35). Knowing the Law had ended, they made no attempt to place gentile believers under it. In 2 Corinthians 3:7–11 Paul affirmed that the Ten Commandments were done away, that what "was engraved in letters on stone" (v. 7) had ended. The writer of Hebrews explained that the Levitical priesthood instituted under the Mosaic Law had ended and been replaced by an eternal Priest, one after the order of Melchizedek. Thus since "there is a change of the priesthood, there must also be a change of the law" (Heb. 7:12).

But if the sacrifice of Christ brought an end to the Mosaic Law, why are some of the commandments still binding on Christians? Does the moral law, the Decalogue, remain in force while the ceremonial law has been abolished? This might have been an acceptable solution had all Ten Commandments been repeated in the New Testament, but the Law regarding the Sabbath is not repeated in the New Testament. Ryrie has offered a reasonable answer by proposing that the Mosaic Law as a code of ethical conduct was done away in its entirety and replaced by the law of Christ. Now the law of Christ contains many new commands but includes some old ones also. In a family, as children mature they live under different codes of conduct imposed by the parents. Some rules may carry over from one code to another, but the old one is abandoned when the new one is adopted. So it is when some of the commandments carry over into the new code of the church age (Charles C. Ryrie, *Basic Theology* [Wheaton, Ill.: Victor, 1986], 305). Certainly those commandments appear as grace principles. The Christian obeys them not to achieve merit, but because through the cross of Christ he *has* received merit, by grace through faith.

The night before His crucifixion Jesus spoke of the New Covenant to be instituted by His death (Matt. 26:17–30). Since the New Covenant replaced the old Mosaic Covenant, new commandments were also needed to guide believers. These were announced by Christ Himself, who said, "A new commandment I give you: Love one another" (John 13:34; see also 1 John 4:21). Believers are to obey Jesus' commands (2:3) because we love Him (John 14:15, 21). "His commands are not burdensome" (1 John 5:3), and obeying them pleases Him (3:22) and results in experiencing more of His love (John 15:10). He has also commanded believers to be His witnesses (Acts 1:8) and to carry each other's burdens (Gal. 6:2). **—DKC**

With God's help keep Christ's commandments, because He said, "Whoever has my commandments and obeys them, he is the one who loves me" (John 14:21).

Condemnation

WHEN AN ADVERSE DECISION or sentence is passed on a person, that person is said to be condemned. In the Old Testament the Hebrew word *rāšāʿ* is almost always translated "to condemn." It is employed with regard to civil matters (Deut. 25:1; Job 34:17; Ps. 94:21) and religious issues (Job 9:20; 10:2; Ps. 37:33; Prov. 12:2; Isa. 50:9; 54:17). These passages show that the basic thought is that of passing judgment against a person and thus treating him as guilty. In some cases a man condemned another without any legal procedure and the person turned out to be innocent, in which case God reversed the verdict (1 Kings 8:32; Ps. 109:31; Isa. 50:9). Christ warned against such false judgments. "Do not condemn, and you will not be condemned" (Luke 6:37).

In the New Testament the Greek word *katakrinō* means "to give judgment against" or "to condemn." Some writers feel a number of related words make a distinction between the sentence and its execution, but in the case of divine condemnation the two cannot be separated.

In the past God has condemned people for their sin (2 Pet. 2:6), and Paul wrote of the condemnation of the entire human race in Adam (Rom. 5:16, 18). The purpose for the coming of Jesus Christ was not to condemn the world, because humanity was already condemned (John 3:17–18). Rather, He came to save the world (3:17), and the clear declaration of Romans 8:1 shows He was eminently successful: "Therefore, there is now no condemnation for those who are in Christ Jesus." Of course, those who reject the Savior and His payment for sin continue under God's condemnation.

Other references in Scripture to condemnation include the statement that one man's godly life can condemn another (Heb. 11:7); that a person is self-condemned by his own words and deeds since they reveal his true character (Titus 3:11); and that a human judge may condemn justly (Luke 23:40–41, NASB).

A related Greek word is *katadikazō*, which refers to rich landlords punishing innocent laborers (James 5:6) and the giving of an account for our words on the day of judgment leading to acquittal or condemnation (Matt. 12:36–37). In 1 John 3:20–21 the Greek word *kataginōskō* speaks of believers' hearts condemning them. In such a case believers must reassure their misgivings by the fact that they "belong to the truth"

(3:19) and by the fact that God knows everything, including their hearts (3:20). Their conscience is not infallible and cannot always be trusted, but God who is greater and more knowledgeable can be trusted. Thus believers can "set [their] hearts at rest in his presence" (3:19).   —**DKC**

*Thank God for His promise that as a believer
you will never face condemnation (Rom. 8:1).*

Confession

ONCE A YEAR, ON THE DAY OF ATONEMENT, the Israelites participated in a ceremony to atone for their sins. Prominent in this event was the high priest's confession of the people's sins. The word *confess* carries the meaning of "acknowledgment," a recognition by the people of their offense against a holy and righteous God (Lev. 16:21). In a graphic way the people understood that forgiveness was based on blood that was sprinkled at the mercy seat.

In Solomon's prayer of dedication for the temple, he stated that confession was necessary for the forgiveness of sins against God (2 Chron. 6:36–39). The need for confession might be shown by a military defeat (1 Kings 8:33; 2 Chron. 6:24) or by the nation experiencing a drought (1 Kings 8:35; 2 Chron. 6:26).

Others who led the Israelites in public confession of their sins were Ezra, Nehemiah, and Daniel. Ezra led the people to confess their sins and to correct specific issues relating to unholy marriages (Ezra 10:1, 11–12). Under Nehemiah's leadership and Ezra's guidance the people were motivated to spend an entire day confessing their sins and listening to the reading of the Scriptures (Neh. 8:1–8; 9:1–3). As Judah's exile in Babylon was coming to an end, Daniel prayed for insight and understanding about the nation's future. His prayer included the confession of sin for himself and for the people. God heard his prayer and told him when to expect Jerusalem and the people to be free from sin (Dan. 9:20–24).

David's experience shows the importance of personal confession. After his heinous sin involving Bathsheba, he sought to cover the evidence and hide his sin. He expressed his anguish over this struggle in Psalm 32:4.

When exposed by Nathan, he acknowledged that what he had done was wrong and was contrary to God's character and law. God accepted his confession, and his sin was forgiven (2 Sam. 12:13). However, he still had many consequences to face in his personal and family life. Confession brings forgiveness but does not cancel the consequences of sin.

In the New Testament "to confess" (Greek, *homologeō*) means to say the same thing, or to acknowledge the truth. Interestingly the New International Version often uses the word "acknowledge" instead of "confess" when translating *homologeō*. Occasionally the confession concerns Christian doctrine and means an avowal of all the Bible says about the subject. When the word *confess* relates to sin, it means to acknowledge our agreement with God about the guilt of what we have said or done. To confess is to understand and recognize that one's sin is exactly what God has declared it to be. Genuine confession is not just repeating words; it is a deep conviction within the heart.

In the New Testament confession is mentioned in connection with acknowledging the truth about Jesus Christ and the tenets of doctrine revealed in Scripture. Jesus Himself said true disciples must acknowledge (confess) Him before men (Matt. 10:32). John the Baptist confessed that Jesus is the promised Messiah (John 1:20–23). Paul taught the need to confess Jesus as Lord because God raised Him from the dead (Rom. 10:9). Embodied in Paul's statement is the reference to the death of Christ. No one receives salvation who has not affirmed the death of Christ and the need for deliverance from sin. Jesus Christ's death and resurrection constitute the gospel (1 Cor. 15:3–4). According to the apostle John, both the incarnation and the deity of Christ should be confessed by every believer (1 John 4:2, 15). Someday every person, whether saved or unsaved, will acknowledge that Jesus is all He claimed to be and will confess this to the glory of the Father (Phil. 2:11).

Salvation does not eliminate the possibility of sin in the lives of believers (1 John 1:8, 10). Jesus alluded to this in the Upper Room when He washed the disciples' feet (John 13:10). To receive forgiveness and restoration of fellowship with God, who is faithful and just, Christians are to confess their sins (1 John 1:9). Confession expresses to God that we see our sins as He sees them, and we agree that sin is contrary to His holy character. Continually praying for forgiveness of some specific sin is unnecessary because He promised to forgive sin once it is confessed.

Confession restores fellowship with God and with others in the family of God as well (1:3).

—WGJ

Don't fail to confess each sin to the Lord because He will forgive.

Conscience

THE GREEK WORD translated "conscience" (*syneidēsis*) literally means "seeing together with." It came to mean "comprehension" or "understanding." Originally it involved the idea of looking back on one's past and evaluating it, from which quickly developed the meaning of conscience. Apart from a textually disputed clause in John 8:9 (NKJV) and three references to conscience by Peter (1 Pet. 2:19, NKJV; 3:16, 21), all the uses of the word are in Hebrews (9:9, 14; 10:22; 13:18) and in Paul's epistles.

Conscience, the capacity to evaluate personal actions and thoughts as right or wrong, good or bad, virtuous or evil, is innate in human beings. Apparently it functions in conjunction with an innate standard, because Paul wrote that "Gentiles, who do not have the law [the Ten Commandments], do by nature things required by the law" (Rom. 2:14) and thereby "show that the requirements of the law are written on their hearts, their consciences also bearing witness" (2:15). But a person's conscience can be "seared as with a hot iron" (1 Tim. 4:2) and "corrupted" (Titus 1:15).

Paul recognized that one's conscience is not necessarily a valid guide to divine approval. He testified often to a "good conscience" (Acts 23:1), a "conscience clear before God and man" (24:16; see also 2 Tim. 1:3), and a conscience that testified that he had conducted himself "in the world . . . in the holiness and sincerity that are from God" (2 Cor. 1:12). Nonetheless he stated, "I do not judge myself. My conscience is clear, but that does not make me innocent. It is the Lord who judges me" (1 Cor. 4:3–4). He also said that his conscience confirmed by the Holy Spirit the fact that he was speaking the truth (Rom. 9:1).

As Paul presented the gospel of Jesus Christ and the truth of God, he said, "We commend ourselves to every man's conscience" (2 Cor. 4:2; see also 5:11). He recognized, however, that some believers have weak consciences and do not have the freedom in Christ to eat food that had been offered to idols and then sold in the market (1 Cor. 8:4–8). As a result Christians with freedom to eat food offered to idols should be careful not to let their freedom "become a stumbling block to the weak" (8:9) and "wound their weak conscience" (8:12). To do so would be to sin against them and against Christ. Today food offered to idols is not an issue, but many debatable practices fall under the same guidelines.

When Christians are invited to meals by unbelievers, Paul advised them to eat what is served without asking questions (10:27). If the fact that the food had been offered to idols is stated, however, "do not eat it, both for the sake of the man who told you" and for his conscience's sake (10:28–29). He also urged Christians "to submit to authorities, not only because of possible punishment but also because of conscience" (Rom. 13:5).

Paul urged Timothy to hold "on to faith and a good conscience" (1 Tim. 1:19; see also 1:5), and the qualifications for a deacon—undoubtedly for an elder as well—include holding "the deep truths of the faith with a clear conscience" (3:9). The sensitivity and accurate response of the conscience are undoubtedly sharpened and strengthened by saturation in God's Word, a life of prayer, and a daily walk in the Holy Spirit.
—JAW

Gauge God's approval of your thoughts and actions by
His indwelling Holy Spirit and His Word, not by your conscience alone.

Conversion

IN THE OLD TESTAMENT the Hebrew verb *šûb* means "to turn" or "to return." The verb is used literally to describe, for example, Abraham returning to a particular place (Gen. 18:33). It is used figuratively for the turning or returning from a sinful course of life toward the Lord God of Israel (1 Kings 8:35; Mal. 3:7). As a nation, Israel often had to return to its God (Jer. 4:1), as did individuals like King David (Ps. 51). Those who disobeyed God's laws and steadfastly refused to return to the Lord were promised various forms of punishment, including ultimate banishment from the land in captivity (Deut. 28). Conversely, those who did return were promised forgiveness (Isa. 55:7), exemption from divine punishment (Jon. 3:9), and productive service (Ps. 51:13).

In the New Testament the Greek verb *epistrephō* similarly means "to turn" or "to return." Twice it is used in the negative sense of being turned from what is right to what is wrong (Gal. 4:9; 2 Pet. 2:21). But it usually describes the opposite—a turning from the wrong pathway to the right one. As such, the term is employed of both unbelievers and believers. In the case of believers it describes a return to a right relationship with God, after fellowship has been marred by moral failure (Luke 22:32) or doctrinal departure (James 5:19–20). When "conversion" is used with reference to unbelievers, it connotes the turning of a soul from sin to God. Paul wrote that the Thessalonian believers "turned to God from idols to serve the living and true God" (1 Thess. 1:9). Conversion, unlike regeneration and justification, which are acts of God, is considered an act of the individual, but one he or she is unable to perform apart from the work of the Holy Spirit.

Conversion is closely related to repentance. John the Baptist preached the need for Israel to convert or repent (Matt. 3:2; Mark 1:4; Luke 3:3), calling for a change in actions to show the reality of the conversion (Matt. 3:8; Luke 3:8). Jesus preached the same message (Matt. 4:17; Mark 1:15).

The conversion of Saul of Tarsus (Acts 9) is a dramatic example of conversion. Apostolic preaching called for people to turn from sin to God (Acts 26:20), and the result was the conversion of many people (9:35).

—DKC

Pray that the consistency of your walk will testify to the reality of your conversion.

Conviction

THE GREEK WORD *elenchō*, found eighteen times in the New Testament, means "to bring someone to a realization of his guilt." It is an antecedent to repentance and faith and is the work of the Holy Spirit, who removes the satanic blindness from people's eyes so that they are able to see themselves as God sees them—guilty and incapable of saving themselves (2 Cor. 4:3–4).

The central passage on conviction is John 16:7–11. Jesus explained to His disciples that it was necessary for Him to leave them, even though the separation would be painful and difficult. Unless He departed (by means of His death, resurrection, and ascension), He would not be glorified and He could not send the Comforter (the Holy Spirit).

The Holy Spirit confronts human beings regarding sin, righteousness, and judgment (16:8). These three elements constitute the substance of the Spirit's revelation to the unsaved. First, He convicts people of the heinousness of sin, specifically the sin of failing to believe in Jesus (see 3:18; 15:22, 24). Since Christ paid the penalty for all sin in His death, the only issue that remains is acknowledging what He has done and receiving Him as Savior (1:12).

Second, the Holy Spirit convicts the lost regarding righteousness (16:10). This probably refers to Christ's own personal righteousness, which was impugned by the act of the Jewish leaders crucifying the One they considered unrighteous. Only a wicked individual would be hanged on a tree, indicating he was under the curse of God (Deut. 21:23; Gal. 3:13). But by His resurrection and ascension Jesus was convincingly demonstrated to be God's righteous servant (Acts 3:14–15; Isa. 53:11). The Spirit thus affirms the righteous, in fact impeccable, character of the Savior. The unsaved, who have no righteousness to offer God, find in Jesus Christ all the merit and righteousness they need (2 Cor. 5:21).

Third, the convicting work of the Spirit involves judgment. This clearly alludes to the cross of Christ, by which "the prince of this world now stands condemned" (John 16:11; see also John 14:30; Col. 2:15). The unsaved should also contemplate the fact that there is a future judgment from which the only escape is found in Jesus Christ (Acts 17:30–31).

In addition to describing the convicting work of God's Spirit, the Greek word *elenchō* is also used of the practice of reproving, rebuking, or correcting within the Christian community. This theme is frequently seen in the Pastoral Epistles (1 Tim. 5:20; 2 Tim. 4:2; Titus 1:9, 13; 2:15). The procedure believers are to follow in this ministry of reproof is spelled out in Matthew 18:15–17. **—DKC**

Pray that the Holy Spirit will convict your lost friends and relatives of sin, righteousness, and judgment.

Covenants

THE OLD AND NEW TESTAMENTS both refer to several covenants between God and man, as well as between human beings. In the Old Testament the most prominent word is *berît,* and the most prominent New Testament term is *diathēkē,* which occurs more than thirty times.

A general definition of a covenant is difficult because of the varied use of this term. The divine covenants with people frequently have the force of a unilateral promise of God, with humankind being part of the covenant only in the sense of being the recipients. While a covenant is made with a group, its enjoyment by an individual may be conditioned on faith and obedience.

Old Testament covenants that bind equal parties are considered parity covenants. Two examples are those between David and Jonathan (1 Sam. 18:3–4) and Jacob's covenant with Laban (Gen. 31:53–54).

In the Old Testament a number of covenants were made between God and humans, in which God promised to accomplish certain things. These include the Edenic Covenant, having to do with God's promise to Adam and Eve in the Garden of Eden (Gen. 2:16–17); His covenant with Noah after the Flood (Gen. 8:21–9:17); His covenant with Abraham, introduced in Genesis 12:1–3; His covenant with David concerning the coming kingdom (2 Sam. 7:4–17); and the New Covenant (Jer. 31:31–37), which relates to peace between God and believers. These were not negotiated; they were introduced by God Himself. As such, they are not conditional, though, as stated earlier, the enjoyment of the covenant by individuals may be conditioned on faith, even though the fulfillment of the covenant concerning a group such as the nation Israel is absolutely certain. The Mosaic Covenant was a conditional covenant, which was fulfilled and abolished by the death of Christ.

Another covenant mentioned in the Old Testament is the covenant of marriage (Mal. 2:14), a two-way commitment between husband and wife.

In the New Testament the word *covenant* is used for a testament or will of a person that becomes effective when he or she dies. The concept of a covenant as a testament is particularly observable in the Epistle to the Hebrews, which includes over half of the New Testament references to covenants. The covenant of Jesus Christ is said to be better than the Mosaic Covenant (Heb. 7:22). He is the Mediator of this New Covenant (9:15;

12:24). At the Lord's Supper the Lord pointed out that His shed blood constituted the basis for His New Covenant (Matt. 26:28; 1 Cor. 11:25).

The interpretation of the fulfillment of the covenants is conditioned somewhat on the interpreter's view of the Millennium as variously held by the amillenarians, postmillenarians, and premillenarians.

Of special interest is the relationship of the New Covenant with Israel (Jer. 31:31–37) and its relationship to the church. Some combine these by regarding the church as the "new Israel," though this is rejected by premillenarians. While various solutions have been offered, it seems preferable to see the New Covenant as based on God's grace. This grace, secured by Jesus' death on the cross, is the basis for Israel's future restoration, which is apart from merit and will proceed entirely from grace. The same thing is true of the salvation of Christians in the New Testament era. Thus on the basis of the death of Christ not only Israel's future but also the salvation of believers in the present church age and in the future are assured. In addition this covenant is the basis for the salvation of all who are saved from Adam to the last person saved. It is therefore similar to the theological concept of the covenant of grace, which God promised in eternity past (Eph. 1:4–10).   —JFW

Enjoy the personal benefits God has given every Christian through the New Covenant, which was made possible by the death of Christ.

Creation

NOTHING DESCRIBES THE BEGINNING of all things with more finality, logic, and truth than the opening sentence of the Bible: "In the beginning God created the heavens and the earth" (Gen. 1:1). No explanation of this intricate, orderly universe, including planet earth with animal and human life, demands more blind faith than the theory that everything evolved by haphazard, mindless chance from a small cloud of inert cosmic dust. On the other hand, no explanation is more reasonable and satisfying than that this finite, limited universe—vast as it is—is the purposeful product of an eternal, infinite, omniscient person—the Lord God Almighty.

Consistently from Genesis through Revelation the Bible presents creation as having come by God and made from nothing (Gen. 14:19, 22; Job 38:4–7; Pss. 33:6–8; 148:1–6; Isa. 42:5; 45:12, 18; Mark 13:19; Rom. 1:25; Eph. 3:9; Rev. 4:11; 10:6). In Psalms God is frequently called "the LORD, the Maker of heaven and earth" (Pss. 115:15; 121:2; 124:8; 134:3; see 146:6), and elsewhere He is called "the Maker of all things" (Eccles. 11:5). Solomon instructed his readers, "Remember your Creator in the days of your youth" (12:1).

The Bible indicates that all three persons of the Trinity were involved in creation.

The apostle John wrote concerning "the Word" (John 1:1) that "through him all things were made; without him nothing was made that has been made" (1:3, 10). The apostle Paul likewise wrote concerning Christ that "by him all things were created: things in heaven and on earth, visible and invisible, whether thrones or powers or rulers or authorities; all things were created by him and for him" (Col. 1:16), and Hebrews states that God "made the universe" through the Son (Heb. 1:2).

God the Father is normally assumed to be the Creator, and one passage specifically refers to "the Father, from whom all things came" (1 Cor. 8:6). That same verse also speaks of "Jesus Christ, through whom all things came." The Holy Spirit, too, is identified as the Creator (Gen. 1:2; Job 33:4; Ps. 104:30). The triune God may be in view when "God said, 'Let us make man in our image, in our likeness'" (Gen. 1:26). In attempting to describe the order of the Godhead in creation, theologians speak of creation being from the will of the Father through the agency of the Son by the power of the Spirit.

The order of creation, especially for planet earth, is found in Genesis 1. This does not include the creation of angels (Ps. 148:2–5; Col. 1:16), nor does it include the creation of the "guardian cherub" (Ezek. 28:14–16), elsewhere called the devil and Satan. Presumably God's creation of angels preceded the creation of the universe, though this cannot be determined with certainty. The statement that "the earth was formless and empty" (Gen. 1:2) may suggest that an original creation was judged by God in conjunction with angelic sin (Isa. 14:12–15), because God "did not create" the earth "to be empty" (45:18). The creation of Adam on the sixth day (Gen. 1:26–31) was the capstone of God's creative work (2:1).

The time involved in God's total work of creation cannot be determined from Scripture. The original cosmic creation may have been millions of years ago. Furthermore, although the six creative days were most probably literal days (1:5, 8, 13, 19, 23, 31), large periods of time may have expired between them. The only thing Scripture does indicate is that the creation of humankind is comparatively recent. Because gaps may exist in the biblical genealogies, Bishop Ussher's date of 4004 B.C. for the creation of man cannot be accepted. Yet it is difficult to reconcile the biblical evidence with a date of more than ten thousand years ago.

Although on the seventh day God "rested from all the work of creating that he had done" (2:3), the entrance of sin and separation from God into human experience brought the necessity of creating once again. This involved the creating of new creatures in the Lord Jesus Christ. As Paul said, "Therefore, if anyone is in Christ, he is a new creation" (2 Cor. 5:17; see also Eph. 4:24). Elsewhere he wrote, "What counts is a new creation" (Gal. 6:15), "for we are God's workmanship, created in Christ Jesus to do good works" (Eph. 2:10).

Since God's judgment of human sin involved a curse on the earth as well, God's provision of deliverance and salvation for humanity will also ultimately include the restoration of the cosmic creation (Isa. 11:6–9; Rom. 8:18–22). Then, after the destruction of the present heavens and earth (2 Pet. 3:7, 10–12), God will create "a new heaven and a new earth, the home of righteousness" (2 Pet. 3:13; see also Isa. 65:17; 66:22; Rev. 21:1). —JAW

Rejoice in and care for God's beautiful creation, which glorifies Him (Ps. 19:1).

Cross

WITHOUT DOUBT THE MOST RECOGNIZABLE EMBLEM in all the world is the cross. It is synonymous with Christianity. In the Roman Empire the cross, two sturdy but crude wooden beams, was a method for administering the death penalty. Though He had committed no crime, Jesus suffered an ignominious death reserved for criminals. As

Isaiah the prophet had said, the Messiah would be "numbered with the transgressors" (Isa. 53:12). Apart from the crucifixion of Christ and the two robbers with Him, no other crucifixion is recorded in the Bible. The simplicity of the Gospel accounts is powerful, as all four say essentially the same thing: "They crucified him." Crucifixion was common in that day, and no additional words were needed to convey the shame, agony, and devastation of death on a cross.

New meaning was given to the term *cross* by Jesus' teachings. Even before His crucifixion He used the word to convey the concept of discipleship. On at least three occasions Jesus spoke about the cross. During His third tour of Galilee, He selected twelve disciples and challenged each one to take up his cross and follow Him. The disciples understood Jesus to be asking for total commitment to Him even at the risk of their lives (Matt. 10:37–39).

When Jesus was with His disciples in Caesarea Philippi, He announced His own death and resurrection. The message stunned His friends, and Peter rebuked Him for thinking those thoughts. Once again Jesus used the cross to explain discipleship (Matt. 16:21–26; Mark 8:31–37, Luke 9:22–25). Just a few months before His crucifixion in Jerusalem, Jesus reiterated words about the cross with an even stronger challenge, this time emphasizing the cost to follow Him, which could even mean separation from one's family (14:22–35). Jesus was not advocating self-crucifixion; He was explaining what was involved in total commitment.

When Jesus was dying on the cross, He said, "It is finished" (John 19:30). By these words He was signifying that He had completed the purpose for which He was sent by God (Matt. 26:39, 42). His death satisfied the demands of God's righteousness and brought redemption for humankind (1 Pet. 3:18).

The cross stands at the center of Paul's theology (1 Cor. 1:23). He saw this humiliating and cruel instrument in a new light—as the extraordinary opportunity to boast in his Savior (Gal. 6:14). The shameful cross stood for everything the world despised and thus His allegiance to Christ separated him from the world. Jesus' death was like a magnet drawing the outcasts of the world to Christ (John 12:32). It makes human wisdom foolish (1 Cor. 1:27) and weak people strong (1:25), and it breaks the spirit of the proud and lifts up the meek and humble

(1:28). Because of His death Jesus breaks the shackles of those in bondage who believe in Him. The Cross brings peace to those in fear (Heb. 2:14–15), and it unites Jews and Gentiles into one body (Eph. 2:16). The Cross brought complete fulfillment to the system of the Mosaic Law and did away with all the regulations standing against humanity (Col. 2:14–18). Because of the Cross, God gives eternal life to those who believe (Rom. 5:18). The Cross, which to the world seemed proof of defeat, became the means of triumph (Col. 2:15).

Paul saw the cross as an integral aspect of the Christian life. He said he desired to be like Christ in His death (Phil. 3:10). Comprehending the meaning of the Cross enables believers to reflect on His humility and deep concern for others (2:3–8).

The author of the Epistle to the Hebrews exhorted believers to stay focused on the Cross (Heb. 12:2) in order to avoid losing heart or growing weary. No one has faced adversity such as that of the Lord Jesus Christ on the cross (12:3). The message of the cross of Christ brings redemption and changes lives. **—WGJ**

Realize daily the significance of the death of Christ in your life
and find ways to tell others about the Savior's death for them.

Crucify

EARLY IN HIS EARTHLY MINISTRY Jesus revealed that He came to earth to die and that He would be lifted up as Moses lifted up the brass serpent in the wilderness (John 3:14). Few understood the meaning of His words at that time. Even when He clearly stated that He would be killed in Jerusalem and raised on the third day (Matt. 16:21; Mark 8:31; Luke 9:22), His disciples were shocked and in disbelief. Sometime later Jesus was tried by the Jewish leaders and then turned over to the Romans because the Jews were not permitted to carry out a death sentence (John 18:31). He was crucified in Jerusalem and died the same day. Historical records chronicle the gruesome details of death by crucifixion and the suffering endured by those who were victims. The Bible provides a minimal description of the actual event, but the significance of the crucifixion of Christ is thoroughly discussed. His death was not by accident; He was destined for the cross by the Father to become the Savior of the world (Isa. 53:10; Luke 22:42; 1 Pet. 1:19–20).

When Jesus spoke about crucifixion, He normally was referring to the well-known practice of nailing a person to a wooden construction designed for the death penalty. On several occasions before His crucifixion Jesus spoke of the reality of the cross to challenge His disciples (Matt. 16:24–25; Luke 14:25–33). He was not advocating self-crucifixion, nor was He suggesting that they would all be martyrs. In challenging them to take up their cross, He was graphically portraying the need for each believer to be totally committed to the Lord and His mission, regardless of the potential danger.

After His crucifixion and resurrection Jesus spent time with His disciples explaining the kingdom of God (Acts 1:3). During that time He opened their understanding to the significance of His crucifixion (Luke 24:45–47). Not surprisingly, then, the apostles' preaching centered in Jesus' crucifixion and resurrection. Peter emphasized that the death of Christ is the basis of forgiveness of sins (Acts 3:18–19; 10:43), available to both Jews and Gentiles (11:18). Years later when Peter wrote to scattered believers, he frequently mentioned the crucifixion of Christ (1 Pet. 1:18–21; 2:24; 3:18; 4:1), clearly stating that Jesus' death on the cross was the payment for sin. The doctrine of salvation is based on the crucifixion of Christ. In Paul's letter to the Galatians he wrote that Jesus was crucified to free us from the curse of the Law (Gal. 3:13). Each believer is identified with the crucifixion of Christ ("I have been crucified with Christ," 2:20). The apostle looked back to Calvary as bringing freedom from the Law and providing power to live by faith (2:20). He also claimed that the crucifixion of Christ separated him from the world system (6:14). What took place at Calvary brought him to his knees, and from the moment of his conversion Paul's preaching focused on Jesus and His death (1 Cor. 1:23; 2:2).

The message of the Cross is the power of God to save those who believe (1:18, 24). In essence the gospel Paul proclaimed consists of the fact of the death and resurrection of Christ (15:3–4). This was his message of reconciliation to the Gentiles, because when Jesus was crucified God was in Christ reconciling the world to Himself (2 Cor. 5:18–19). Justification, redemption, and reconciliation result from faith in Christ because of His crucifixion (Rom. 3:24–25; 5:10). Apart from the death and resurrection of Christ humankind would be lost forever, separated from God and without hope (3:23; Eph. 2:12).

Paul's development of the Christian life also centers around the death of Christ. Sanctification has its basis in the crucifixion (Rom. 6:1–14), for believers have been united to Christ in His death and resurrection. Because of this identification and union, the power of sin has been broken, believers have new life in Christ, and sin need no longer rule over them (6:5–7). Victory in the Christian life means the believer does not need to be defeated or dominated by sin, because of what Christ accomplished on the cross and because of the power of His resurrection. Christians need to recognize this truth and live in light of it (6:11).

Paul did not say Christians are to crucify themselves or their sinful nature. Rather, they need to recognize that this was already accomplished through the crucifixion of Christ (6:6). Therefore because of what Christ has done, the believer is to put off the old self and its practices (Eph. 4:22). When Paul said, "Put to death, therefore, whatever belongs to your earthly nature" (Col. 3:5; see also Rom. 6:11), he was reminding the Colossians to recognize what Christ had already done and to count it a reality in their lives. They had already taken off the old self and put on the new (Col. 3:9–10).   —WGJ

Realize at the beginning of each day that you died with Christ
and that you are free to live for Him and not be a slave to sin.

Curse

THE WORD *curse* IS NOT USED in the Bible in the modern sense of profanity. One of the Ten Commandments, however, is "You shall not misuse the name of the LORD your God" (Exod. 20:7; see also Lev. 19:12), and Jesus warned against speaking to others in a rude or scornful way (Matt. 5:22).

In the Bible a curse is an imprecation calling down the judgment of some false deity or the true God on a person or group of people. For example, Goliath the Philistine, "cursed David by his gods" (1 Sam.

17:43). Similarly, Balak, king of Moab, fearing the advancing Israelites, summoned the prophet Balaam, saying, "Now come and put a curse on these people" (Num. 22:6).

The Bible also indicates that some human beings curse God. This is an accusation of injustice and wrongdoing against God for one's afflictions and trials. Satan told God that if He destroyed Job's possessions and struck him with a disease, he would "surely curse you to your face" (Job 1:11; 2:5). After Job lost his possessions and all his children and was physically afflicted, even his wife advised him, "Curse God and die!" (2:9). But Job refused to charge God with wrongdoing (1:22; 2:10).

When the Bible speaks of God cursing a person, a place, or a thing, it signifies a judgment from God that may be executed immediately, in the future, or both. Thus the serpent in Eden was cursed by God to crawl on his belly then (Gen. 3:14) and ultimately to have the woman's offspring—the Lord Jesus Christ—crush the serpent's head (3:15). God told Adam, "Cursed is the ground because of you" (3:17), and later God told Cain, "Now you are under a curse" (4:11). After God's judgment on the human race and the earth with the Flood, He told Noah, "Never again will I curse the ground because of man" (8:21).

When God called Abram to leave his country, people, and father's household for a land He would show him, He promised that "whosoever curses you I will curse" (12:3). Following the directions given by Moses (Deut. 27:1–26), Joshua divided the people of Israel on Mount Gerizim and Mount Ebal and ratified the Palestinian Covenant with all its curses and blessings (Josh. 8:30–35). Later, because they had forsaken the Lord, the priests of Israel were cursed (Mal. 2:2), as were the people of Israel (3:9).

Paul wrote, "All who rely on observing the law are under a curse, for it is written: 'Cursed is everyone who does not continue to do everything written in the Book of the Law'" (Gal. 3:10; see also Deut. 27:26). He added, however, that "Christ redeemed us from the curse of the law by becoming a curse for us, for it is written: 'Cursed is everyone who is hung on a tree'" (Gal. 3:13; see also Deut. 21:23; Acts 5:30). As He hung on the cross, Jesus prayed for the people and priests who taunted Him and hurled insults at Him (Matt. 27:39–44), saying, "Father, forgive them, for they do not know what they are doing" (Luke 23:34). Likewise He taught His followers to "bless those who curse you" (6:28). —JAW

Be grateful that the hardships and trials God permits to enter your life are not curses from an angry deity but are blessings from the heavenly Father.

Dd

Darkness

IN THE BIBLE DARKNESS IS THE ANTITHESIS to God and light. This is true in both the physical and the spiritual sense. The apostle John wrote, "God is light; in him there is no darkness at all" (1 John 1:5). James described God as "the Father of the heavenly lights, who does not change like shifting shadows" (James 1:17). Especially in the spiritual sense, darkness represents everything that is opposed to God. It is identified with Satan (Acts 26:18) and his demonic forces (Eph. 6:11–12).

Because unsaved people are controlled by Satan (2:1–3), they are called "darkness" (5:8) and are under "the dominion of darkness" (Col. 1:13). They "sat in darkness" (Ps. 107:10), to be "living in darkness" (Matt. 4:16; Luke 1:79), and to be "walking in darkness" (Isa. 9:2). They love "darkness instead of light because their deeds [are] evil" (John 3:19), and "the way of the wicked is like deep darkness" (Prov. 4:19).

Despite its opposition to God and light, darkness as presented in the Bible is not equal to God, a view held by some forms of philosophical and religious dualism. Scripture presents God as in control of both physical and spiritual darkness (2 Sam. 22:29; Pss. 18:28; 107:14; Isa. 42:16; 49:9). In fact, God said, "I form the light and create darkness" (Isa. 45:7), a claim demonstrated on the first day of earthly creation (Gen. 1:3–5).

Darkness describes the chaotic condition of the waters covering the earth (1:2) following God's creation of "the heavens and the earth" (1:1). It is coupled with distress (Isa. 5:30; 8:22), drought and desert (Jer. 2:31; see also 2:6), gloom (Joel 2:2; Zeph. 1:15), and terror (Job 24:17).

God can dispel darkness physically (Gen. 1:3; Josh. 10:12–14) and spiritually (Isa. 58:10; 1 Cor. 4:5; 2 Cor. 4:6). In salvation He calls believers "out of darkness into his wonderful light" (1 Pet. 2:9) so that they no longer are "in darkness" (John 12:46). Furthermore He can see in the dark and knows people's hearts and thoughts (Job 34:21–22; Ps. 139:11–12; Dan. 2:22). God can also produce darkness, as He did when

He made a covenant with Abram (Gen. 15:7–21), judged Egypt with a plague of darkness (Exod. 10:21–23), separated the pursuing Egyptian army from the fleeing Israelites at the Red Sea (14:19–20; Josh. 24:7), and when "darkness came over all the land" for three hours while Jesus bore God's judgment for the sins of humanity on the cross (Matt. 27:45–46).

Darkness is identified with God's judgment in a number of ways. When God descended on Mount Sinai to deliver the Ten Commandments to Israel through Moses, it was covered with fire and smoke (Exod. 19:16, 18; 20:18), and "Moses approached the thick darkness where God was" (20:21; see also Deut. 4:11; 5:22–23). Moses explained that this display of God's glory and power was designed "to test you, so that the fear of God will be with you to keep you from sinning" (Exod. 20:20). God's judgment of Israel was called darkness (Jer. 13:16; 23:12), as was His judgment of Egypt (Ezek. 32:7–8).

God's final time of judgment—"the day of the LORD" (Amos 5:18) is called "darkness, not light" (5:20; see Ezek. 34:12; Joel 2:2, 31; Acts 2:20; Rev. 16:10). The ultimate destiny of unregenerate humanity is eternal separation from God; it is called darkness (Matt. 8:12; 22:13; 25:30), even "pitch darkness" (Prov. 20:20) and "blackest darkness" (2 Pet. 2:17; Jude 13). **—JAW**

In the darkness of this world let your light for Christ shine
to point others to faith in Him and thus glorify God the Father.

Day, days

THE WORD *day* has both natural and theological meanings in Scripture. The Jewish method of measuring a literal day was from sunset to sunset. The Babylonians on the other hand began their day at sunrise, and Egyptians and Romans viewed a day as extending from one midnight to the next.

According to the Old Testament the daylight hours were divided into morning, noon, and evening (Ps. 55:17). The only day of the week given a name was the Sabbath, although the day before the Sabbath came to be called the Preparation Day (Matt. 27:62).

The plural "days" is used to express "in the time of," in the case of Abraham (Gen. 26:18) and Noah (Matt. 24:37). The plural noun also describes the duration of human life as in Genesis 5:5, "So all the days that Adam lived were nine hundred and thirty years" (NASB). God the Father is named "the Ancient of Days" (Dan. 7:9, 13).

Frequently, especially in the New Testament, the word *day* is used in a figurative sense. Jesus said, "As long as it is day, we must do the work of him who sent me. Night is coming, when no one can work" (John 9:4). Similarly, Paul wrote, "The night is nearly over; the day is almost here. So let us put aside the deeds of darkness and put on the armor of light" (Rom. 13:12).

The days of creation have been the focus of much discussion by Bible students. Some understand the days of creation to be twenty-four-hour or solar days. Others support the day-age view, which posits that the creation days were actually long ages, thus accommodating the ages of uniformitarian geology. A mediating view holds to solar days of creative activity separated by long periods of time, that is, the geologic ages. Still another view is that the days of creation were "revelatory days" when on successive days God revealed to Moses what He purposed to do over a period of time.

Advocates of the day-age view note that the word *day* (Hebrew, *yôm*) in Genesis 2:4 (NASB) refers to God's creative acts as occurring over an extended period of time. Thus *yôm* in this verse would contradict the previous reference to six twenty-four-hour days. However, the Hebrew word can mean either a solar day or in a more general sense such as "at the time when" ("in the day that" in Gen. 2:4, NKJV, is rendered "when" in the NIV). Furthermore, whenever a numerical adjective is attached to the Hebrew word for *day* its meaning is always restricted to a solar day. Also some argue for the day-age view by pointing out that since the sun was not created till the fourth day the first three days were of indefinite duration. But solar-day advocates say possibly God created a temporary localized astronomic light on the first day to begin the day-night cycle. They also argue that the reference to day and night in Genesis 1:18 makes sense only in reference to solar days. What would be the meaning of day and night if the creative days were ages? Also Exodus 20:11 and 31:17 declare that God created everything in six days and rested on the seventh day. This clear analogy to man's cycle of work and rest suggests that Israelites would have understood the days of creation to be twenty-four hours.

In Israel special days were set aside for worship of God, including the Sabbath (Gen. 2:3; Exod. 20:8–11), the Passover (Exodus 12:14), and the Day of Atonement (Lev. 16:29–31). Work was forbidden and special rituals were carried out on those days.

Other references to *days* have an eschatological reference. Of major importance is the Day of the Lord, an expression that can denote (a) any divine intervention in history for judgment, (b) eschatological judgments of the future Tribulation period, or (c) the blessings of the millennial kingdom. The outcome of the Day of the Lord is described in Isaiah 2:17, "The arrogance of man will be brought low and the pride of men humbled; the LORD alone will be exalted in that day."

The Day of the Christ refers to the period connected with the coming of Christ for church saints. It is the time when the dead in Christ will be raised and living saints will be translated and taken to be with Christ in heaven (1 Thess. 4:13–17). There saints will appear before the judgment seat of Christ and receive rewards (2 Cor. 5:10). The Day of Christ is referred to in 1 Corinthians 1:8; 2 Corinthians 1:14; and Philippians 1:6, 10; 2:16. It will come to an end when believers return to the earth to reign with Christ.

Some interpreters identify the Day of God, an expression in 2 Peter 3:12, with the Day of the Lord. Peter, however, related it to the passing of the present creation and the coming of the new heavens and new earth, that is, the coming of the eternal day. A similar expression, "the great day of God Almighty" (Rev. 16:14), clearly refers to the battle (or campaign) of Armageddon at the time of Christ's return to the earth.

The term *last days* may refer to Israel or the church. With respect to Israel, it often describes the character of that nation's last days on earth, that is, the days of her kingdom glory (Isa. 2:2–5). In Zechariah 12–14 the frequent expression "on that day" refers to events surrounding the return of Christ and the millennial kingdom as they relate to Israel. The final days of the church before the Rapture will be evil in character (1 Tim. 4:1–5; 2 Tim. 3:1–5; Heb. 1:1–2; James 5:3; 2 Pet. 3:1–9; 1 John 2:15–19; Jude 17–19). In these and other passages the readers are often said to be living in the "last days," because those days, which began with the first advent of Christ, focus especially on the time of degeneration and apostasy at the end of this present church age. The New Testament writers saw that evil will be especially prominent in the final days. In essence, our present age is the last historical era before God intervenes to carry out His ultimate plans and purposes.

Other uses of the word *day,* especially in the New Testament epistles, refer to the day of wrath (Rom. 2:5; Rev. 6:17), the day of judgment (2 Pet. 2:9; 3:7), the day of redemption (Eph. 4:30), and the day of salvation (2 Cor. 6:2).

The word *day* is found over two thousand times in the Old Testament and over 350 times in the New Testament. Great care needs to be exercised in discovering how the word is used, either in a natural or a theological sense. **—DKC**

Thank God that this is still the day of salvation.

Death

VIEWED AS THE CESSATION OF PHYSICAL LIFE on earth, death is universally regarded as a mystery. Why should man, the crown of God's creation, have a briefer lifespan than some forms of plant and animal life? In fact, since man was made in the image of God, why should he die at all? The scriptural answer is that human death is a consequence of sin. Genesis 2:17, the Bible's first reference to death, records God's warning to Adam: "But you must not eat from the tree of the knowledge of good and evil, for when you eat of it you will surely die."

Paul in his Roman epistle describes death as the penalty for sin, tracing the entrance of sin into the human family to Adam: "Therefore, just as sin entered the world through one man, and death through sin, and in this way death came to all men, because all sinned" (Rom. 5:12). Theologians differ on the meaning of "all sinned." Some hold that it means that each person sins and therefore dies. But the words "all sinned" are connected with one man, Adam. We are to understand then that all sinned when Adam sinned. That is, Adam contained the seed of all humanity so that when he sinned all sinned. Another example of this concept is found in Hebrews 7:9–10, in which the writer explained that

Levi, though not born until two centuries later, actually paid tithes in Abraham, his great-grandfather. Thus Abraham, in a sense, contained his descendant, as Adam likewise contained his descendants, namely, the entire human race. Since the participants in Adam's sin were universal, the penalty—human death—is universal.

The Old Testament views death as a common fact of human experience (see, for example, Gen. 5, with its monotonous repetition of the doleful expression "and he died"). The happy exception of Enoch (5:24) introduces a glimmer of hope that death in some distant future may be overcome. Yet death was feared (Pss. 6:1–5; 88:1–14), especially an early death (2 Kings 21:1–11). Psalm 90, on the other hand, teaches that even a full life span is brief and ends because of God's wrath. God, nevertheless, is in control of death, for He sometimes granted escape from death (Ps. 68:20); restored dead persons to life (1 Kings 17:22, 2 Kings 4:34; 13:21); and promised that death will be overcome by resurrection (Isa. 25:8; 26:19; Ezek. 37:11–12; Dan. 12:2; Hos. 13:14).

In the New Testament the dominating theme is the death and resurrection of Christ by which He "has destroyed death and has brought life and immortality to light through the gospel" (2 Tim. 1:10). Believers in Christ are granted spiritual (eternal) life, but they remain subject to physical death because that is the last enemy to be destroyed (1 Cor. 15:26). For the Christian, death will be banished when Christ returns and the believing dead are raised imperishable (15:52). Then death will be swallowed up in victory (15:54). As for the unbelieving dead, they will be raised to stand before the Great White Throne for judgment. John concluded his description of that grim scene with the words, "Then death and Hades were thrown into the lake of fire. The lake of fire is the second death. If anyone's name was not found written in the book of life, he was thrown into the lake of fire" (Rev. 20:14–15). Thus the second death, the separation of the soul and spirit from God, is eternal death. The second death has no power over believers (20:6), for they are the heirs of eternal life.

The New Testament distinguishes between physical death and spiritual death. The former is the lot of everyone (Heb. 9:27) except for those who will be alive at the Lord's coming for the church (1 Thess. 4:16–17). The writer to the Hebrews said the death of Christ destroyed the one who held the power of death—the devil—and freed those "who all their lives were held in slavery by their fear of death" (Heb. 2:14–15).

Whereas physical death is the separation of the soul and spirit from the body, spiritual death is the separation of the soul and spirit from God. All persons are born spiritually dead (Eph. 2:1–3; Col. 2:13). Spiritual death began with the sin of Adam and was transmitted to each person by heredity from one's parents. The remedy for spiritual death is regeneration.

The ancient world had a dark and depressing view of death. Theocritus, a third-century B.C. Greek poet, wrote, "Hopes are among the living. The dead are without hope." Likewise, Lucretius, a first-century B.C. Roman philosopher, stated, "No one awakes and arises who has once been overtaken by the chilling end of life." In bold contrast, because of Christ's redemptive work the fear of death is overcome, the sting of death is removed, and departing this life by death brings positive gains for the Christian (Phil. 1:21). **—DKC**

The resurrection of Christ gives us confidence
that death has been defeated and we too will be raised.

Decrees

A DECREE IS A COMMAND or a statement of certainty, usually of earthly rulers who issue laws, but occasionally it refers to God's orders. In 2 Chronicles 30:5 it is translated "proclamation"; Ezra 6:11, Esther 1:20, and Daniel 6:7 translate it "edict"; and Ezra 5:13, Daniel 3:10, Luke 2:1, and Acts 17:7 record examples of human decrees. The conclusions of the Council of Jerusalem are called "decisions" (Greek, *dogmata;* Acts 16:4).

In contrast to the decrees of earthly rulers, however, God issued decrees, which refer to His plans (Job 23:14; Jer. 40:2) or His commands and statutes (Deut. 4:5; 1 Kings 9:4, 6; Ezra 7:11). In the latter sense *decrees* occurs twenty-two times in Psalm 119. The divine decree in Psalm 2:7 pertains to God the Son. "I will proclaim the decree of the LORD: He said to me, 'You are my Son; today I have become your father.'"

In theology *decree* (used in the singular) is regarded as including all God's plans and purposes for the future. It can also refer to some particular aspect of His all-encompassing plans. This decree embraces all things, including not only what God Himself does but also His rendering certain the actions of the entire universe. Election and predestination are included in this decree, but this differs from fatalism. The latter views events as happening without purpose, with humans powerless to change them. In God's decrees, individuals, as moral creatures, may obey or disobey, but all their actions are rendered certain by God. The supreme illustration of such a decree accompanied by human responsibility is the death of Christ. Decreed by God, it was absolutely essential to fulfill God's purposes, but at the same time its accomplishment rested on the decisions of individuals. "This man was handed over to you by God's set purpose and foreknowledge; and you, with the help of wicked men, put him to death by nailing him to the cross" (Acts 2:23). Peter and John said that those who crucified Jesus "did what [God's] power and will had decided beforehand should happen" (4:28).

—JFW

Accept the fact that God is in control of every aspect of life,
remembering that He will fulfill His purposes for your life.

Demons

THE ENGLISH WORD *demon* is a transliteration of the Greek noun *daimōn*, used once in the New Testament (Matt. 8:31), and the translation of the diminutive *daimōnion*, which occurs frequently. Demons also are called "deceiving spirits" (1 Tim. 4:1) and "evil spirits" (Luke 8:2). In some verses the word translated "evil" is literally "unclean" (Matt. 10:1; Mark 1:23; Luke 4:33; Acts 5:16). References to demons are found mostly in the Gospels in connection with the ministry of Jesus Christ, occurring infrequently in the rest of the New Testament and only twice in the Old Testament (Deut. 32:17; Ps. 106:37), where the word refers to pagan deities.

Outside of the Bible, especially in early Greek philosophy, *demons* referred to both positive and negative forces in the world. As time passed, the word was used increasingly of evil spirits who oppose people. In the Bible demons are opposed to God, the Lord Jesus Christ, and believers.

They indwell men (Matt. 9:32), women (Luke 8:2), and children (Matt. 17:17–18; Mark 7:25–30), and they can inflict physical and mental harm on some of those they indwell (Matt. 8:28; 9:32–33; 12:22; Luke 9:42).

Demons are spirit beings, but they obviously desire to indwell and control a human person or some body (Mark 5:12–13). More than one demon can indwell the same person (Luke 11:24–26), even as many as a legion (8:30), that is, six thousand or more. Because of this desire for embodiment, some people say demons are the disembodied spirits of the dead, especially the wicked or unburied. But the Bible does not support this view.

Like everything else, demons are under God's control. The Bible does not directly discuss their origin, but it does identify them with Satan as his agents (Matt. 12:24, 26), also called rulers, authorities, powers, spiritual forces of evil (Eph. 6:12). As a result they are identified as some of the angels created by God who joined Satan in his rebellion against God (Isa. 14:12–15; Ezek. 28:12–17; 2 Pet. 3:4). Like Satan, they are confirmed in their opposition to God and His program on earth among humankind and are destined for punishment forever in "the eternal fire" (Matt. 25:41; see Rev. 20:10). Some of the fallen angels are already confined, awaiting judgment (2 Pet. 2:4; Jude 6), but other demons are free to carry out Satan's program.

Although superior to human beings, demons are not infinite like God. They are finite, limited, and localized. They are spirit beings, but apparently they are able to assume visible forms (Rev. 9:1–11; 16:13). They have power far greater than human power, so that one demon-possessed man broke his chains when "chained hand and foot" (Luke 8:29), and another overpowered and beat the "seven sons of Sceva" (Acts 19:14–16). They are more intelligent than human beings, both innately and because they have been alive since before the creation of Adam and Eve. As a result, they knew who Jesus is (Mark 1:24), and they knew about Paul (Acts 19:15). They know God and His plan of salvation (James 2:19) and are aware of their final judgment (Matt. 8:29). They develop and promote false teachings (1 Tim. 4:1–3).

Demons have been active throughout human history; they are the spirit beings behind gentile nations (Dan. 10:12, 20) and pagan idols (Deut. 32:17; Ps. 106:28; 1 Cor. 10:20–21). However, they were especially active during the earthly life and ministry of the Lord Jesus Christ

(Matt. 4:24; 8:16, 28–33; 9:32–33; 12:22; 17:18; Mark 7:26–30; Luke 4:33–35). Jesus gave His disciples authority and power to cast out demons (Mark 3:15), a power they used (6:13; Luke 10:17) successfully most of the time (Matt. 17:14–21). In the early church the apostles had power over demons (Acts 5:16), as did Philip (8:7) and Paul (16:16–18) and Christians throughout church history (Mark 16:17). The activity of demons apparently will increase in the end times (1 Tim. 4:1; Rev. 9:20), undoubtedly as they, together with Satan, their leader, realize that their time of judgment is near and they are given greater freedom with the removal of the Holy Spirit's work of restraining sin (2 Thess. 2:7).

Jesus' enemies, the Pharisees, on numerous occasions accused Him of casting out demons "by Beelzebub, the prince of demons" (Matt. 12:24; see 9:34) and of being demon-possessed (John 7:20; 8:48, 52; 10:20), as they also accused John the Baptist (Matt. 11:18). Jesus pointed out the illogic of their accusation, stating, "Every kingdom divided against itself will be ruined" (12:25), and turned it back on them, asking, "And if I drive out demons by Beelzebub, by whom do your people drive them out?" (12:27). —JAW

In view of the demonic forces all around us,
"be strong in the Lord and in his mighty power" (Eph. 6:10).

Depravity

THE WORD *depravity* is used twice in the New International Version (Rom. 1:29; 2 Pet. 2:19), and *depraved* is used five times (Ezek. 16:47; 23:11; Rom. 1:28; Phil. 2:15; 2 Tim. 3:8). Neither word is used in the King James Bible, and *depraved* is used only twice in the New American Standard Bible (Rom. 1:28; 2 Tim. 3:8). These other translations use the words *corrupt, perverse,* and *reprobate.* As a result the word *depravity* is more of a theological term based on biblical testimony. This doctrine, frequently called "total depravity," refers to people in their unregenerate condition of spiritual death and separation from God with their inability to be or do anything to make themselves acceptable to God. Acceptance by God can come only when an individual receives by faith God's gracious provision of salvation from sin's consequences and penalty through Jesus Christ's death on the cross.

Humankind's state of depravity began when Adam and Eve disobeyed God's command by eating "from the tree of the knowledge of good and evil" (Gen. 2:17; see 3:6–7). Their spiritual death and separation from God began immediately and is seen in their hiding "from the LORD God among the trees of the garden" (3:8). The transmission of depravity to their offspring is demonstrated by Cain's murder of his brother, Abel (4:8). Its mushrooming manifestation in the generations following is described in Genesis 6:5, 11–12, and led to God's decision to destroy everyone, except for righteous Noah and his family, with a flood (6:7–10, 13). David confessed, "Surely I was sinful at birth, sinful from the time my mother conceived me" (Ps. 51:5).

Paul described the depths to which depravity will go when people refuse to glorify God and to give thanks to Him. Then "their thinking became futile and their foolish hearts were darkened" (Rom. 1:21). People became idolaters (1:23) and God "gave them over" (1:24, 26, 28) to practice "every kind of wickedness" (1:29). Although this undoubtedly describes the expression of human depravity which led to God's judgment by the Flood, it also portrays the depths of depravity since the time of the Flood and up to the present.

It is important to remember that depravity, although it may and frequently does express itself in wickedness of all kinds, means in essence spiritual death and separation from God. As a result an unregenerate person who is honest and moral and upright is depraved, just as is a moral pervert. Jesus told the righteous Pharisee, Nicodemus, "No one can see the kingdom of God unless he is born again" (John 3:3). The prophet Isaiah stated, "All our righteous acts are like filthy rags" (Isa. 64:6).

Because of their depravity, unsaved people cannot save themselves. In addition, "The god of this age has blinded the minds of unbelievers, so that they cannot see the light of the gospel of the glory of Christ" (2 Cor. 4:4). As a result, the convicting (John 16:7–11) and enlightening ministry of the Holy Spirit is required for individuals to be able to respond by faith to the gospel. Salvation is totally by the grace of God. Depravity does not mean everyone is as sinful as he could be; it does mean that sin affects every aspect of human thoughts and actions (Gal. 5:18–19).

When an individual responds by faith to the message of the gospel through Jesus Christ, the Holy Spirit takes up permanent residence in the believer's heart and life (2 Cor. 1:22; Eph. 1:13–14). The sin nature in the individual is not eradicated from the believer, however (Rom. 7:14–8:14). Because the indwelling Holy Spirit wars against the sin nature (Gal. 5:17), believers can have victory over sin by living in the power of the Holy Spirit (Rom. 8:4; Gal. 5:25). **—JAW**

When witnessing for Christ, be aware of the depraved hearts of unbelievers and trust the Holy Spirit to convict and save.

Disciple

THE WORD *disciple* comes from the Latin *discipulus,* an equivalent of the Greek word *mathētēs.* Both mean a pupil or learner. In Greek culture a disciple or learner was considered a philosopher's follower or sometimes an apprentice learning a trade. Scarcely mentioned in the Old Testament (1 Chron. 25:7; Isa. 8:16; 50:4), the concept nonetheless is found there with Samuel's, Elijah's, and Elisha's understudies, "the sons of the prophets."

In the New Testament the term *disciple* is found exclusively in the Gospels and Acts, where it is used in different ways. First, it describes the Twelve: Simon Peter, Andrew, James of Zebedee, John, Philip, Nathanael (also known as Bartholomew), Thomas, Matthew (called Levi), James son of Alphaeus, Simon the Zealot or Canaanite, Judas the brother of James (sometimes called Thaddaeus), and Judas Iscariot. Radical demands were placed on these men since Jesus, as an itinerant Teacher, was constantly on the move. Therefore a disciple of Jesus must literally be His follower (a word used some eighty times in the Gospels to describe the relationship between Jesus and His companions). The word *follower* in fact became a synonym for *disciple.* As a literal follower of Jesus the disciple had to give up his occupation (Mark 1:18–19), his parents (10:29), and "everything" (10:28). Thus the disciples of Jesus were in a unique and honored position not only to benefit from His teachings but also to be witnesses of the unfolding drama of redemption.

The term *disciple* is also used of the followers of other teachers, most notably the disciples of the Pharisees (Matt. 22:16; Luke 5:33) and of John the Baptist (Matt. 11:2; Mark 2:18; Luke 5:33; John 1:35–37). Mention is also made in the Gospels of the disciples of Moses, latter-day followers of his teachings (John 9:28).

In its widest sense the word *disciple* includes all who believed Jesus' words (John 8:30–31) and came to learn from Him (Matt. 5:1–2). These disciples composed a large number (Luke 6:17) and represented a cross-section of society from sinners to scribes (Matt. 8:18–22; Mark 1:16–20; Luke 6:14–16; John 19:38). Although many of these disciples were initially attracted to Jesus, many of them did not make a firm commitment to Him and defected when they found His teachings too difficult to accept (John 6:60–66). True disciples were expected to follow Christ wholeheartedly and to fulfill the crucial obligation of discipleship, namely, to make disciples of others (Matt. 28:19).

While the word *disciple* appears in Acts, it is used there as a general term for a Christian (Acts 9:25 and 19:1 are exceptions). Acts 11:26 declares, "The disciples were first called Christians at Antioch." This apparently marks the beginning point of the change in the designation of believers. Significantly, the writers of the Epistles did not use the word *disciple* a single time, perhaps because a disciple-teacher relationship with the earthly Jesus was no longer possible. To facilitate Christlikeness, the goal of discipling according to Luke 6:40, the Epistles emphasize the role of the Holy Spirit (2 Cor. 3:18), the indwelling Christ (Gal. 2:20), and the fellowship of believers. This goal of Christlikeness will only be ultimately and perfectly achieved at Jesus' return. "But we know that when he appears, we shall be like him" (1 John 3:2). **—DKC**

Strive to be a true disciple of Jesus,
depending on the Holy Spirit to help make you more Christlike.

Discipline

A FATHER'S DISCIPLINE of his son blends instruction and correction (Deut. 8:5; Heb.12:5–11). The concept of teaching and training—which includes attaining wisdom and doing what is right and proper—comes from the meaning of the words used in both Old and New Testaments. Solomon told his son not to despise the LORD's discipline, "because the Lord disciplines those he loves, as a father the son he delights in" (Prov. 3:11–12). The predominant emphasis in both Testaments is toward positive growth and development, although there is an aspect of the subject that relates to chastisement. Punishment is never seen as an end in itself. Rather it is to bring out the best in an individual and ultimately to cause him or her to glorify God. At least four areas of discipline can be found in the Bible: discipline of Israel as a nation; of individuals (both Old and New Testament believers); discipline by local churches; and parental discipline of their children.

Before the people of Israel entered the Promised Land, Moses reminded them of how God had spoken from heaven and demonstrated His power on earth through great and awesome deeds to discipline them (Deut. 4:32–36). One of the purposes of the Book of Numbers was to record God's actions in disciplining His people so we could learn from those experiences (1 Cor. 10:11; Heb. 4:11). Although God's actions seemed severe at times, they were based on His love for them (Deut. 4:37). The demands of the Lord are clearly described in Scripture, and without assistance the standards are often unattainable. Because God's discipline is anchored in His love and grace, His provisions are equally great.

The heart of the teaching on this subject comes from the Book of Proverbs. Given initially to Israel, these instructions apply to believers in any age. According to Solomon those who respond positively to discipline are good examples for others (Prov. 6:23; 10:17). Ignoring discipline will result in poverty and shame and reveal that people don't care about themselves (13:18; 15:32). The person who loves discipline loves knowledge (12:1), but the one who rejects instruction is a fool (15:5). Folly, Solomon said, is undisciplined, lacks knowledge, and is the opposite of wisdom (9:13). Because God disciplines in love, we should not resent His corrections (3:11). Solomon exhorted parents not to neglect disciplining their children even if it means using a rod (22:15). Failure to provide proper discipline can contribute to a child's ruin (19:18). Parental neglect of discipline demonstrates hatred instead of love (13:24).

The New Testament instruction on individual discipline amplifies the Old Testament teaching. The central passage is Hebrews 12. Jesus, who willingly endured the cross, is the perfect example for all believers who struggle with difficult experiences in life. These hardships are to be endured as discipline for they provide evidence of a close relationship to God (Heb. 12:7). Just as earthly fathers use discipline with their children, so the heavenly Father disciplines His children for their good. Discipline is not pleasant; in fact, the opposite is true (12:11). Yet it is God's way of making our lives productive in holiness, righteousness, and peace. If we respect our earthly fathers because they disciplined us, how much more should our hearts respond in love and gratitude to our heavenly Father whose discipline results in eternal benefits.

Another aspect of this subject is church discipline. Peter dealt with an issue in the early church at Jerusalem. Had he not done so, it ultimately could have been devastating to the entire church family. Ananias and Sapphira pretended to give all their proceeds from a property sale to the Lord, but they kept part of it for themselves. Peter, guided by the Holy Spirit, challenged them for lying. The physical death of this couple taught the church an important lesson (Acts 5:11). This and other passages in the Epistles provide some principles for church discipline. Action is necessary when individuals have sinned against the Lord, and it affects the life of the whole congregation (5:4; 1 Cor. 11:27–31). It is the responsibility of the leadership of the church to deal with issues within the church (5:12). If the individuals continue in sin after having been confronted, then certain restrictions are necessary (5:11). Disciplinary action should have as its goal the good of the individual as well as the preservation of the congregation (5:5). Once an individual has responded properly to church discipline, it is important to forgive him so Satan does not take advantage of the situation.

Another area where discipline is to be exercised is the family. Paul exhorted fathers to bring up their children "in the training and instruction [literally, 'discipline'] of the Lord" (Eph. 6:4). Those who are in church leadership are called to manage their families well with special reference to children (1 Tim. 3:4, 12). More specifically Paul told Titus that leaders' children are to be believers and are to conduct themselves in a godly manner (Titus 1:6). Bringing up children in the way of the Lord was considered a good deed (1 Tim. 5:10).　　　**—WGJ**

When God disciplines you, don't lose heart;
instead respond positively and learn from those experiences.

Disobedience

DISOBEDIENCE IS REFUSAL TO RESPOND positively to what is required. In theology it means failure to hear and do what God requires. Disobedience may be simply neglect (Heb. 2:1–2) or it may be active, outright refusal (Ps. 95:7–11; Heb. 3:16–18). At the root of this attitude is a heart that has been hardened, as was true of the people of Israel in the wilderness. Such a heart is said to be sinful and unbelieving (3:12). Unbelief and disobedience are linked, because failure to trust the Lord results in failure to do what He commands.

Examples of disobedience in the Scriptures are numerous. Even before God created Adam, some angels sinned. Satan was an angelic being whose attitude toward God was hostile. When he blatantly disobeyed God, he was immediately cast from His presence (Isa. 14:12, 15). Other angels followed Satan and are now under judgment (2 Pet. 2:4; Jude 6). Adam and Eve disobeyed God's explicit instruction and plunged the world under the condemnation of sin (Gen. 3:6–11; Rom. 5:12, 18). Moses disregarded God's command to speak to the rock and dishonored the Lord before all Israel (Num. 20:12, 24). Because the Israelites failed to believe that God would give them the land He promised (Deut. 1:26–27), they wandered in the wilderness for forty years. One man's secret defiance spelled disaster for Israel after an overwhelming victory over Jericho (Josh. 7:15–26). Failing to obey instructions, King Saul offered a sacrifice that displeased the Lord (1 Sam. 15:1–27), and this began his downfall. Samuel told Saul that God wants obedience far more than He wants sacrifices (15:22). The prophet Jonah rebelled against the Lord's orders and suffered deeply before God used him to spark a revival among the people of Nineveh.

A similar pattern is found in the New Testament. Disobedience resulted in the first sin in the church at Jerusalem when Ananias and Sapphira lied to the Holy Spirit and took credit for something they didn't do (Acts 5:1–11). In describing the last days, Paul indicated that disobedience would be prevalent (2 Tim. 3:1–2). He said it was an indication that the spirit of the adversary is at work (Eph. 2:2). The history of the church reveals that disobeying God brings devastating consequences.

Disobedience brought about the necessity of the death of Christ. Nowhere in Scripture is this so clearly seen as in Paul's letter to the Romans. Through the disobedience of one man, Paul said, many were made sinners (Rom. 5:19). This one trespass brought condemnation to all (5:18). Adam's sin was a blatant act, a breaking of a command (5:14). Christ's obedience, however, stands in sharp contrast to this one man's sin (5:19). Peter called Jesus the precious Stone for believers and a stumbling stone for those who disobey the message (1 Pet. 2:7–8). In this passage unbelief and disobedience are synonymous, although not all disobedience is a result of unbelief.

Several admonitions concerning disobedience are given in the Bible. Church leaders are to have children who believe and are not characterized as wild and disobedient (Titus 1:6). Christians are to be submissive to people who are in authority over them, both in society and in the church, because disobedience is a mark of unbelievers (3:1, 3). Believers should not associate with those who disobey God's Word (2 Thess. 3:14). The gracious conduct of a believing wife can be the means of winning over a husband who is disobedient to the Word of God (1 Pet. 3:1).

—WGJ

Learn God's commands in the Scriptures and determine,
with the Holy Spirit's help, to obey them.

Dispensation

THE WORD *dispensation* comes from the Greek word *oikonomia*, which means a stewardship or an administration. This word, which occurs nine times in the New Testament, comes from *oikos* ("house") and *nomos* ("a law"). An *oikonomos* was a person who ran a household or an estate as a steward or manager. The word *dispensation* does not in itself involve the concept of time, but the fact that one dispensation replaces another dispensation at a certain time suggests it. Thus dispensationalism refers to the view that God has administered the world in various stages of revelation and according to various principles or standards. Four times Paul used *oikonomia* of a divine stewardship or administration (Eph. 1:10; 3:2, 9; Col. 1:25).

The dispensations build on the idea that in Scripture there is progressive revelation, beginning in the Garden of Eden and having its ultimate fulfillment in the millennial kingdom. In each dispensation the "rule of life" for humanity involved certain obligations, and in each dispensation mankind failed to live up to God's standards. A number of dispensations can be identified, each of which to some extent built on God's revelation in previous dispensations but which involved additional revelation that dramatically changed the situation. In Eden the obligation was not to eat of the forbidden fruit. When conscience was given to the human race following the Fall, the rule of life was what the conscience indicated was right or wrong. This in turn was succeeded by human government in the time of Noah, which embodied the rule that murderers should be executed. To some extent conscience was continued. Following the failure of human government at the tower of Babel, God chose a new direction in His covenant with Abraham, which involved blessings on him personally, blessings on him as the progenitor of the nation Israel, and blessings to the entire world (Gen. 12:1–3).

The Mosaic Law introduced the most dramatic change in the dispensations in the Old Testament. Though it concerned only Israel, it revealed God's concern for the details of human life. While obedience to the Law evidenced saving faith, the Mosaic Law did not provide salvation. "No one is justified before God by the law" (Gal. 3:11). Works are never the basis of salvation (Eph. 2:8–9), but they do give evidence of it.

The present church-age dispensation began on the Day of Pentecost (Acts 2; see 11:15) and will end at the Rapture. The final dispensation will be the Millenium, when Christ will reign on the earth. Paul called this "the dispensation [*oikonomia*] of the fullness of the times" (Eph. 1:10, KJV). The Scriptures give extended revelation about three of these divine "economies"—the Mosaic Law, the present church age, and Christ's future reign on earth.

Though Christ's death abolished the Law of Moses as a way of life, as Paul argued in Galatians, many of its moral commands are repeated in the New Testament. No one is under the Law of Moses (Gal. 3:25). Believers are not slaves to the Law; instead, living under the rule of grace, they are sons and heirs of Christ (4:7).

God's rules of life change for mankind under subsequent revelation. But in every dispensation people are saved only by grace through the death of Christ.

All branches of theology recognize the existence of dispensations to some extent. Even nondispensational theologians recognize at least two dispensations. Some theologians see the dispensations as divisions of the covenant of grace. A branch of dispensationalism known as ultra-dispensationalism attempts to divide the present age into two divisions, one Jewish and one church-related.

Dispensationalists hold that Scripture maintains a clear distinction between God's program for Israel and His program for the church.

—JFW

List the provisions God has made for you in this present age,
as revealed in the New Testament, and appropriate these in your daily life.

Dreams and Visions

DREAMS ARE FORMS OF MENTAL ACTIVITY when a person is asleep. To some extent dreams relate to problems, fancied or real, that the individual is concerned with when awake. Most dreams have no theological significance, but in the Bible God often used a dream as a means of divine revelation. For example, God revealed to Jacob in a dream that his descendants would inherit all the land around him (Gen. 28:12–15).

Other dreams in which God revealed truths were given to Joseph (Gen. 37:5–11), two prisoners of Pharaoh (40:5–22), Pharaoh himself (41:1–32), a Midianite soldier (Judg. 7:13–15), Nebuchadnezzar (Dan. 2:1–45; 4:4–28), and Daniel (7:1–28). Other dreams, however, were entirely natural and nonrevelatory (Job 20:8; Pss. 73:1–20; 126:1; Eccles. 5:3; Isa. 29:7–8).

In the New Testament God gave dreams as a means of revelation to Joseph (Matt. 1:20–23; 2:12–13, 19–20, 22) and Pilate's wife (27:19). In Acts 2:17 Peter quoted the prediction in Joel 2:28, "Your old men will dream dreams," indicating that people will experience dreams and visions in the last days. These might be bona fide revelations.

Sometimes false prophets claimed to convey God's message by their dreams (Deut. 13:1–3). But such dreams are false or unreliable (Zech. 10:2).

A vision is an experience in which God appears and communicates some revelation to His servant. Visions in the Scriptures often occurred when the recipient was dreaming, but not always.

Individuals who received visions from God include Abraham (Gen.

15:1; 17:3), Jacob (46:2), Samuel (1 Sam. 3:15), Iddo (2 Chron. 9:29), Isaiah (Isa. 1:1), Ezekiel (Ezek. 1:1; 8:3–4; 11:24; 40:2; 43:3), Daniel (Dan. 1:17; 2:19, 49; 7:1–2, 7, 13, 15; 8:1–2, 13–19, 26–27; 9:21, 23–24; 10:1, 7–8, 14, 16), Obadiah (Obad. 1), Micah (Mic. 1:1), Nahum (Nah. 1:1), Zechariah the prophet (Zech. 1:8; 13:4), Zechariah the father of John the Baptist (Luke 1:22), Cornelius (Acts 10:3), Peter (10:17–20), Paul (9:10, 12; 16:9–10; 18:9; 26:19; 2 Cor. 12:1), and John (Rev. 9:17). Nathan and Habakkuk each received information from God in a vision. The New International Version translates "vision" in 2 Samuel 7:17 and Habakkuk 2:2–3 by the word *revelation*, thereby conveying the point that visions communicate information. Usually the person receiving a vision from God realized it was supernaturally conveying a message from Him. Since the completion of the New Testament, God no longer communicates new revelation by means of visions.   —JFW

Guard against any inclination to equate any dream
or personal experience with the revealed Word of God.

Ee

Election

THE BIBLE ADDRESSES several aspects of divine election. One is the election of Israel. God chose the nation Israel and set her apart as a special people among the nations of the world. This is frequently noted in the Old Testament (Deut. 4:37; 7:6–7; 10:15; 14:2; 1 Kings 3:8; Pss. 33:12; 105:6, 43; 135:4; Isa. 41:8–9; 43:20; 44:1; 45:4; Ezek. 20:5).

This electing of Israel is a completely sovereign act of God, not based on any conditions or the idea that Israel was better or worse than any other nation. God selected Israel so she would be a channel of revelation to others about His person, work, and will.

Because of her special relationship to God, Israel is regarded as a holy people (Exod. 19:6; 22:31), that is, a people set apart to Him. In a special sense, Israel is God's possession (Deut. 14:2; Pss. 33:12; 135:4). Therefore she is to praise Him (Isa. 43:21). God's special dealings with the nation express His nature, perfections, and love (Exod. 9:16; 32:9–14; Ps. 106:8, 47; Isa. 43:25; 48:9–11; 63:12–14; Ezek. 36:21–24).

In addition to being elected as a nation, certain persons and tribes in Israel had a special place in God's plan (Num. 16:5; Deut. 18:1–5; 1 Sam. 10:24; 2 Sam. 6:21; 2 Chron. 6:6; Ps. 78:68). However, the fact that Israel is an elect nation does not mean each individual Israelite has a personal revelation. This is stated clearly in Romans 9:8. Nevertheless, through Israel, God manifests His marvelous grace, as seen in Genesis 12:3 and elsewhere.

Another aspect of election is God's election of Christ. He is God's "chosen One" in whom God the Father delights (Isa. 42:1). At the Transfiguration God the Father said, "This is my Son, whom I have chosen; listen to him" (Luke 9:35). Though rejected by men, He was chosen by God the Father as "the living Stone" and "a chosen and precious cornerstone" (1 Pet. 2:4, 6; see also 1:20), that is, as the foundation of our faith.

God's election to salvation is unconditional, resulting totally from

His sovereign grace. In eternity past, God chose some individuals to salvation, as indicated in Ephesians 1:4 ("before the creation of the world"), 2 Thessalonians 2:13 ("from the beginning"), and 2 Timothy 1:9 ("before the beginning of time"). Related to predestination (Eph. 1:4–5, 11), election to salvation is an act of divine grace, for no saved person can merit salvation (Rom. 11:5; Eph. 1:7; 2:8–9). God chose to give new birth to those who believe in Him (James 1:18). Church-age believers, called God's elect (2 Tim. 2:10; Titus 1:1; 1 Pet. 1:1), are His "chosen people" (1 Pet. 2:9). Believers are to lead Christ-honoring lives (Col. 3:12) and to bear spiritual fruit (John 15:16). The "elect" in Matthew 24:22, 24, 31 are those who will be saved in the Tribulation, for the elect of the church age will already have been raptured before the Tribulation.

God's election is to be distinguished from fatalism. Fatalism is the belief that events are fixed without any intelligent end or motivation, whereas election is part of God's willful purpose for the world.

It is also important to distinguish between the omniscience of God, by which He is aware of every possible plan or modification, and His foreknowledge, which is a result of His determining what His purposes will include.

The death of Christ was absolutely certain (predetermined by God), and yet the wicked men who crucified Him were doing what they willfully chose to do (Acts 2:23; 4:28). Even though human choice was involved, the end result was absolutely certain. Similarly, God's electing some to salvation and not electing others was in accord with His purpose. But individuals must believe in order to be saved. As Luke wrote of Paul and Barnabas's ministry, "All who were appointed [by God] for eternal life believed" (13:48).

Christians are exhorted to make their election "sure" (2 Pet. 1:10), not in the sense that their decisions render it certain but that it should be clear to the individual that he is elected on the basis of his faith in Christ. It is possible for a person to have a false sense of security, thinking he was elected when he was not because he has not trusted in Christ.

The Bible also speaks of other forms of election. Some individuals are said to be chosen by God for special ministries, including David (Ps. 78:70), the twelve apostles (Luke 6:13; John 6:70; Acts 1:2), Stephen (6:9), and Paul (9:15; 22:14). Also some angels are called elect (1 Tim.

5:21). These are unfallen angels, whose election is based on the fact that it is absolutely certain that they will continue as holy angels, having decided in eternity past to serve God. Yet they cannot experience salvation from sin.

—JFW

Recognize that being chosen by God is an act of grace,
and respond to Him in gratitude and worship.

Endurance

GOD WILL ENDURE FOREVER. Even though creation, the work of His hands, will perish, He will remain, and His years will never end (Ps. 102:25, 27). Also God's Word (19:9; 1 Pet. 1:23–25), His name (Pss. 72:17; 135:13), and His kingdom (Heb. 12:28) will endure. Since God endures or is immutable, the qualities that are true of Him will also endure forever (for example, His love, Ps. 136:1–25).

Most biblical references to endurance refer to the subjective or experiential aspect of endurance by people. At least eight words are used to express endurance in the Old Testament and seven in the New. They provide various shades of meaning all relating to the concept of holding up or being strong (especially under pressure and adversity), bearing patiently, and being long-suffering. Endurance is closely related to perseverance, and English Bible translators render the Greek word *hypomonē* by both "perseverance" and "endurance."

Those who have trusted in the Lord (for example, Moses) are said to have endured (Heb. 11:27, NASB). They endured because of their faith in God. A review of Old Testament saints mentioned in Hebrews 11 provides a vivid picture of the difficulties these people faced—yet they endured because they were aware of God's presence and promises. Job is another example of someone who endured and was vindicated by the Lord (James 5:10). Paul said Abraham did not waver in his faith. He endured many years of frustration because he believed the promises of God (Rom. 4:20). Faith is the basis of endurance.

The greatest example of endurance is Jesus Christ. The writer of Hebrews said Jesus endured the cross, remaining steadfast in doing the

Father's will and even bearing shame and opposition from the adversary (Heb. 12:2–4). Believers are to follow His example so that we do not grow weary or lose heart. Reflecting on the crucifixion of Christ, Peter exhorted believers to follow in the Savior's steps, that is, to endure suffering (1 Pet. 2:20–21). In fact, Peter said it is commendable before God if a believer suffers for doing good and endures it. One of the marks of a true believer is the manner in which he or she exhibits endurance in the midst of the struggles of life.

Endurance is expected of all believers because of the Lord's gracious provisions that enable us to endure the challenges of life. It all begins with explicit trust in Him, believing He is faithful (Heb. 10:19–25). He is the source of our endurance. When we go through times of testing, suffering, or difficulties, our faith will sustain us and this results in endurance (James 1:4). At the end of our earthly life our endurance will give evidence that God has been at work in us, conforming us to the image of His Son (Rom. 8:29). We endure because of our hope in the Lord Jesus Christ and all He has provided through His death and resurrection (1 Thess. 1:3). Christians also have the indwelling Holy Spirit, who can produce qualities within us such as patience (Gal. 5:22).

Highlighting the believer's responsibility in endurance, Peter said we are to make every effort to allow qualities such as endurance to increase in our lives (2 Pet. 1:5–8). Those who trust the Lord can avail themselves of the complete armor God has provided in order to stand against Satan's attacks (Eph. 6:13). Paul prayed that the believers at Colosse would understand the power of God, which would bring them great endurance and patience (Col. 1:10–11). Paul himself was a model of endurance for Timothy as the apostle faced persecution, sufferings, and all kinds of adversity in serving the Lord (2 Tim. 3:10–11). Endurance validates the grace of God in our lives. **—WGJ**

Be encouraged through the strength the Lord gives you to remain steadfast in the midst of difficult circumstances and temptations.

Eternity

THE WORD *eternity* occurs only once in the King James Version (Isa. 57:15) and only three times in the New International Version (Ps. 93:2; Prov. 8:23; Eccles. 3:11). However, the words *eternal*, *everlasting*, and *forever* occur frequently. The fact that God has always existed and always will is mentioned often in both the Old and New Testaments. Infinite in His being, He has no beginning and no ending. This truth is summed up in Psalm 90:2, "Before the mountains were born or you brought forth the earth and the world, from everlasting to everlasting you are God" (see also Neh. 9:6; Isa. 40:28; Hab. 1:12).

"Eternal" is also used of something that has a beginning in time but then is of infinite duration. This applies to many things in Scripture, such as the everlasting covenants: the Abrahamic Covenant (Gen. 17:7, 13, 19; 1 Chron. 16:17; Ps. 105:10), the Davidic Covenant (2 Sam. 23:5), and the New Covenant (Ezek. 37:26; Heb. 13:20); the fact that God's arms (loving support) are everlasting (Deut. 33:27); and that Christians have eternal life (John 3:15–16, 36; 5:24; 10:28; Rom. 6:23; 1 John 5:11), which is called an "eternal inheritance" (Heb. 9:15).

In the New Testament the adjective *aiōnios*, "eternal," is used of damnation as well as the life God bestows on believers (Matt. 25:46; 2 Thess. 1:9). The chains binding fallen angels are said to be everlasting (Jude 6). At the end of the Millennium, Satan will be "thrown into the lake of burning sulfur," where he "will be tormented day and night for ever and ever" (Rev. 20:10).

Because God is eternal, everything about Him is everlasting, including His love (Ps. 103:17; Jer. 31:3), righteousness (Ps. 119:40), kindness (Isa. 54:8), power (Rom. 1:20), and purposes (Eph. 3:11). Believers have an "eternal house in heaven" (2 Cor. 5:1), where they will enjoy "eternal glory" with Christ forever (2 Tim. 2:10). Meanwhile they experience His eternal joy (Isa. 61:7) and encouragement (2 Thess. 2:18).   **—JFW**

Live each day with the realization that life in Christ does not end at death.

Evangelism

FROM BEFORE THE CREATION OF THE WORLD, the redemption of humankind was on the mind of God (1 Pet. 1:19–20), and it always will be until the final judgment of all who have rejected His Son (Rev. 20:11–15). Old Testament writers clearly taught that salvation from sin is the work of God (for example, Isa. 49:25–26; 55:6–7), and faith is the means of appropriating this provision (Heb. 11:6).

Evangelism is the term that best describes the activity of believers who proclaim the good news about salvation. By the very nature of the message, evangelism is primarily concerned with the ministry of people who have lived after the death, resurrection, and ascension of Christ. Israelites were not commanded to evangelize other people, even though in their national identity they were to be witnesses to the power and character of God (Isa. 43:11–13). During the time of Christ the message of salvation was given primarily to "the lost sheep of Israel" (Matt. 10:5–6), and that message concerned the nearness of the kingdom (4:17; 10:7). Certainly there were notable exceptions, but the major thrust was to Israelites. Not until Christ rose from the dead was a specific command given to believers to go to all nations, taking them the message of salvation (28:19–20; Luke 24:47). While Jesus was on the earth, He spent much of His time preparing His disciples for this task.

The importance of evangelism cannot be overstated. God loved the world and sent His Son to be the Savior, and those who do not believe in Christ are lost (John 3:16, 36). Apart from the death and resurrection of the Lord Jesus, there is no other way of salvation (Acts 4:12). Apart from hearing the good news, unbelievers will not have the opportunity to receive Christ (Rom. 10:14–15). One reason the Lord has not returned is that He longs for many more to come to Him (2 Pet. 3:9).

Evangelism is the responsibility of everyone in the body of Christ. Paul taught that all who have received Christ and have been reconciled to God have been entrusted with the ministry of reconciliation (2 Cor. 5:18). Believers are to be ambassadors for Christ (5:20) and His witnesses (Acts 1:8). The gospel was so important to the apostle Paul that he felt compelled to proclaim it (1 Cor. 9:16), considering himself a slave to everyone so he could win as many to Christ as possible (9:19–23). The work of evangelism is possible because of the power of the gospel (Rom. 1:16), the convicting ministry of the Holy Spirit (John 16:8), the authority and clarity of the Bible (2 Tim. 3:16; Heb. 4:12), and the prayers of God's people (Rom. 10:1). God does give the spiritual gift of evangelism to some (Eph. 4:11), but this gift is not necessary in order for a believer to be able to lead a person to Christ. Paul challenged Timothy to "do the work of an evangelist," which should be the model of every Christian (2 Tim. 4:5). Evangelism is possible, not only by what we say but also by the way we live (1 Pet. 3:1–2, 4).

The message of evangelism is clear and uncomplicated. Paul wrote to the Corinthians about the gospel he preached, which they received and was the foundation of their life in Christ. The message concerned Christ's death for sins and His subsequent burial and resurrection (1 Cor. 15:1–4). The death of Christ paid for the sins of the world, and because of the resurrection He imparts eternal life to every sinner who believes (Titus 3:5–7). Paul declared that those who trust in Christ become a new creation (2 Cor. 5:17). Salvation is described as a gift from God apart from any human effort or work, and this gift is appropriated by faith (Acts 16:31; Rom. 10:9–10; Eph. 2:8–9). Though the message of evangelism is easily stated, it cannot be comprehended and received apart from the enlightening work of the Holy Spirit (John 16:8–11; Rom. 8:9; 1 Cor. 2:14). This is why the effective ministry of evangelism involves more than presenting a clear and accurate message. Salvation is dependent on the power of God rather than the eloquence or persuasiveness of the evangelist (2:4).

The details of the conversion experiences in the Book of Acts vary, but a pattern is evident. Salvation is always preceded by the convicting work of the Holy Spirit. God used different means to convict people, but no one came to Christ who was not drawn by the Spirit. Faith in Christ was always the means of true conversion. In Acts, faith included repentance, though it was not considered a separate step or condition (Acts 20:21). Baptism followed one's faith in Christ and never preceded the act of believing; it was not considered efficacious or necessary for salvation (1 Cor. 1:17; Eph. 2:8). Paul considered his own conversion experience as an example for those who would believe in Christ (1 Tim. 1:15–16).

Of course, not everyone who hears the gospel responds by trusting Christ. This is illustrated by the first three soils in Jesus' parable of the sower (Matt. 13:3–7, 18–22) and by the fact that many people who heard Paul preach the gospel opposed him and his message.

Once a person received Christ as his or her Savior, growth in the spiritual life was expected, and believers joined together for fellowship and the study of the apostles' teaching (Acts 2:42). The Epistles were written to assist the growth of the believers in their walk with the Lord (Titus 3:14; 2 Pet. 1:5–9). One of the evidences of salvation was the desire on the part of believers to tell others about Christ (1 Pet. 1:4–10), and because of this, evangelism has always been a high priority in the church. **—WGJ**

Ask the Lord to give you a burden for souls who are lost, and plan to witness for Christ when the opportunities arise.

Ff

Faith

MILLIONS OF PEOPLE experience fellowship daily with a God whom they have never seen, an experience possible only by faith. This faith is based on the inerrant Word of God, the written revelation of God Himself.

The writer of Hebrews makes it clear that from the time of creation people have been notable because of their faith in God. Abel, Enoch, and Noah were early illustrations of the fact that salvation in Old Testament times came through faith in God, and without faith it was impossible to please Him (Heb. 11:4–7). The most detailed account of someone exercising faith toward God was that of Abram. Genesis 15:6 states that he "believed in the Lord." God declared Abram righteous when he believed, and his faith in the Lord became an example for the New Testament writers when they explained the significance of trusting in Christ for salvation and justification (Rom. 4:18–25; Gal. 3:6; James 2:23).

Theologians differ on the object of faith for those who lived before Christ. The Reformed view is that the object of faith was always the coming Messiah and His sacrificial death; the dispensational view is that God Himself was the object of faith and that Old Testament believers did not understand that the Messiah would have to die. Instead, they trusted in the God who had created them and revealed Himself to them in various ways. Before the Law was written, God often revealed Himself directly to people (Gen. 3:9; 4:6; 6:13). To Abram He made Himself known in a vision (15:1; 17:3) and to Jacob in a dream (28:12–15). In every situation those who trusted the Lord knew who He was, and they respected and revered Him.

The Mosaic Law was the rule of life for Israel, but salvation came, as it always does, by faith, not from keeping the Law. With the Law came a greater realization of God's character and a deeper understanding of their unrighteousness. The Law demanded complete obedience to every detail, something impossible to do. Centuries later when the apostle Paul was explaining Israel's failure, he stated that lack of faith is what caused the nation to fall out of favor with God (Rom. 9:30–32).

The covenant relationship God established with Moses and Israel, the Law itself, and the manner in which God appeared to them was an effort to bring them to trust in the Lord (Exod. 19:3–9; Deut. 1:30–32). But Israel wandered in the wilderness for almost forty years because of unbelief (Heb. 3:12–4:2). Before the people entered the land, Moses reminded them that they were to love the Lord and obey Him and that this could happen only if their hearts were right and they held fast to Him, implying faith (Deut. 30:16–17, 20).

The significance of faith in the personal life of an Israelite can be seen from the expressions used in the Book of Psalms. David said he trusted in the unfailing love of the Lord (Pss. 13:5; 52:8). He lamented over those who put their trust in idols rather than in the Lord (31:6). Trust in the Lord gave meaning to David's life and resulted in his having the desires of his heart (37:3–5). The word *bātaḥ*, "to trust or have confidence in," used in those verses, conveys the concept of faith, much like the word *ʾāman*. Another word in the Psalms, *ḥāsâ*, "to seek refuge in," was used in a figurative way to express placing trust in someone. David used this word in Psalms 5:11; 7:2; 25:20 and elsewhere to describe his trust in the Lord. Belief in God brought salvation to people who lived in Old Testament times. Those who trusted the Lord endeavored to be obedient to Him, and in that way they were witnesses to God's greatness (Isa. 43:10).

Jesus Christ is now the object of our faith, since He came to reveal the Father in human form (John 1:14–18). Those who believe in Him become children of God (1:12). Whoever trusts in Christ receives eternal life (3:16, 36). Jesus stated that to believe in Christ also means believing in His words (6:63, 68–69). Belief in Christ means belief in what He accomplished on the cross and in His resurrection (3:15–16; 11:25–26). The miracles He performed were for the specific purpose of bringing people to faith in Him (20:30–31).

Jesus taught that faith is the way to appropriate all God has for His children (Mark 9:23). Faith is simply the means, and not the basis, of appropriating His promises. The amount or quantity of faith does not save (11:22–24). Even circumstances that seem to be impossible from a human perspective do not call for more faith. Instead we are to rely by faith on the grace of God (Luke 17:1–6). The effectiveness of faith is totally dependent on the credibility of the object toward which faith is directed.

The Book of Acts demonstrates the importance of faith in the spread of the gospel. Peter declared that the crippled man by the temple gate was healed because of his faith (Acts 3:16). This incident gave Peter courage to proclaim the message of salvation to the Jewish leaders in Jerusalem (4:5–12). Because of his preaching on the resurrection of Christ, many believed and received salvation (4:4).

Through the miracles performed by the apostles many put their faith in Christ (5:12–14). Belief in Christ is the reason many Samaritans were converted (8:12). Saul's conversion (Acts 9) was the result of his faith in the risen Savior (Phil. 3:9). When the message went to the Gentiles, Peter testified to the fact that they were saved by faith in Christ (Acts 11:14, 17). Under Paul's ministry Sergius Paulus was saved by believing the message about the Lord (13:12). Faith in Christ became the theme of Paul's preaching (13:38–39). The Philippian jailer believed in the Lord Jesus Christ and was saved (16:30–31). Paul told the Ephesian elders that he had been faithful in preaching the message of faith in Christ to both Jews and Greeks (20:21).

The New Testament Epistles repeatedly affirm the truth that salvation and justification come by grace through faith in Christ (Rom. 1:16; 3:28; 10:9–10; 1 Cor. 1:21–23; Eph. 2:8–9; Gal. 2:16). The Christian life is a life of faith from beginning to end (Rom. 1:17; Gal. 2:20; 3:11; Heb. 10:38). One's faith in Christ provides a foundation for Christian growth (2 Pet. 1:5–8). Trust in the Lord sustains believers in the trials of life (1 Pet. 1:5–7), which in turn helps develop spiritual maturity (James 1:2–4). Faith gives victory to overcome the world (1 John 5:4–5), and it helps guard against the attacks of Satan (Eph. 6:16; 1 Thess. 5:8). James echoed the teaching of Christ by showing the importance of praying with faith (James 5:15; compare Matt. 21:21–22).

The apostle Paul also mentioned that the spiritual gift of faith is given by the Holy Spirit to assist in the ministry to the church (1 Cor. 12:9). All believers are to walk by faith, but the spiritual gift of faith is a God-given capacity to attempt great things for God.

Several times the term *faith* was used in an objective sense to refer to the system of biblical truth which Christians believed (1 Tim. 1:2; 3:13; 2 Tim. 4:7; Titus 1:13; Jude 3, 20). The term is often used this way in the modern world—"the Christian faith."   **—WGJ**

Trust in the unlimited power of God
as you face every obstacle and challenge in life.

Faithfulness

FAITHFULNESS DESCRIBES, on the one hand, God's constant, complete reliability and, on the other hand, a person's confidence in God in association with faith in Him. Thus in Scripture God is said to be faithful (1 Cor. 1:9; 10:13; 1 Thess. 5:24), and people can be faithful to others and to God (Matt. 24:45; 25:21, 23). God's faithfulness stems from His infinite perfections, whereas a person's faithfulness is often a reflection of his faith or confidence in another, such as in God. Faithfulness, by its nature, is related to faith toward God.

God is faithful in His work of creation and providence, in providing redemption through the coming Messiah, and in making various covenants in which He made promises to man. In redemption God is faithful in keeping His promises to those who trust in Him. Fulfilled prophecy confirms His faithfulness to His Word, His being true to what He says He will do. Moses said God is the "faithful God" (Deut. 7:9; 32:4). The psalmist wrote that "the LORD is faithful to all his promises" (Ps. 145:13) and that He "remains faithful forever" (146:6), "through all generations" (100:5; 119:90). His faithfulness, Jeremiah wrote, is "great" (Lam. 3:23).

Paul too stated that God "is faithful" (1 Cor. 1:9; 10:13; 2 Cor. 1:18) and will always "remain faithful" (2 Tim. 2:13). He is faithful in protecting believers from Satan (2 Thess. 3:3) and in forgiving believers who confess their sins (1 John 1:9). Christ is the believers' faithful High Priest (Heb. 2:17; 3:6), and when He returns to earth He will bear the title "Faithful and True" (Rev. 19:11). God's faithfulness to His own is like a protective shield for them (Ps. 91:4).

On the human side, faithfulness refers to a person's response to divine promises by believing in God and conducting oneself properly in keeping with this divine relationship. Human faith is confidence in what He is and what He has promised. To believe is to place one's trust in God for salvation. Believers are then to be faithful in their Christian walk, to be reliable, truthful, consistent. Believers are to be faithful in serving the Lord (2 Chron. 19:9; Matt. 25:21, 23; 3 John 5), as God's stewards (1 Cor. 4:2), and faithful in prayer (Rom. 12:12).

One of the important New Testament Greek words is *pistis* ("faith"), which is sometimes rendered "faithfulness." It is related to the verb *pisteuō*, "to believe or trust in." This shows that apart from faith in God, a person cannot be faithful to Him. The Christian life rests on the faithfulness of God on the one hand and on one's faithfulness to God on the other.

—JFW

Be encouraged by the truth that God is totally dependable,
and trust Him to help you meet every challenge in life triumphantly.

Fall, The

THE FALL refers to the account in Genesis 3 of Adam and Eve's disobedience to God, which resulted in their loss of innocence and perfection. The entire human race came under the burden of their sin (Rom. 5:12).

Adam and Eve had been created in innocence, that is, they had not sinned and they had no innate propensity to sin. God gave them the simple command not to eat of the tree of the knowledge of good and evil. A serpent, apparently indwelt and dominated by Satan, tempted Eve to disobey this command by God. By saying she must not touch the tree (Gen. 3:2–3), Eve made the command more strict than it really was. The serpent immediately replied, "You will not surely die" (3:4). It is characteristic of temptation, first, to make God more strict than He is, and second, to question the goodness of God in His commands. Satan told her, "For God knows that when you eat of it your eyes will be opened, and you will be like God, knowing good and evil" (3:5). What Satan said was partially true. They would increase their knowledge of good and evil, but they would not have the power to resist the evil. In both of his statements, Satan perverted the truth and misrepresented the situation.

Eve was susceptible to this temptation and partook of the fruit, and Adam, who apparently understood that it was wrong, also ate of it. First Timothy 2:14 indicates that Adam did this willfully and was not deceived.

The results were catastrophic. Adam and Eve became subject to a sin nature, and in the material realm God's judgment affected the whole earth, including the "cursing" of the ground (Gen. 3:17–19). Also Satan was cursed and was destined for ultimate destruction, and the serpent was condemned to crawling on the ground (3:14). In addition, God said there would be enmity between Satan and the woman and between his offspring and her offspring (3:15). The prediction, "You will strike his heel," refers to Satan's attempt to destroy Christ. Yet Christ will defeat Satan, as seen in the words, "He [Christ] will crush your head" (3:15). Women would have pain in childbearing and would be subject to the rule of their husbands (3:16). Adam—and all his offspring—were condemned to a life of labor in order to have enough food to live (3:17–19). Knowing the Fall would occur, God planned the redemption of sinners, even from before the foundation of the world. Adam's posterity inherited his act as the head of the race, much as Christ died as the Head of the new creation (Rom. 5:12–19; 1 Cor. 15:21–22, 45–49). Every person except Christ sins, because he or she is born in sin with a sin nature and is spiritually dead (Eph. 2:1). —JFW

Acknowledge the effects of sin in the world but don't be defeated by sin, for Christ died to bring freedom from sin's bondage.

Family

THE FAMILY WAS ESTABLISHED BY GOD as the capstone of the creative order. After creating male and female, "God blessed them and said to them, 'Be fruitful and increase in number'" (Gen. 1:28). "No suitable helper" (2:20) was found for Adam, so God created Eve from one of

Adam's ribs and brought her to Adam as his companion and helper (2:21–22). After Adam received and acknowledged her, God said, "For this reason a man will leave his father and mother and be united to his wife, and they will become one flesh" (2:24).

As husband and wife Adam and Eve formed the nucleus of the first family. Then children became part of the family, starting with Cain (4:1). God intends for married partners to reproduce (1:28), but this is subject to His timing.

As established by God, the basis of the family is the monogamous, loving relationship between a man and a woman. Although Lamech married two wives (4:19) and polygamy soon became widespread, the Bible maintains God's endorsement of monogamy. Difficulties that came into polygamous families are clearly portrayed.

The monogamous relationship was designed to be of lifelong duration. Only death separates a person from his flesh, and so only death should separate a man and a woman from their marriage relationship, for they are "one flesh" (2:24). In God's regulations for Israel He made allowance for polygamy (Deut. 21:15–17) and divorce (24:1–4), but these conditions are not the ideal in marriage. The Lord Jesus endorsed lifelong monogamous marriage (Matt. 19:4–6) and explained, when questioned (19:3, 7), that "Moses permitted you to divorce your wives because your hearts were hard. But it was not this way from the beginning" (19:8; see also 5:31–32).

It is important to note that the woman was created and brought to the man as a helper and companion (Gen. 2:18, 20–23), not as a possession or property. The woman, like the man, was created "in the image of God" (1:27). Order is necessary in the family, with the husband being the head of the home (1 Cor. 11:3) and the wife being submissive to him (Eph. 5:22–24; Col. 3:18; 1 Pet. 3:1–6). Conversely the husband is to "be considerate" of his wife, to "treat [her] with respect" (3:7), and to love her as his own body (Eph. 5:28, 33; Col. 3:18), even "as Christ loved the church and gave himself up for her" (Eph. 5:25). Harmony in the family prevails when such order is maintained.

The human family illustrates the relationship of people to God. In the New Testament the title "Father" is frequently applied to God (Matt. 6:1, 4, 6, 8–9, 14–15, 18; John 20:17; Rom. 1:7; 2 Cor. 1:2–3; Eph. 5:20; James 3:9; 1 Pet. 1:2, 17; 1 John 3:1), but God is also addressed as the

Father of Israel in the Old Testament (Ps. 89:26; Isa. 63:16; 64:8; Jer. 3:4, 19; Mal. 2:10). God directed Hosea to restore his unfaithful wife (Hos. 1:2–3; 3:1–3) as a way of portraying His future restoration of unfaithful Israel as His earthly people. The church is called "the family of believers" (Gal. 6:10) and "the family of God" (1 Pet. 4:17). Paul wrote, "I kneel before the Father, from whom his whole family in heaven and on earth derives its name" (Eph. 3:14–15). The harmonious Christian family, therefore, serves as a witness to the love, joy, and peace that flows from being identified with God the Father through faith in the redemption and eternal life provided by the Lord Jesus Christ.   **—JAW**

As you rejoice in the joy of knowing God as your Father,
remember that you are only one child in an ever-growing family of God.

Fasting

THROUGHOUT BIBLICAL HISTORY fasting was a common practice. The Israelites were commanded to fast once a year on the Day of Atonement (Lev. 16:29, 32). The Jews in captivity fasted on certain days in the fourth, fifth, seventh, and tenth months (Zech. 8:19), although this was not commanded by the Lord. The prophet Joel called the nation to repentance, exhorting them to return to the Lord with fasting (Joel 2:12) and to declare a holy fast (2:15). Certainly fasting was a frequent practice throughout Old Testament times, as numerous Scripture references indicate.

Jesus fasted when He faced temptations from the devil in the wilderness (Matt. 4:1–2; Luke 4:1–2), and Paul fasted after his conversion experience on the road to Damascus (Acts 9:9). Jesus did not forbid fasting. In fact, He suggested there would be times in the future when it would be appropriate for the disciples to fast (Matt. 9:14–15; Luke 5:33–34). The church at Antioch fasted and prayed before they sent out Saul and Barnabas (Acts 13:2–3); and Paul and Barnabas fasted when they appointed elders for the churches in Lystra, Iconium, and Antioch (14:23). Apart from these references there is no indication that fasting was a regular part of the early church life. Paul's epistles are silent about fasting, as are all the remaining New Testament books.

In its broadest definition fasting is the abstinence from food and/or drink for a relatively brief period of time. Usually it is an expression that has religious implications, although it could also be done for medicinal purposes. Pagans practiced fasting, and in some cases it was for evil purposes (1 Kings 21:9–10). A conspiracy was formed among some of the Jews who refused to eat or drink until they had murdered Paul (Acts 23:12–15). Normally the practice is self-instigated, and the benefit is primarily individual. Because of the limited instruction about fasting in the Bible, any attempts to develop a theology of fasting must be derived from the examples rather than from specific instructions.

The examples and descriptions of fasting in the Bible are varied. Apart from the Day of Atonement, as stated above, no fast was required. People fasted on various occasions, such as in worship (Acts 13:2), times of calamities and approaching danger (2 Chron. 20:3; Ezra 8:21; Jon. 3:5–6), times of war (1 Sam. 7:6; 28:20), or when tragedy struck (31:13; 20:34; 2 Sam. 1:12). David fasted during the illness of his son (12:16), Moses fasted when he was devastated by the idolatrous actions of the people of Israel (Deut. 9:18, 25), and David fasted when wicked men spoke out against him (Ps. 109:24–25). The people of Israel fasted when they were seeking guidance in light of a difficult situation (Judg. 20:26), and Zechariah spoke of a future occasion when fasting would be associated with joy (Zech. 8:19).

No uniformity is found in the examples given as to the length of time people fasted. In Old Testament times it normally was from sunrise to sunset (Judg. 20:26; 1 Sam. 14:24). It could even be for a shorter period of time (Dan. 6:18). References also indicate three days (Esth. 4:16; Acts 9:9), seven days (1 Sam. 1:13; 2 Sam. 12:16–18), and on one occasion it was for three weeks (Dan. 10:1–2). Moses and Jesus each fasted for forty days (Exod. 34:28; Matt. 4:2). The genuineness of fasting was not determined by the length of the fast.

Isaiah 58 provides an extensive analysis of fasting. Isaiah revealed that one's spiritual relationship to God is to be the basis of the act. Fasting does not necessarily bring a person closer to the Lord, nor does the act itself bring about a response from God (58:3–4). A person is not humble because of the experience, but the fasting can reflect the true attitude of the heart. According to Isaiah, when fasting was done out of pure motives and came from the heart, it would be manifested through righteous actions. There would be proper consideration of others (58:3), peace instead of discord (58:4), efforts to help those in need (58:6), the sharing of abundance with others (58:7), and a tongue that is under control that otherwise could be destructive (58:9).

Prayer is not necessarily more effective if accompanied by fasting, although the two are sometimes mentioned together (Acts 13:3; 14:23). Fasting does not guarantee that our prayers will be answered (Ps. 35:13; Jer. 14:11–12). It might seem from Mark 9:29 in some Bible versions (for example, NKJV) that prayer *and* fasting are necessary to experience God's power in difficult situations. However, most versions, including the New International Version, omit the word *fasting* in that verse because of lack of strong Greek manuscript evidence. Even if the word was included in the original manuscript of the Gospel of Mark, there is no basis for making the act of fasting more significant than prayer. Jesus was dealing with the attitude of the disciples who had lost sight of the fact that any power or ability they possessed was from God, not themselves.

When done with a sincere heart, fasting does have benefits. It gives time for meditation and reflection on the Lord and His Word. Personal discipline is strengthened through self-control. Fasting frees us from concentrating on ourselves and our needs. It can make us more aware that we do not live by bread alone. David seemed to indicate that fasting for his enemies who were ill helped him have a better understanding of them (Ps. 35:11–14). If this was true for enemies, then it certainly should give us more empathy for those around the world who have been deprived of food through no fault of their own.

The nature of fasting makes it subject to abuse. Fasting can lead to pride and presumption. Jesus told a parable to highlight this danger (Luke 18:9–12). The act itself can be used as an attempt to manipulate God. At various times in church history, fasting was viewed as a means of achieving merit before God. It can diminish the importance of prayer, Bible study, and dependence on the Spirit. Paul wrote to Timothy that everything created by God was good, including food, and it should not be rejected if it is received with thanksgiving (1 Tim. 4:3–4). A proper balance between food and exercise can be of some value to believers (4:8).

—WGJ

Be willing to sacrifice time, money, and material privileges such as food to spend time in prayer and fellowship with the Lord.

Fatherhood

IN THE OLD TESTAMENT, fathers had all-encompassing authority over their children, as illustrated in Abraham's willingness to offer Isaac as a sacrifice. Later, however, the Mosaic Law prohibited offering human sacrifices. The Law also forbade fathers to force their daughters into prostitution (Lev. 19:29) or to sell their daughters as slaves to a foreigner. Fathers could marry their children to whomever the fathers chose, but often the daughters expressed their opinion about the choice. Some children who were rebellious could be stoned (Deut. 21:18–21).

Fathers were considered teachers of their children (4:9; 6:7; 31:13; Prov. 2:1–5; 3:1; 4:1, 10, 20; 5:1; 22:6), and fathers were to exercise discipline over them (13:24). The influence of a father over his son continued even after marriage, as illustrated in the case of Terah, Abram's father (Gen. 11:31). The relationship between a father and child illustrates God's relationship to believers. Just as children are to obey their fathers (Eph. 6:1–2; Col. 3:20), so all believers are to obey God, their heavenly Father.

The Bible frequently speaks of God the Father's love for His children (Ps. 103:13). As a faithful Father, He disciplines them (Deut. 8:5; Prov. 3:12; Heb. 12:5–11) to encourage them to return to fellowship with Him. In one sense God is the Father of all creation, but in a special sense He is the Father of only those who trust His Son and are thus born again as His children. Because Israel is God's chosen people, He has a special relationship to Israel as her Father (Isa. 63:16; 64:8).

A unique aspect of God's Fatherhood is the relationship of God the Father to Jesus Christ, God's Son. God is the "Father of our Lord Jesus Christ" (Rom. 15:6; 2 Cor. 1:3; Eph. 1:3; Col 1:3; 1 Pet. 1:3). Christ frequently spoke of this relationship, often calling God His "Father" (John 5:18; 10:30, 38; 20:17). This relationship does not deny monotheism. While God is distinguished in three divine persons, there is only one God (Deut. 6:4–5; Mark 12:29; Rom. 3:30). Of course, a major difference exists between the relationship of the Father to the Son and the relationship of God to human beings.

By adoption believers are recognized as God's sons (Rom. 8:14, 15; Gal. 4:6). Those who trust in Christ as their Savior become children of God (John 1:12; Rom. 8:16; Eph. 5:1; 1 John 3:2), and He is their "heavenly Father" (Matt. 6:14, 26, 32; 15:13) and "the Father of us all" (Rom. 4:16; see also Eph. 4:6).　　　　　　　　　　　　　　　　　　　　　**—JFW**

*Count all the benefits you as a believer can enjoy
because God is your heavenly Father.*

Fear of God

THE NATURAL RELATIONSHIP between sin and the fear of God in the normal sense of the word *fear* (as "dread") is displayed by Adam and Eve. Apparently God made a practice of fellowshipping with them "in the garden in the cool of the day" (Gen. 3:8). After they had disobeyed God by eating the fruit of the tree of the knowledge of good and evil, however, "they hid from the LORD God" and Adam confessed, when confronted by God, "I was afraid" (3:10). Later, after Cain, their firstborn killed his younger brother, Abel, Cain expressed his fear when he told God, "whoever finds me will kill me" (4:14).

God's demonstration of His awesome power to the Israelites at the giving of the Ten Commandments at Mount Sinai produced fear as well. Moses wrote, "On the morning of the third day there was thunder and lightning, with a thick cloud over the mountain, and a very loud trumpet blast. Everyone in the camp trembled" (Exod. 19:16; 20:18). Even godly Isaiah cried, when he received a vision of the Lord in the temple, "'Woe to me! . . . I am ruined! For I am a man of unclean lips, and I live among a people of unclean lips, and my eyes have seen the King, the LORD Almighty'" (Isa. 6:5).

In time, the fear of God in the sense of fear or terror, developed into the concept of awe and reverence. This is evident in the use of the phrase "the fear of the LORD" in Job 28:28; Psalms 19:9; 9:10; 22:4. 32:11; 111:10; Proverbs 1:7; 8:13). This is particularly true in the New Testament after the incarnation of Christ and the emphasis on God as a loving heavenly Father (Matt. 6:8; 32-33; Luke 12:30–31). It is important to remember, however, as the Epistle to the Hebrews reminds us, "It is a dreadful thing to fall into the hands of the living God" (Heb. 10:31). Today the tendency is to lose all fear of God by thinking of Him as only a doting grandfather and forgetting that He is the eternal, infinite Creator to whom all are accountable. "There is no fear of God before their eyes" (Rom. 3:18).

Believers are to "walk in the fear of our God" (Neh. 5:9), remembering that "the fear of the Lord is the beginning of wisdom" (Ps. 111:10; Prov. 1:7; 9:10; see also Job 28:28). Fearing God is also associated with serving Him (Deut. 6:13; Josh. 24:14; 1 Sam. 12:14; Ps. 2:11), trusting Him (Ps. 115:11), obeying Him (Eccles. 12:13), and worshiping Him (Rev. 14:7), Every believer should "know what it is to fear the Lord" (2 Cor. 5:11). —JAW

Address your heavenly Father, the eternal,
infinite Creator of all things, in reverential awe.

Fellowship

THE STORY OF THE BIBLE is one of fellowship. The plurality of the Godhead suggests, among other things, a relationship between the Father, Son, and Holy Spirit. When God created man, He made him in His own image, and the earliest scenes in the Book of Genesis depict God having fellowship with Adam. God enjoyed His creation and it was good. Eve was created so Adam could have fellowship, and when they became one flesh it was the most intimate of human relationships (Gen. 2:24).

The glimpses of God's fellowship with those He created are many. Such a relationship was true of Enoch, who "walked with God" (5:22, 24). The Lord appeared to Abram and established a relationship with him so that he was called a friend of God (James 2:23). A dynamic fellowship existed between Moses and God. The Lord promised that He would go with Moses, and God revealed His glory to him (Exod. 33:18–23). Perhaps the epitome of fellowship was between God and David, for David was a man after God's own heart (1 Sam. 13:14; see also Acts 13:22). This relationship was confirmed in many psalms written by

David. On one occasion David said the Lord confides in those who trust in Him (Ps. 25:14).

Jeremiah is a superb example of the fellowship the prophets had with God. The Book of Jeremiah is filled with personal illustrations of God and Jeremiah in communion with each other. In the Old Testament even the average believing Israelite had fellowship with God, although it was in the prescribed way through the Levitical system (Lev. 7:11–21).

The concept of fellowship is greatly enhanced in the New Testament. The incarnation of Christ brought a new dimension never before known on the earth. God was living among the people, and those who believed in Jesus followed Him throughout Judea, Samaria, and Galilee.

The death, resurrection, and ascension of Christ brought an even closer relationship for His followers. The night before He was crucified Jesus began preparing His disciples for this new relationship (John 13–16). He didn't expect them to understand it fully at that time, but later they would (13:7–14). This new relationship would be possible because the Father would send His Spirit to dwell in them. The Spirit had been *with* them, but after Pentecost He would be *in* them (14:17), and Jesus and the Father would come and make their home with those who would obey His words (14:23). Using the figure of the vine and the branches, Jesus described this close relationship in terms familiar to the disciples (15:4–10).

Some of the results of this close fellowship were a desire to love others (13:34), a strengthening of their prayer life (14:13), and a peace that would sustain them even in their most difficult days (14:27).

The teaching of fellowship reached its zenith in the epistles of Paul and John. These apostles used the word *koinōnia* to describe this unique relationship. This word and its derivatives carry the meaning of partnership. Writing to the church at Corinth, Paul said that God had called those believers into fellowship with His Son, Jesus Christ (1 Cor. 1:9). This partnership was a result of God's grace. As partners they were recipients of God's gifts and promises, and they were exhorted to live in harmony with each other. There were to be no divisions in the body of Christ (1:10). In a later letter to the same church Paul warned that their close association with Christ left no room for partnership with unbelievers (2 Cor. 6:14–16). One way believers expressed this partnership with the Lord was through participating in the Lord's Supper. Eating the bread and drinking of the cup made them partners in the blood and body of Christ (1 Cor. 10:16–17).

This wonderful fellowship was also expressed in other ways. Paul said believers should share their material resources with others (Rom. 15:26–27; 2 Cor. 8:4; 9:13; Phil. 1:5; 4:15). They were to share in each other's sufferings (2 Cor. 1:7; Phil. 1:7) and to be like-minded, having the same attitude as Christ (2:1–2). This close fellowship was indispensable in living for Christ in a hostile world.

Paul's personal desire was to know Christ in the most intimate and meaningful way. This involved a knowledge of Christ's resurrection and the power related to it (3:10). The Resurrection was the source of his daily strength and his hope for the future.

In the same verse Paul wrote that knowing Christ also meant a partnership with Him in His sufferings. Paul wanted to share in His humility and to know more fully what it meant to be obedient to the will of the Father. When believers are humble before God and obedient to His will, they find strength in weakness. Fellowship with Christ involves both enablement by His resurrection power and the helplessness of suffering.

To the apostle John the supreme concept of fellowship is the believer's relationship with God, who is absolutely holy (1 John 1:3–7). To enjoy such a relationship, believers must live in a way that reflects that holiness. This is possible because Christ died and removed the barrier of sin. Even when a Christian sins, fellowship can be restored because forgiveness is assured when confession is made (1:9). Walking in fellowship with God also brings us into partnership with others in the body of Christ. —WGJ

Enjoy the unique relationship that believers have in Christ
and encourage others to enjoy this privilege.

Firstfruits

THE ISRAELITES WERE REQUIRED by the Mosaic Law to bring "the best of the firstfruits of [their] soil" to the tabernacle (Exod. 23:19). This act acknowledged that the land and its produce were God's gift to His people. God claimed the firstborn son of men and animals (13:2) as well as the firstfruits of the land (22:29–30). The offerings of the firstfruits included grain, fruit, honey, and wool, described as that which is "first ripe." Firstfruits also included the results of man's labor, such as flour, oil, wine, dough, and bread (34:18, 22; Lev. 23:16–20). The manner in which the firstfruits were to be brought to the tabernacle (and later the temple) is described in Deuteronomy 26; however, the amount to be offered is nowhere stipulated. In times of revival and reform (for example, in Hezekiah's reign), the amounts offered were abundant and amply cared for the daily needs of the priests (2 Chron. 31:5). After the Captivity the exiles returning to Jerusalem covenanted to be faithful in bringing the firstfruits to the temple (Neh. 10:37). However, during Nehemiah's subsequent absence the people stopped the practice; when he returned he sternly urged them to support the priests and Levites (13:10–12). Prosperity was promised in the Book of Proverbs to those who honored the Lord with their firstfruits (Prov. 3:9).

Israel celebrated the Feast of Firstfruits (Lev. 23:9–14) at the beginning of the barley harvest. The first sheaf of the new crop was waved before the Lord, acknowledging that the harvest came because of His blessing and that it all belonged to Him. The "wave sheaf" also served as a sample of the abundant harvest to follow. On the fiftieth day after the Feast of Firstfruits, the Feast of Pentecost ("Pentecost" means "fiftieth") celebrated the completion of the wheat harvest. At this time the firstfruits of the wheat were to be presented to the Lord (Exod. 34:22; see also 23:16; Lev. 23:15–21).

The term *firstfruits* is also used in Scripture in a metaphorical or figurative sense. The nation Israel is described as "the firstfruits of his harvest" (Jer. 2:3), that is, as a nation holy to God. In the New Testament the most significant occurrence of firstfruits is with reference to Christ in His resurrection. "But Christ has indeed been raised from the dead, the firstfruits of those who have fallen asleep" (1 Cor. 15:20). When Christ appeared in heaven in His glorified human body, He represented the vast harvest of those who will follow Him in their resurrection bodies (Phil. 3:20–21). As the first one to rise from the dead, Christ's resurrection constitutes both a pledge of more to come and a sample of the rest of the "harvest."

Believers are described as "a kind of firstfruits" (James 1:18), that is, they are a guarantee of many more who would come to Christ for salvation. Also Christians possess "the firstfruits of the Spirit" (Rom. 8:23), which means God's children have a foretaste of what awaits them in heaven. In addition, the first converts in a given locality were spoken of as spiritual firstfruits (Rom. 16:5; 1 Cor. 16:15).

The term *firstfruits* also describes the saved remnant in Israel in the present age (Rom. 11:16), as well as the 144,000 in the future Tribulation period (Rev. 14:4). The latter are seen as the firstfruits of the coming kingdom. In that millennial age, according to Ezekiel's vision and prophecy, the priests once again will receive the firstfruits (Ezek. 44:30).

—DKC

Rejoice that God has guaranteed the resurrection of all saints because Christ is the "firstfruits of those who have fallen asleep" (1 Cor. 15:20).

Flesh

THE CONCEPT OF FLESH appears many times in the Bible with various natural or theological meanings. In the Old Testament "the flesh" (Hebrew, *bāśār*) often refers to the human race (for example, Gen. 6:12, "people"). Other times it indicates physical bodies of animals or people. Still other times it refers to the mortal aspect of the human race, as in Genesis 6:3, where God said, "My Spirit will not contend with man forever, for he is mortal [literally, 'flesh']." "Flesh" also often points to the frailty of humanity (for example, 2 Chron. 32:8). "Flesh" in the Old Testament does not convey the idea of a sin nature, as it does in the New Testament.

The New Testament word for "flesh" is *sarx,* which refers to the human race (John 17:2, "people"), the physical body (Acts 2:31; Gal. 2:20, "body"; 2 Cor. 12:7, "flesh"), or the sin nature (Col. 2:11, "sinful nature"; 1 Pet. 4:2, "evil human desires"). Sometimes *sarx* refers to individuals (Rom. 3:20, "no flesh will be justified," NKJV; Gal. 1:16, "man") or to the mortal aspect of human beings (2 Cor. 4:11). Obviously the translation "sinful nature" is partly an interpretation, an attempt to get at the meaning of *sarx* when it is referring to the inner inclination of human beings to sin. Except for Christ, every person born into the world is born with a sin nature, that is, an innate capacity or propensity for sin.

In the New Testament the flesh is regarded as weak and unable to achieve holiness by itself. In sanctification the Holy Spirit indwells a person at his or her new birth, thereby enabling the person to achieve a measure of holiness, as indicated in Galatians 5:16: "Live by the Spirit, and you will not gratify the desires of the sinful nature ['flesh']." The sin nature is contrary to what the Holy Spirit desires in the life of a believer (5:17). A list of the acts of the sinful nature is given in 5:19–21. By contrast, the fruit of the Spirit, that is, the work of the Holy Spirit in the life of a believer, produces "love, joy, peace, patience, kindness, goodness, faithfulness, gentleness and self-control" (5:22–23).   —JFW

Avoid the desires of the human nature that would hinder the work
of the Holy Spirit in your life.

Foreknowledge

THE SCRIPTURES UNIFORMLY ASSERT that God knows from eternity past everything that would happen in creation (Job 28:23–24; 37:16; Pss. 44:21; 139:1–4; Isa. 46:9–10; 48:2–3, 5; Jer. 1:5; 1 Cor. 2:10–11; 1 John 3:20). Nothing is hidden from Him. The foreknowledge is part of God's omniscience or total knowledge of everything, past, present, and future. It is also related to God's omnipotence, because all that happens happens because He causes it; He has the power to make happen what He wishes, and He foreknows what this will be. In His omniscience God knows not only what will eventuate but also what will not occur.

God is not related to the time of our world in the same way we are. He created our time when He created the universe and He stands outside it. Some of the difficulties and controversies relating to the issues of divine foreknowledge and human free will result from our ignorance as to God's relationship to time.

Calvinists and Arminians differ on what happens when a person is saved, with Calvinists tending to make God the determining factor and Arminians making a person's choice the determining factor. Scripture implies that God's foreknowledge is absolutely certain and that He can both predict actions and render them certain while still holding the human race responsible for their sin.

Because each member of the human race (other than Jesus Christ) is spiritually dead and unable to comprehend the truth of God, a supernatural work of God is required for an unbeliever to understand and receive the gospel. It is necessary for the Spirit of God to convict the world of its guilt, of God's righteous standards, and of His judgment on sin (John 16:7–11). What happens when a person believes in Christ is somewhat inscrutable because the human and the divine are both involved. On the one hand, individuals by themselves cannot understand or come to God in faith. As Christ expressed it, "No one can come to me unless the Father who sent men draws him" (John 6:44). On the other hand, no one is saved contrary to his or her own will. In other words, God enables people to exercise faith in Him (John 6:37, 44–45, 65; Rom. 8:5–9; Phil. 1:29; 2 Pet. 1:1).

Ephesians 2:8–9 reads, "For it is by grace you have been saved, through faith—and this not from yourselves, it is the gift of God—not by works, so that no one can boast." Some readers assume that the word "this" refers to "faith," which implies that faith itself is given by God. However, "faith" in the Greek is feminine and "this," a relative pronoun, is neuter. The verse then is saying that a person is saved by grace through exercising faith but that "this," that is, the whole work of salvation, is the gift of God.

How human choice and divine influence combine in a person believing in Christ continues to be a disputed point in theology. In foreknowledge God knows what each person will do in advance, based on natural and supernatural influences. God can be absolutely certain that when a person believes in Christ he is saved, but God at the same time does not make the decision of faith Himself. Rather, the exercise of faith involves human choice. Though God influences a person to believe, belief in Christ is an act of the human will. However, as already stated, it must be enabled by God.

Yet while their belief is certain, that does not mean He *coerces* people to believe. Certainty is not the same as coercion. Some things God accomplishes through natural laws and other things through human choices. All these events are absolutely certain because God knows completely what will eventuate in every human choice.

While all things are absolutely certain from eternity past, having been decided by God and therefore subject to His foreknowledge, it is also clear that God is not responsible for the sin of humankind. While human agency and determination is a part of the plan, it is nevertheless true that God approved the total plan and therefore has rendered certain all of its events.

First Peter 1:2 seems to say foreknowledge precedes election, that is, that God knew who would be saved and so He chose them. However, the Greek word rendered "foreknowledge" means more than advance knowledge, though it includes it. The same is true of the Greek verb rendered "foreknew" in Romans 8:29. It means "to have regard for, to have loving concern for, to choose." Thus those whom God chose in love, He elected (1 Pet. 1:2) and predestined (Rom. 8:29).   —JFW

Realize that God's knowledge and planning do not absolve personal responsibility.

Forgiveness

THE DRAMA SURROUNDING THE ACTIVITY of Adam and Eve in the early chapters of Genesis ended in tragedy when the first couple sinned against God. On that day with the coming of sin came a desperate need for forgiveness. Forgiveness is God's act of grace whereby He pardons a sinner, so that he or she no longer faces eternal condemnation for sin.

The Mosaic Law had specific instructions concerning forgiveness. Sin required a sacrifice for individuals as well as for the Israelite community (Lev. 4:20, 26, 31, 35). The word used in these verses is *sālaḥ*, "to forgive, pardon," and was used only in relation to God's forgiveness. Solomon used this term in his prayer to God when the temple was dedicated (2 Chron. 6:21, 25, 27, 30, 39).

Forgiveness was real to David, as expressed in a psalm written after his sin with Bathsheba (Ps. 32:1–2). He used three Hebrew words to explain what God had done with his sin: *nāśaʾ*, "to lift, carry away"; *kāsâ*, "to cover"; and *ḥāšab*, "to count, impute." In even more graphic language David described his sins as being removed as far as the east is from the west (103:12).

The prophets spoke mostly about forgiveness for the nation Israel, an important message with great hope for the people (Isa. 1:18). Jeremiah expressed this hope as he wrote about the New Covenant God will make with His people in the future. At the second coming of Christ, the Lord will pardon their sins and restore their land (Jer. 33:6–8). Micah closed his book with a series of statements about the forgiveness that will come to Israel. God will pardon sin, forgive transgression, tread sins underfoot, and hurl iniquities into the depths of the sea (Mic. 7:18–20).

Though the forgiveness provided in the Old Testament was real and effective for those who lived by faith, it was incomplete because ultimately the forgiveness of sins was to be based on the finished work of Christ at Calvary. Paul proclaimed this in Romans 3:24–26. The writer of Hebrews concurred, declaring that Christ is the supreme Sacrifice for sins and the only Sacrifice bringing eternal redemption (Heb. 9:11–14; 10:3–11).

In the New Testament two words are used to express the concept of forgiveness: *aphiēmi*, "to send away, to let go," and *charizomai*, "to show favor, to pardon or forgive." Paul used this latter word in 2 Corinthians 2:7, 10; Ephesians 4:32; Colossians 2:13; and 3:13.

John the Baptist introduced Jesus as the sacrificial lamb who would take away the sin of the world (John 1:29). Nothing more was said in the Gospels about the death of Jesus as the basis of forgiveness until the night before the Crucifixion. On that occasion Jesus instituted what is commonly known as the Lord's Supper. Explaining the significance of the bread and the cup, He stated specifically that His blood would be poured out for the forgiveness of sins (Matt. 26:28). Understanding that the death of Christ is the basis of forgiveness of sins, Peter emphasized this truth in his preaching (Acts 10:43; 13:38). Paul's writings also state this truth (Rom. 3:25; Eph. 1:7; Col. 1:14).

Jesus has authority to forgive sins, and He demonstrated this when He healed a paralytic (Matt. 9:5–8; Mark 2:10–12). Forgiveness is available to anyone who believes in the Lord, regardless of that person's station in life. Luke recorded the touching story of a woman who had lived in sin but who received forgiveness because of her faith (Luke 7:48–50). Luke also detailed the heartrending parable of the prodigal son, which demonstrates the love of the Father in seeking the lost (15:11–32).

A major theme in the New Testament is the Christian's responsibility to forgive others. Of Jesus' seven last sayings, two related to forgiveness (Luke 23:34, 43). The followers of Christ should manifest the gracious qualities He had, including forgiving even our enemies.

In one of His early messages Jesus taught the importance of forgiveness. If one's attitude is not right toward others, how can he expect God to grant forgiveness to him? (Matt. 6:14). The debt we owe God is much greater than what anyone could owe us (18:15–17). Forgiveness should be the hallmark of the Christian. Forgiveness should have no limit and should be genuine, not superficial (18:21–35).

The Epistles reinforce the teachings of Jesus on forgiveness. Spirit-controlled believers should reflect the kindness and compassion of the Lord and forgive each other just as God has forgiven them (Eph. 4:32). Christians are to clothe themselves with the graciousness of Christ and forgive whatever grievance they may have against another person (Col. 3:13).

The apostle John wrote that because of the death of Christ all the sins of the world were paid for by the Savior (1 John 2:1–2). The children of God are to walk in fellowship with the One who is absolutely holy and with others in the family of God (1:7). Daily sins disrupt our fellowship, but forgiveness is promised when we confess them, that is, when we view our sins the same way God sees them (1:9). This regular cleansing allows us to walk in the Light and to be in harmony with other believers.

—WGJ

*Each believer should have the same attitude of forgiving others
that Christ has manifested.*

Freedom

CAPTIVITY IS A SOMBER THEME throughout the pages of the Bible. The fear of death has held people captive since the fall of Adam and Eve (Heb. 2:14–15). Our adversary, the devil, has a viselike grip on unbelievers, a hold that makes them slaves to do his will (2 Tim. 2:26). Sin holds people captive, and even Christians find themselves struggling to be free from sin's power (Rom. 6:14; Gal. 4:4–7). Even the Law of Moses put people under bondage and left them powerless to fulfill its demands

(Rom. 7:6). Creation, too, longs for the day when it will be free from its slavery to corruption (8:21). Because the human heart desires freedom, it is not surprising that false teachers offer unsuspecting people a fraudulent freedom that actually drags them into bondage (2 Pet. 2:17–19). It is to this downtrodden and desperate world that genuine and lasting liberty is available from the Maker of heaven and earth, who experiences freedom as an integral part of His nature (Ps. 146:5–9).

One of the momentous acts of God was His deliverance of the Israelites from bondage in Egypt (Exod. 6:6–8). This event was one of the greatest demonstrations of God's power prior to the resurrection of Christ. Yet Israel was often subject to bondage to surrounding nations. In reviewing the history of Israel the psalmist reminded the people of the many times God had freed them when they were held captive (Ps. 106:43).

Individual freedom was also something the Israelites cherished. Slaves were to be freed after six years of service and sent away with gracious provisions (Lev. 25:39–42; Deut. 15:12–15). Every fifty years was to be a jubilee, and liberty was to be proclaimed throughout the land (Lev. 25:10). Isaiah spoke to the people about the freedom the Messiah would bring (Isa. 42:7; 61:1). God promised freedom for the captives on the day of salvation (49:8–9). Jerusalem, Isaiah said, will one day throw off the chains that enslave her (52:2). Because of God's desire to provide freedom for the Israelites, He expected them to give freedom to their own people, especially those bound in the chains of injustice (58:6–7).

The hope of freedom was in the hearts of the people when God sent His Son to the earth (Luke 1:68–71). Early in His Galilean ministry Jesus said that His preaching the good news to the poor and proclaiming freedom for the oppressed (Luke 4:16–19) was in fulfillment of Isaiah's prophecy in Isaiah 61:1–2. Toward the later part of his ministry He explained that true spiritual freedom can come only from Him (John 8:31–36). This is in harmony with His statement that whoever believes in Him is delivered from death and has eternal life (5:24). James states that God's Word brings freedom (James 1:25; 2:12).

Much of the New Testament teaching on freedom comes from the writings of the apostle Paul. In Galatians, possibly his first letter, Paul discussed the issue of freedom from the Mosaic Law. It is important to understand that when Paul discussed freedom from the Law, he was not saying that the divine principles on which the Law was established were invalid. Moral principles were valid even before the Law was given. But freedom in Christ means freedom from the Law (Gal. 5:1). Paul emphasized that no one can be justified or sanctified by the Law (2:16; 3:2–3). He also taught that freedom has its restraints and that in Christ there is freedom to serve others (5:13). Peter echoed the words of Paul in his letter when he instructed the believers to use their freedom to live as servants of the Lord (1 Pet. 2:16).

When Paul wrote to the church at Rome, freedom was a significant issue. He taught that Christ died so that believers would not have to be slaves to sin (Rom. 6:6–7). Since they had been freed from sin, they were now slaves to righteousness and to God (6:18, 22). Through Christ Christians have complete freedom from the law (that is, the ruling principles) of sin and death (8:1). To the Corinthians Paul taught that freedom does not mean license. Freedom in Christ is to be controlled by concern for others (1 Cor. 10:23–24). Paul's desire to reach others for Christ made him willing to be a slave to everyone (9:19). When freedom in Christ is properly understood, it brings humility, love, patience, and a desire to magnify Christ above everything else. **—WGJ**

Enjoy the freedom you have in Christ,
and never allow your freedom to be a stumbling block to your friends.

Fruit

IN THE OLD TESTAMENT "fruit" often describes the product or yield of the ground. Examples of this usage are in Genesis 4:3; Leviticus 25:19; Psalm 72:16; and Jeremiah 7:20. The same Hebrew word also refers to offspring, that is, children or other descendants, as in Genesis 30:2; 49:22; Deuteronomy 7:13; 2 Kings 19:30; Psalm 21:10, 132:11; and Micah 6:7. A figurative use of the term is illustrated in Proverbs 1:31, "They will eat the fruit of their ways and be filled with the fruit of their schemes." See also Isaiah 3:10; Jeremiah 17:10; and Micah 7:13 (NKJV).

The song of the vineyard in Isaiah 5:1–7 is an outstanding example of the figurative use of the concept of fruit bearing. The vineyard in this familiar passage is a symbol of Israel (see also Ps. 80:9–16 and Jer. 12:10). God gave Israel every possible advantage in a fertile land and He expected good fruit, namely, justice and righteousness, but instead there was bad fruit: bloodshed and cries of distress. Consequently God's protective hedge was removed and Israel was devastated by invaders.

In the New Testament the Greek word for fruit is used in the same three ways as the Hebrew word, that is, of agricultural produce (Matt. 21:19; 26:29; Luke 22:18), of children or other descendants (Luke 1:42; Acts 2:30), and of a person's actions that result from his or her true character. When John the Baptist saw the Pharisees and Sadducees coming to scrutinize his baptisms, he charged them, "Produce fruit in keeping with repentance" (Matt. 3:8; Luke 3:8).

In John's Gospel and in Paul's epistles fruitfulness is viewed not so much as the product of one's character as it is the result of the work of God who indwells believers. An important New Testament passage on fruit bearing is found in John 15, in which Jesus identified Himself as the "true vine" in contrast to the vine (Israel), which God had previously chosen and nurtured but which produced rotten fruit. God desires good fruit of His children. The key, Jesus said, was a disciple's continual abiding in Him and His indwelling the believer. "If a man remains in me and I in him, he will bear much fruit" (John 15:5).

Another key New Testament passage on fruit bearing is Galatians 5:16–26. Here Paul drew a stark contrast between "bad fruit" (the fruit of our sinful human nature) and "good fruit" (the fruit the Holy Spirit produces in and through us). The "bad fruit," which originates with the sinful nature, is described as "sexual immorality, impurity and debauchery; idolatry and witchcraft; hatred, discord, jealousy, fits of rage, selfish ambition, dissension, factions and envy; drunkenness, orgies, and the like" (Gal. 5:19–21). These vices include sexual sins, religious sins, societal sins, and sins associated with alcohol. A person, declared Paul, who lives continually on such a level of moral corruption demonstrates that he or she is not a child of God.

There is, however, no need for a Christian to produce evil fruit. Rather, as Paul explained, the "fruit of the Spirit," the good fruit, can and should characterize the lives of believers. The fruit in verses 22 and 23 consists of "love, joy, peace, patience, kindness, goodness, faithfulness, gentleness and self-control." The word *fruit* here is singular, indicating that these qualities constitute a unity, all of which should be found in a believer who lives under the control of the Spirit. In an ultimate sense this fruit is simply the life of Christ lived out in a Christian.

Thus the Old and New Testaments speak with a united voice concerning the fact that God expects His children to be fruitful. Though this has always been foreign to fallen human nature, in this dispensation believers enjoy the blessing of the permanent indwelling of the Holy Spirit, who enables them to produce qualities that are pleasing to God.

—**DKC**

Pray that you may learn how to depend on the Holy Spirit
so that He may produce good fruit in your life.

Gg

Gentiles

IN A GENERAL WAY THE WORD *Gentiles* refers to nations as a whole. This word translates the Hebrew *gôyîm* and the Greek *ethnoi*.

The whole world was considered gentile until the events of Genesis 12, when God selected a new people descending from Abraham in contrast to other nations.

In His promise to Abram God said, "I will make you into a great nation" (12:2). By this He meant He was making a distinction between Abram's descendants and all other nationalities. The nation Israel stems from the twelve sons of Jacob, Abraham's grandson. Though descendants of Abraham other than those from Jacob—such as Ishmael's and Esau's descendants—are Semites, they are regarded as Gentiles. Yet they are referred to in God's promise that Abraham would be "the father of many nations" (17:4).

Old Testament promises and prophecies about Israel are therefore to be distinguished from prophecies relating to other "peoples on earth" (12:3).

In the Old Testament a few Gentiles are spoken of as having placed their faith in the God of Israel. They include Rahab (Josh. 2:1, 11), Ruth (Ruth 1:16; 2:12), the widow of Zarephath (1 Kings 17:24), Naaman (2 Kings 5:15), and Nebuchadnezzar (Dan. 4:37). But most Gentiles were worshipers of idols.

Although Jesus' ministry did affect some Gentiles, like a Roman centurion (Luke 7:1–10) and some Greeks (John 12:20–22), His teaching and healing were mainly focused on the Jewish people. In fact, He commanded His disciples to go only to the people of Israel (Matt. 10:6). This changed, however, after Jesus' resurrection when He commissioned the disciples to go to the world (Mark 16:15). Soon after the Day of Pentecost the Ethiopian official and Cornelius, both Gentiles (Acts 8:26–40; 10:1–48), were saved. Then Jewish believers realized that "God has granted even the Gentiles repentance unto life" (11:18).

—JFW

Rejoice that God's grace is available to the Gentiles as well as to Israel.

Glory

THE GLORY OF GOD is the outward display or manifestation of His inherent perfections or attributes. His perfections are revealed in the world ("the heavens declare the glory of God," Ps. 19:1) and in humankind (God "crowned him [man] with glory and honor," 8:5). Because of God's presence in heaven, "glory" is sometimes used as a synonym for heaven's splendor (for example, Heb. 2:10).

Moses wanted to see God's glory, but he was told he could not see His face and live (Exod. 33:18, 20). *Kābôd*, the Hebrew word for "glory," is related to a verb that means "to be heavy or weighty." This noun is sometimes used of a person's "weighty" reputation or honored status. The Exodus brought glory to God (14:4), that is, it revealed His splendor. So Moses referred to God as "awesome in glory" (15:11). The glory of the Lord, that is, the evidence of His presence, filled the tabernacle (40:34) and the temple (2 Chron. 5:14; 7:1) in the form of a cloud when they were both dedicated. This was so impressive that Moses could not enter the tabernacle (Exod. 40:35), nor could the priests enter the temple (2 Chron. 7:2).

David spoke of seeing God's power and glory (Ps. 63:2), and he wrote that kings should sing to the Lord because "the glory of the LORD is great" (138:5). An anonymous psalmist stated, "The LORD is exalted over all the nations, his glory above the heavens" (113:4). In Isaiah's vision of the Lord angelic beings known as seraphs exclaimed, "Holy, holy, holy is the LORD Almighty. The whole earth is full of his glory" (Isa. 6:3). God's presence, Jude wrote, is indeed "glorious" (Jude 24).

The supreme revelation of God is Jesus Christ, "the radiance of God's glory" (Heb. 1:3). John wrote of "the glory of the One and Only" (John 1:14), and James called Him "our glorious Lord Jesus Christ" (James 2:1). When Jesus became a man, His glory was veiled to some extent. But in His Transfiguration this limitation was temporarily lifted, and Peter, James, and John saw Christ in His glory as His face shone and His clothes were brilliantly white (Matt. 17:2). Peter spoke of the three disciples being "eyewitnesses of his majesty" (2 Pet. 1:16). All of Christ's works on earth reflected God's glory, for Jesus prayed to God the Father, "I have brought you glory on earth by completing the work you gave me to do. And now, Father, glorify me in your presence with the glory I had with you before the world began" (John 17:4–5). The glory of Christ was inherent in His deity for all eternity, as 17:5 implies. In His resurrection He received a "glorious body" (Phil. 3:21), and at His ascension He was "taken up in glory" (1 Tim. 3:16).

The gospel of salvation through Christ is glorious (1 Tim. 1:11), for it reveals God's attributes of grace, mercy, and love.

When Christ comes to the clouds to take believers to Himself in the Rapture of the church, His coming will be so splendorous that Paul called it a "glorious appearing" (Titus 2:13). Believers "will appear with him in glory" (Col. 3:4). In heaven believers will share in His glory, that is, we will experience the splendor of His presence in heaven (Rom. 8:17; 1 Pet. 5:1), for we are called "to his eternal glory" (5:10). When He comes, believers will be "overjoyed" (4:13); therefore they "rejoice [now] in the hope" of the coming manifestation of God's glory (Rom. 5:2).

When Christ returns to earth to establish His millennial reign, He will come "with power and great glory" (Matt. 24:30), and He will reign "on his throne in heavenly glory" (25:31; see also 19:28). In the Millennium everyone will know of "the glory of the LORD" (Hab. 2:14).

According to the Westminster Catechism, "man's chief end is to glorify God." To glorify Him means to manifest His qualities in one's life. Believers are to live for "the praise of his glory" (Eph. 1:12, 14). Everything a Christian does should reflect the Lord's splendor. "Whatever you do, do it all to the glory of God" (1 Cor. 10:31; see also Phil. 1:11). To glorify God (Rom. 15:6) or to give Him glory (Jer. 13:16) means to show forth His virtues (1 Pet. 2:9). Our worship is to give Him glory (Rev. 4:11; 5:12). Even answers to our prayers bring glory to the Father (John 14:13). His glory will be rewarded in believers when they are in His presence in heaven (Rom. 8:18). As Paul wrote, God is the One "to whom be glory for ever and ever" (Gal. 1:5). —JFW

Display in your daily life the qualities of the Holy Spirit
that will allow others to see Christ in you and to glorify God.

God

THE WORD *God* refers to any deity, whether the true God of the Bible or the gods of polytheism and pagan religions. In every use, however, it implies something more than human ability and normally relates to a person of supernatural character.

In the Bible God is portrayed as the infinite, eternal, all-powerful Creator who is infinite in all His acts and ways.

The Scriptures give many facts about God's person, works, and attributes. The Hebrew word *Yahweh*, which is God's name, is used first in Genesis 2:4 and appears several thousand times in the Old Testament. In Exodus 3:13–15 God told Moses the meaning of His name. "Moses said to God, 'Suppose I go to the Israelites and say to them, "The God of your fathers has sent me to you," and they ask me, "What is his name?" Then what shall I tell them?' God said to Moses, 'I AM WHO I AM. This is what you are to say to the Israelites: "I AM has sent me to you."' God also said to Moses, 'Say to the Israelites, "The LORD, the God of your fathers— the God of Abraham, the God of Isaac and the God of Jacob—has sent me to you." This is my name forever, the name by which I am to be remembered from generation to generation.'"

Yahweh refers to God as the self-existing One who has always existed in the past and will always exist in the future. As such He is the supreme God of the universe.

A number of Bible versions render the Hebrew *Yahweh* as LORD. *Jehovah* is an older English form of *Yahweh*.

The Old Testament words *'ĕlōhîm*, *'ēl*, or *'ĕlŏah* are more general terms for God, and are used of false gods as well as of the God of Scripture. Because *'ĕlōhîm* has a plural ending, some suggest that this implies the Trinity. Others say this is a "plural of majesty." Since the Bible does teach Trinitarianism, it is possible that *'ĕlōhîm* hints at and anticipates the fuller revelation of the Trinity in the New Testament.

The Old Testament word *'ădōnāy* means "Lord" or "Master." It empha- sizes the fact that the Lord is Master and Ruler of our lives. Both *Yahweh* and *'ădōnāy* are often combined with other adjectives or titles. Yahweh is often linked with *'ĕlōhîm*, as in Exodus 34:6. Also Yahweh is linked to *Jireh*, meaning "the Lord will provide." *Yahweh-Rapha* (15:26) refers to God as the One who heals. *Yahweh-Nissi* (17:8–15) means "the Lord is my banner" under whose authority the believer is victorious. *Yahweh-Sabaoth* (1 Sam. 1:11) refers to the fact that God is over His hosts (angels). *Yahweh-Shalom* (Exod. 34:6) means "the Lord is our peace." *Yahweh-Shammah* (34:6; Ezek. 48:35) means "the Lord is there," and *Yahweh-Tsidkenu* (Exod. 34; Jer. 23:6) means "the Lord is our righteousness."

In the New Testament *theos* ("God") is used a thousand times, and *kyrios* ("Lord") occurs about five hundred times. *Kyrios,* similar to the Old Testament *ʾădōnāy,* is the equivalent of *Yahweh,* but it was also used to mean simply "sir" or "master." Debate continues over which usages emphasize that Jesus is Master and which stress His essential eternal existence.

While there were foreshadowings of the Trinity in the Old Testament, the New Testament clearly indicates that God exists in three persons, God the Father, God the Son, and God the Holy Spirit. Yet there is only one God, as affirmed in Deuteronomy 6:4, "Hear, O Israel: The Lord our God, the Lord is one." Literally, this verse reads "*Yahweh,* our *ʾelôhîm Yahweh* is one." The Hebrew word for "one" (*ʾeḥād*) suggests that the persons of the Godhead are a unit. The same word is used in Genesis 2:24 of the unity of a husband and a wife. Also Paul wrote that "God is one" (Gal. 3:20).

In Jesus' baptism God the Father was seen as being in heaven, Christ was being baptized, and the Spirit of God became visually present as a dove (Matt. 3:16–17). Further, God the Father said that Jesus Christ is the Son whom He loves and with whom He is well pleased (3:17). The baptismal formula indicates that Jesus' disciples should be baptized "in the name of the Father and of the Son and of the Holy Spirit" (28:19). Each person of the Trinity has the same attributes as the two other persons. Each one possesses full deity and also the attributes of personality, that is, intellect, sensibility, and will. The Father is regarded as the first person, the Son as the second person, and the Holy Spirit as the third person. Paul's benediction in 2 Corinthians 13:14 mentions the grace of the Son, the love of God, and the fellowship of the Holy Spirit.

God's eternal nature is affirmed in John 1:1, and His immutability is stated in Hebrews 1:12. He is omnipotent (all-powerful), omnipresent (Ps. 139:7; Acts 17:27), and omniscient (all-knowing). Additional attributes such as holiness, goodness, grace, love, mercy, faithfulness, justice, and wisdom are all ascribed to God.

In summary the Scriptures fully support the concept that God is infinite in all His attributes. As such He is the God who is able to save and keep those who put their trust in Him and will in eternity reward those who have been faithful. **—JFW**

Make the worship of the Lord a priority,
and be sure the purpose of your life is to accomplish His will.

Gospel

THE ENGLISH WORD *gospel* comes from the Anglo-Saxon *godspell,* meaning "Godstory" or "good story." It translates the Greek word *euangelion,* "good news." In the Septuagint, the Greek translation of the Old Testament, *euangelion* is found only once (2 Sam. 4:10), yet the concept is certainly found in such passages as Isaiah 52:7, "How beautiful on the mountains are the feet of those who bring good news, who proclaim peace, who bring good tidings, who proclaim salvation," and 61:1, "The Spirit of the Sovereign LORD is on me, because the LORD has anointed me to preach good news to the poor." Jesus read the latter passage in the synagogue at Nazareth and declared that it was descriptive of His mission (Luke 4:18–21).

Euangelion, which occurs more than seventy-five times in the New Testament, is often modified by such phrases as "the good news of God" (Mark 1:14), "the gospel about Jesus Christ" (Mark 1:1), "the gospel of his Son" (Rom. 1:9), "the good news of the kingdom" (Matt. 4:23; 9:35; see 24:14), "the gospel of God's grace" (Acts 20:24), the "gospel of peace" (Eph. 6:15), and "the eternal gospel" (Rev. 14:6).

The gospel message is simply that "Christ died for our sins according to the Scriptures, that he was buried, that he was raised the third day according to the Scriptures, and that he appeared to Peter, and then to the Twelve" (1 Cor. 15:3–5). Paul said this was the gospel he preached to the Corinthians and it was the message by which they received salvation. Also expressions of the gospel are found in the form of early Christian hymns (Phil. 2:6–11), creedal statements (1 Tim. 3:16), and the apostolic sermons of Peter and Paul. In connection with the latter there was always a historical declaration of the death, resurrection, and exaltation of Jesus, followed by an explanation of the person of Jesus as both Lord and Christ, concluding with a solemn call to believe and receive divine forgiveness of sins.

Dispensational interpreters believe that when the New Testament speaks of "the gospel of the kingdom," it is referring to the good news that God will establish an earthly kingdom in fulfillment of the Davidic Covenant (2 Sam. 7:16). This is the kingdom Jesus offered as He presented Himself as the prophesied King, the Son of David. This kingdom was proclaimed by John the Baptist (Matt. 3:1), Jesus (4:17), and the disciples (10:7) until the Jewish rejection of the Messiah (Luke 17:25). According to Matthew 24:14 it will be proclaimed again during the Great Tribulation, heralding the second advent of the King in glory. The message will be, "The King is coming!" Also at that time "the eternal gospel" will be announced by an angel to earth dwellers (Rev. 14:6). This will be an announcement of coming judgment, not a message of salvation; yet it will be good news to believers on earth because wicked persecutors will be judged. Believers will then be assured that God is in control and that righteousness will triumph.

In the Pauline Epistles the apostle used *euangelion* sixty times. It was one of his favorite terms, found in each of his epistles except Titus. Paul wrote that he was "set apart for the gospel" (Rom. 1:1) and that preaching the gospel to the Gentiles was his special task (Gal. 2:7). He felt a special compulsion to fulfill his task, asserting, "Woe to me if I do not preach the gospel" (1 Cor. 9:16).

Paul's defense of the gospel is nowhere more fervent than when he rebuked and warned Galatian believers who were "turning to a different gospel—which is really no gospel at all" (Gal. 1:6–7). Paul insisted that a gospel of legalism which adds works to faith is not the same kind of gospel he preached and by which they were saved. Those who proclaimed such a false gospel were placed under God's terrible anathema by the apostle.

The gospel is good news because it is a gift of God and not something that can be achieved by human effort. It is the gospel of God's grace (Act 20:24) because it originates in His lovingkindness, and it is the gospel of salvation (Eph. 1:13) because "it is the power of God for the salvation of everyone who believes" (Rom. 1:16).　　—DKC

Thank God for the good news of the gospel,
the message by which we received salvation.

Government

IN THE ULTIMATE EXERCISE OF AUTHORITY, direction, and justice, government rests in the hands of God, the sovereign Creator and Ruler of the universe (Exod. 15:18; 1 Chron. 29:11–12; 2 Chron. 20:6; Pss. 10:16; 22:28). God did not create the physical universe to operate by inherent laws while He served as an absent landlord (Col. 1:17; Heb. 1:3), nor did He create people to be autonomous. God is continually working both directly and providentially to fulfill His eternal plan (Eph. 1:11; 3:11) to His glory. God uses both spiritual and human agents, but He remains in ultimate authority and control.

The foundation for authority and government on the human level was established after the Flood by God's pronouncement to Noah about the sanctity of human life, because "in the image of God has God made man" (Gen. 9:6). As a result He said, "And from each man, too, I will demand an accounting for the life of his fellow man" (9:5). Human government was undoubtedly established to carry out this objective. The particular form of human government is not specified, but the patriarchal era that developed after Noah undoubtedly gave rise to an autocratic form such as the monarchy. In any case, as Paul wrote, "There is no authority except that which God has established. The authorities that exist have been established by God" (Rom. 13:1).

God's control of human government is demonstrated graphically in His dealings with King Nebuchadnezzar of Babylon. Daniel knew that God "sets up kings and deposes them" (Dan. 2:21). As a result he explained to Nebuchadnezzar when interpreting his dream of "a large statue" (2:31) that "the God of heaven has given you dominion and power and might and glory; in your hands he has placed mankind and the beasts of the field and the birds of the air. Wherever they live, he has made you ruler over them all" (2:27–38). In interpreting Nebuchadnezzar's second dream Daniel explained that the king would be inflicted with insanity for seven years "until you acknowledge that the Most High is sovereign over the kingdoms of men and gives them to anyone he wishes" (4:25). A year later, as Nebuchadnezzar was boasting of his power and accomplishments (4:28–30), he was struck with insanity until he acknowledged that God's "dominion is an eternal dominion; his kingdom endures from generation to generation" and that "he does as he pleases" (4:34–35).

When God established His chosen people Israel as a nation, He governed it directly as a theocracy through appointed human leaders, including Moses (Exod. 3:10, 12–15; Num. 12:1–2; 6–8), Joshua (Deut. 31:7–8, 14, 23; Josh. 1:1–9), and then the successive judges until Samuel (1 Sam. 3:19–21; 7:15), when Israel asked for "a king to lead us, as all the other nations have" (8:5). God directed Samuel to grant the people's request, explaining that "it is not you they have rejected, but they have rejected me as their King" (8:7).

The future worldwide millennial kingdom of Jesus Christ (Isa. 9:6–7; 11:1–9; Luke 1:30–33) demonstrates that, when the throne is occupied by God's appointed King, the monarchy is the best, most efficient form of government. Until Christ returns to establish His kingdom, however, some form of government by the people through elected representatives is preferable. No matter the form of government, Scripture directs us to submit to "the governing authorities" (Rom. 13:1; see also Titus 3:1; 1 Pet. 2:13–14), because they are ordained by God. Christians are also enjoined to pray "for kings and all those in authority" (1 Tim. 2:1–2). We must remember that Paul and Peter gave these directions to believers while Nero, one of the most despicable and dissolute despots of history, was ruler of the Roman Empire.

In His first coming Jesus Christ, the eternal Son of God (John 1:14, 18), set the example of submission to human government. When the Pharisees and Herodians tried to trap Him by asking, "Is it right to pay taxes to Caesar or not?" (Matt. 22:17; Mark 12:14; Luke 20:22), Jesus asked to be shown the coin used to pay taxes, a denarius (Matt. 22:19). When given one, He asked, "Whose portrait is this? And whose inscription?" (20:20). When His tempters responded, "Caesar's," Jesus said, "Give to Caesar what is Caesar's, and to God what is God's" (20:21). Jesus also recognized the divine source of human authority. When Pilate asked, "Don't you realize I have power either to free you or to crucify you?" (John 19:10), Jesus responded, "You would have no power over me if it were not given to you from above" (19:11).

There are occasions, however, when God's people must refuse to obey human authorities, being willing to suffer the consequences. Daniel's three friends, Shadrach, Meshach, and Abednego, refused to bow to Nebuchadnezzar's golden image, being willing to be thrown into the blazing furnace (3:12–18). Later Daniel disobeyed Darius's decree to pray only to him for thirty days (6:6–9). He continued to pray to the Lord, and so he was thrown into the den of lions (6:10, 16). When Peter and John were ordered by the Sanhedrin "not to speak or teach at all in the name of Jesus" (Acts 4:18), they replied, "Judge for yourselves whether it is right in God's sight to obey you rather than God. For we cannot help speaking about what we have seen and heard" (4:19–20). Later, Peter and the other disciples responded to the high priest, "We must obey God rather than men" (5:29).

Because of the secular nature of most human governments, some Christians oppose participation in them beyond obeying laws and paying taxes. The Scriptures, however, provide several examples of godly persons who were used greatly in the pagan governments in which they lived. The first example is Joseph, who was placed second to Pharaoh in the rule of Egypt (Gen. 41:37–47) and who recognized God's providential control in his being sold into slavery by his jealous brothers (45:4–8; 50:19–21). Other examples are Daniel, Shadrach, Meshach, and Abednego in Babylon (Dan. 1:19–20; 2:48–49; 3:30; 5:29; 6:28), Esther (Esth. 4:12–14), Mordecai (10:3), and Nehemiah (Neh. 1:11). God's control of human governments is seen in His calling Nebuchadnezzar "my servant" (Jer. 27:6), and Cyrus His "anointed" (Isa. 45:1) and "my shepherd [who] will accomplish all that I please" (44:28). Although Paul did not participate in government affairs, on several occasions he insisted on his rights as a Roman citizen (Acts 16:22–24, 35–40; 22:23–29; 25:8–12, 21, 25–27; 26:32).

The resurrected Lord gave the apostles human authority and leadership for the soon-to-be-inaugurated church (Matt. 28:18–20; John 20:21–23; Acts 1:8). The numerical growth of the Jerusalem church soon convinced the apostles of the need to share the authority and ministry. They directed the disciples to choose seven wise, Spirit-filled men to care for the widows' physical needs (6:2–4). Thus was born the office of deacon, and in local congregations the elders took the place of the apostles in providing spiritual leadership (14:23; 20:17; 1 Tim. 5:17;

Titus 1:5; James 5:14; 1 Pet. 5:1–3). Official leaders are provided in the local church for orderly direction and spiritual development.   —JAW

Take part in our system of government by voting and by doing what you can to help bring about justice.

Grace

THE CONCEPT OF GRACE unfolds gradually in Scripture. It has its roots in the Old Testament, where the Hebrew word *ḥēn* describes the compassionate response of a superior to an inferior, suggesting that the kindness is undeserved. Thus Moses prayed, "Now therefore, I pray, if I have found grace in Your sight, show me now Your way, that I may know You and that I may find grace in Your sight" (Exod. 33:13, NKJV). The Hebrew word *ḥesed* is also related to the concept of grace and emphasizes God's loving-kindness or loyal love toward Israel, His covenant people (Exod. 20:6; Deut. 7:12; 2 Sam. 7:15; Jer. 31:3).

In the New Testament the concept of grace is fully developed (the Greek word is *charis*). With the coming of Christ, grace took on its complete meaning (John 1:17). The apostle Paul in his epistles used the word *grace* to describe the vital difference between exerting human efforts to attempt to win God's favor and receiving God's gift of salvation, which is an expression of His grace. In Ephesians 2:4–5 Paul pointed out the relationship of three important doctrinal words, *love, mercy,* and *grace:* "But because of his great love for us, God, who is rich in mercy, made us alive with Christ even when we were dead in transgressions—it is by grace you have been saved." *Mercy* may be defined as God's compassion which moved Him to send a Savior for the lost world. But if salvation could have been provided simply on the basis of God's mercy alone, the sacrificial death of Christ would have been totally unnecessary. Divine *love,* on the other hand, was the motivating force behind all God did in providing salvation. Yet God's infinite love could not realize its desire to save sinners unless there was a total satisfaction for sin. This was provided in the atoning death of Christ, and only then could God's grace be freely bestowed on the lost. *Grace* can be defined therefore as God's unmerited favor in the giving of His Son, through whom salvation is offered to all.

Because grace proceeds from God's graciousness and is His free decision to favor us because of Christ, it must function apart from all human works (Eph. 2:8–9). The Mosaic Law has no power to justify the unsaved; rather sinners are "justified freely by his grace through the redemption that came by Christ Jesus" (Rom. 3:24). Paul affirmed dogmatically, "You are not under law, but under grace" (6:14).

Grace provides acceptance with God (3:24), gives enablement to live for God (Col. 1:29; Titus 2:11–12), establishes the believer in a new position (1 Pet. 2:9), and bestows on the saved every spiritual blessing for this life and the life to come (Eph. 1:3–14).

Many of the Epistles open and close with the hope that grace will be experienced by the readers, and the New Testament closes with the benediction, "the grace of the Lord Jesus be with God's people. Amen" (Rev. 22:21). **—DKC**

Rejoice today in God's grace, His unmerited favor toward us.

Guilt

THOUGH COMMONLY REGARDED today as a feeling, guilt in Scripture is considered a fact. It is a legal and moral condition resulting from any violation of God's standards. Further, the biblical concept includes the elements of sin and punishment. Though in a given passage of Scripture emphasis may be placed on just one of these elements, little or no distinction is made between them.

Various Hebrew words are used in the Old Testament to describe guilt, especially *'āšām*, the common word for "trespass offering." Its frequent uses describe guilt as something that can be incurred, enlarged, cleansed, punished, pardoned, remembered, and/or eliminated. Guilt in the Old Testament was both individual (2 Kings 14:6) and collective (Dan. 9:5). The coming Messiah, described by Isaiah as the Suffering Servant, is the prophesied *'āšām* or offering for the guilt of our sin (Isa. 53:10).

Guilt in the New Testament is often viewed as a legal term certifying criminal responsibility. For example, the Greek word *hypodikos*, found only in Romans 3:19, is translated "guilty" (NKJV) and "held accountable" (NIV). The world, Paul stated, is accountable to God and is declared guilty in divine court.

Other Greek words viewing guilt as a judicial concept are *aitia* and *aitios*, meaning a "charge" or "accusation." These words are used in the Gospels with reference to the accusations or charges brought against Jesus by His enemies (Matt. 27:37; Mark 15:26; Luke 23:4, 14, 22; John 18:38; 19:4, 6). They are found as well in Acts in describing the accusation or charges brought against Paul in Jerusalem, Caesarea, and Rome (Acts 22:24–25; 23:35; 25:7, 18, 27; 28:18).

Enochos, "worthy of punishment," occurs in Matthew 5:22; Mark 3:29; 1 Corinthians 11:27; James 2:10; and elsewhere.

Scripture is abundantly clear that people are guilty of transgressing God's laws (Rom. 3:23) and therefore stand in grave jeopardy of incurring His judgment (Heb. 9:27). But the good news is that the guilt brought by sin can be removed through faith in Christ whose death made a complete and final payment for sin. To be "in Christ" is to be free from condemnation and guilt (Rom. 8:1). For believers the verdict of "guilty" has been finally and fully reversed.   **—DKC**

*Thank God for His verdict of "not guilty"
because you have accepted Christ's final payment for sin.*

Hh

Hardening

BECAUSE OF THEIR SIN NATURE, many unbelievers rebel against God and refuse to accept divine truth. A pattern of refusal results in the heart being hardened, which was Pharaoh's response to each of the first five plagues (Exod. 7:13, 22; 8:15, 19, 32; 9:7). God then hardened Pharaoh's heart (9:12; 10:1, 20, 27; 11:10; 14:4, 8) *after* he had hardened his own heart against God.

God's hardening of Pharaoh simply confirmed what Pharaoh had already done in refusing to obey God. God's hardening resulted in greater glory to Himself (10:1; 11:9; Rom. 9:17), for it demonstrated the Lord's superiority over Pharaoh.

A special line of this truth is related to Israel. Paul wrote in Romans 11:7–10 that Israel's lack of comprehension of divine truth led them into hardening against further revelation. As a result, Gentiles in the present age have taken over a large portion of God's present purposes in the church. Yet Israel's blindness or hardening is for a time and is only partial. "I do not want you to be ignorant of this mystery, brothers, so that you may not be conceited: Israel has experienced a hardening in part until the full number of the Gentiles has come in. And so all Israel will be saved, as it is written, 'The deliverer will come from Zion; he will turn godlessness away from Jacob. And this is my covenant with them when I take away their sins'" (Rom. 11:25–27). However, at the Rapture there will be a special deliverance of Israel from their blindness with the result that many will come to Christ and believe the gospel. The lesson from this is that in order to understand God's truth, we must accept and respond to what He has previously revealed. This then becomes a stepping-stone to understanding more truth. In contrast to those who are hardened and do not receive the truth, those who accept Christ are enlightened by God's truth.　　　　　　　　　　　　　　　　—JFW

Respond always to the convicting work of the Spirit, never allowing your heart to become insensitive to the truth of God.

Headship

ALTHOUGH THE WORD *headship* does not occur in the Bible, the concept is used in a number of ways. It signifies a position of leadership and authority and is developed from the position and use of the head, the controlling and directing part of the human body, occasionally identified in Scripture as the person (2 Chron. 6:23; Ezek. 33:4–5; Acts 16:6).

The most significant headship, of course, is that of God, who, as sovereign Creator of all things, is Head of all creation (1 Cor. 11:3; 3:23; 15:28). In His sovereign plan God the Father appointed His Son, the Lord Jesus Christ, as "the head over every power and authority" (Col. 2:10; see also 1 Cor. 15:25–37; Eph. 1:21). In the permissive will of God, Satan—who "has been sinning from the beginning" (1 John 3:8) and who led some angels into rebellion against God with him—rules and serves as head or "prince of demons" (Matt. 12:24).

Of special importance to the believer is the fact that the Lord Jesus was appointed by God "to be head over everything for the church, which is his body" (Eph. 1:22–23). As a result Christ is described as "the head of the church, his body, of which he is the Savior" (5:23) and "the head of the body, the church" (Col. 1:18). Later Paul explained that Christ, as Head, is the one "from whom the whole body, supported and held together by its ligaments and sinews, grows as God causes it to grow" (2:19; see also Eph. 4:16). Believers are to "grow up into him who is the Head, that is, Christ" (4:15), for they "are members of his body" (5:30).

Another significant headship is in the family. Paul explained that "man did not come from woman, but woman from man; neither was man created for woman, but woman for man" (1 Cor. 11:8–9; see also Gen. 2:21–24). As a result "the head of the woman is man," just as "the head of every man is Christ" (1 Cor. 11:3). In another place Paul wrote that "the husband is the head of the wife as Christ is the head of the church, his body" (Eph. 5:23). Therefore, "as the church submits to

Christ, so also wives should submit to their husbands in everything" (5:24; see 1 Pet. 3:1).

On the other hand, "In the Lord, however, woman is not independent of man, nor is man independent of woman. For as woman came from man, so also man is born of woman" (1 Cor. 11:11–12). Therefore Paul wrote that husbands are to love their wives "just as Christ loved the church" (Eph. 5:25; see also 5:28, 33). Peter also instructed husbands to "be considerate as you live with your wives, and treat them with respect as the weaker partner and as heirs with you of the gracious gift of life" (1 Pet. 3:7). In the final analysis, in this relationship there should be a mutual consideration, love, respect, and submission "to one another out of reverence for Christ" (Eph. 5:21).   —JAW

Obey the Lord Jesus, the Head of the church,
so that you can participate with Him in accomplishing His work.

Healing

PHYSICAL AND MENTAL INFIRMITIES create the need for healing. Ever present are the desire, hope, and prayers for wellness, whether the malady results from an accident or a disease. The root of all sickness and death is the fall of Adam and Eve (Gen. 2:17). Their sin brought spiritual death and immediate separation from God, and it also started the process of physical decline toward death. This does not mean that sickness always results from specific sins, though this was a prevailing view during the time of Christ (John 9:2). Sometimes God permits sickness and suffering, as was true of Job (Job 2:4–7). Whenever this occurs it is to accomplish the purposes of God, even if those purposes are unknown to the one who is suffering (2:8–10; John 9:3).

The Old Testament contains numerous references to illness and specific healings. For example, Abraham prayed for the physical healing of Abimelech and his household and God restored them to health (Gen. 20:17). In response to Hezekiah's prayer, God healed him and extended his life for fifteen years (2 Kings 20:5–6). Jeremiah used the same word for healing (*rāpā'* to describe God's restoration of the nation of Judah after a time of captivity (Jer. 33:6–8). The prophets also used this word for healing when referring to the forgiveness of sins and spiritual restoration (Isa. 57:19; Hos. 14:4).

The New Testament words for healing describe either medical (physical) or spiritual healing, though restoring the body predominates. The Gospels are replete with examples of Jesus' healing power (Matt. 4:24; 9:35). On many occasions He healed those who were demon-possessed (8:16; Mark 1:32–34; Luke 4:40–41). The healing ministry of Jesus gave evidence that He is the Messiah (Matt. 11:2–5). John called the miraculous work of the Lord "signs," which included His power to heal (John 4:54; 5:8; 9:1–7). Jesus also gave His disciples the authority to heal every kind of disease and sickness (Matt. 10:1). However, physical healing was not the major purpose of Christ's ministry, as He reminded those He had sent out (Luke 10:19–20). When the risen Christ uttered the words commonly called the Great Commission, He made no reference to healing or miracles of any kind (Matt. 28:19–20).

Healing continued in the early church, as recorded in the Book of Acts. God used Peter, John, and other apostles to heal others (Acts 3:1–10; 5:12–16). These healings were signs that authenticated their ministry. Paul's ministry included healing but Luke records only a few incidents (14:8; 16:18; 28:8). Writing to the Corinthians, Paul defended his apostleship and referred to the miraculous signs that had been performed in their midst (2 Cor. 12:12).

The Epistles are almost silent on this subject. Paul lists healings as one of the gifts given by the Spirit to the church (1 Cor. 12:9, 30). Apparently this gift was not sought after, as was the gift of tongues, for no instructions were given as to its use nor did Paul have to correct its misuse. Toward the end of his ministry Paul did not exercise this gift. During Paul's imprisonment Epaphroditus was ill and almost died (Phil. 2:25–30). When Trophimus was in Miletus with Paul, he became sick but he was not healed by the apostle (2 Tim. 4:20). No recorded effort was made to heal Timothy of his frequent illnesses (1 Tim. 5:23). It is clear from Paul's own words that healing was not part of the gospel proclamation (1 Cor. 15:1–4). When Peter wrote his two letters, he made no mention of physical healing. Besides Paul, only James wrote about the subject of bodily healing (James 5:13–16). In this passage James was dealing with sickness resulting from unrighteous behavior or sin (5:15).

It was an issue within the church since the elders were called to intervene (5:14). The oil was not medicinal since the passage states that healing came through prayer offered in faith (5:15).

Today God in His grace and mercy often brings about healing when people pray, but yet it is evident that God does not heal everyone who asks (2 Cor. 12:7–10). No valid evidence exists to suggest that the gift of healing has been exercised since the first century. However, God has given people ability to learn about all kinds of sickness and disease, and today great strides have been made in the medical field to assist people who are ill. Even Paul took advantage of the medical skills available through his beloved companion and medical doctor, Luke (Col. 4:14). Ultimately, all who trust in Christ will find perfect healing when He will make all things new and will wipe away every tear, and there will be no more death, crying, or pain (Rev. 21:3–4). **—WGJ**

Pray earnestly for those who are sick,
knowing that God delights in healing people when it is His will.

Heart

THE WORD *heart* is used more than eight hundred times in Scripture. Only a few times does it refer to the physical organ of the human body (for example, Exod. 28:29–30; 2 Sam. 18:14; 2 Kings 9:24; Job 37:1). It almost always refers to the inner person, that is, the inner life that controls a person's thoughts, emotions, and actions.

The unregenerate person, since he is spiritually "dead in . . . transgressions and sins" (Eph. 2:1) and controlled by Satan (2:2–3), is described as having "every inclination of the thoughts of his heart . . . only evil all the time" (Gen. 6:5; see also 8:21). God stated that "the heart is deceitful above all things and beyond cure. Who can understand it?" (Jer. 17:9). As a result every individual needs to be born again (regenerated), for "if anyone is in Christ, he is a new creation; the old has gone, the new has come!" (2 Cor. 5:17). "What counts is a new creation" (Gal. 6:15).

The word *heart* is used of the mind, the seat of knowledge, thoughts, and wisdom (Prov. 2:2, 10; 3:1; 23:12, 15–16). It is capable of discerning good (1 Kings 3:9, 12; 2 Chron. 6:7–8) or bad (Pss. 58:1–2; 64:6; Prov. 6:14, 18). As the Lord Jesus explained, "for out of the heart come evil thoughts, murder, adultery, sexual immorality, theft, false testimony, slander" (Matt. 15:19).

The "heart" also refers to the seat of human emotions, both positive and negative. It can experience hatred (Lev. 19:17), pride (Deut. 8:14), despair (28:65), fear and terror (28:67; 1 Sam. 28:5), grief and sorrow (2:33), sadness (Neh. 2:2), resentment (Job 36:13), anguish (Ps. 55:4), and stubbornness (Jer. 16:12; 18:12). It can also experience gladness (Exod. 4:14), generosity (25:2; Deut. 15:10), joy (1 Sam. 2:1; 1 Kings 8:66; 2 Chron. 7:10), devotion (17:6), and cheer (Prov. 15:15).

Jeremiah asked concerning the heart, "Who can understand it?" (Jer. 17:9), anticipating the response, "No one." Humanly speaking, he was right; but God, since He is the Creator, replied, "I the LORD search the heart and examine the mind" (17:10; see also 1 Sam. 16:7; 1 Chron. 28:9; Prov. 17:3; Jer. 11:20; 20:12; Rom. 8:27; Rev. 2:23). God indeed knows the heart (Acts 1:24; 15:8). Because of that, David prayed, "Search me, O God, and know my heart; test me and know my anxious thoughts" (Ps. 139:23), and "examine my heart and my mind" (26:2).

Besides knowing the human heart, God, as the omnipotent Sovereign, also controls it as He purposes. Repeatedly the Scriptures state that "the LORD hardened Pharaoh's heart" (Exod. 9:12; 10:20, 27; 11:10) after promising Moses, "I will harden Pharaoh's heart" (4:21; 7:3; 14:4). Pharaoh was not merely an automaton, however, because he of his own will hardened his heart (8:32; 7:13–14, 22; 8:15, 19; 9:7, 35). To prepare Saul to minister as king of Israel "God changed [his] heart" (1 Sam. 10:9). Centuries later "the LORD moved the heart of Cyrus king of Persia" (2 Chron. 36:22; see Ezra 1:1, 5) to allow Jews to return to their homeland. God had put Solomon's astounding wisdom in his heart (1 Kings 10:24; 2 Chron. 9:23), and Nehemiah wrote that "God had put in my heart" his plans for Jerusalem (Neh. 2:12; 7:5).

God Himself is said to have a heart and to experience emotions and thoughts. Since God is Spirit, this is a figure of speech known as an anthropomorphism. But it does describe God's ability to think and feel. When God saw the wickedness of the human race before the Flood, He "was grieved . . . and his heart was filled with pain" (Gen. 6:6). God told Eli that He would raise up "a faithful priest, who will do according to what is in my heart and mind" (1 Sam. 2:35), and He described David as "a man after his own heart" (13:14; see also Acts 13:22). After Solomon built the temple, God told him, "My eyes and my heart will always be there" (1 Kings 9:3; 2 Chron. 7:16). Israel is a nation "close to his heart" (Ps. 148:14).

God's basic command to His people Israel was, "Love the LORD your God with all your heart and with all your soul and with all your strength" (Deut. 6:5), a command He repeated a number of times (10:12; 11:13; 13:3; 30:2, 6, 10; Josh. 22:5). In addition he told them to serve Him wholeheartedly (1 Sam. 12:20, 24). All believers are to work with all their heart, that is, completely and enthusiastically, and are to "trust in [Him] with all [their] heart" (Prov. 3:5).   —JAW

Be sure your heart is right with God through faith in Jesus Christ,
so that you will have concern for others, both saved and unsaved.

Heaven

THE JEWISH NOTION that the heavens are divided into seven different strata finds no support in Scripture. Paul however, spoke of being "caught up to the third heaven" (2 Cor. 12:2). This statement has led many Bible scholars to speak of three heavens, the first being the atmospheric heaven that surrounds the earth. Scripture speaks of this as the region of the clouds (Ps. 147:8), winds (Zech. 2:6, 6:5), rain (Deut. 11:11), thunder (1 Sam. 2:10), dew (Deut. 33:13), frost (Job 38:29), hail (Josh. 10:11), air (Gen. 1:26, 30; Matt. 6:26), and sky (Prov. 23:5).

The second heaven embraces the stellar spaces with the sun, the moon, the planets, and the stars. These heavenly bodies were created as "lights in the expanse of the sky" (Gen. 1:14). Genesis 15:5 refers to the stars in the heavens and Job 9:9 and 38:31 name two constellations of stars, Pleiades and Orion. In contrast to the heathen, the Hebrews were expressly forbidden to worship the heavenly bodies (Exod. 20:4; Deut. 4:19).

The dwelling place of the triune God—the Father, the Son, and the Holy Spirit—is in the "highest heaven" or the "heaven of heavens" (Deut. 10:14; 1 Kings 8:27; Pss. 68:33; 148:4). This no doubt is the counterpart to Paul's expression, "the third heaven." In Solomon's prayer at the dedication of the temple he declared, "The heavens, even the highest heaven, cannot contain you. How much less this temple I have built!" (1 Kings 8:27). God indeed is omnipresent, and yet in a particular way heaven is His habitation (Isa. 57:15; 63:15).

Jesus taught that heaven is the dwelling place of God (Matt. 6:9). He repeatedly claimed to have come from heaven (John 3:13; 6:33–51), where He had lived eternally (17:5). Just before His trial and crucifixion Jesus told His disciples that heaven was a specific place and that He was going there to prepare abodes for them (14:1–2). In His high priestly prayer Jesus referred to His eternal preexistent glory with the Father in heaven (17:5). After His resurrection He spoke of His ascension to heaven (20:17), a dramatic event described by Luke (Luke 24:51; Acts 1:9). Two angels reminded the disciples that Jesus will return from heaven someday (Acts 1:10–11), a promise Jesus Himself had affirmed (John 14:3) and Paul later expanded and reaffirmed (1 Thess. 4:13–18). In the present age Christ is in heaven "at the right hand of God and is also interceding for us" (Rom. 8:34).

In addition to the glorified Christ, the present inhabitants of heaven include the redeemed souls of Old and New Testament saints. Paul taught that believers "prefer to be away from the body and at home with the Lord" (2 Cor. 5:8). To the dying thief Christ said, "Today you will be with me in paradise" (Luke 23:43). Two Old Testament saints, Enoch and Elijah, were translated into heaven (2 Kings 2:1, 11; Heb. 11:5). Long before God created Adam and Eve, angels were in heaven, where they serve and praise God (Ps. 148:2; Heb. 12:22). From heaven the angels go forth to minister to people living on earth, especially those who are heirs of salvation (Heb. 1:14).

Skeptics have sometimes said people have no certain knowledge of heaven because no one has returned from there to tell about it. Occasionally sensationalist preachers have made fraudulent claims to such an experience, but the only reliable and trustworthy accounts are found in Scripture. Christ, of course, is the first such authentic eyewitness of heaven, which was His home from eternity past. Another eyewitness to heaven was the apostle Paul, who was "caught up to the third heaven," (2 Cor. 12:2), probably when he was almost stoned to death in Lystra (Acts 14:19–22). He was prohibited from revealing what he saw and heard and was given a "thorn in the flesh" to remind him of the restriction (2 Cor. 12:7). A third eyewitness was John, who while on Patmos saw and heard remarkable things. He wrote, "After this I looked and there before me was a door standing open in heaven. And the voice I had first heard speaking to me like a trumpet said, 'Come up here, and I will show you what must take place after this'" (Rev. 4:1). In the Book of Revelation, John faithfully described the stunning revelations he received of God on His throne and of the judgments and glories to come.

Appropriately John was given the privilege of disclosing a great deal about heaven. (The word *heaven* occurs fifty-two times in the Book of Revelation.) Of particular interest is John's description of the New Jerusalem, the heavenly city (21:1–22:5). John wrote that he saw "the Holy City, the new Jerusalem, coming down out of heaven from God" (21:2). This city, which Jesus went to prepare for His saints (John 14:1–3), will descend from the third heaven to the earth. This will occur after the Great White Throne judgment. Thus at the beginning of the eternal state, heaven will come to earth! It will be the eternal abode of the redeemed of all ages.

A number of things will be absent from heaven. For example, there will be no marrying or giving in marriage (Luke 20:35). There will be no tears, sorrow, pain, death, or night. Nor will there be any need of light because the Son of God will be heaven's light (Rev. 21:23, 22:5). In contrast to these negative references are the lavish and magnificent descriptions of the heavenly city with its foundations, gates, and walls. Above all, it is a city in which the glory of God will be fully revealed (21:11). The cities of earth may reflect the glory of man, but the celestial city will reflect only the glory of God.

While heaven will be a place of rejoicing and rest, it will not be a place of inactivity. As stated in the final chapter of the Bible, in heaven the saints will serve God, will see His face (that is, will have immediate access to His presence), and will reign with Christ forever (22:3–5).

—**DKC**

Look forward with eager anticipation to heaven, your real home, where every believer will worship and serve the Lord forever.

Hell

THE ENGLISH WORD *hell* translates the Old Testament word *sheol,* which is used more than sixty times in the Old Testament. In some cases this seems to refer to the grave, where dead bodies are buried, and in other occurrences it is used of the present (intermediate) state of the unsaved. Charles Hodge, the late Presbyterian theologian of Princeton Seminary, taught that *sheol* had two compartments, one for the saved and the other for the lost, and that in cases where the intermediate state is meant, it refers to this two-compartment situation. However, W. G. T. Shedd, a contemporary of Hodge's, held that the two-compartment theory was borrowed from Greek mythology and was not the case in the Old Testament. He held that the term *sheol* should always be translated "grave." The New International Version tends to follow Shedd and translates *sheol* as "the grave" in all but a few instances. For instance, in Deuteronomy 32:22 *sheol* is translated "realm of death below," in Job 17:16 it is rendered "gates of death," and in Job 26:6 *sheol* is translated "death."

In Jesus' account of the rich man and Lazarus, the rich man was in *hades,* the equivalent of *sheol,* and was able to carry on a conversation with Lazarus, even though there was a great gulf between them (Luke 16:19–31). The attempt to write off this account as a parable is hindered by the fact that the poor beggar was named, whereas in all of Jesus' parables no names were ever used.

In the New Testament a number of Greek words are used for hell. Some of them refer to the temporary or intermediate state of the wicked, and others refer to their eternal state. Like *sheol,* hades can refer to either the grave (of the unsaved) or their present conscious condition after death. Hades, populated entirely by unsaved people, is a temporary place for the unsaved. Immediately after the Great White Throne judgment they will be cast into their permanent place of punishment in what is called "the lake of fire" (Rev. 20:15). In contrast to hades is the word *gehenna,* a word Jesus used several times in referring to the final destiny of the lost. It is apparently the equivalent of the lake of fire, because it does not refer to a temporary situation. The nature of hell as eternal fire and torment is most explicit in Jesus' teachings (see, for example, Matt. 18:9; 25:46; Mark 9:44, 48).

Tartarus (2 Pet. 2:4), another word for hell, is either the same as *gehenna,* or a present place of confinement for fallen angels until they too, are cast into the lake of fire.

Though the concept of hell as eternal punishment is difficult for human intelligence to comprehend, it is the clear teaching of Scripture. Our difficulty stems from the fact that we do not understand the infinite character of sin and God's righteous nature which must judge all sin that is not forgiven through an individual's faith in Christ. A clear instance of eternal punishment is found in Revelation 20:10, which states that the devil will be thrown into the lake of fire (or "burning sulfur"), where the beast and the false prophet, Satan's leaders in the Great Tribulation, were cast a thousand years before. All three "will be tormented day and night for ever and ever."

According to Christ's own words, the lake of fire was "prepared for the devil and his angels" (Matt. 25:41). Those who do not receive Christ as Savior will share the destiny of the devil and the fallen angels.

Evangelical expositors agree that in the present age when a Christian dies his soul goes immediately to heaven rather than to *sheol* or hades. The believer in heaven is conscious in the presence of the Savior, while awaiting the resurrection of his body at the Rapture. Thus if there were two compartments in *sheol* in the Old Testament, this is not the case now.

—JFW

Pray daily for those who are blind to the gospel
so they will escape God's judgment on unbelievers.

Heresy

THE ENGLISH WORD *heresy* is close to a transliteration of the Greek word *hairesis,* which means a choosing or a choice, then what is chosen, or an opinion. In classical Greek the word came to be used for those who held a particular opinion or view, such as the Stoics or the Epicureans, without regard to approval or disapproval of the view. In this sense Scripture speaks of "the party [*hairesis*] of the Sadducees" (Acts 5:17) and "the party [*hairesis*] of the Pharisees" (15:5; see also

26:5). The word is used pejoratively when Paul was called "a ringleader of the Nazarene sect" [*hairesis*] (24:5; see also 28:22).

Paul used this word to speak of "differences" of opinion (1 Cor. 11:19; "factions," NASB). These different opinions in the church at Corinth resulted in "divisions" (11:18), a condition he regretted. "Factions," as Paul wrote in Galatians 5:20, are one of the "acts of the sinful nature." Peter identified the views of false prophets and false teachers as "destructive heresies," for they denied the sovereign Lord who bought them (2 Pet. 2:1).

Primarily as a result of Peter's use of the word *hairesis*, a heresy became identified as a departure from an essential truth of the Christian faith. From Christianity's earliest years believers have had to identify and deal with false views, that is, heresies. For example, Paul had to respond to those who said "there is no resurrection of the dead" (1 Cor. 15:12–19), and John warned against "the man who denies that Jesus is the Christ" (1 John 2:22). Jude urged his readers "to contend for the faith that was once for all entrusted to the saints" because of the "godless men, who change the grace of our God into a license for immorality and deny Jesus Christ our only Sovereign and Lord" (Jude 3–4). Having to identify and denounce heresies has actually helped the church through the centuries, and the early church in particular, in establishing the essential doctrines of the Christian faith. **—JAW**

Draw a line between accepting a doctrinal difference of opinion
and tolerating a heresy concerning a key biblical truth.

Holiness

HOLINESS IS A FOUNDATIONAL ATTRIBUTE of God; He is said to be "majestic in holiness" (Exod. 15:11). He has "sworn by [His] holiness" (Ps. 89:35; Amos 4:2), and He reveals "the holiness of [His] great name" (Ezek. 36:23; see also 38:23). When God redeems and restores Israel in the future, the Gentiles "will acknowledge the holiness of the Holy One of Jacob" (Isa. 29:23). Israel was commanded to worship Him for "the splendor of his holiness" (1 Chron. 16:29; 2 Chron. 20:21; Pss. 29:2; 96:9).

Several times God is called "the Holy One" (Job 6:10; Ps. 22:3; Prov. 9:10; 30:3; Isa. 40:25) and frequently the "Holy One of Israel" (2 Kings 19:22; Pss. 71:22; 78:41; 89:18; Jer. 50:29; 51:5; Ezek. 39:7, including more than two dozen times in the Book of Isaiah). Frequent references to God's "holy name" (Lev. 20:3; 1 Chron. 29:16; Pss. 97:12; 106:47; 145:21; Ezek. 36:20–23; Amos 2:7; see also Isa. 57:15)—abbreviated sometimes simply to "the Name" (for example, Lev. 24:16; 1 Chron. 13:6)—refer to God Himself.

From the use of the words "holy" and "holiness" in Scripture, as well as from the meaning of the Hebrew and Greek words (qōdeš and its derivatives in Hebrew, and hagios and its derivatives in Greek), the concept signifies something or someone who is separate and set apart or consecrated. God is holy because He is unique, totally separate in nature from all His creatures. The words also mean moral purity or separateness from evil. God is holy in the sense of being morally pure. Habakkuk wrote concerning God, "Your eyes are too pure to look on evil; you cannot tolerate wrong" (Hab. 1:13).

God alone is inherently holy, but He is also able to make His creatures holy in the sense of being separated or consecrated to Him and His service and in the sense of being morally pure.

By choosing Israel to be His special nation, God made the Israelites holy, that is, separated from other peoples and consecrated to Him (Exod. 31:13). Israel is described as "a people holy to the LORD your God" (Deut. 7:6; 14:2, 21; 26:19) and God's "holy nation" (Exod. 19:6) and "holy people (22:31; Deut. 28:9). As a result of this "positional" holiness, God expected the Israelites to manifest holiness (morality) in their conduct. God told Israel to "be holy, because I, the LORD your God, am holy" (Lev. 19:2; see also 11:44–45). "I am the LORD," God said, "who makes you holy" (20:7).

God also makes many inanimate objects holy in the sense of setting things apart for sacred use (Exod. 29:37; 40:9–10; Lev. 2:3, 10; 6:25–27; Num. 4:15–16; 16:37). Obviously no moral purity resides in these things, but they are dedicated to the service of God and therefore are holy. In the same way, some events (Gen. 2:3; Exod. 16:23; 20:8, 11) and places (3:5; 26:33–34; 1 Chron. 29:3; Pss. 11:4; 20:6) are called holy.

In the New Testament, holiness is ascribed primarily to the Lord Jesus Christ and the Spirit of God rather than to God the Father. Since the Old

Testament only hints at the Trinity, the New Testament emphasizes the existence of the second and third persons of the triune Godhead. In the light of the New Testament, Old Testament references to God's "Anointed One" and His "Son" (Ps. 2:2, 7) speak of the second person of the Trinity. Although the Old Testament frequently mentions the "Spirit of God" and "Spirit of the LORD" (for example, Gen. 1:2; Judg. 3:10), He is called the "Holy Spirit" only three times in the Old Testament (Ps. 51:11; Isa. 63:10–11). On the other hand, the New Testament often speaks of the third person of the Trinity as "the Holy Spirit."

Jesus was called "the Holy One" by the angel Gabriel in his announcement to Mary (Luke 1:35), by a demon that He was exorcising (Mark 1:24; Luke 4:34), and by Simon Peter (John 6:69). Two other occurrences of "the Holy One" could refer to either Jesus Christ or God the Father (1 John 2:20; Rev. 16:5). In light of Peter's application of Psalm 16:10 in Acts 2:27 and Paul's reference in Acts 13:35, the "Holy One" is understood as referring to the Lord Jesus. Peter also called Jesus Christ "the Holy and Righteous One" (3:14) and the believers who were led in prayer by Peter and John called Him God's "Anointed One" (4:26) and "holy servant Jesus" (4:27, 30). The glorified Christ identified Himself to the church in Philadelphia as "him who is holy and true" (Rev. 3:7).

Christians are occasionally spoken of as holy in the sense of being separated to God (2 Tim. 2:21; 1 Pet. 2:9), but more often the emphasis is on holiness as moral purity. Through Christ's sacrificial death Christians have been made holy in the sight of God the Father (Heb. 2:11; 10:10, 14; 13:12). As a result they are often called saints (for example, Rom. 1:7; 1 Cor. 6:1–2; 2 Cor. 13:13) and are said to be holy (Eph. 5:3; Col. 1:2; 2 Thess. 1:10).

Because God views Christians as holy and blameless, He exhorts them to become as morally pure in their daily lives as possible by help of the indwelling Holy Spirit. Being holy means maintaining purity of thoughts and attitudes (Heb. 4:12; Ps. 139:23), in addition to correct deeds. Peter summed up this responsibility when he wrote, "But just as he who called you is holy, so be holy in all you do; for it is written; 'Be holy, because I am holy'" (1 Pet. 1:15–16). "It is God's will that you should be sanctified" (1 Thess. 4:3), Paul wrote, and therefore each believer is urged "to live a holy life" (4:7; see also 2 Tim. 1:9).

—JAW

*Strive to translate your holiness in your position in Christ
into holiness in daily living.*

Holy Spirit

THE HOLY SPIRIT IS A PERSON, possessing all the qualities of personality, and at the same time He is a member of the Godhead, coequal with
the Father and the Son. Evidence that the Holy Spirit is a person, not a
principle or an object, includes the fact that He communicates as a person (testifying of Christ, John 15:26; speaking, 16:13; and revealing,
16:15) and acts as a person (believers can have fellowship with Him,
2 Cor. 13:14; He intercedes for believers, Rom. 8:27; He leads believers,
Gal. 5:18; He gives them spiritual gifts, 1 Cor. 12:4, 11; and He appoints
them to service, Acts 13:2). Also, people can respond to Him as a person
(people have lied to Him, Acts 5:3; grieved Him, Isa. 63:10; Eph. 4:30;
and insulted Him, Heb. 10:29).

The Scriptures clearly teach the deity of the Holy Spirit. He is identified as God (Acts 5:3–4), He is associated with God the Father and
God the Son and is coequal with them (Matt. 28:19; 2 Cor. 13:14; 1 Pet.
1:2). He does works that only God can do. He led men to write Scripture
(2 Pet. 1:21), He was involved in the creation of the world (Gen. 1:2), He
searches and knows the mind of God (1 Cor. 2:10–11), He raised Jesus
from the dead (Rom. 8:11), He convicts the world of sin (John 16:7–11),
He regenerates (Titus 3:5), and He sanctifies (1 Pet. 1:2).

In the opening chapter of Genesis the Holy Spirit is related to creation. In verse 2, He is seen as the Organizer of the order of creation,
who turned chaos into order. Though the Scriptures state that each of
the persons of the Godhead was involved in creation, the Holy Spirit
seems to have been particularly related to its beauty and order (Job
26:13; 33:4; Pss. 33:6; 104:29–30; Isa. 40:13). Job 26:13 speaks of the
Holy Spirit as causing the sky to become fair (the NKJV of this verse says
the Holy Spirit "adorned the heavens"). Also the Holy Spirit continues
to sustain the physical world (Ps. 104:29–30).

God revealed Himself to individuals through the Holy Spirit (2 Sam.
23:2–3; Isa. 59:21; Acts 28:25).

On the Day of Pentecost the Holy Spirit began a new work, for He came then to form the church, the body of Christ. Of significance is His work in regeneration, providing life for those who are spiritually dead when they place their faith in Christ. All three persons of the Trinity are involved in giving a person spiritual life, including the Father (James 1:17–18), the Son (John 5:21; 1 John 5:12), and the Holy Spirit (John 3:5–6, 8).

Other new works the Spirit began on the Day of Pentecost are indwelling and sealing. While some individuals in the Old Testament were temporarily filled by the Holy Spirit, beginning on the Day of Pentecost every believer is indwelt by the Holy Spirit at the moment of salvation and His body becomes a temple of God. This was anticipated in Jesus' words in John 14:17 ("he lives with you and will be in you"). This indwelling ministry is mentioned often in the New Testament (John 7:37–39; Rom. 5:5; 8:9, 11; 1 Cor. 2:12; 6:19–20; 2 Cor. 5:5; Gal. 3:2; 4:6; 1 John 3:24; 4:13). If a person is not indwelt by the Holy Spirit, he or she is not saved (Rom. 8:9; Jude 19). By indwelling the believer, the Holy Spirit is God's seal or evidence of possession and protection (Eph. 4:30).

Another ministry of the Holy Spirit is the baptism of the Spirit (which was predicted in Matt. 3:11 and Acts 1:5, 8). In this new ministry, which He began on the Day of Pentecost, every believer is baptized into one body, that is, the church, the body of Christ, of which He is the Head. This points to the church as a distinct body of believers, not known in the Old Testament. Because this work of the Spirit occurs for every believer at salvation, it is not an experience to be sought subsequent to the new birth.

Though the filling of the Spirit may occur at the same time as the baptism of the Spirit, the two works differ. The baptism is once for all, but the filling can be repeated many times.

Most important in the work of the Spirit is the filling of the Spirit, which is possible for any Christian. Before the church age began, some individuals were filled with the Spirit temporarily (Exod. 31:3; 35:31; Luke 1:15, 41, 67; 4:1). This filling was to enable individuals to carry out special forms of service for God. Since Pentecost, however, each believer can be filled with the Spirit if he meets the conditions set forth in the Scriptures. The filling of the Spirit does not mean getting more of the Spirit; instead, it refers to the Spirit taking complete charge of a Christian and empowering him or her. An immature Christian can be filled with the Spirit, even though maturity takes time and the full evidence of God's work in the believer may not always be evident immediately.

On the Day of Pentecost all the apostles were filled with the Spirit (Acts 2:4). Subsequent experiences of being filled are frequently mentioned in the Book of Acts (4:8, 31; 6:3; 7:55; 11:24, 13:9, 52).

Three conditions are necessary for a believer to be filled with the Spirit. First, Christians should not "quench" the Spirit (1 Thess. 5:19, NKJV), that is, they are not to "put out the Spirit's fire" (NIV). This means that believers should yield to the Spirit and not resist His guidance and empowerment. A second condition is stated in Ephesians 4:30, "Do not grieve the Holy Spirit of God," which means confessing sin in order to restore one's fellowship with Christ (1 John 1:9). The third command is to "live by the Spirit" (Gal. 5:16), or, perhaps better, to "walk by the Spirit." The idea is that one should constantly depend on God for victory over sin.

As believers are filled with the Spirit, they can enjoy the "fruit" of the Spirit (Gal. 5:22–23), by which He produces holiness in the life of the believer. Other results from the filling of the Spirit include being guided by the Spirit, enjoying the assurance of salvation, expressing love for God, seeing answers to prayer, and experiencing the power of God.

—JFW

Be sensitive to the many ways the Spirit of God can enrich your life.

Homosexuality

ONE OBVIOUS PURPOSE God has for every one of His children is to be holy (1 Thess. 4:3). God does not call anyone to an impure life, and to deviate from His will is to neglect or reject Him (4:7–8). When Christian people know something is displeasing to the Lord, it must be taken seriously. This is true with regard to what the Bible says about the practice of homosexuality. Though Scripture passages on that subject are few, the message is unmistakably clear. God is not pleased when men and women violate His purposes for human sexuality.

The basis for understanding this teaching is rooted in the creation account in the Book of Genesis. God made male and female in His image (Gen. 1:27), and what He created was very good (1:31). God did not intend for Adam to live alone because he would have been incomplete. So He created woman and the two became one (2:18; 21–24). Of significance is the fact that the Lord did not create another male for Adam. Instead He made someone who was different from him but yet one who would complement him. This was also the way God would populate the earth, which would not have been possible with the creation of a same-sex individual. The relationship of man and woman was ideal until sin entered the world. Sin had far-reaching effects on man and woman and on all of creation (Rom. 8:18–22).

Unholy relationships brought God's judgment on the whole earth by the Flood (Gen. 6:1–7). And another devastating event involved the people of Sodom and Gomorrah. God destroyed these two cities and all their inhabitants except Lot and his family (19:24–25). The Bible provides a brief glimpse of the conduct of the people whose actions were so grievous to God (18:20). All the men from every part of the city of Sodom came to Lot and demanded to have sex with the men who were visiting in Lot's home (19:5). To "have sex with" (NIV) translates the verb *yādâ*, "to know," which is used in the Old Testament at least eleven other times to refer to sexual relations. Because this word is also translated "to become acquainted" in other places in the Old Testament (Gen. 29:5; Ruth 2:11), prohomosexual advocates claim that this is its meaning in Genesis 19:5. However, this word is used in the same context to explain that Lot's daughters were virgins and had not "known" man (Gen. 19:8) or had "not had relations with man" (NASB). The traditional interpretation of Genesis 18–19 about the men's rampant evil practice is confirmed in the New Testament by Jude, who described the sin of Sodom and Gomorrah as sexual immorality and perversion (Jude 7). Second Peter 2:6–10 also adds support to this translation of the Genesis account.

The Mosaic Law includes specific teaching on the subject of homosexuality. The Lord told Moses to speak to the people concerning practices that He would not allow in the land of Israel. A man was not to lie with another man in the same manner that a man would lie with a woman (Lev. 18:22). This kind of conduct, God said, was detestable and would defile them as well as the land (18:24–25). Because of His holy nature God would not tolerate this kind of lifestyle.

Leviticus 20:13 states that homosexuals were to be punished by death. It is true that the Mosaic Law as a system has ended (Rom. 12:4; 2 Cor. 3:7–11), and the penalty for the practice of homosexuality in this dispensation is not immediate death. However, the moral principles on which the Law was established never change because they are evidence of God's holy character, and are supported by the New Testament teaching against homosexual practice.

Jesus did not deal with this issue directly, but His teaching on marriage was based on the Genesis account, and He reiterated the fact that marriage is to be between male and female (Matt. 19:4–6).

Paul wrote that one of the reasons for the manifestation of God's wrath in his day was the practice of homosexuality that was so prevalent in the Greek world (Rom. 1:18–32). The apostle called homosexual activity unnatural" (1:26–27). He described its practices as indecent acts and perversion (1:27). Though the judgment was not immediate, death was deserved (1:32). But God gave those who were practicing homosexuality up to their passions, which was His judgment on them (1:26, 28). There is no evidence that what is being practiced today by homosexuals is any different from what Paul was describing in Romans and what the Law prohibited in Leviticus.

In two other passages Paul warned believers about actions that displease God. He wrote that homosexual activity is not something that characterizes those who are to inherit the kingdom of God (1 Cor. 6:9–10). Some of the people in the church at Corinth had been involved in the sinful practices Paul outlined, but because of God's grace they had been redeemed and sanctified from those practices (6:11). In 1 Timothy 1:10 Paul also warned about homosexuality activity ("homosexuals," NASB; "perverts," NIV). This practice is contrary to sound doctrine and thus is not pleasing to the Lord.

In light of the biblical teaching about homosexuality Christians who have an inclination toward or are susceptible to this lifestyle need to heed Paul's admonition in Colossians 3:5–6. The sin of homosexual activity can be forgiven, because Christ died for all the sins of the world. Those who are attracted to this kind of sexual activity need to realize that this sin need not master them (Rom. 6:13–14). Homosexuals who love Christ can find power and encouragement when they seek the Lord's help, as is true of any believer struggling to overcome sin. The danger individuals encounter when dealing with sin is to seek to minimize or justify actions rather than turning to the mercy of the Lord and seeking forgiveness and deliverance from its dominance.

As to certain other questions about homosexuality, such as its causes or its removal as a sexual orientation, the Bible contains no explicit teaching. —**WGJ**

Ask God for a patient and sensitive heart
in dealing with those who struggle with sexual temptations.

Hope

IN CASUAL CONVERSATION the word *hope* conveys a desire or even a fantasy that is uncertain of fulfillment. Doubt is attached as if the hope or wish will probably not come to pass. Thus Luke 23:8 states that Herod "hoped" to see Jesus perform a miracle, and according to Acts 24:26 Felix "was hoping" Paul would give him a bribe. The word *hope* is only rarely used in this way in Scripture; most often it conveys the meaning of a confident or certain expectation.

In the Old Testament various Hebrew words for hope express the ideas of trust or of expectation. Job, for example, raised the plaintive cry, "If the only home I hope for is the grave . . . , where then is my hope? Who can see any hope for me?" (Job 17:13, 15). In the end Job found the same answer as the later psalmist, "LORD, what do I look for? My hope is in you" (Ps. 39:7). The psalms are replete with expressions that affirm the believer's hope or trust in God. He is seen as a deliverer, who will certainly act on behalf of believers someday. Meanwhile the godly are invited to wait and hope. "But the eyes of the LORD are on those who fear him, on those whose hope is in his unfailing love, to deliver them from death and keep them alive in famine" (33:18–19). Other verses that express the same hope are Psalms 31:23–24; 62:5–7; 71:5, 14; 119:49–50; 130:7; 146:5–7.

The Old Testament prophets stressed the importance of hope, even in the face of the catastrophic Babylonian exile. Jeremiah addressed God as the "Hope of Israel" (Jer. 14:8), and he reassured the Jews, "[You] will return from the land of the enemy. So there is hope for your future" (31:16–17).

In both Testaments hope sometimes has to do with temporal or earthly concerns or desires. These include the hope of bearing children (Ruth 1:12), of finding water (Job 6:19), of the repayment of a loan (Luke 6:34), of deliverance from a storm (Acts 27:20), of sharing in a harvest (1 Cor. 9:10), and of visiting someone (Rom. 15:24; 1 Cor. 16:7; 1 Tim. 3:14). In the New Testament the word *hope* occurs frequently in the Epistles and was a favorite term of the apostle Paul (Rom. 12:12; 15:13; Eph. 1:18; Titus 1:2). Christ Himself is the believer's hope (Rom. 5:2; Col. 1:27; 1 Tim. 1:1). The fountainhead of that hope is the death, burial, and resurrection of Christ (1 Pet. 1:3). Thus God has given believers hope through the gospel (Col. 1:23; Heb. 6:18–19). That hope has an eschatological significance. Because Jesus was resurrected bodily, believers will be resurrected (Acts 23:6; Rom. 8:18–25). In fact everyone, both the righteous and the wicked, will be resurrected (Acts 24:15). Because of this hope (or what J. B. Phillips called a "happy certainty") that believers will be raised to be with Christ, we are not "to grieve like the rest of men, who have no hope" (1 Thess. 4:13) and are "without hope" (Eph. 2:12). Closely associated therefore with the believer's resurrection is "the blessed hope" of the return of Christ for His own (Titus 2:13), at which time we will receive resurrection bodies (1 John 3:2).

The Christian's hope pertains not only to the future. It also has present benefits. John declared that the hope of Christ's return has a sanctifying effect on the believer. "Everyone who has this hope in him purifies himself, just as he [Jesus] is pure" (1 John 3:3). Further, Paul explained that the Christian's troubles or afflictions produce perseverance, and that perseverance produces a tested and proved character, which in turn strengthens our hope (Rom. 5:3–4). Later Paul commended the Thessalonian believers for their endurance, which was "inspired by hope in our Lord Jesus Christ" (1 Thess. 1:3).

God's words to Jeremiah provide a fitting summary: "For I know the plans I have for you, declares the LORD, plans to prosper you and not to harm you, plans to give you hope and a future" (Jer. 29:11).   **—DKC**

Contemplate what life would be like without our hope in Christ.

Humility

CONSIDERING OTHERS AHEAD OF ONESELF and taking a position lower than what may be deserved is diametrically opposed to the philosophy of the world. Yet humility is one of the most desirable virtues for Christians (Eph. 4:2; Col. 3:12). Isaiah the prophet summed up the significance of being humble before the Lord with these words: "This is the one I esteem: he who is humble and contrite in spirit, and trembles at my word" (Isa. 66:2). Micah stated that God requires believers to walk humbly with Him (Mic. 6:8). Jesus declared that humility is necessary for entrance into the kingdom of God (Matt. 18:3–4). Both James and Peter quoted Proverbs 3:34, which emphasizes that God gives grace to those who are humble (James 4:6; 1 Pet. 5:5).

Solomon's magnificent personal prayer at the dedication of the temple shows his humility. The attitude of humility along with a turning away from sin is what God honors and makes prayer effective (2 Chron. 7:12–16). The remaining chapters in 2 Chronicles are a running commentary on God's response to humility. When Shishak, king of Egypt, threatened to overrun Jerusalem, the leaders of Israel, including King Rehoboam, humbled themselves before the Lord, and because of this God spared them from judgment (12:6–7, 12). Asa's failure to humble himself before God brought disaster at the end of his life and left a tragic blot on his record (16:7–12). Amaziah's pride was the reason for his defeat at the hands of Jehoash, king of Israel (25:19–21). In Hezekiah's reign the Lord honored the humility of the people of Israel and allowed them to celebrate the Passover in Jerusalem (30:11–12). Judgment from God was averted because Hezekiah and his people humbled themselves (32:24–26). Even when Manasseh, whose wickedness was devastating to the nation, humbled himself, God responded (33:12–13). Jerusalem finally fell into the hands of the Babylonians because of the refusal of Amon and Zedekiah to humble themselves before the Lord (33:23; 36:11).

The life and teachings of Christ are marked by humility. When He began His public ministry in Galilee, He emphasized the importance of humility with the words, "Blessed are the poor in spirit" (Matt. 5:3). How strange this was to the ears of the scribes and Pharisees. In counteracting the teachings and actions of the Pharisees, Jesus often told parables that revealed their proud hearts (23:1–12; Luke 14:7–11). He explained the meaning of humility by using a child as an object lesson (Matt. 18:1–5). Unless people are willing to change their attitudes and become like little children, they cannot receive what God has for them. By this illustration Jesus taught that humility means to place ourselves in a position below what may be rightfully ours. For an adult to become like a child cannot be done without a willful decision. Perhaps the strongest admonition concerning humility was expressed by Jesus when He called for those who were weary and burdened to come to Him. They were to learn from Him, the epitome of humility, the One who is "gentle and humble in heart" (11:28–30).

Central to the teaching on humility in the Bible is the Lord's own example of humility by His death on the cross. Paul's description of this in Philippians 2:5–11 may be one of the most beautiful expressions of this truth in all of Scripture. This passage is significant for it records Jesus Christ's actions as the ultimate example of humility. While retaining His deity as the Son of God, Jesus voluntarily took on Himself the form of a servant (2:7). He consciously and willingly took a position lower than what He had. He did this to please the Father and to accomplish His will (Eph. 1:9), and in so doing He demonstrated His great love for humanity (John 3:16).

God exalted Jesus to the highest place and gave Him a name above all other names (Phil. 2:9). This act of humility and exaltation will ultimately glorify God the Father, when everyone will bow down before the Lord Jesus Christ (2:10–11). Paul exhorted every believer to follow the example of Christ by having the same attitude He had (2:5).

The night before He was crucified Jesus gave a graphic illustration of humility: He washed the disciples' feet, thereby taking the role of a servant. To Peter this seemed demeaning until he understood the purpose behind the act. Years later, when Peter was writing to Christians scattered throughout present-day Turkey, Peter reflected on that occasion and called on believers to be like Christ by clothing themselves with humility toward each other (1 Pet. 5:5). If Christians humble themselves before God, Peter said, then He can lift them up (5:6).

Jesus claimed humility (Matt. 11:29), as did Paul (Acts 20:19), so it is possible for Christians to be aware of their own humility without being proud of it. There is no formula that guarantees humility; it is an attitude of the heart and mind. The expression of this attitude is always to God but it should also be expressed to others. Our attitude toward others may be the best indicator of our humility or lack of it. God knows people's hearts, whereas others only see our actions and hear our words. Every believer should desire to be like Christ by following His attitude of humility. —WGJ

Walk each day in the steps of Christ,
exhibiting the same meekness that characterized His life,
and don't be self-centered.

Ii

Idolatry

IDOLATRY MEANS THE WORSHIP OF IDOLS or the paying of divine honors to any created thing. People have always wanted to have some tangible manifestations of the divine. The worship of inanimate things such as trees, rivers, and stones is called animism. Animate things, including bulls, serpents, and birds, have also been objects of worship. People have reverenced the sun, moon, and stars as well as the forces of nature (fire, water, and storms). The worship of deceased ancestors, of emperors and kings, of the fertility principle, and even of abstract ideas such as wisdom and justice are known practices.

The Old Testament records many stern warnings against idolatry, which infiltrated Israel from her heathen neighbors, including the Egyptians, the Canaanites, and the Mesopotamian nations of Assyria and Babylon. The Egyptians had a staggering array of deities numbering in the thousands. The Pyramid texts alone mention two hundred gods, and the Book of the Dead lists some twelve hundred. Most of the Egyptian deities were portrayed as animals, though the chief gods were pictured in human form. Egypt also worshiped cosmic deities, such as Re, the sun god. The pharaohs themselves were viewed as incarnations of deity. Though Egyptian religion with its multiplicity of gods and grotesque idols must have repulsed the Hebrews, it nonetheless had a strong influence on them, as seen in the golden calf incident at Mount Sinai (Exod. 32).

Scholars believe Babylon exerted a greater influence on Israelite religion than either Egypt or Canaan. Terah, Abraham's father, was an idolater (Josh. 24:2), and Abraham himself was probably a worshiper of the Babylonian gods before God called him to leave his home in Ur. Some scholars estimate there were more than fifteen hundred gods in the Babylonian pantheon, including Shamash, Marduk, Sin, and Ishtar, the goddess of lust and procreation. The Assyrians were similarly idolatrous and were considered more cruel and sadistic than other nations of the ancient Near East.

The fertility cults of Canaan with their orgiastic worship of nature and the productivity principle were characterized by unbounded license and moral abandonment. The chief Canaanite deities, El, Baal, and Astarte, were pictured as morally degenerate. Sacred prostitution was a legalized part of the cult. Canaanite religion had a strong appeal to illicit sexual desires. Moses clearly warned the Israelites against the dangers of this debasing form of paganism (Deut. 7:4; 20:18).

The history of idolatry among the Israelites is a discouraging story. In no period of Hebrew history were they totally free from the worship of idols until the Babylonian exile. The Old Testament Scriptures specifically prohibit idolatry for God's people, beginning with the second commandment, which forbids the representation of God in any form (Exod. 20:4–5; Deut. 5:8–9). The prophets often heaped ridicule on those who made an idol with their hands and then worshiped it (Isa. 40:19–20; 44:9–20; Jer. 10:2–10; Hos. 8:5; Hab. 2:18).

Sadly, Israel frequently disobeyed God's command to avoid idolatry. Rachel, wife of Jacob, took the teraphim (household gods) when the family fled from Laban (Gen. 31:34). During the Egyptian sojourn the Israelites worshiped idols (Josh. 24:14; Ezek. 20:8–18; 23:3–8) and persisted in doing so at Sinai when Moses was receiving the Law from God (Exod. 32). At the end of the wilderness wanderings in the plains of Moab they angered God by worshiping Baal (Num. 25:1–3). Just before the Israelites conquered Canaan, Moses warned them not to make and worship idols and not to marry members of the native populace (Deut. 4:15–19; 7:1–5). Because Israel disobeyed the command to destroy the Canaanites completely, it was repeatedly led into apostasy and idolatry (Judg. 2:11–13; 6:25–32; 17:1–13). Samuel explained to the people that their defeat by the Philistines was because of their idolatry; but deliverance from that dread enemy would come, he said, if they put away their false gods (1 Sam. 7:3–4). During the period of Israel's united kingdom Solomon opened the door for a great apostasy to idolatry by taking many foreign wives, each of whom worshiped a false god, including the abominable Chemosh and Molech. In his old age Solomon, too, worshiped these false deities (1 Kings 11:1–8), and as a consequence God divided his kingdom (11:9–13). Jeroboam, the first king of the northern tribes of Israel, set up golden calves at Dan and Bethel to keep the people from returning to Jerusalem to worship.

Thereafter he was labeled "Jeroboam, who sinned and who made Israel sin" (14:16, NKJV).

Calf worship, launched by Jeroboam, and Baalism, imported by Ahab, dominated the religious scene in the Northern Kingdom until its conquest by the Assyrians in 722 B.C. Although a few kings in the Southern Kingdom led spiritual revivals (Asa, Jehoshaphat, Jehoash, Azariah, Hezekiah, and Josiah), royal apostates (Rehoboam, Ahaz, and Manasseh) also appeared on the scene to sponsor idolatry. The Babylonian exile came as a direct result of Judah's idolatry (Jer. 19:3–9; 20:4). (The same lot had befallen Israel for the same reason more than a century earlier when the Assyrians invaded Israel; 2 Kings 17:7–18.) The Jews recognized they were captives in a foreign land because of their idolatry. Babylon was saturated with idols, and the Jews there developed an abhorrence to idols that has characterized Judaism ever since.

Gentile idolatry was still widespread in the world of the first century; thus early Christians unavoidably came in contact with it. Paul had much to say about idolatry, warning believers to avoid events involving idol worship (1 Cor. 10:14). While he insisted that an idol had no real existence, he stated that demons were involved in their worship, and so idol feasts were to be avoided (10:18–21). In a classic passage Paul described the pervasive idolatry of the pagan world, stating that it not only involves rejection of the true God but also has moral implications (Rom. 1:18–32). The apostle clearly rejected the theory that idolatry was a primitive form of religion to be replaced by higher forms. Rather, he saw it as a retrogression and a perversion of the genuine worship of the one and only God. In Athens Paul observed that idol worship was so common that the Athenians had even erected an altar to an unknown god (Acts 17:23). In Ephesus his protest against idolatry resulted in the business of the makers of images of the goddess Diana being severely curtailed (19:23–27). In Jerusalem the council of apostles and elders exhorted gentile believers to "abstain from food sacrificed to idols" (15:29). The apostle John wrote that in the Tribulation, people will "not stop worshiping demons, and idols of gold, silver, bronze, stone and wood—idols that cannot see or hear or walk" (Rev. 9:20). John also recorded a dire warning against any who worship an image of the beast or antichrist (13:14–15; 14:9–11; see also Matt. 24:15–16).

The term *idolatry* was also employed by Paul in a figurative sense to designate covetousness or greed (Eph. 5:5; Col. 3:5) and gluttony (Phil. 3:19). In effect, the apostle charged people with making a god out of their passions and appetites.

At the end of his first epistle John wrote, "Dear children, keep yourselves from idols" (1 John 5:21). Since believers know "the true God" (5:20) why turn to the false and embrace the moral laxness that accompanies idolatry? This was a relevant message for those living in the world of John's day, and it remains relevant today if the meaning of idolatry is understood as including anything that takes the place in a believer's heart that belongs to God alone. **—DKC**

Beware of making a god out of your appetites, your passions, your possessions.

Image of God

GOD MADE MAN THE CAPSTONE of His creative activity. "God said, 'Let us make man in our image, in our likeness. . . . So God created man in his own image, in the image of God he created him; male and female he created them'" (Gen. 1:26–27). This fact of humanity's creation in the image of God is stated again at the beginning of the written record of Adam's descendants ("When God created man, he made him in the likeness of God"; 5:1) and when explaining the value of human life in warning against murder (9:6). Further evidence that the image of God in humanity persists after the Fall is stated twice in the New Testament (1 Cor. 11:7; James 3:9).

What constitutes the image of God in humankind? It obviously is not our physical nature, including uprightness of posture. Scripture explains that "the LORD God formed man from the dust of the ground" (Gen. 2:7); but, as Jesus stated, "God is spirit" (John 4:24). In the visions that some men had of God, they described Him by using anthropomorphisms (Exod. 33:18–23; Isa. 6:1; Dan. 7:9; Rev. 4:2–3), but those descriptions are vague and do not portray a bodily form.

The image of God relates to our immaterial nature, the result of God's breathing "into [Adam's] nostrils the breath of life" so that he "became a living being" (Gen. 2:7). It includes the elements of person-hood—self-consciousness and self-determination—and the capacities of intellect, sensibility, and will. God possesses all the elements of per-sonhood to an infinite degree, whereas He has given them to humans only finitely to varying degrees. God's purpose was for people to "rule over the fish of the sea and the birds of the air, over the livestock, over all the earth, and over all the creatures that move along the ground" (1:26; see also 1:28). This responsibility reflects God's infinite sover-eignty and is also a part of the image of God in humankind.

Adam and Eve's innocent holiness as they came from the creative hand of God also must be a part of the image of God, because "God saw all that he had made, and it was very good" (1:31). This included man. Later Solomon wrote, "God made mankind upright" (Eccles. 7:29), meaning righteous, but, he continued, "men have gone in search of many schemes." This describes the loss of original righteousness as the result of Adam and Eve's sin, which was a loss of at least a part of their image of God.

To what extent did sin impact the image of God? Loss of original righteousness (or innocence) is obvious, but how was the rest of the image of God affected? Some scholars insist it was totally destroyed when Adam and Eve sinned, but Scripture, as stated, speaks of the image persisting after the Fall. Since the Fall men and women still possess intellect, sensibility, and will, but those qualities have been impacted and misdirected so that people cannot find God apart from His gracious revelation of Himself.

In a unique sense the Lord Jesus Christ is described as "the image of God" (2 Cor. 4:4; Col. 1:15). John declared, "No one has ever seen God, but God the One and Only Son, who is at the Father's side, has made him known" (John 1:18). When Philip said, "Lord, show us the Father" (14:8), Jesus responded, "Anyone who has seen me has seen the Father" (14:9; see also 12:45; Heb. 1:3). As the eternal Word (John 1:1–2), Jesus Christ is the image of God the Father. Throughout His earthly life and ministry the incarnate Son of God, the Lord Jesus Christ, perfectly and sinlessly displayed the image of God.

Although the introduction of sin into the human race by the fall of Adam and Eve did not destroy or remove the image of God in humankind, it did distort and pervert it. As a result, when an individual receives the Lord Jesus Christ as his or her Savior by faith and is born again and indwelt by the Holy Spirit, the Lord begins the process of help-ing that person become "conformed to the likeness of his Son" (Rom. 8:29; see also 1 Cor. 15:49; Eph. 4:24; Phil. 3:21; Col. 3:10; 1 John 3:2–3).

—JAW

Though you, as a human being, display the image of God marred by sin,
as a Christian seek to reflect the image of Christ.

Immortality

NOT BEING SUBJECT to the human limitations of death and decay, only God possesses immortality inherently.

Romans 1:23 refers to "the immortal God," 1 Timothy 1:17 refers to God as "the King, eternal, immortal," and in 1 Timothy 6:16 Paul stated that God "alone is immortal." His immortality is attributed to His essen-tial being as the infinite God from eternity past to eternity present without change. It is linked to His eternity as the living God (Pss. 18:46; 90:2; 115:3–8; Jer. 10:11). Being immortal, God is far above humanity, whose bodies die.

Because of the Fall, death (mortality) was imposed as a judgment on sin. Because Adam sinned, he died (Gen. 2:17; 3:19), and the entire human race sinned in Adam and died (Rom. 5:12). Thus every human being is mortal, subject to death. Yet though they die, they will exist for-ever after death in either heaven or hell. God is *inherently* immortal; mankind *receives* immortality. For those who believe in Christ and thus have eternal life, immortality means that though their bodies die they will be resurrected. Immortality for believers is available through the work of Christ (2 Tim. 1:10).

Some Christians will not face death if they are alive at the time of the Rapture. And at the Rapture those church-age believers who have died will be resurrected. All believers at the Rapture, including those who have died and those who will still be living, will be given immortal, res-urrected bodies. Christ "will transform our lowly bodies so that they will be like his glorious body" (Phil. 3:21). "We shall be like him" (1 John 3:2). "So will it be with the resurrection of the dead. The body that is sown is perishable, it is raised imperishable; it is sown in dishonor, it is raised in glory; it is sown in weakness, it is raised in power; it is sown a natural body, it is raised a spiritual body" (1 Cor. 15:42–44). Deceased believers will receive imperishable bodies, and believers still living at the Rapture will be transformed so that their mortal bodies will become immortal. Then death for church-age saints will be overcome (15:54–55).

At the end of the Millennium all the wicked dead will be resurrected from their graves, will be judged at the Great White Throne judgment, and then will be thrown into the lake of fire (Rev. 20:11–15), where they will suffer eternal torment (Matt. 25:46) as punishment for their sin (2 Thess. 1:9). —JFW

Live every day in the light of the eternal life you possess in Christ.

Imputation

FOUND ONLY IN VERBAL FORM in Scripture, "to impute" means "to set to one's account," or "to reckon something to someone." The Hebrew verb *ḥāšab* appears over one hundred times in the Old Testament and is translated "to impute, reckon, esteem, purpose, account." The Greek verb *logizomai,* similarly translated, is used forty-one times in the New Testament. The idea of imputation is illustrated in the letter to Philemon when Paul wrote to his friend about the runaway slave Onesimus, "If he has done you any wrong or owes you anything, charge it to me" (Philem. 18).

The theological concept of imputation is set forth in Scripture in three ways: the imputation of Adam's original sin to the entire human race, the imputation of the sin and guilt of the human race to Christ, and the imputation of divine righteousness to the believer.

The doctrine that Adam's sin was imputed to his posterity is based on Genesis 3:1–19; Romans 5:12–19; and 1 Corinthians 15:21–22. Although the Genesis narrative describes only the consequences of sin for Adam and Eve, human experience and further biblical revelation show that their tragic sin has affected the entire human race. Paul, in the

Romans 5 passage, taught that Adam's sin was every man's sin. "Sin entered the world through one man, and death through sin, and in this way death came to all men, because all sinned" (5:12). Paul did not mean that people sin and therefore die, but that all sinned when Adam sinned and thereby all inherit the penalty of physical death. This truth is repeated in various expressions: "if the many died by the trespass of the one man" (5:15); "as the result of one trespass was condemnation for all men" (5:18); and "through the disobedience of the one man the many were made sinners" (5:19). Further evidence that Adam's sin has been charged to the entire human family is found in 1 Corinthians 15:22, where Paul said, "in Adam all die."

Theologians differ in their views on how the human race participated in Adam's sin. Some hold that when Adam sinned, he acted as the head and representative of the human race (the "federal headship" view). Others believe Adam's sin was not only imputed to his posterity but that they were genetically present in Adam so that his sin was truly theirs (the "seminal" or "realistic" view). The latter theory is supported by the affirmation that Levi was in Abraham's loins when his great-grandfather paid tithes to king Melchizedek (Heb. 7:9–10).

While the Bible does not explicitly say that humanity's sin was imputed to Christ, nevertheless the idea is clearly present in various Scriptures. The Old Testament sacrificial system typifies the imputation of sin to Christ. The sins of the offerer were transferred symbolically to the sacrificial animal. The ritual of the scapegoat on the Day of Atonement graphically portrays this truth (Lev. 16). The prophet Isaiah affirmed that mankind's guilt was reckoned to the Servant of Yahweh. "Surely he took up our infirmities and carried our sorrows . . . the LORD has laid on him the iniquity of us all . . . he bore the sin of many" (Isa. 53:4, 6, 12). The apostle Paul similarly wrote that "God made him [Christ] who had no sin to be sin for us" (2 Cor. 5:21) and that "Christ redeemed us from the curse of the law by becoming a curse for us" (Gal. 3:13). The apostle Peter declared, "He himself bore our sins in his body on the tree" (1 Pet. 2:24). With the guilt of all mankind charged to the account of the sinless Son of God, His impassioned cry from the cross, "My God, my God, why have you forsaken me?" (Matt. 27:46), is more easily understood.

The third biblical imputation, also "judicial" rather than "real," is the crediting of the righteousness of God to the believer. An event in the life of Abraham illustrates the imputation of righteousness in response to God's promise regarding his descendants. "Abram believed the LORD, and he credited it to him as righteousness" (Gen. 15:6). No person, the Bible asserts, possesses the righteousness God demands (Rom. 3:10). Yet God graciously provides the righteousness He requires, a righteousness that fully satisfies the demands of His holy character. Specifically, God imputes Christ's righteousness to the believer (2 Cor. 5:21). This is a judicial act by which the believer is *declared* righteous, God's work in which He grants the believer, at the moment of salvation, a righteous standing before a holy God. This imputation is not an experience as such, that is, the believer is not *made* righteous; instead this is a fact of divine reckoning. Some erroneously teach that when God justifies a believer he or she is made righteous, that is, the individual is infused with holiness rather than having Christ's holiness imputed and received by faith alone.

The imputation of divine righteousness to the believer is one of the most important doctrines of the New Testament and is a major theme in Romans (Rom. 3:21–5:21). This divine act reverses the disastrous effect of the imputation of Adam's sin to the human race for those who believe and is the sole basis for acceptance with God.   —DKC

Praise God that He provides for the believer the righteousness
He requires for us to be in His presence.

Incarnation

THE WORD *Incarnation* does not occur in Scripture, but evidence for the doctrine is found throughout the Bible, primarily in the New Testament. The truth that the eternal second person of the triune Godhead joined Himself with a complete human nature and was born as Jesus, the God-Man, is expressed in the apostle John's statement, "The Word became flesh and made his dwelling among us" (John 1:14).

When the angel Gabriel announced that Mary would "be with child and give birth to a son" (Luke 1:31), Mary asked, "How will this be . . .

since I am a virgin?" (1:34). Gabriel explained the miracle of the Incarnation in this way: "The Holy Spirit will come upon you, and the power of the Most High will overshadow you. So the holy one to be born will be called the Son of God" (1:35). Since Mary was betrothed to Joseph, an angel (probably Gabriel) told him not to "be afraid to take Mary home as your wife, because what is conceived in her is from the Holy Spirit" (Matt. 1:20).

This union of the eternal second person of the Godhead with a human nature at conception by the Holy Spirit in the womb of a virgin and His birth as the God-Man provides the answer to the false teachings concerning the Lord Jesus Christ that arose in the early church. The earliest was Docetism, which taught that Jesus only seemed to have a human body (1 John 4:2–3; 2 John 7). To refute this false view John emphasized that the apostles "have heard . . . have seen with our eyes . . . have touched . . . the Word of life" (1 John 1:1) and that the "Word became flesh" (John 1:14; see also 6:51–58). If Jesus only appeared to have a human body, then He was not identified with humanity and He did not really die on Calvary and provide a redemptive sacrifice for sin.

A second error concerning the person of Christ is called adoptionism. According to this view Jesus was conceived and born simply as a human being, who was adopted and indwelt by the divine Logos, probably at His baptism. The Logos left Jesus on Calvary, so that He died simply as a human being. If this were true, Jesus' death would have no redemptive value and He would have been conceived as an illegitimate child.

Another misunderstanding about the Incarnation grows out of Paul's statement that Jesus Christ "emptied himself" (Phil. 2:7, NASB). Some scholars conclude that this means that when Jesus became incarnate He laid aside His divine attributes of omnipotence, omnipresence, and omniscience. But if He had done that, He would have become less than God. Furthermore, Jesus manifested those very attributes (Mark 4:39; Luke 8:24–25; John 1:47–48). Rather than discarding some attributes, the incarnate Son of God veiled His divine glory (except to Peter, James, and John on the Mount of Transfiguration; Matt. 17:1–2), and He did not use His divine attributes for His own gratification.

Although Jesus possessed the divine nature as the eternal Son of God and a human nature derived from Mary, He was one person, the God-Man, not two persons experiencing the struggle of a split personality.

The two natures worked harmoniously to be expressed in the actions, emotions, and thoughts of the one person.

The Incarnation was a part of God's eternal plan and program. This helps explain why John called Jesus Christ "the Word" (John 1:1–2, 14); He was the one designed to reveal God to humanity (14:7–11). As part of that plan, the Incarnation was prophesied in the Old Testament, beginning vaguely with God's judgment on the serpent that the offspring of the woman "will crush [the serpent's] head" (Gen. 3:15). Somewhat less vague are the promises to Abraham that "through your offspring all nations on earth will be blessed" (Gen. 22:18; see Gal. 3:16) and to David (2 Sam. 7:11–16; see also Pss. 89:3–4, 20, 26–37; 132:10–12, 17–18; Luke 1:32–33). Still more specific are the prophecies in Isaiah 7:14 (see Matt. 1:23), Isaiah 9:6–7 (see Luke 1:32), and Micah 5:2–4 (see Matt. 2:1–12).

Paul wrote, "But when the time had fully come, God sent his Son, born of a woman, born under the law, to redeem those under law, that we might receive the full rights of sons" (Gal. 4:4–5; see also Eph. 1:10; 1 Tim. 2:6; Titus 1:3). Paul also pointed out that the Incarnation had a redemptive as well as a revelatory purpose and objective. Having begun in time, the Incarnation will continue forever. The glorified incarnate Lord Jesus Christ is now seated at the right hand of God the Father (Rom. 8:34; Eph. 1:20; Col. 3:1; Heb. 1:3; 8:1; 10:12; 12:2). He will return to earth (Rev. 19:11–16) to establish His kingdom of righteousness and peace for a thousand years (20:4–6). After the Great White Throne judgment of the unbelieving dead (20:11–15) and the beginning of the eternal state (1 Cor. 15:24-28), the incarnate Lord Jesus Christ will reign forever with God the Father and God the Holy Spirit (Rev. 21:1–2, 22–27; 22:1–5).

—JAW

Through the power of the indwelling Holy Spirit and the written Word of God, seek to "live out" the ascended Christ in your life.

Inheritance

IN THE EARTHLY, PHYSICAL SENSE an inheritance is an estate that is passed from one generation to another, and in the spiritual sense an inheritance speaks of believers entering the presence of God in heaven.

When God chose and called Abram (later Abraham) to leave Haran and led him to Canaan, He promised, "To your offspring I will give this land" (Gen. 12:7; see also 13:14–17; 15:18–21; 17:7–8; Acts 7:4; Rom. 4:13; Gal. 3:18; Heb. 11:8–10). This promise of the land as an inheritance was repeated to Isaac (Gen. 26:2–3) and Jacob (28:13).

When the people of Israel were at Mount Sinai after the exodus from Egypt, God identified them as "a people holy to the LORD your God," a people for his own possession (Deut. 7:6; see 4:20; 14:2; 26:18–19; Exod. 19:5). God directed Moses to lead Israel to possess the land promised to the patriarch's descendants for an inheritance (Exod. 33:1; Num. 26:52–56; 33:50–55; 34:1–12; Deut. 1:8).

When the Israelites refused at Kadesh-Barnea to heed Caleb and Joshua and enter the Promised Land, God denied that inheritance to those who were twenty years of age and older, except Caleb and Joshua. These older Israelites were sentenced to die in the wilderness (Num. 14:22–23, 29–35; 26:64–65; 32:11–13; Deut. 1:34–36; 4:21–22, 26). The younger generation was promised they would inherit and possess the land (Num. 33:53–54; 34:13, 16–18, 29), with the two tribes of Gad and Reuben and the half-tribe of Manasseh receiving their inheritance on the east side of the Jordan River in return for helping the other tribes conquer Canaan (Num. 32:5, 16–22, 29–33; Deut. 1:12–20; Josh. 1:12–16; 22:1–4).

God directed that the promised land of Canaan, when conquered, was to be divided for an inheritance by lot according to the size of the tribes and families (Num. 26:52–56; 33:53–54; 34:1–2, 13–15; Josh. 14:1–5). Ownership of the allotted land was to be passed down from generation to generation, according to specific regulations, to maintain possession in the family to whom it was originally given (Num. 27:1–11; 36:1–9). The land could not be sold permanently (Lev. 25:23), though it could be leased (25:14–17). It could be redeemed at any time by either the seller (25:26–27) or his kinsman (25:25; see Ruth 4:1–11). If not redeemed previously, ownership reverted automatically to the seller or his heirs in the Year of Jubilee (Lev. 25:8–10, 13, 28, 31, 33). These regulations were important, the Lord explained, "because the land is mine and you are but aliens and my tenants" (25:23). God also considered the people of Israel as His inheritance (Deut. 4:20; 9:29; 32:9; see also 9:26; Exod. 34:9; Ps. 33:12).

Even though the people of Israel have been dispersed from the land

of their inheritance and scattered throughout the world, their ownership of the land is still valid by divine promise, and God will restore
them to it (Deut. 30:1–5; Jer. 29:14; 30:3; Zech. 8:2–3, 7–8, 15; 10:9–10).
This restoration has spiritual as well as physical significance, because it
will involve the return of the people of Israel to God and their spiritual
regeneration (Deut. 30:2, 6, 8; Jer. 31:31–34).

The inheritance of Christians is spiritual, the result of their trusting
the Lord Jesus Christ as their Savior. That inheritance is salvation (Heb.
1:14) and the hope of eternal heavenly blessedness in God's presence
(Col. 1:12; Titus 3:7; Heb. 9:15; James 2:5; 1 Pet. 1:3–5), guaranteed to
believers by the indwelling Holy Spirit (Eph. 1:13–14). The Holy Spirit
witnesses to us "that we are God's children" and thus "are heirs—heirs
of God and co-heirs with Christ" (Rom. 8:16–17). As a result, Christians
will share in the inheritance of Christ, who has been "appointed heir of
all things" (Heb. 1:2; see Ps. 2:8). And Christ's inheritance includes all
believers (Eph. 1:18).   —JAW

In view of the tremendous spiritual inheritance
reserved in heaven for you, don't live as a spiritual pauper in this life.

Inspiration

THE DOCTRINE OF THE INSPIRATION of the Scriptures affirms that
the Bible was produced through men who were directed by God. In
inspiration God directed the human authors of Scripture without
destroying their individuality, personality, literary style, or the languages with which they were familiar, so that they accurately recorded
His complete revelation. In some instances God dictated Scripture but
usually it was written by the writers of Scripture, who were permitted to
express freely their thoughts, emotions, even their doubts and fears. Yet
the ultimate record is exactly what God wanted said and expresses without error the truth of God's revelation. When evangelicals speak of
plenary inspiration, they mean that the Bible is inspired in its entirety.

Some writers contended that inspiration means that the ideas, but
not the words, of the Bible were inspired. So evangelicals added the

word *verbal* to their statements about inspiration. Then others suggested that the Bible has errors, so evangelicals added the word *infallible.* Then when there were attempts to weaken this also, the word *inerrant* was added. This teaches that the Bible never states as a fact something that is in error. Of course the Bible may record the opinions of men or even Satan without necessarily approving them. But everything affirmed in the Scriptures is truth without error. The Bible's inspiration then is verbal, plenary, infallible, and inerrant.

The Scriptures themselves provide abundant evidence of their infallibility. Scriptures record the actions of God in creation before humans were created and also reaches forward in prophecy to the end of time. Of the approximately one thousand passages which can be classified as prophetic, five hundred have already been literally fulfilled, a fact that testifies to the accuracy of Scripture and the impossibility of human ingenuity to devise such prophecies.

Christ Himself affirmed the accuracy of the Scriptures. He declared, "The Scripture cannot be broken" (John 10:35). The Gospels record many fulfilled prophecies (for example, Matt. 1:22–23; 4:14; 8:17; 12:17; 15:7–8; 21:4–5, 42; 22:29; 26:31, 56; 27:9–10, 35). Interestingly many of these fulfilled prophecies are quoted from the books that some critics have disputed, such as Deuteronomy, Daniel, and Jonah. Jesus' mention of Daniel as a prophet (Matt. 24:15) affirms the inspiration and accuracy of the Book of Daniel. The inspiration of the New Testament is regarded as equal to that of the Old Testament; for example, in 1 Timothy 5:18 Paul quoted both Deuteronomy 25:4 and Luke 10:7 as inspired. And in 2 Peter 3:15–16 Peter called Paul's epistles "Scriptures."

The central passage on inspiration is 2 Timothy 3:16: "All Scripture is God-breathed and useful for teaching, rebuking, correcting and training in righteousness." The term "God-breathed" is from the Greek *theopneustos,* which means "breathed out by God" or "proceeding from God." Thus in the process of inspiration the human authors were uniquely and supernaturally writing what God directed them to write.

The process by which human authors could write without error is defined in 2 Peter 1:21: "For prophecy never had its origin in the will of man, but men spoke from God as they were carried along by the Holy Spirit." In other words, in inspiration what they wrote was a product of their being personally carried along by God to express truth without error. The frequent expression "Thus said the LORD" occurs approximately two thousand times in the Old Testament and indicates that what was written was from God.

When we speak of the Bible's inerrant inspiration, we refer to the original manuscripts. Of course, we do not possess the original manuscripts; the Scriptures we have are translations of copies of the originals. Yet there is abundant evidence that the copying was done so accurately that what we have is essentially the same as what was originally provided. Many confirmations of this have come from research, such as the fact that a copy of Daniel dating from the first century B.C. is essentially the same as the copy in our Bibles, which was about A.D. 900. Virtually no variations developed in all those years.

Each book of the Bible witnesses to its inspired and inerrant quality. Apocryphal books, which are included in some Bible versions, lack evidence of divine inspiration and the quality and accuracy of the Bible's sixty-six books. Of Christ's many affirmations on the truthfulness of Scripture, probably the most direct statement is in Matthew 5:18. "I tell you the truth, until heaven and earth disappear, not the smallest letter, not the least stroke of a pen, will by any means disappear from the Law until everything is accomplished." "The smallest letter" refers to the *yôd*, the smallest character of the Hebrew alphabet, and "the least stroke" refers to a small portion of a Hebrew letter.

Even radical critics agree that Jesus accepted without question the authority of the Old Testament. His arguments in Matthew 22:43–45 and John 10:34–35 rest on the accuracy of a single word of the Bible. To deny the Bible is thus to deny the deity and integrity of Christ Himself. To this is added the extensive testimony of the apostles Paul and Peter as well as other writers of Scripture. As a result of the inspiration of the Holy Spirit the Bible is just as accurate and true in its factual statements as if God Himself had taken a pen and written the words.

—JFW

Study the Scriptures with confidence,
knowing they are trustworthy because they are from God.

Intermediate State

THE TERM *intermediate state* refers to the state of a soul between death and resurrection.

After death the soul continues to be conscious (2 Cor. 5:6–9). The believer in Christ, after death, is "at home with the Lord" (5:8), but his or her body remains dead until the time of resurrection. In heaven the souls of Christians are alive and experience various things. Among these is the judgment seat of Christ (5:10) in which Christians will be judged and rewarded according to the quality of their lives.

One of the questions about the intermediate state is whether believers in heaven before their resurrection will have some kind of body. The fact that people who will be saved in the Tribulation will each receive a white robe (Rev. 6:11) may suggest that they will have temporary bodies. Paul spoke of believers after death being "clothed with our heavenly dwelling" (2 Cor. 5:2, 4). This may refer to the intermediate state, or it may refer instead to the resurrected body.

In the Old Testament the word *sheol* often refers to the grave, the place of death, but at other times it refers to the intermediate state. In the New Testament the word *hades* is used as a synonym of *sheol*. In both the Old Testament and the Gospels the righteous and the unrighteous exist in an intermediate state, as illustrated by the rich man and Lazarus (Luke 16:19–31). The intermediate state, however, is viewed as temporary, for the saved will be resurrected (1 Thess. 4:15–16; Rev. 20:6), and the lost will be resurrected and judged at the Great White Throne and cast into the lake of fire (20:11–15). The lake of fire is not occupied now but it will be the permanent place of punishment for the unsaved.

Christ referred to the intermediate state as "paradise" (Luke 23:43), the portion of hades in which the righteous existed. But after His resurrection the Scriptures regard paradise as being in the very presence of God (2 Cor. 12:3–4; Rev. 2:7). At the present time, therefore, hades is occupied only by the unsaved.

The important point is that in the intermediate state between death and their resurrection, individuals, whether saved or lost, continue to exist and are conscious forever.   —JFW

Be comforted by the promise that after death
God has prepared a place for us to live with Him.

Interpretation

MANY PEOPLE ARE CONFUSED about how to interpret the Bible. Often this stems from ignorance or neglect of several standard rules of interpretation. The most important point in interpretation of the Bible is to recognize that the Bible is normally a literal expression of what God wants to communicate. The idea that the Bible is a book of hidden, non-literal meanings arose from the school of theology in Alexandria, Egypt, toward the end of the second century A.D. and became a dominant factor in the church's interpretation of the Scriptures. While this attempt to interpret all the Bible nonliterally was rejected by the church, difficulty was faced in establishing a literal interpretation of the Bible's prophetic writings. The problem of interpretation, however, is far greater than the issue of prophecy, for it extends to various types of revelation in the Scripture.

A basic rule is to interpret the Bible in its natural sense unless there is good reason for believing that a figure of speech has been used. It is helpful to keep in mind the question, What did the author mean here? What did he intend for us to understand? If the author intended us to understand a statement in a figurative or nonliteral way, that will be indicated in the context. The meaning of a passage lies in what the author intended when he penned the words.

Another rule is to interpret verses in the light of their immediate context. When symbols or other figures of speech are used, the context often helps convey the meaning. An example is the ten horns mentioned in Daniel 7:7; verse 24 indicates that they represent ten kingdoms. Similes, metaphors, personifications, hyperboles, symbols, and other figures of speech are literary forms that depict literal truths in a picturesque way.

Another basic rule is to interpret obscure passages, in which the meaning is not clear, by passages that are not obscure. In most important doctrinal matters, the Bible states plainly and clearly in normal terms what God is communicating.

When misinterpretation arises, it is usually because Scripture has not been carefully studied, the details have not been examined adequately, the context has been neglected, or preconceived ideas have been brought to the text.

A fundamental principle of interpretation is that God intended the Bible to communicate to those who have spiritual discernment. And while the work of the Holy Spirit in illuminating the Scriptures is essential in enabling believers to understand it, nevertheless the Bible is not a book of vague revelations. The Bible has communicated all that God wants us to know in this life about Himself and His plans.   —JFW

Ask the Holy Spirit to help you understand the truths in God's Word, and then apply them to your life.

Israel

THE NAME *Israel,* which the Lord gave to Jacob after he wrestled with God (Gen. 32:28), means "he wrestled with God" or "God rules." From then on the term *Israel* was applied to the nation about twenty-five hundred times in the Old and New Testaments in recognition of the fact that Jacob was the father of the twelve tribes of Israel. Israelites are also called Jews, with the first instance being in Ezra 4:12. The term *Jew* comes from the name of the tribe of Judah, Israel's principal tribe.

Because of famine Jacob moved to Egypt along with his entire family to be with his son Joseph, and for the next several hundred years Jacob's descendants, the Israelites, grew from a family of about seventy to a people of perhaps two million. They were made slaves in Egypt and were greatly oppressed, as recorded in Exodus.

After they were in Egypt four hundred years God raised up Moses and inflicted ten plagues on the land of Egypt. The pharaoh finally allowed the Israelites to leave Egypt for the Promised Land, Palestine. But because of their unbelief, God allowed them to wander for forty years in the desert of the Sinai Peninsula. After Moses died, Joshua led them across the Jordan River and they began to conquer and possess the land.

Before his death Moses gave Israel what is called Deuteronomy, "the second law," in which he summarized what God had revealed about His will for them. He told them that if they kept the Law they would be blessed and protected in the land, but if they broke the Law they would eventually be expelled. Israel neglected and disobeyed the Law for many years, and so the Assyrians conquered the ten northern tribes in 722 B.C. and the Babylonians conquered Judah and Benjamin in 586 B.C., destroying the city of Jerusalem and its beautiful temple.

Just before the Babylonian Captivity God had raised up three major prophets. Jeremiah ministered to those in the land and almost lost his life because he said the nation should surrender to the Babylonians. The rulers in Jerusalem ignored this, resulting in their being slaughtered and their city and temple destroyed. The second, Daniel, was a teenager carried off into captivity in 605 B.C. After interpreting Nebuchadnezzar's dream (Dan. 2), Daniel was appointed chief executive to Nebuchadnezzar throughout the remaining forty years of his reign and no doubt did much to alleviate Israel's sad condition. The third, Ezekiel, was among the early captives taken to Babylon in 597 B.C., and he ministered near Babylon to the captives there.

After seventy years of captivity in Babylon some of the Jews were allowed to return to their homeland, as God had predicted (Jer. 29:10). Nearly fifty thousand Jews returned to reestablish themselves in their land. Hindered by enemies, they were unable to complete the building of the temple until 516 B.C. Not until 444 B.C. was Nehemiah able to rebuild the fallen walls of Jerusalem. Then over several decades the city of Jerusalem and other Judean cities were restored. As a result Christ was born in Bethlehem, not Babylon, just as Micah 5:2 had predicted.

Israel, however, continued to depart from God. Roman soldiers destroyed Jerusalem in A.D. 70, and many Jews were scattered to other nations, with about fifteen thousand Jews remaining in the land.

One of the main features of Israel's future, however, is the frequent prediction in the Old Testament that they will be regathered and restored as a nation in the end times.

In the Tribulation, following the rapture of the church, Israel will experience a terrible time of trouble (Jer. 30:5–11) but will then be rescued by God at Christ's second coming and will be regathered from all over the world (Ezek. 39:25–29). The rebels, that is, Jews who will not have come to Christ in the preceding period, will be eliminated (20:33–38). But godly Israelites, those who will have received Christ in the period preceding His second coming, will be given the Promised Land. This will be in fulfillment of God's promises that she will ultimately possess the land. This promise was originally given to Abraham (Gen. 15:18–21). The land will be partitioned into twelve sections, with one for each of the twelve tribes (Ezek. 47:13–48:35). Israel's possession of the land will be fulfilled in the Millennium, the period after the Second Coming. Jesus Christ, Israel's Messiah, will rule the millennial kingdom as the Son of David on the Davidic throne (Isa. 9:7).

—JFW

God's faithfulness to the nation Israel is a reminder
that He will never leave us or forsake us.

Jj

Jerusalem

THIS CITY HAS BEEN CALLED "the world's most significant city" and "the spiritual capital of the world." It is sacred to the three foremost monotheistic faiths—Christianity, Judaism, and Islam. The etymology of the name Jerusalem is uncertain. At one time it was thought to mean "city of peace" (from the Hebrew *šālōm*). Some modern scholars believe the two parts of the name, *uru* ("city") and *salim* (a divine name), define the meaning as "the city of (the god) Salim," a member of the Amorite pantheon. Jerusalem was also known as Salem (Gen. 14:18), Jebus (Judg. 19:10–11), Ariel (Isa. 29:1), the City of David (2 Sam. 5:7, 9), Zion (Ps. 87:1–3), the City of Righteousness (Isa. 1:26), and the holy city (Isa. 48:2; 52:1; Rev. 21:2). Muslims call Jerusalem *al-Quds* meaning "the Holy [Town]."

Jerusalem is located fourteen miles west of the northern tip of the Dead Sea and thirty-three miles east of the Mediterranean coast at an elevation of 2,550 feet. Jerusalem, like Rome, is a city set on hills. Jerusalem's five hills are bordered on all sides except the north by deep ravines. The psalmist wrote of Jerusalem, "It is beautiful in its loftiness, the joy of the whole earth" (Ps. 48:2). The history of Jerusalem is long and complex and is filled with a succession of sieges, surrenders, restorations, and rebuildings. In about 3000 B.C. nomadic tribes settled on the city's southeastern hill, where later they left kitchen pots and flint tools. In patriarchal times Abraham paid tithes to Melchizedek, the priest-king of Jerusalem (Gen. 14:18–20). During the period of the Conquest and settlement of Canaan, Adoni-Zedek, king of Jerusalem, gathered a coalition and unsuccessfully opposed Joshua's conquest (Josh. 10:1–26). Though the tribe of Judah captured Jerusalem, it was reoccupied by the Jebusites, who possessed it until the time of Israel's monarchy. David conquered the city (2 Sam. 5:6–7) and made it the capital of his kingdom, an empire that ultimately stretched from Egypt to the Euphrates River. David's plan was to establish Jerusalem as a religious capital as well as a political capital. He therefore brought the ark of the covenant into the city and laid plans for the building of a temple where God's presence would be evident. Solomon, David's son, was the actual builder of the temple, a task that required seven years (1 Kings 6:1). At its dedication the ceremonies were climaxed by the coming of the presence of God (8:10). Solomon also made Jerusalem a cosmopolitan commercial center with revenues from land caravans from Egypt and Babylonia and sea trade from Elath, the Red Sea, and Ophir. The "golden age" of Solomon, however, came to a tragic end and the divided monarchy left Judah and Jerusalem weak and vulnerable.

A few years after the schism Shishak, pharaoh of Egypt, invaded Judah and exacted heavy tribute from Jerusalem (14:25–26). The city was plundered by the Philistines and Arabs in the reign of Jehoram (2 Chron. 21:16–17). When Athaliah, Ahab and Jezebel's daughter, was on the throne of Judah, Jerusalem became the center of a revived Baal worship (2 Kings 11; 2 Chron. 22:10–23:15). The city was attacked and plundered again by Jehoash of Israel (2 Kings 14:8–14), but it was restored in glory and influence by King Uzziah (2 Chron. 26:7–8). Another crisis for Jerusalem arose when Ahaz was king and the armies of Syria and Israel laid siege to the city. Ahaz was encouraged by Isaiah (Isa. 7:4–9), but was forced to pay heavy tribute to the king of Assyria, to whom Ahaz had appealed for help (2 Kings 16:7–9). An even greater crisis befell Jerusalem in 701 B.C., when the Assyrians, under Sennacherib's leadership, invaded Judah and laid siege to the city. Even though Hezekiah had armed the people, repaired the walls, and safeguarded the water supply, it took divine intervention to save the city from destruction (18:13–19:37).

The rise of Babylon as a world power and the prowess of its ruler Nebuchadnezzar spelled the beginning of the end for Jerusalem. After Babylonian invasions in 605 and 597 B.C. a final attack on Jerusalem occurred in 586 B.C., and the city was decimated. The Solomonic temple and palace were destroyed, the city walls were demolished, and large numbers of the people were deported to Babylon. The prophet Jeremiah observed and lamented the tragic scene (Lam. 1:1–19).

The fall of Babylon brought the rise of Persia as the new world power. This in turn brought new hope for the city of Jerusalem, for under Cyrus, the Persian ruler, the Jews were allowed to return to their homeland to rebuild their beloved Jerusalem (Ezra 1). Following a twenty-year period of indifference, the second temple was completed at the urging of Haggai and Zechariah. It was dedicated in 516 B.C. (6:13–22). Jerusalem itself, however, was sparsely populated, its walls were broken, and its gates burned down. Not until 444 B.C. did there appear on the scene a leader who would serve as a catalyst to bring about the complete rebuilding of the walls and the resettlement of the city. That leader, Nehemiah, left a secure post in the court of the king of Persia and with vision and energy spurred the people of Jerusalem to complete what had been considered an impossible task—rebuilding the walls and gates in just fifty-two days!

Another major crisis took place in the second century B.C. in the intertestamental period. The Seleucids of Syria wrested control of Palestine from the Ptolemies of Egypt and sought to impose Hellenistic culture on the Jews. In the process Jerusalem was captured by the Syrian forces, and the temple was desecrated. The worship of God was abolished, and a statue of the Olympian Zeus was installed in the temple. Three years later, in 165 B.C., Jewish patriots led by the Maccabean family recaptured Jerusalem. The temple was cleansed and rededicated at the Feast of Lights. Jews continue to celebrate this feast (Hanukkah) to the present day.

During a time of civil strife between several Jewish sects the Roman general Pompey besieged and then broke into Jerusalem, dissolved the Maccabean government, and annexed Jerusalem and Judea to the Roman province of Syria (63 B.C.).

During the period of Roman rule, Jerusalem was the religious center of the Jews. Each year throngs of pilgrims gathered in the city on Passover and other religious feast days. While Jesus was born in Bethlehem and grew to manhood in Nazareth, He visited Jerusalem on numerous occasions. At the age of eight days He was presented at the temple (Luke 2:21–38); at twelve he dialogued with the teachers in the temple (2:41–50); after His baptism, Jesus was taken by Satan to Jerusalem to stand on the high point of the temple (4:9–12). John recorded four visits of Jesus to Jerusalem (John 2:13–3:21; 5:1–47; 7–10; 12–20) and the Synoptic Gospels add much detail, particularly regarding the events of the Passion Week. Jesus' death, resurrection, and ascension all took place in and about the city of Jerusalem.

The history of the early church also centered in Jerusalem. The Book of Acts is replete with references to the activities and sufferings of the early Christians, including Peter and Paul, in the city. Following a four-year rebellion of the Jews, the Roman general Titus breached the walls of Jerusalem in A.D. 70 and burned the temple, just as Jesus had predicted (Mark 13:2).

In the postbiblical period the Jews rebelled again under Bar Kochba in A.D. 134. The city once more was razed, but it was quickly rebuilt by the Romans as a pagan city called Aelia Capitolina. Since then, Jerusalem has gone through nine periods of rule: Roman, to 330; Byzantine, to 638; Arab, to 1099; Crusader, to 1187 and from 1229 to 1244; Arab, to 1516; Turkish, to 1917; British, to 1948; Jordanian, to 1967; and Israeli, to the present.

With the return of Christ to the earth at His second advent, Jerusalem once again will assume a place of biblical significance. Christ will descend to the Mount of Olives and will rescue the believing Jewish remnant from a besieged Jerusalem (Zech. 14:1–4). The city will be the Messiah's millennial capital (14:20–21) and the home of a temple whose sacrifices will be memorial.

The final biblical reference to Jerusalem is found in Revelation 21–22. John, in a glorious vision of the eternal state, saw "the Holy City, the new Jerusalem, coming down out of heaven from God" (Rev. 21:2). This city, anticipated by Abraham (Heb. 11:10, 16) and promised by Christ (John 14:2–3), is "the heavenly Jerusalem, the city of the living God" (Heb. 12:22), "Jerusalem that is above" (Gal. 4:26). As the final and eternal home of redeemed humanity, the New Jerusalem will shine with the glory of God. In contrast to man-made cities, which display only human achievements, this heavenly city, which will come to earth, will be ablaze with light, the light of the glory of God. At last Jerusalem will deservedly be called the Holy City.
                                                              —DKC

Rejoice in the fact that the believer's final home will be
in the glorious holy city,
the New Jerusalem.

Judgment

AS "THE JUDGE OF ALL THE EARTH" (Gen. 18:25; see 1 Sam. 2:10) and "all men" (Heb. 12:23), God judges with equity (Ps. 96:10), justice (Acts 17:31), impartiality (1 Pet. 1:17), righteousness (Ps. 9:8), and truth (Rom. 2:2). The Scriptures affirm that God is the Judge of all activities on the earth. His authority is without limit in heaven and earth, and there is no possibility of questioning the accuracy of His judgments (Pss. 58:11; 99:4). His judgments are based on His absolute justice, as the Scriptures often affirm (Gen. 18:25; Deut. 32:4; Pss. 33:5; 89:14; Jer. 11:20; 33:15; Ezek. 33:20; Rom. 3:5–6; 1 Pet. 2:23; Rev. 16:7; 19:2). He "loves justice" (Pss. 11:7; 99:4), and He has the power to carry out His judgment because of His omnipotence.

Jesus' death on the cross was an act of God's justice, as well as His grace and love, in that Jesus carried the punishment of the sins of the entire world "in his body on the tree" (1 Pet. 2:24). Isaiah wrote that "the LORD has laid on him the iniquity of us all" (Isa. 53:6), and Paul wrote, "God made him who had no sin to be sin for us" (2 Cor. 5:21). Jesus Christ died on our behalf "to demonstrate his [God's] justice" against sin (Rom. 3:25–26). That is, He did not overlook sin; He had to pay its penalty.

The Bible records a number of instances in the past in which God judged individuals and nations for their sins. His ultimate judgment on individuals does not come, however, until after death. "Man is destined to die once, and after that to face judgment" (Heb. 9:27).

Many people assume there will be only one final judgment of the saved and unsaved at the end of the age. The Scriptures, however, speak of a series of coming judgments. One of the first of these is the judgment seat of Christ, which will take place after the rapture of the church. In that judgment in heaven believers will be judged on the basis of what they have done for Christ and will receive or not receive rewards (2 Cor. 5:10). During the Tribulation, the seven-year period between the Rapture and the Second Coming, many judgments will be poured out on the earth because of human wickedness (Rev. 6–18). Many have wrongly tried to tone down the severity of these judgments by saying they are not to be taken literally.

Several other judgments will take place when Christ returns to the earth. The armies that will gather to fight it out in the Holy Land will turn at Christ's coming to fight the armies from heaven but they will be immediately destroyed (Rev. 16:13–16; 19:19). The Antichrist, called "the beast," and his cohort, called the false prophet, will be cast into the lake of fire (19:20). Then Satan will be judged by being rendered inactive for a thousand years, starting with the second coming of Christ (20:1–3). Jews who survive the Tribulation will be judged, and believing Jews will be given a place of blessing in the millennial kingdom.

Judgment on Gentiles who survive the Tribulation is mentioned in Matthew 25:31–46. The sheep represent the saved, who will enter the millennial kingdom in their natural bodies, and the goats represent the lost, who will be judged by everlasting punishment in hell.

In the Millennium Christ will reign with an absolute rule and will judge any open rebellion against Him. At the end of the thousand years Satan will be loosed, judged, and cast into the lake of fire (Rev. 20:7–10), and the wicked will be judged at the Great White Throne judgment (20:11–15). While unpleasant to contemplate, the eternal punishment of the lost is an act of divine justice because sin cannot go unpunished. As Paul wrote, "God is just" (2 Thess. 1:6).

Christians are told not to judge fellow believers needlessly (Matt. 7:1–5). Yet they should call sin sin, doing so in a spirit of gentleness and recognizing that they themselves are sinners (Gal. 6:1). When Christians come to the Lord's Table, they should judge themselves, to be sure they have no unconfessed sin in their lives (1 Cor. 11:27–32).

God the Father has committed all judgment to Jesus Christ, His Son (John 5:22, 27). —JFW

Be gracious in dealing with others,
knowing that God alone judges impartially and in righteousness.

Justice

JUSTICE INVOLVES what is right or correct, as conveyed by several Hebrew words in the Old Testament (primarily *mišpat*) and Greek words in the New Testament (mainly *krisis* and *dikaiosynē*). For all practical purposes justice is equivalent to righteousness, both English words being used to translate the Hebrew and Greek words. As a result, justice (that is, righteousness) or its opposite, injustice (that is, unrighteousness), describe a person's dealings with another individual. This is true of dealings with God as well as with other individuals.

Justice begins with God, who is infinitely just by nature and is always just in all His dealings with all His creatures. Isaiah declared that "the LORD is a God of justice" (Isa. 30:18); Elihu said, "I will ascribe justice to my Maker" (Job 36:3; see also Ps. 9:16; Isa. 5:16); and Paul wrote "God is just" (1 Thess. 1:6). Isaiah quoted God as stating, "I, the LORD, love justice; I hate robbery and iniquity" (61:8). This emphasis on God's justice is almost invariably found in contexts that speak of His grace, love, and mercy, thus showing that it involves much more than simply retributive justice. God will exercise retributive justice, however, because He is properly identified as "the Judge of all the earth" (Gen. 18:25; see also Pss. 58:11; 94:2), who "has entrusted all judgment to the Son" (John 5:22).

Because of His justice by nature and in action, God is concerned that justice prevail in people's dealings with each other. This is especially true for those who are in authority over others and have the opportunity to misuse their position and power. Before the Israelites entered Canaan, Moses told them to "follow justice and justice alone," and at Sinai he warned them not to "pervert justice by siding with the crowd" (Exod. 23:2; see also 23:6; Lev. 19:15; Deut. 1:17; 16:19). Later through Zechariah God told Israel, "Administer true justice" (Zech. 7:9), which involved showing "mercy and compassion to one another," not oppressing "the widow or the fatherless, the alien or the poor," and not thinking "evil of each other" (7:10).

Of necessity, the exercise of justice involved the establishment of laws and their application. As quoted above, God said, "I hate robbery and iniquity" (Isa. 61:8). Laws can be interpreted and administered so rigidly, however, that no place is given for clemency. This is illustrated by the Pharisees, who condemned Jesus' disciples for plucking and eating heads of grain to satisfy their hunger on the Sabbath (Matt. 12:1–2) and criticized Him for healing on the Sabbath (John 5:1–16; see also Matt. 12:9–14; Mark 3:1–6; Luke 6:6–11). Justice requires that laws be executed with wisdom.

The exercise of justice also required the establishment of governmental authorities with power to achieve justice. These, including even ungodly ones, have been ordained by God (Rom. 13:1), which explains why Christians are commanded to submit to them (13:1–7; Titus 3:1; 1 Pet. 2:13–14). The final exercise of perfect justice awaits the millennial kingdom of the Lord Jesus Christ (Isa. 2:2–4; 42:1–4; 2 Thess. 1:6–7; Rev. 19:11). —JAW

Be vigilant to exercise justice and fairness in every area of your life.

Justification

JUSTIFICATION IS THE ACT OF GOD by which a sinner who believes in Christ is declared righteous on the basis of what Christ has done for him or her on the cross. While the death of Christ was sufficient to justify all men, it becomes a reality in an individual's life only when he trusts in Christ as his Savior. Romans 3:28, Galatians 2:16, and 3:24 speak of being "justified by faith," and Romans 3:24 and Titus 3:7 state that we are justified "by his grace." An Old Testament example of justification is Abraham: "Abraham believed the LORD, and he credited it to him as righteousness" (Gen. 15:6). In justification God's righteousness is credited to the believer so that God sees him or her in a right standing before God (Rom. 4:5, 23–24).

Though Christ did not speak at length on justification, He did say that a tax collector who prayed, "God, have mercy on me, a sinner," "went home justified before God" (Luke 18:13–14).

The apostle Paul frequently wrote about justification, and he related it to many other terms such as redemption, reconciliation, righteousness, and others. He explained that no one can be justified by works (Gal. 2:16; 3:11; Rom. 4:5) because no amount of self-produced good actions can change a person's past or his or her sin nature. Justification is a judicial act in which God declares a sinner righteous because God sees in him the perfections of the work of His Son. The death of Christ on the cross is the basis by which God justifies believing sinners. This is why Paul wrote that we are "justified by his blood" (5:9).

Justification includes forgiveness of sins, but it is more than that.

Forgiveness is subtraction of guilt, whereas justification involves imputing or reckoning the righteousness of Christ to the believer. Justification is an act of God's grace, but it is also an act of righteousness because Christ bore the penalty Himself. The Christian doctrine of justification is in stark contrast to that of world religions, which base justification on human efforts. —JFW

Because of your right standing as a believer before God,
reflect God's righteousness in your dealings with others.

Kk

King

THE FIRST REFERENCE IN SCRIPTURE to a king or supreme political leader is in Genesis 14. Several kings had captured Lot, who was residing in Sodom. But Abram, Lot's uncle, was able to defeat those kings, rescue Lot and other captives, and retrieve the plunder. Immediately following this rescue, Melchizedek, king of Salem (that is, Jerusalem), blessed Abram. Melchizedek was also known as "priest of God Most High" (14:18), and in recognition of that position Abram gave him a tenth of his possessions (14:20).

Throughout history, kings continued to rule over nations, and often the political leader of even a city was called a king.

The nation Israel was a theocracy, that is, God was her leader. But the people wanted to have a king like other nations (1 Sam. 8:5, 20). Samuel, God's prophet and Israel's spiritual leader at the time, warned them that a king would be oppressive in many ways (8:11–18). The people insisted, so God told Samuel to choose Saul, son of Kish, as king. Saul eventually turned from God, and Samuel anointed David as king (16:12–13). David did not succeed Saul until after his death, and even then David's control of all twelve tribes was delayed. After David died, his son Solomon was appointed. When Israel divided into two kingdoms in 931 B.C., ten tribes formed the Northern Kingdom known as Israel, and the remaining two tribes, the Southern Kingdom, were known as Judah. The nineteen kings of the South were all of the tribe of Judah, but the twenty kings of the North were of other tribes. Only eight of the kings of Judah were good kings, and all twenty in the North were bad.

The Lord God is Israel's King in the sense of being her Sovereign (Isa. 33:22; 43:15; Zeph. 3:15). And of course He has always reigned over the universe (Pss. 9:8; 47:7–8; 99:1).

In His first advent Jesus Christ presented Himself to Israel as her King, but the nation rejected Him (Luke 7:30; 17:25). At His trial and crucifixion Jesus was mockingly derided as the "King of the Jews" (Matt.

27:29, 37), another indication of the nation's rejection of His offer of the kingdom. So His reign on the earth awaits His second coming when He will reign on David's throne (Isa. 9:7).

In an important prophecy in 2 Samuel 7 God told David that his descendants would rule over the house of Israel forever. Ultimately Jesus Christ, a direct descendant of David of the tribe of Judah, will fulfill this prophecy. Amillenarians say this Davidic kingdom is entirely a spiritual reign in which Christ is reigning today in heaven. Premillenarians, however, interpret the millennial promises of the Old and New Testaments literally and believe that Christ will rule on the earth for one thousand years in a political kingdom over Israel and over the entire world as the King of kings and the Lord of lords (1 Tim. 6:15; Rev. 19:16; see also 17:14).   —JFW

Praise God for the realization that the day is coming
when Christ will be recognized as the Ruler over all the earth.

Kingdom

THE BIBLE REFERS TO SEVERAL KINGDOMS, realms ruled by kings: secular kingdoms, such as the political rule of a city or a state with the leader who is designated king; the kingdom of heaven; the kingdom of God; the future kingdom of David with Jesus the Messiah ruling on the earth; and God's rule as the Creator and Sovereign of the whole earth (2 Kings 19:15; 1 Chron. 29:11; Pss. 47:2, 7–8; 103:19).

Amillennial theology stresses that there is one kingdom with various subdivisions, including the rule of God as Creator, His rule of Israel in Old Testament times, and most preeminently, His rule in a spiritual sense over all humanity and especially over those who believe in Him.

Premillennialism, on the other hand, emphasizes different forms of the kingdom, with each one having its own characteristics. God's rule over creation arises from His having created the world, and it includes all humanity, whether believers or unbelievers, as well as the world of nature. In the Old Testament the kingdom of Israel was a political kingdom over the territory of Israel. After the nation began as a monarchy under King Saul, David, of the tribe of Judah, became the next king. After David's son Solomon reigned, the kingdom of Israel divided, with ten tribes constituting the Northern Kingdom, called Israel, and the remaining two tribes of Benjamin and Judah constituting the Southern Kingdom, known as Judah. Though a remnant returned from exile under Zerubbabel, Ezra, and Nehemiah, the nation Israel was never the same. Many Jews scattered to other parts of the world.

When Christ returns to the earth, the nation Israel will be restored to her land (Jer. 31:17; Ezek. 36:24; Amos 9:11–15) and the kingdom of David will be established (2 Sam. 7:12–16; Isa. 9:7; Luke 1:31–33). David will be raised from the dead and will reign with Christ in Jerusalem (Jer. 30:9; Ezek. 34:23–24; 37:24–25). In Christ's millennial rule of one thousand years (Rev. 20:6) He will reign in justice (Isa. 2:2–5; 11:1–5; 32:1) on David's throne (9:7).

Just before His ascension the disciples asked Jesus if He was going to restore the kingdom to Israel then (Acts 1:6). They were speaking of the Messiah's reign on earth, which they thought He would establish then. But it is delayed until He comes back to the earth.

After the Millennium, in which Christ will "reign until he has put all his enemies under his feet" (1 Cor. 15:25; see also Pss. 8:6; 110:1), He will hand over the kingdom to God the Father (1 Cor. 15:24).

Premillenarians interpret these prophecies literally, whereas amillenarians take them in a nonliteral sense and apply them to God's present spiritual rule over believers.

The New Testament speaks of the kingdom of heaven and the kingdom of God. Most expositors regard these two kingdoms as one without noting the differences. True, sometimes these terms are used synonymously, but when they are contrasted the kingdom of heaven is regarded as a sphere of profession, that is, it includes not only believers but also some who profess Christ but are not actually saved. The kingdom of God, however, includes only those who are genuine believers.

The term *kingdom of heaven* is found only in Matthew. Bible teachers who equate the kingdom of heaven with the kingdom of God argue that because the Jews feared using the term *Yahweh*, when they came to a phrase like the *kingdom of God (Yahweh)*, they used the term *kingdom of heaven*. However, even in Matthew there are four instances where the term *kingdom of God* is used (Matt. 12:28; 19:24; 21:31, 43). According to these verses those who are in the kingdom of God are saved; there is no false profession of salvation. In Jesus' parables of the kingdom of heaven in Matthew 13, the sphere of false profession is indicated by the weeds in the field (13:24–30, 36–42) and the bad fish in the net (13:47–50). These parables illustrate the kingdom of heaven, but they are never used of the kingdom of God. Whether this distinction is held does not affect dispensational prophecy as a whole.

In John 3:3, 5 Jesus said the kingdom of God includes only those who are born again, that is, those who receive eternal life by trusting in Him as their Savior. The kingdom of God is the spiritual rule of God in the hearts of believers. Believers, Paul wrote, have been brought "into the kingdom of the Son" (Col. 1:13; see also 4:11).

The major contrast between the premillennial and amillennial points of view on the kingdom is that premillennialism holds that in a future literal political kingdom on earth Christ will reign from Jerusalem, whereas amillennialism denies that such a literal event will occur after the Second Coming.   —JFW

Count it a privilege that every believer is under the rule of God now and will participate in serving the Lord in the coming millennial kingdom.

Ll

Lamb

ANIMALS HAVE A SUBORDINATE but significant role in the Scriptures. Animal sacrifices were offered from the time of Abel to the days of the prophet Malachi. One of the first references to the offering of a lamb was in the life of Abraham (Gen. 22:7–8). The Hebrew word used in those verses was *śeh,* "one from the flock," which could refer to a lamb or a kid. This was also the word used of the sacrifice Abel brought to the Lord (4:4). The same word appears in Exodus 12:1–5, as instructions were given to Moses from the Lord about the animal to be selected for the Passover meal the night before the judgment of God came on the Egyptians and their gods. This was to be an unblemished one-year-old male lamb or kid.

A more definitive term, *kebeś,* was used to describe the lambs for the daily sacrifices in the tabernacle (Exod. 29:38–41; Num. 28:1–8). One lamb was to be offered in the morning and the other at twilight, and those sacrifices would be a "pleasing aroma" to the Lord. Besides the daily offerings, lambs were also used for Sabbath offerings (Num. 28:9–10) and monthly offerings (28:11–15), and on the Passover (28:16–25), the Feast of Weeks (28:26–31), the Feast of Trumpets (29:1–6), the Day of Atonement (29:7–11), and the Feast of Tabernacles (29:12–40). When lambs were sacrificed for a sin offering, a female without blemish was to be given (Lev. 4:32). A lamb could be sacrificed for purification after childbirth (12:6), and three lambs were to be offered when a person was being ceremonially cleansed after being healed of an infectious disease (14:10).

Since lambs were part of the daily lives of the Israelites, the term *lamb* was often used in a metaphorical sense. In recounting the power of God in bringing Israel out of Egypt, a psalmist described the mountains quaking like the skipping of lambs (Ps. 114:1–4). Isaiah spoke of a lamb to express the tranquillity that will characterize the Millennium (Isa. 11:6; 65:25). The Messiah is pictured as carrying the people of

Israel in His arms as a shepherd would carry his lambs (40:11). The lamb portrays the meekness of Messiah (53:7), as well as the submission of the enemies of Israel when judgment comes (Jer. 51:40).

When John the Baptist announced the coming of Christ, he identified Him as "the Lamb of God" who takes away the sin of the world (John 1:29, 36). The Greek word *amnos* is used in those two passages to describe the lamb. This term appears four times in the New Testament, always in reference to Jesus as our Sacrifice for sin. Peter wrote that believers have been redeemed "with the precious blood of Christ, a lamb without blemish or defect" (1 Pet. 1:19). *Amnos* also occurs in Acts 8:32, in Luke's record of the passage the eunuch read (Isa. 53:7). Paul referred to Jesus as "the Passover Lamb, who has been sacrificed" (1 Cor. 5:7), but the word *lamb* has been supplied by the New International Version translators. Though the writer of Hebrews did not use the word *lamb,* he did consider Jesus the Sacrifice offered to God for the sins of humankind (Heb. 9:14; 10:10, 14; 13:12).

Like the prophets, Jesus used the term *lamb* in a figurative sense when describing the precarious circumstances His disciples would face in fulfilling their responsibilities (Luke 10:3). In His conversation with Peter after the Resurrection, Jesus again used the word metaphorically as He exhorted Peter to feed His lambs (John 21:15).

The entire Book of Revelation centers around Christ, the Lamb of God. More than two dozen times John refers to the "Lamb," using the Greek word *arnion.* Although this word differs from the word for lamb that is used in the Gospels and the Epistles, no clear distinction between the terms is apparent.

The future of the world will revolve around the Son of God, the Lamb who has been slain (5:6). The Lamb is the only One worthy to break the seals and unleash the judgments that will come on the earth in the Tribulation (5:1–10). People from all walks of life will fall down before the Lamb as He alone has the authority to judge (6:15–17). Those saved during the Tribulation will be redeemed by the blood of the Lamb (7:12). The Lamb is also the Shepherd, who provides eternal life (7:17). As the Lamb, Christ will triumph over Satan, the great adversary of Israel (12:7–12). Israel's hope and salvation during the Tribulation will be the Lamb (14:1–5). The Lamb will also triumph over the kings and rulers of the earth (17:14). A scene revealed to John depicted the wed-

ding of the Lamb to His bride (19:6–9). The final two chapters of
Revelation describe the new heavens and the new earth and the splendor of life in the presence of the Lamb (22:3–5). Throughout eternity
believers will enjoy the salvation of the Lamb and will worship and serve
Him forever (21:27; 22:3–5).   **—WGJ**

Always be thankful that Jesus, the Lamb of God,
gave Himself for the sins of the world.

Last Days

THE BIBLE USES THE PHRASES "the last days" and "the last times"
with reference to several different time periods. Since the coming of
God's promised Messiah is identified with the last days, there is a sense
in which they began with the incarnation of Jesus Christ: "In these last
days he [God] has spoken [finally, once for all] to us by his Son" (Heb.
1:2), and "He was chosen before the creation of the world, but was
revealed in these last times for your sake" (1 Pet. 1:20).

Broadly speaking, therefore, the last days include the earthly life and
ministry of Jesus Christ, the entire history of the church to the present,
as well as all events prophesied in the Scriptures that are still unfulfilled.
Even near the beginning of the church's history John pointed out that
the "many antichrists [who] have come" are evidence that this "is the
last hour" (1 John 2:18).

Although these predicted events may point to the last days in a
broader sense than just the life of the church, Paul warned Timothy that
"there will be terrible times in the last days" (2 Tim. 3:1). Then he
described the character of people, ending with the clause, "having a
form of godliness but denying its power" (3:5). Both Peter and Jude
warned that in the last days "scoffers" will come (2 Pet. 3:3; Jude 18).
Although such opposers of the Christian faith appeared in the early
generations of church history, they apparently will increase and become
more active as the church approaches its last days.

In the Old Testament the last days are identified with God's yet-future
blessings of restoration and salvation for His chosen people Israel (Deut.

30:1–10). God will pour His Spirit on the people of Israel and save them (Jer. 23:3–8; Joel 2:28–32). The people of Israel will return to the Lord (Hos. 3:5), and God will restore them to the Promised Land and Jerusalem will become the capital of all nations (Isa. 2:2–5; Mic. 4:1–8). Numerous other prophecies speak of these future blessings for Israel without using the phrase "the last days."

Before that future time of blessedness will occur, a time of conflict and judgment will come in which God will defeat both His human and His satanic enemies (Joel 2:30–31; 3:9–15). This time of tribulation is called "the day of the LORD" (Isa. 13:6, 9–13; Zeph. 1:14–18; Mal. 4:1–3, 5). It in turn will be followed by "the coming of salvation" (1 Pet. 1:5) and the fulfillment of Christ's promise of resurrection "at the last day" (John 6:39–40, 44, 54).

—JAW

Anticipate the Lord's coming for His own at any moment,
since we are already in the last days.

Law

THE PRIMARY Old Testament and New Testament words for "law," *tôrā* and *nomos,* have the basic meaning of a controlling or guiding principle or precept. From this has developed the idea of a regulation or requirement to be obeyed under threat of punishment. Laws can be both positive, demanding certain actions, and negative, prohibiting certain actions.

In a real sense law begins with God, since He is the Creator and Sovereign of all things (Isa. 45:5–7, 18), who is fulfilling His eternal plan to His glory and praise. This is true even of the laws of godless nations, because "there is no authority except that which God has established. The authorities that exist have been established by God" (Rom. 13:1). In fact, law began in the Garden of Eden when God commanded Adam not to "eat from the tree of the knowledge of good and evil," warning that "when you eat of it you will surely die" (Gen. 2:17).

Law controlling people's relationships to one another was given by God to Noah and his family when He said He would "demand an accounting for the life of his fellow man" (9:5), declaring, "Whoever sheds the blood of man, by man shall his blood be shed; for in the image of God has God made man" (9:6). All laws of capital punishment, the death penalty, spring from this divine pronouncement.

In a special sense law is identified with the people of Israel and the multitude of regulations God gave them to control their relationship with Him and with one another. These are crystallized in the Ten Commandments (Exod. 34:28; Deut. 4:13; 10:4), known by the Jews as "the Ten Words" because the Hebrew word translated "commandments" literally means "words." The English word *commandment* focuses attention on the authoritarian, regulatory nature of the statements, while the Hebrew word for *word* emphasizes their revelational character as a message from God to His people.

Since the Ten Commandments, as well as all the other civic, religious, and social regulations God gave His people Israel, were communicated to them through Moses, they are frequently called "the Law of Moses" (for example, 1 Kings 2:3; 2 Kings 23:25; Dan. 9:11; Luke 2:22; 24:44; John 7:23; Acts 13:39; 1 Cor. 9:9) or simply "the Law" (for example, Neh. 10:34, 36; Isa. 2:3; Mic. 4:2; Matt. 5:17–18; Luke 2:27; John 1:45). To emphasize its divine origin it is called "the law of the LORD" (for example, 2 Kings 10:31; 1 Chron. 16:40; Pss. 1:2; 19:7; 119:1; Isa. 5:24; Luke 2:23, 39).

The Law signifies more than the Ten Commandments; it also applies to the entire Pentateuch, a fact demonstrated by the phrase this "Book of the Law" (Deut. 28:61; Josh. 1:8; 2 Kings 22:8; Neh. 8:3, 18; 9:3). The phrase cannot mean simply the Book of Exodus or the Book of Deuteronomy because many of the regulations are stated in Leviticus, and many of the judgments that carried the force of the Law are recorded in Numbers. Identifying the Law with the entire Pentateuch is further substantiated by the phrase "the Law and the Prophets" (Matt. 7:12; Acts 13:15; Rom. 3:21; see also Luke 16:29, 31; 24:27; Acts 28:23), which speaks of the entire Old Testament.

It is important to remember that the Ten Commandments and all the laws God gave Israel through Moses were not a way to earn salvation and eternal life, but a means of demonstrating obedience to God and maintaining fellowship with Him. Israel was already God's chosen people (Exod. 19:5–6; Deut. 7:6–8; 4:20; 14:2; 26:18) on the basis of a covenant established and confirmed with their forefathers. Obedience to God's laws would mean His continuing blessing; disobedience would bring His judgment. The Ten Commandments were given to Israel to express God's perfect standard and to lead people, when they fail, to turn to Him in faith for His forgiveness and salvation provided for Israel through the sacrifices in anticipation of the final redemptive sacrifice of the Lord Jesus Christ, the Savior.

Jesus did tell the rich young man, "If you want to enter life, obey the commandments" (Matt. 19:17), and this is true. However, this is impossible for any human being to achieve, as the young man proved. Upright as he was, he was violating the first and second commandments, because his wealth was his idol, replacing God as first in his life (19:21–22; Exod. 20:3–4). As Paul stated, by observing the Law no one will be justified (Rom. 3:20; Gal. 2:16).

What then is the purpose of the Law? First, "through the law we become conscious of sin" (Rom. 3:20; 7:7). "Sin is not taken into account when there is no law" (5:13; see also 4:15). Second, "the law was put in charge to lead us to Christ that we might be justified by faith" (Gal. 3:24).

Paul added, "Now that faith has come, we are no longer under the supervision of the law" (3:25). Then he warned the Galatian Christians against "turning back to those weak and miserable principles" (4:9), because "when the time had fully come, God sent his Son, born of a woman, born under law, to redeem those under law" (4:4–5). He illustrated this principle by marriage, which is in force so long as both partners are living but is abrogated when one of the spouses dies (Rom. 7:1–3). As believers we "also died to the law through the body of Christ" to "belong to another, to him who was raised from the dead" (7:4).

Does Paul's teaching nullify the Lord Jesus' statement that "until heaven and earth disappear, not the smallest letter, not the least stroke of a pen, will by any means disappear from the Law until everything is accomplished" (Matt. 5:18; Luke 16:17)? Of course not! Paul agreed with Jesus and David that "the law of the LORD is perfect" (Ps. 19:7–10). Paul called the Law "holy . . . righteous and good" (Rom. 7:12, 16) and "spiritual" (7:14). He insisted that justification by faith does not "nullify the law," saying "Not at all! Rather, we uphold the law" (3:31). Later Paul explained that "through Christ Jesus the law of the Spirit of life set me free from the law of sin and death. For what the law was powerless to do in that it was weakened by the sinful nature, God did by sending his own Son in the likeness of sinful man to be a sin offering. And so he condemned sin in sinful man, in order that the righteous requirements of the law might be fully met in us, who do not live according to the sinful nature but according to the Spirit" (8:2–4).

Nine of the Ten Commandments—all except the one "to observe the Sabbath day" (Deut. 5:15; Exod. 20:8–11)—are repeated in the New Testament Epistles. However, church-age believers are to live on a higher level, being empowered by the indwelling Holy Spirit. Paul wrote the Galatian Christians to "live by the Spirit, and you will not gratify the desires of the sinful nature" (5:16). The verb translated "live" signifies the constant walking about of one's daily life. Paul explained that "if you are led by the Spirit, you are not under law" (5:18).

After listing the fruit of the Holy Spirit (5:22–23), Paul stated, "Against such things there is no law" (5:23). By this he meant that those nine virtues of the Spirit are on a higher plane than the Mosaic Law. When a Christian is not walking under the leadership of the Holy Spirit and violates the Law, however, the Law condemns his action. That Christian has fallen to the level of the Law, God's perfect standard for human conduct. Therefore "since we live by the Spirit, let us keep in step with the Spirit" (5:25). The verb translated "keep in step" is a military term meaning "to walk in a row" as on parade, and it emphasizes continuing action. Living each day under the leadership of the Holy Spirit is God's desire for each Christian and should be the desire and goal of every believer.   **—JAW**

Fulfill God's "law" by displaying the fruit of the Holy Spirit in your life.

Laying On of Hands

IN ANCIENT ISRAEL the practice called "laying on of hands" was used for a variety of purposes. It was a symbol of blessing, demonstrated when Jacob laid his hands on the heads of his grandsons Ephraim and Manasseh, and blessed them (Gen. 48:14–20). It was also a symbol of identification for consecrating Aaron and his sons as priests when they placed their hands on a bull and a ram that were then slain (Exod. 29:10–21; Lev. 8:14, 18).

On the Day of Atonement, after slaying both a bull and a goat as sin offerings for the priests and the people, the high priest was "to lay both hands on the head of the live goat and confess over it all the wickedness and rebellion of the Israelites—all their sins—and put them on the goat's head" (16:21). The goat was then released into the desert as a scapegoat.

Individual Israelites similarly identified themselves with their fellowship offerings (3:1–2, 6-8, 12–13) and sin offerings (4:27–29, 32–33) by laying their hands on the heads of sacrificial animals. The elders of Israel placed their hands on the sin offering for the community (4:13–15), as the priest or other leader did for his sin (4:3–4, 22–24).

Laying on of hands was also a symbol of consecration to ministry, as with the Levites (Num. 8:10, 12–14), and commissioning, as with Joshua (27:18–20, 22–23; Deut. 34:9). The rite also was used at the execution of a blasphemer. All the Israelites who heard the blasphemy were "to lay their hands on his head" and then "the entire assembly [was] to stone him" (Lev. 24:13–14).

The Lord Jesus Christ used laying on of hands as a sign of His blessing, something He did for the little children who were brought to Him to be blessed and prayed for (Matt. 19:13–15; Mark 10:13–16; Luke 18:15–17). Jesus also laid His hands on people when He healed them (Matt. 9:18–19, 25; Mark 5:22–24; 6:5; Luke 4:40). At His ascension, although Jesus apparently did not lay His hands on the apostles' heads, He "lifted up his hands and blessed them" (24:50).

Laying on of hands continued in the apostolic church as a symbol of consecration to an office and a ministry. After seven men were chosen to care for the daily distribution of food (Acts 6:1–5), the seven were presented to the apostles, "who prayed and laid their hands on them and sent them off" (13:3).

In the apostolic church the laying on of hands was involved in ordination to ministry. Paul ordained Timothy to the ministry "through the laying on of my hands" (2 Tim. 1:6; see also 1 Tim. 4:14) and warned him against being "hasty in the laying on of hands" (5:22) in ordaining others. In the apostolic church the laying on of hands symbolized the fact that those who received the Holy Spirit were united with other believers (Acts 8:12–13, 14–17; 19:1–7). This bestowal of the Holy Spirit through the laying on of hands was a power wrongly sought by Simon the sorcerer (8:18–21). Paul and undoubtedly others in the apostolic church used laying on of hands in performing miracles of healing (28:8; Mark 16:18). It may or may not have been involved in the anointing with oil, coupled with prayer, to heal the sick (James 5:14–15).

Through the centuries, churches have continued the practice of laying on of hands as part of the ritual of ordination.　　　**—JAW**

*Whether or not you receive the laying on of hands by others,
seek the Lord's approval in your life.*

Leadership

THE BIBLE HAS MUCH TO SAY about leadership. In one of his acrostic psalms David gave a breathtaking summary of God as the ultimate Ruler over His everlasting kingdom (Ps. 145:13). It was the Lord who raised up men like Abraham, Isaac, Jacob, Moses, and Joshua to be leaders in Israel. The role of these men lacked the formality of modern-day leadership but there was never a question about their call and authority to lead. After the days of Joshua God raised up eleven men and one woman to be judges in Israel and to provide leadership for the people. Besides governing, they also were to be military leaders to rescue their people from oppression.

Later, the ultimate leadership role in Israel was exercised by the king. Moses gave specific instructions from the Lord on the process of selecting a king (Deut. 17:14–20). The people were to look to the Lord for the man of His choosing, and this man was to rule in accord with instructions in the Word of God. Of all the kings of Israel, one man, David, stood out from all others as the epitome of a godly and gifted leader (Ps. 78:72; Acts 13:22, 36).

Leadership in the Old Testament was not limited to kings. When those in the royal palace turned away from God and became unfaithful to the laws of the nation, then the Lord called on others to provide spiritual leadership. These included men like Elijah, Elisha, Isaiah, Jeremiah,

Ezekiel, Daniel, and a host of other qualified people. These men were not always acclaimed as leaders, but what they accomplished for God has forever been recorded in the pages of Scripture.

In the New Testament a whole new order of leadership was established, following the example of the Lord Jesus Christ. The writer of Hebrews called Jesus our Apostle and High Priest (Heb. 3:1). Jesus had all the credentials of a successful leader. He was sent by the Father to accomplish His will (10:5–10). All authority in heaven and on earth had been given to Him (Matt. 28:18); yet His leadership style was more like that of a shepherd than a king. Jesus called Himself "the good shepherd" (John 10:11). Peter called Him "the Chief Shepherd" (1 Pet. 5:4), and declared that His style of leadership should be followed by all leaders in the church (5:2–3).

In examining the leadership of the Lord Jesus, several thoughts emerge. First, leadership involves an individual being willing to take responsibility, and Jesus willingly came to this earth to lay down His life (John 10:14–18). This basic concept was captured by Paul as the qualities for church leaders were formulated (1 Tim. 3:1). Second, as a leader, Jesus acted as guide, out in front of people, helping them stay focused on the proper goals. Often Jesus rebuked His disciples because they had lost sight of His purposes (Matt. 16:22–27). Third, leaders should be goal-oriented, and Jesus had an overall goal, namely, to fulfill the Father's will.

The first New Testament leaders were called apostles. They were appointed by Christ and were given the authority to carry out their mission (Mark 3:13–15). The apostles along with Christ were the foundation on which the church was built (Eph. 2:20). Besides the original Twelve, a few others, most notably Paul, were called apostles (1 Cor. 15:6–9).

The pattern for church leadership was established early, though no prescribed details are given in Scripture. The need for organization came as a result of growth. New converts coming to Christ needed to learn the apostles' doctrine and to be graciously initiated into the life of the church. Also problems developed, and that made organization essential and called for more leadership (Acts 6:1). By the end of the first decade elders were serving in the church at Jerusalem, but there is no indication as to when they were appointed (11:30). When Paul and

Barnabas went on their first missionary journey, they established the pattern of appointing elders in all the churches (14:23). Basic to effective spiritual leadership was selecting leaders who were "full of the Spirit and wisdom" (6:3).

In Paul's impromptu and informal gathering with the elders from the church in Ephesus he mentioned some of the responsibilities of elders. They were to be concerned with the spiritual growth of the congregation (20:28), the doctrinal purity of the people and the leadership team (20:29–31), and the teachings of the grace of God (20:32), with an emphasis on serving and giving as opposed to receiving (20:33–35).

Later in Paul's ministry he emphasized specific qualities that should characterize elders (1 Tim. 3:2–7; Titus 1:6–9). Paul noted that an elder should desire to serve and be willing to take responsibility. His personal life is to be exemplary and his marriage strong. His life is to be under control so he will be respected. He is to be open to everyone in the church, to have the ability to communicate, to possess a gentle spirit, not to be affected by wealth, able to manage his own family, a mature believer with a healthy respect for the cleverness of the devil, known outside the church for leading a Christlike life, and knowledgeable about the teachings of the church so he can teach others and detect error.

The office of deacon emerged as churches experienced numerical growth and the need for qualified assistance in the work of the Lord. The term *deacon* means "servant" or "minister." Specific details as to the creation of this office are not given in Scripture. Some believe that when seven men were chosen to serve the Twelve in Acts 6, that is where it began, though the passage gives no specific evidence to support this view. What is evident from the passage is that organization developed out of need, that growth required additional leadership.

The initial occurrence of the term *deacon* in an official capacity appears in Paul's salutation to the leaders of the church in Philippi (Phil. 1:1). This establishes the fact that deacons were viewed as having an authoritative role along with elders. By the time Paul wrote his letters to Timothy, the office of deacon was well established (1 Tim. 3:8–13). In this passage the apostle described some of the qualities a deacon should possess. These men should demonstrate a consistent growth in spiritual matters, exhibiting qualities that demand respect (3:8, 10). They must give evidence of a deep commitment to the truths of the Christian faith (3:9), must have a wholesome family life (3:12), and their wives must be considered partners in ministry (3:11).

Some believe the Greek term *gynaikas* in 1 Timothy 3:11 should be translated "women" rather than "wives," thus suggesting that they were deaconnesses. The word *gynaikas* does leave the door open to consider the possibility of women ministering in an official capacity. A growing number of people in the early church were women, and some would have had special needs, as Paul addressed them later in the letter (5:3–16). Paul did seem to anticipate these needs, which could be handled informally by deacons' wives or officially by deaconesses.

The teaching of the New Testament is clear that leadership in the church originates with God, who gives gifted people to the church (Eph. 4:11), and who through His Spirit gives gifts to enable those chosen to carry out their tasks effectively (Rom. 12:8; 1 Cor. 12:28). Leaders are to be respected, encouraged, honored, and appreciated (1 Thess. 5:12–13; Heb. 13:7, 17).   —WGJ

Pray about how God wants to use you in relationship to leaders in the body of Christ and the cooperation you may offer to facilitate the work of God.

Life

LIFE IS MYSTERIOUS and unexplainable. Scientists are able to observe life, but are hard pressed to define what it means. If a body were to be weighed both before and after death, the weight would be the same, yet something, life itself, has departed. Life then is what gives consciousness or sensibility to the body.

In the Old Testament two main words are used for life. The first is *hayyîm*, meaning physical life, with special reference to its duration (1 Kings 4:21). It also is used of a life that enjoys the favor of God, with resultant spiritual and material blessings (Deut. 30:15–20; Pss. 30:5; 42:8).

The second major Hebrew word for life is *nepeš*, which is translated in various ways such as "soul," "life," or "breath" (its root meaning). In

Genesis 2:7, 19 God is said to be the Source of life. In these verses both humans and animals are called "living beings," combining the two Hebrew words for life. The human race, however, is distinct from animals, for people have been given the image and likeness of God. The importance of human life is emphasized in passages on capital punishment: "Show no pity: life for life" (Deut. 19:21; see also Gen. 9:5–6; Exod. 21:23). In the sacrificial system of the Mosaic Law God provided an atonement for sinners by the blood of an animal, "For the life of a creature is in the blood, and I have given it to you to make atonement for yourselves on the altar; it is the blood that makes atonement for one's life" (Lev. 17:11). God accepted life for life—the animal's for the human's.

The Old Testament also stressed conditions related to life on earth for Israel. Before the Israelites crossed into Canaan, God spoke to His people through Moses in the Plains of Moab: "This day I call heaven and earth as witnesses against you that I have set before you life and death, blessings and curses. Now choose life, so that you and your children may live" (Deut. 30:19). A few references to life in the Old Testament refer, in the judgment of some, to eternal life (Pss. 16:10–11; 21:4–6; Prov. 12:28; Isa. 26:19; Dan. 12:2).

The New Testament uses three words to describe and explain life: *bios, psychē,* and *zōē.* The first word, *bios,* refers to the external conditions of a person's present earthly life (Luke 8:14; 1 Tim. 2:2; 2 Tim. 2:4, NKJV). It or its derivatives also describe one's lifestyle (Acts 26:4, 1 Pet. 4:2–3), and means of support (Mark 12:44; Luke 15:12, 30; 1 John 2:16; 3:17). This word is never used of eternal life.

The word *psychē,* used over one hundred times in the New Testament, is often translated "soul" (for example, Mark 8:36; 1 Pet. 2:11; 3 John 2) and occasionally it is rendered "life." *Psychē,* corresponding to the Hebrew word *nepeš,* is a multifaceted word that refers to the inner person or personality, that is, the self. In Matthew 20:28 Jesus said He came "to give his life as a ransom for many." According to Luke 12:22–23 Jesus challenged His followers with the words, "Do not worry about your life, what you will eat; or about your body, what you will wear. Life is more than food, and the body more than clothes."

Zōē is used in diversified ways. On occasion it is employed of natural or physical life (Acts 17:25; 1 Cor. 15:19). It also speaks of the life of God (John 5:26) and of the life of Christ residing in the believer (2 Cor.

4:10–11; Col. 3:4). This life is received by faith (John 3:16) and is a present possession (5:24). It extends through death to eternity (2 Cor. 5:4).

Though the mystery of life cannot be fully fathomed, it must be acknowledged as a gift of God. This is true of both natural or physical life and eternal life. Though man's natural life on earth is transient (James 4:14) and subject to physical death, existence is nonetheless endless for both the saved and the unsaved. The unsaved will exist eternally apart from God, whereas the eternal destiny of the saved involves unending communion in heaven with the triune God, Father, Son, and Holy Spirit. Only then will believers understand and appreciate the full meaning of the eternal life they received while on the earth.

—DKC

Thank God for physical life and for eternal life through Jesus Christ our Lord.

Light

LIGHT IS ONE OF THE GREATEST BENEFITS God has bestowed on the inhabitants of earth. The first recorded words of God are "Let there be light" (Gen. 1:3), and on the fourth creative day God set the light-bearing sun, moon, and stars in the sky (1:14–17). But what was the source of light before the appearance of the light-bearing bodies? Some suggest it was a cosmic light that was not centered anywhere, perhaps something like that of the aurora borealis. On the other hand it should be noted that in eternity's new Jerusalem, "The city does not need the sun or the moon to shine on it, for the glory of God gives it light" (Rev. 21:23).

In addition to creating light God provided special light for the Israelites on at least two occasions. During one of the plagues in Egypt the Israelites had light in their homes while the Egyptians were in thick darkness (Exod. 10:22–23). When the Israelites left Egypt, they were led by a pillar of cloud by day and a pillar of fire to give them light by night (13:21; 14:20; Ps. 78:14). God also favored His people with light when the Shekinah glory appeared at the completion of both the tabernacle (Exod. 40:34–38) and the temple (1 Kings 8:11; 2 Chron. 5:13–14).

"Light" is used in a metaphoric or figurative sense throughout Scripture. God is declared to be light (1 John 1:5) and the "Father of the heavenly lights" (James 1:17). He is described as One who "wraps himself in light as with a garment" (Ps. 104:2), and "who lives in unapproachable light" (1 Tim. 6:16). Frequently light symbolizes God's blessings (Job 12:22; 29:3; Pss. 18:28; 27:1; 97:11; 118:27). The expression "the light of his countenance" appears frequently in Psalms and usually connotes God looking with favor on His people (4:6; 44:3; 89:15). Sometimes it means that nothing, not even secret sins, escape God's close scrutiny (90:8). Light is connected with justice (Isa. 51:4) and with good conduct (Prov. 4:18; 6:23). It is a perversion when darkness is regarded as light and light as darkness (Isa. 5:20). The Word of God is compared to a light (Ps. 119:105), and a righteous king, David, was identified with light, that is, he was considered a source of illumination for his subjects (2 Sam. 21:17; 1 Kings 11:36).

New Testament references to light are both literal and figurative. Among the former are the supernatural brightness of the Transfiguration scene (Matt. 17:2), the bright light at Paul's Damascus road conversion (Acts 9:3), the light of day (John 11:9), and ordinary lamps (Acts 20:8).

Of all the New Testament writers John most frequently used symbols, particularly that of light. The Greek word for light, *phōs*, is found twenty-three times in the first twelve chapters of John's Gospel and almost always refers to Jesus or His teachings. Jesus is called the "light of men" (John 1:4), "the true light" (1:9), and "the light of the world" (8:12). He declared, "Light has come into the world, but men loved darkness instead of light because their deeds were evil" (3:19). Just before withdrawing from the crowd to be with His disciples in the upper room, Jesus said to the people, "You are going to have the light just a little while longer. Walk while you have the light, before darkness overtakes you.... Put your trust in the light while you have it, so that you may become sons of light" (12:35–36). But, as Paul later explained, Satan blinds the minds of the lost lest they see "the light of the gospel." God, however, overcomes Satan's opposition and causes the believer to receive "the light of the knowledge of the glory of God in the face of Christ" (2 Cor. 4:4–6). Such a transaction having taken place, believers are expected to live as "children of light," producing such fruit as "goodness, righteousness, and truth" (Eph. 5:8–9).

In his first epistle John also emphasized what is required of those who walk in the light. "God is light" (1 John 1:5), and as such He exposes and condemns people's sins. A Christian therefore cannot claim to have communion with God while living in darkness (sin). The only way to have fellowship with God is to live in the light where He is. Then there is openness to the light of divine truth and cleansing from every sin by the shed blood of Christ (1:6–7). Cleansing takes place when the believer acknowledges the failure revealed by the light of God (1:9). John then mentioned the specific sin of hating a fellow believer, behavior that is typical of the realm of darkness (2:9). The believer, on the other hand, who loves other Christians "lives in the light, and there is nothing in him to make him stumble" (2:10; see also Rom. 13:8–10).

The challenge to believers reaches its high point in Christ's words to His followers, "You are the light of the world" (Matt. 5:14; see 5:16). (Jesus also said He is the Light of the world; John 8:12.) He came to bring "life and immortality to light through the gospel" (2 Tim. 1:10). Like John the Baptist, believers are to be witnesses to the light, that is, to Christ (John 1:8). But because dangers loom in a dark world, Paul urged Christians to put on "the armor of light" (Rom. 13:12) and to keep themselves apart from false teachers. He asked the pointed question, "What fellowship can light have with darkness?" (2 Cor. 6:14).

—DKC

Walk in the light by allowing the piercing, cleansing brightness
of Christ's holiness to destroy all hidden corners of fear,
jealousy, greed, and selfishness in our hearts.

Logos

THE WORD *logos* IS A TRANSLITERATION of the Greek noun that is normally translated "word" in the sense of concept, idea, or thought resulting in communication (1 Cor. 14:9, 19). As a result, occasionally in the singular (John 6:60; 14:23) but usually in the plural (Matt. 7:24; 10:14; Mark 8:38; Luke 1:29; John 2:22), the Greek noun refers to a statement or even an entire teaching. In this sense it is used to refer to God's message to humankind (Mark 7:13; 1 Cor. 14:36; Phil. 1:14).

Of special significance is the apostle John's message concerning the Word (*logos*) in the opening verses of his Gospel (1:1–5) and his identification of the Word with the Lord Jesus Christ (1:14, 18). This identification is confirmed when John called the Rider on the white horse at the Second Coming from heaven "Faithful and True" and "the Word of God" (Rev. 19:11, 13).

John's affirmations concerning the Word in his prologue to his Gospel are stupendous. He drew an obvious comparison to Genesis 1:1 by opening with the clause, "In the beginning was the Word." This states that at whatever point the beginning is affirmed, at that point the Word already was; thus John was affirming the eternal existence of the Word. This is restated for emphasis in verse 2. "He [literally, 'this one'] was with God in the beginning." The preposition translated "with" followed by the accusative case signifies close face-to-face proximity in fellowship. In other words the Word shares eternality with God the Father. The equality of the Word with God has already been stated in the clause, "the Word was with God" (1:1).

"The Word was God," the final affirmation in verse 1, states that the Word has the character or quality of God. Because the word "God" in the Greek text does not have the definite article with it, Jehovah's Witnesses translate the clause, "the Word was a god." However, in the Greek the subject has the definite article (*ho logos*), and the predicate (*theos*), which does not have the definite article, appears first in the sentence to emphasize the character of the subject. Thus the verse states that the Word (Jesus Christ) possesses the quality of deity. A parallel Greek construction occurs in Jesus' statement to the Samaritan woman at the well, "God is spirit" (John 4:24).

John explained that this eternal Word "became flesh" and lived as a man "for a while" (1:14). His incarnation enabled people to behold "his glory, glory as of an only-born from a father full of grace and truth" (literal translation). Since "God is spirit," "no one has ever yet seen God; the only-born God, the one being in the bosom of the Father, that One has led him forth" (1:18, literal translation). As the eternal Word equal with God the Father, He manifested God's infinite power and wisdom in creation (1:3, 10); and as the incarnate Word He manifested and revealed God's glory, grace, love, and mercy (10:38; 12:45; 14:9–11). Creation and Incarnation are appropriate functions of this One who is the Word, the One who manifests and communicates God and His plan.

Although John is the only biblical author to use *logos* ("Word") to speak of the eternal, coequal, Creator God who became incarnate as Jesus Christ, the truths John stated about Him are presented by others. Paul wrote of Christ's equality with God (Phil. 2:6; Col. 2:9), His eternal existence (1:17), and His work of creation (Rom. 8:3; Gal. 4:4; Phil. 2:7–8). The author of Hebrews also wrote of the deity and eternality of Christ, His involvement in creation (Heb. 1:2–3, 10–11), and His incarnation (1:5–6).

Of significance are the reasons why John used the term *logos* of the eternal, preincarnate Lord Jesus Christ. First, at the close of the apostolic century, when John wrote his Gospel, Greek philosophy was beginning to impact the Christian church. Gnosticism taught that a Logos, sometimes called a demiurge, mediated as a subordinate god between the ultimate Deity and humankind and the material world. Some believed in a long chain of subordinate gods sometimes called *logoi* (plural of *logos*), and Gnosticism taught that by increasing in special knowledge (*gnōsis*) a person could become a lesser god. John wrote of the *logos* as he did to refute this false teaching.

Second, although the Old Testament never wrote of the Word as God Himself, as John did, it did speak of creation being accomplished "by the word [*dābār*] of the Lord" (Ps. 33:6, 9; compare Gen. 1:3, 6, 9, 14, 20, 24, 26, 29; Ps. 148:5; Heb. 11:3). God's word is identified with Him (Ps. 147:15, 18) and given an almost personal character (107:20; Isa. 55:1; Hos. 6:5). In Proverbs, wisdom, which comes from God, is personified (Prov. 1:20–21; 8:1–21, 32–9:6) and is described as eternal and involved with God in the work of creation (3:19–20; 8:22–31). In the intertestamental Jewish Wisdom Literature, wisdom is coupled with the Word of God. Philo of Alexandria, a Jewish philosopher who lived when Jesus Christ did, combined the Jewish and Greek concepts of wisdom and *logos*, presenting *logos* as a subordinate force or person in an emphasis on strict Jewish monotheism. John's teaching concerning the *logos* thus refuted Philo's view.

"Word" is also used of God's message to a person, as in the phrase "the word of the Lord" (for example, Gen. 15:1, 4; Num. 3:16, 51; 1 Sam. 15:10; 1 Kings 6:11; Zech. 1:1). Subsequently the phrase "the word of God" is used for all or any portion of the Scriptures (Luke 3:2; 8:11; Acts 6:2, 7; 2 Cor. 2:17; Eph. 6:17; Heb. 4:12) and for the proclaimed message of God (Acts

12:24; 13:46; 17:13). Sometimes that phrase is reduced simply to "the word" (6:4; 8:4; 14:25; 1 Cor. 15:2; 2 Tim. 4:2). Whether referring to the Lord Jesus or the Scriptures, the Word (*logos*) is the revelation of the nature, message, and plan of God.   —JAW

Thank the Lord that He has revealed Himself to us
through Jesus Christ and the Scriptures.

Lordship

JESUS SPOKE IN A VOICE that only a small group could hear, but what He told them to do would have an impact around the world. Just before His ascension Jesus announced to His disciples that all authority in heaven and on earth had been given to Him (Matt. 28:18). This proclamation was all-encompassing and all-inclusive; He has "all authority in heaven"—over angels and dead believers—and authority over everything "on earth." All is under His domain. By this powerful statement Jesus Christ claimed He is Lord. No one but God could utter those words.

The theme of lordship is not incidental in the New Testament. Though writing from different perspectives, the Gospel writers left no doubt that the One they wrote about is the Lord. Each Gospel ends with an affirmation of the lordship of Christ (Matt. 28:16–20; Mark 13:26; Luke 24:44–48; John 20:28). Paul painted many word pictures of Jesus as Lord, and Colossians 1:15–20 is an appropriate example. The Book of Hebrews begins with an eloquent presentation of Jesus' superiority to angels and of the fact that He is worthy of our worship (Heb. 1:1–13). The Book of Revelation prophesies the return of the Lord to the earth in triumph, with believers giving Him all praise, honor, and glory accorded to Him (Rev. 19:1–8; see also 4:8–11; 5:12–13). He truly is the sovereign Lord.

The lordship of Jesus is directly related to His triumph on the cross (Phil. 2:8–9) and His resurrection from the dead (Acts 2:36; Rom. 1:4). He has always been the Son of God and the title of Lord applies to Him just as it does to each person of the Godhead (Ps. 110:1; Luke 20:42).

Even when Jesus became man through the Incarnation, the angel Gabriel spoke of Him as "Christ the Lord" (Luke 2:11). In the Incarnation Christ did not lose or relinquish any of His attributes (Phil. 2:6), but in keeping with His humanity He didn't use His divine attributes for personal convenience. His death and resurrection were God's means of bringing salvation to the world. Because He is exalted as Lord, someday everyone will acknowledge His lordship (2:9–11).

Implications of His lordship are seen throughout the New Testament. Because He is Lord, and thus sovereign, He is to be worshiped. Jesus rebuked Satan and reminded him that only God is to be worshiped (Luke 4:4–8). When Peter realized that Jesus is Lord, he worshiped Him and felt unworthy in His presence (5:8). The disciples who witnessed His ascension worshiped Him (24:52), and after the Day of Pentecost the believers worshiped Him every day (Acts 2:36–42).

The Lord was the focal point of the preaching by the apostles (10:36; 2 Cor. 4:5). As Lord He is head over the church, the body of Christ, which is subject to Him (Eph. 1:22–23; Col. 1:18; 1 Pet. 3:22). And all prayer is to be directed to the Father through Him (John 14:13–14; 16:23–24; Eph. 2:18; Heb. 7:25). He gives gifts and gifted people to the church (Eph. 4:7–11); as the wisdom of God He provides guidance needed to accomplish His purposes (1 Cor. 1:30–31; 2 Cor. 2:12); and He gives strength to His own (12:8–10; Phil. 4:10–13). Because He is Lord, Christians need not fear death (1 Cor. 15:25–26); they recognize that ministry for the cause of Christ will never be in vain (15:28); they have hope because of the Lord's promise to come back for those who believe in Him (1 Thess. 4:13–18). Since He is Lord, every believer is accountable to Him for the way he relates to others in the body of Christ (Rom. 14:4–12).

To submit to the lordship of Christ should be the desire of every believer. This subjective yielding is not a requirement for salvation, but results from the sanctifying work of the Holy Spirit in the life of the believer (Rom. 6:8–14; 12:1–2; Eph. 4:1–5; 5:20–32; Phil. 3:10–16; Col. 3:1–10). Some of the practical outworkings of our submission to Christ are noted in 1 Peter 2:11–3:7.   **—WGJ**

Worship the Lord regularly and rejoice in the truth that Jesus is Lord over everything and that someday this will be recognized by everyone.

Lord's Supper

ALTHOUGH THIS PHRASE is used only once in the New Testament (1 Cor. 11:20), the establishing of the Lord's Supper by the Lord Jesus is described in the three Synoptic Gospels (Matt. 26:26–29; Mark 14:22–25; Luke 22:19–20). The apostolic church referred to it as the practice of "the breaking of bread" (Acts. 2:42, 46; 20:7), a title some groups still use for the observance.

More liturgical groups call the Lord's Supper the Eucharist, from the fact that the Lord Jesus "gave thanks" (*eucharistēsas*) before breaking the bread (Matt. 26:26; Mark 14:22; Luke 22:19; see 1 Cor. 11:24) and also most likely before passing the cup of wine (Matt. 26:27; Mark 14:23). Luke and Paul did not specifically mention the Lord's giving thanks before the cup, but they implied it in the phrase "in the same way" (Luke 22:20; 1 Cor. 11:25).

In the phrase "the Lord's Supper" the emphasis is on the word "Lord," because it is the supper established by the Lord Jesus and observed at His direction. Also it concerns Him, as believers remember His finished redemptive sacrifice which provides salvation and eternal life. Participating in the Lord's Supper enhances spiritual fellowship with the ascended Lord and anticipates His imminent return to gather them to Himself.

Because the apostolic "believers were together and had everything in common" (Acts. 2:44; see also 4:32; 6:1–4), they ate their meals together (2:46). This raises the question whether "breaking of bread" simply refers to sharing common meals or to the observance of the Lord's Supper. Apparently both were involved, because Paul's discussion of the procedure is found in the context of rebuking abuses in Corinth at the love feast, which was the common meal (1 Cor. 11:17–22, 27–34).

Apparently at first believers observed the Lord's Supper every day (Acts 2:46). How long this continued is not known, but apparently it was soon reduced to once a week, for when Paul was at Troas (20:6) on his way to Jerusalem (20:16, 22), the Supper was observed "on the first day of the week" (20:7). While some groups observe the Lord's Supper weekly, most churches observe it once a month and on some special occasions. The Lord did not specify the frequency; He simply said, as communicated to Paul, "For whenever you eat this bread and drink this cup" (1 Cor. 11:26; see also 11:25).

The apostolic church also apparently observed the Lord's Supper in the evening (Acts. 20:7). This has been continued by some church groups, but most groups conduct the Lord's Supper as a part of the Sunday morning worship service. Evening observance continued the Lord Jesus' establishment of the ceremony in conjunction with the Jewish Passover meal in the evening (Matt. 26:17–30; Mark 14:12–26; Luke 22:7–20). Although John made no reference to the establishment of the Lord's Supper, he did refer to the Passover and the evening meal (John 13:1–2).

The relationship of the Lord's Supper to the Passover is puzzling but significant. From the Synoptic accounts Jesus established the ceremony in conjunction with the Passover meal (Matt. 26:19–20; Mark 14:16–17; Luke 22:13–14); yet it hardly seems likely that the Jewish leaders would have arrested Jesus and tried Him on Passover night. Furthermore Christian tradition teaches that Jesus was crucified on Passover day as God's "Passover Lamb" (1 Cor. 5:7).

Some scholars solve the puzzle by saying that the evening meal Jesus ate with His apostles was not the Passover meal, but it was simply a meal at that season. Another solution is that two Passovers were observed at that time, the first by Galileans, the Qumran community, and other groups, and the second by the priestly Jerusalem establishment. Jesus and His apostles ate the earlier Passover, and He was taken from Caiaphas to Pilate by the Jewish leaders and crucified during the day of the second Passover that began that Friday evening (John 18:28).

A third and preferable solution is that the preparations for the Passover meal took place on Nisan 14 (Thursday), but the Passover meal was eaten by Jesus and His disciples after sundown. Thus they actually ate the meal on Nisan 15. That same day (according to Jewish reckoning) Jesus was arrested, condemned, and crucified on the Passover day (which corresponds with our Friday). He was indeed God's Passover Lamb, since His crucifixion occurred before sundown, the start of Nisan 16. This Passover day on which Jesus was crucified also marked the preparation for the Feast of Unleavened Bread, which lasted seven days and was sometimes called Passover Week.

On the basis of Jesus' statement concerning the bread, "This is my body" (1 Cor. 11:24) and His statement concerning the cup of wine, "This cup is the new covenant in my blood" (11:25), some groups believe that the elements are transformed into Christ's body and blood by the minister's words. Others believe that Christ becomes present with the elements. Still others hold that He is spiritually present. Undoubtedly believers are spiritually blessed and enriched by observing the Lord's Supper, for Jesus spoke of its observance as a memorial of Him, saying, "do this in remembrance of me" (Luke 22:19; see also 1 Cor. 11:24–25). Since Jesus was holding the unleavened bread and breaking it in His hands and later held the cup of wine, they must be only symbols of His body and blood.

As a memorial observance, the Lord's Supper gives the believers a threefold perspective. First, it looks to the past, reminding Christians of the Lord's redemptive sacrifice on the cross. Second, it looks to the present and the Christians' continuing fellowship with Christ as their Advocate and Great High Priest. Third, it looks to the future in anticipation of the imminent return of Christ.

Although John did not discuss the establishment of the Lord's Supper in his record of Jesus' Passover meal with His disciples (John 13:1–18:1), he did record Jesus' presentation of Himself to the Jews as "the bread of life" (6:35, 48) whose body had to be eaten and his blood drunk to receive and enjoy eternal life (6:50–59). John also recorded Jesus' claims to be the source of "living water" (4:10, 7:37–38) received by faith.

The Lord's Supper is a supreme act of worship. It is to be participated in only after serious self-examination (1 Cor. 11:28), because whoever partakes "in an unworthy manner will be guilty of sinning against the body and blood of the Lord" (11:27). That is what the Corinthian Christians were doing in their love feast that preceded the Lord's Supper (11:17–22, 29–34), thereby negating the purpose and value of the observance. The Lord's Supper is a communion with other believers as well as with the Lord Himself.　　　　—JAW

When you partake of the Lord's Supper,
examine your life and be sure you are in fellowship with Christ.

Love

LOVE HAS BEEN DEFINED as "the greatest thing in the world" (Henry Drummond); "the grandest theme of Scripture"; and as an "exceedingly ambiguous term." The Bible says much about love, both as an attribute of God and as a Christian virtue.

In the Old Testament *'āhēb,* the most common word for "love," is used of the relationship between a father and a son (Gen. 22:2) and a master and a slave (Exod. 21:5). It is also used of love for a neighbor (Lev. 19:18), love for a stranger (Deut. 10:19), love for God, and of God's love for humankind. In particular *'āhēb* is used to explain God's choice of Israel and His commitment to them as a people (Deut. 4:37–38; 7:7–8). The prophets, too, associated God's love with major events of Israel's history (Hos. 11:1; Mal. 1:2–3). Especially strong are God's words to Israel, "I have loved you with an everlasting love; I have drawn you with loving-kindness" (Jer. 31:3). Israel's future too will be blessed with God's love (Isa. 43:1–7; Hos. 14:4).

A second significant Hebrew word for love is *ḥesed,* rendered "loving-kindness" or "steadfast love." This unshakable, steadfast love stood in contrast to the impulsive, capricious moods and actions of heathen deities. God's love as *ḥesed* is closely linked with His covenants. The Sinai Covenant is referred to as a "covenant of love" (Deut. 7:9, 12), and His covenant promises to David are based on love: "I will maintain my love to him forever, and my covenant with him will never fail" (Ps. 89:28). God's unchanging love promises the redeemed deliverance from enemies (6:4; 17:7), safekeeping (21:7; 32:10), forgiveness (25:7; 51:1; Mic. 7:20), answers to prayer (Ps. 66:20), redemption (130:7), and the future establishment of David's throne and kingdom (Isa. 16:5; 55:3).

For all this, God expected a response of wholehearted love and obedience. He called Israel to "love the LORD your God with all your heart and with all your soul and with all your strength" (Deut. 6:5). Such love would be demonstrated by obedience: "These commandments that I give you today are to be upon your hearts" (6:6). In addition to loving God, the people of Israel were also to love their neighbors (Lev. 19:18).

Love, both divine and human, receives its fullest exposition in the New Testament. Of the three common Greek words for love, only two are found in the New Testament. The word not used, though it was common in Greek literature, is *erōs*, sexual love. Another word for love is *phileō* (verb form), meaning a spontaneous natural affection expressed between relatives and friends. The most frequent word is the noun *agapē*, a term that describes believers' love for one another (John 13:35) but that more often conveys the depth of God's love for humans (Rom. 5:8).

The apostle John affirmed that God's love is the foundation of all that happened to bring about salvation. "For God so loved the world that he gave his one and only Son, that whoever believes in him shall not perish but have eternal life" (John 3:16; see also 16:27; 17:23). In John's first epistle he declared that "God is love" (1 John 4:16), and that because God loved us first we in turn should love Him and fellow believers (4:19–21).

In Romans 5:6–8 the apostle Paul wrote what has been called "the finest exposition of God's love found anywhere in the Bible." He explained that what people would scarcely do for the good, God has done for the vile and despicable! Christ, indeed, died for the *ungodly* who are God's *enemies!* Such a demonstration, wrote Paul, demands a response on the part of the believer: "Live a life of love, just as Christ loved us and gave himself up for us as a fragrant offering and sacrifice to God" (Eph. 5:2). The apostle also exhorted, "Serve one another in love. The entire law is summed up in a single command: 'Love your neighbor as yourself'" (Gal. 5:13–14). Paul quoted Leviticus 19:18 and then argued that Christian love is the "fulfillment" or the "carrying out" of the Law. He developed this point in Romans 13:8–10.

Jesus, too, had much to say about love. As He prepared to leave the world, He said to His disciples, "A new command I give you: Love one another. As I have loved you, so you must love one another" (John 13:34). This command was new because it described a special love for other believers based on Jesus' sacrificial love. This love for each other would help the disciples survive in the hostile world they would soon face. Earlier in His earthly ministry Jesus emphasized that His followers were to love even their enemies (Matt. 5:44–48).

The dimensions of God's love for the human race and the demands of such love on the believer seem almost impossible to comprehend. Scripture is clear that the self-sacrificing love of God sent Christ to die for sinners, and that believers are called on to manifest the same love to each other and to unbelievers. Such love, according to Paul, is the "fruit of the Spirit" (Gal. 5:22), something not produced by human effort but by the Holy Spirit working through a Christian who is in vital union with Christ (John 15:1–8).   —DKC

Strive to love other believers as Jesus commanded.

Mm

Marriage

GOD ESTABLISHED MARRIAGE when He formed Eve out of the rib taken from Adam to be a "suitable helper" for him and brought her to him (Gen. 2:20–22). As Scripture states, "For this reason a man will leave his father and mother and be united to his wife, and they will become one flesh" (2:24). This first union created by God was monogamous, and although polygamy was recognized in Scripture (Deut. 21:15–17), monogamy has always been the ideal. Similarly the dissolution of a marriage by divorce was permitted (Deut. 24:1–4), but the ideal was a lifelong union dissolved only by the death of one of the partners.

Lamech, the fifth generation in the line of Cain, was the first to marry more than one wife (Gen. 4:19). A polygamous marriage always created tension in the family, as illustrated by Jacob's experience with Leah and Rachel and Elkanah's experience with Hannah and Peninnah. With several wives David had discord in his family, and Solomon's many wives led him away from the Lord to serve other gods (1 Kings 11:4–6, 9–10). On the other hand Noah, Isaac, and Joseph each had only one wife, and the Old Testament depicts domestic harmony together with monogamy (Ps. 128:1–4; Prov. 31:10–31).

In the Old Testament, endorsement of monogamy rests on God's relationship to Israel, which is likened to that of a husband to his wife (Isa. 54:5–8; Jer. 3:14; Hos. 2:19–20). Because of their forsaking the true God for other gods, both the Northern Kingdom (Israel) and the Southern Kingdom (Judah) were judged by God as adulterous (Isa. 57:3; Jer. 3:6–10; 5:7; 13:24–27; 23:10, 13–14; Ezek. 6:9; 16:32–43). God gave His people Israel a "certificate of divorce" (Isa. 50:1) and "sent her away because of all her adulteries" (Jer. 3:8).

Although God has judged His people Israel for her spiritual adulteries, He has not abandoned her. He directed the prophet Hosea to provide in his family life an object lesson of God's dealings with Israel. Hosea was directed to "take to yourself an adulterous wife" (Hos. 1:2) to illustrate that "the land is guilty of the vilest adultery in departing from the LORD." Hosea married Gomer (1:3), who bore three children, each of whom was given a symbolic name. After her adulterous relationships God directed the prophet to "go, show your love to your wife again, though she is loved by another and is an adulteress. Love her as the LORD loves the Israelites, though they turn to other gods" (3:1). Hosea bought her back to be his wife and directed her not to live with any man (3:3). Similarly after separation and judgment God will restore Israel as His people (2:14–16, 19–20, 23).

Jesus' teachings on marriage, as recorded in the Gospels, are most important. His approval of marriage and the joyous festivities accompanying it are demonstrated by His presence at the wedding at Cana and His performance of His first miracle (changing water into wine to save the bridegroom from embarrassment; John 2:1–11).

When questioned by the Pharisees about the validity of divorce (Matt. 19:3; Mark 10:2), Jesus endorsed monogamous, lifelong marriage by quoting part of Genesis 1:27 and 2:24 and then saying, "So they are no longer two, but one. Therefore what God has joined together, let man not separate" (Matt. 19:6; see Mark 10:8). When the Pharisees then asked Jesus why Moses allowed for divorce (Matt. 19:7; Mark 10:3–4; Deut. 24:1–4), He replied that it was "because your hearts were hard. But it was not this way from the beginning" (Matt. 19:8; Mark 10:5). Jesus then identified "marital unfaithfulness" as the only valid basis for divorce (Matt. 19:9; 5:32).

The statement, "Marriage should be honored by all, and the marriage bed kept pure" (Heb. 13:4), summarizes the New Testament teaching on marriage. Paul endorsed monogamous, lifelong marriage, demanding it of men who serve as elders (1 Tim. 3:2; Titus 1:6) and deacons (1 Tim. 3:12). Although Paul was unmarried and desired others to be as he was (1 Cor. 7:7–8; 9:5), devoted only to the Lord (7:32, 34), he recognized the necessity and validity of marriage (7:2–6). Much of his teaching to the Corinthians concerning marriage was in light of the "present crisis" (7:26) in the church and because "the time is short" (7:29).

Paul deplored divorce (7:10–11) but directed that "if an unbeliever leaves, let him do so. A believing man or woman is not bound in such circumstances" (7:15). He did not approve of a believer marrying an unbeliever (2 Cor. 6:14–15), but a believing partner should not divorce an unbeliever who is willing to live with the believer (1 Cor. 7:12–13). The marriage is sanctified by the believing partner (7:14), and the unbeliever might be saved (7:16; 1 Pet. 3:1). As the gospel of Christ was proclaimed in the first century, many men and women believed whose marriage partners remained unbelievers for a shorter or longer time.

Paul presented the relationship of husband and wife as a portrait of the relationship between the Lord Jesus Christ and His church (Eph. 5:22–33). He described the husband "as the head of the wife as Christ is the head of the church" (5:23; see also 1 Cor. 11:3; Eph. 1:22; 4:15; Col. 1:18; 2:19), and he called on wives to "submit to your husbands as to the Lord" (Eph. 5:22; see also 5:24, 33; Titus 2:5; 1 Pet. 3:1, 5–6). Conversely, he called on husbands to "love your wives, just as Christ loved the church" (Eph. 5:25) and sacrificed Himself for her. He also said husbands are to "love their wives as their own bodies" (5:28) and to "love his wife as he loves himself" (5:33; see 1 Pet. 3:7). Husbands who fulfill these admonitions even to a small degree will find that their wives will lovingly fulfill their own roles. As Paul said concerning the whole subject, "This is a profound mystery—but I am talking about Christ and the church" (Eph. 5:32).   **—JAW**

Whether married or not, every believer is responsible before God
to promote the sanctity of marriage.

Mediator

JOB EXPRESSED HUMANKIND'S NEED for a mediator with God when he said, "If only there were someone to arbitrate between us, to lay his hand upon us both" (Job 9:33), that is, on God and Job. A mediator stands between two estranged individuals or groups to achieve a mutually agreed-on settlement and reconciliation.

In human affairs a mediator can be proposed by either person or group involved and then agreed to by both. In our relation to God, however, only God Himself can provide a mediator. And He has done so. As Paul proclaimed, "For there is one God and one mediator between God and men, the man Christ Jesus, who gave himself as a ransom for all men" (1 Tim. 2:5–6).

The need for a mediator between God and humans was created by the entrance of sin into human experience, when Adam and Eve disobeyed God and ate the fruit of the tree of the knowledge of good and evil (Gen. 2:17; 3:6–7). Before that time they apparently enjoyed fellowship with God, but after that "they hid from the LORD God" when they heard Him "walking in the garden" (3:8). At first God simply spoke to His estranged creatures (3:9, 11, 13, 16–17; 4:5, 9–10, 15; 6:13–21; 7:1–4; 8:15–17; 9:1–16; 12:1–3; 13:14–17), but later He used visions (15:1), angels (19:1), and many chosen men (for example, Moses, Exod. 3:7–10) as mediators to communicate His will, execute His program, and reconcile people to Himself.

Mediators can minister between God and individuals in a number of ways. The first and most frequent way is as recipients and communicators of God's messages. In Old Testament times this ministry was performed first by the Angel of the Lord (Gen. 16:7–14; Exod. 3:2–6; Num. 22:22–35; Judg. 6:11–24), who was a visible appearance of the preincarnate Jesus Christ. Then it was performed by chosen men such as Moses (Exod. 19:3–9) and the prophets (1 Sam. 3:11–21; Ezek. 2:1–10). Jesus served as a Mediator in this sense, for He was recognized as a prophet by the people (Matt. 21:11; John 9:17) and He Himself claimed to be a Prophet (Matt. 13:57; Luke 13:33).

While God is the sovereign Creator and Ruler of the universe, He exercises authority among men on earth, particularly among His chosen people Israel through mediators. This is demonstrated by Moses (Exod. 18:13–16), Joshua (Num. 27:15–23; Deut. 34:9; Josh. 1), the judges (Judg. 2:16, 18), and Israel's kings (1 Sam. 9:16–17; 10:1; 16:12–13; 1 Kings 11:29–39). In a sense this is true of all "governing authorities" (Rom. 13:1–7; Titus 3:1; 1 Pet. 2:13–17). Jesus Christ is the supreme mediatorial Ruler. He is the One to whom "the Lord God will give him the throne of his father David, and he will reign over the house of Jacob forever; his kingdom will never end" (Luke 1:32–33).

Since sin in human experience has broken fellowship with God and created the need for mediators, God has created a third category of mediators to minister on behalf of people before Him. In patriarchal times this priestly ministry of offering sacrifices and prayers was performed by fathers for their families (Gen. 8:20; Job 1:5) or by other persons on behalf of others (Gen. 14:18–20; Job 42:7–9; Heb. 7:1–3).

God designed Moses' brother, Aaron, his descendants, and the tribe of Levi to serve as priests for Israel. Once again our Lord Jesus is the supreme priestly Mediator "in the order of Melchizedek" (Ps. 110:4; Heb. 5:5–10; 6:19–20; 7: 15–17, 20–22, 24–8:2). Jesus offered Himself as the final redemptive sacrifice for sin (Eph. 5:2; Heb. 7:27; 9:14; 10:5–7, 10, 14), and He now ministers at the right hand of God as the believers' "Advocate" (1 John 2:1, NASB) and our High Priest, who "always lives to intercede" for us (Heb. 7:25; see also Rom. 8:34; Heb. 9:24, John 17).

Since Christians are identified with Christ by faith, we have been made "a holy priesthood" (1 Pet. 2:5) and "a royal priesthood" (2:9). Christ has made believers "a kingdom and priests to serve his God and Father" (Rev. 1:6; see also 5:10; 20:6). Christians have the unique privilege to "approach the throne of grace with confidence, so that we may receive mercy and find grace to help us in our time of need" (Heb. 4:16). We can intercede for each other, and we have "the priestly duty of proclaiming the gospel of God" (Rom. 15:16). —JAW

As a Christian, you have an opportunity to be a mediator
for others with God and a mediator with others.

Meditation

BEFORE THE CHILDREN OF ISRAEL entered and possessed the land promised to them, Joshua received a commission from God. The Lord told Joshua He would be with him and asked for his complete obedience to keep the Law given to Moses. The Lord also revealed to Joshua how he and the people of Israel could be successful. Joshua was to keep the "Book of the Law" at the center of his life. He was to meditate on it day and night and do all it required of him (Josh. 1:7–8). The word *meditate* means "to ponder or reflect." Several Hebrew words in the Old Testament convey this concept. The word used in this passage implies that the book was to be pondered in the heart or rehearsed in one's thoughts. For Joshua, it was more than meditating on the Law; it was contemplating God Himself and thinking about His power and greatness.

The importance of meditation for the Israelites is a recurring theme in the Book of Psalms. The very first psalm draws a sharp contrast between the righteous and the wicked. The righteous person is marked by meditation on God's Word day and night, that is, regularly (Ps. 1:2). Often this meditation came when the godly person faced difficult situations. David was in distress, and he found relief as he pondered the goodness of God. He spoke of peace and gladness that flooded his soul in the night (4:4–8). On another occasion, when David was in the house of the Lord, he struggled because of opposition from his enemies. He found strength as he meditated on the beauty of the Lord (27:4, NASB). Though David was facing immediate danger, he felt it necessary to take time to meet with the Lord in the place of worship and to reflect on the One who was his light and salvation. Even in isolated places like the Judean desert David found that meditating on God's love and greatness sustained him. Though he suffered physically, he said he meditated on the Lord at night (63:6, NASB).

In Psalm 77 the psalmist Asaph said he meditated on the power of God as he rehearsed the events associated with God's delivering the Israelites out of Egypt. As he thought about all the Lord's mighty works, he found strength for his present situation (77:11–15).

Central to Israel's worship was meditation on the Word of God. Psalm 119 makes numerous references to the place of Scriptures in the lives of God's people. Purity of life results from meditating on His precepts and considering His ways (Ps. 119:15). The antidote to sorrow is to meditate on the wonders of God revealed in His precepts (119:27–28), and pondering God's truth provides hope when taunted by the enemy (119:42–48). When the enemy speaks lies against them, believers are sustained by reflecting on the truth of God (119:78). In the darkest night they find hope by meditating on God's promises (119:148).

While the New Testament says little about meditation, it was presumably practiced by Jesus and His followers, much as believers in the Old Testament meditated on God's Word and reflected on His ways.

—WGJ

Take time each day to ponder the goodness and
greatness of God as revealed in the Scriptures.

Mercy

GOD'S MERCY IS HIS COMPASSION expressed in the face of dire human need. Moses, while predicting Israel's future failures and punishments, declared, "The LORD your God is a merciful God; he will not abandon or destroy you or forget the covenant with your forefathers" (Deut. 4:31). Micah described the Lord as a God of compassion and as One who "delight[s] to show mercy" (Mic. 7:18–19).

Mercy is a many-sided concept, as illustrated by the variety of Hebrew and Greek words employed in Scripture to define and describe it. The Old Testament reveals God's mercy in rich and different ways in His dealings with Israel. God is portrayed as a Father who has compassion on His children (Ps. 103:13), even though they are sometimes wayward and rebellious (Hos. 11; Jer. 31:20). Hosea described Israel as an unfaithful and adulterous wife to whom God shows compassion and mercy (Hos. 1–3; see also Isa. 54:4–8). Isaiah portrayed God as a mother who has compassion on the child at her breast (49:15). During a time of revival for the restored remnant in Nehemiah's time, the Levites led the congregation in a moving prayer of confession. In reviewing the history of Israel from the call of Abraham to the Babylonian exile, Nehemiah showed how God responded to the frequent sins of the people with His mercy and forgiveness (Neh. 9:5–31). Israel often petitioned the Lord for mercy and forgiveness in times of need (Pss. 6, 40, 51, 69, 79, 130, 143). The Lord responded to all such petitions by affirming, "I will have mercy on whom I will have mercy, and I will have compassion on whom I will have compassion" (Exod. 33:19).

In His mercy Jesus responded to various human needs. Blind men pleaded for sight (Matt. 9:27; 20:30–31; Mark 10:46–48; Luke 18:35–39). A Canaanite woman implored Jesus to deliver her daughter from demons (Matt. 15:22). A father sought help for a demon-possessed son (17:15); and ten lepers asked for healing (Luke 17:12–13).

The Gospels show that mercy is not only something God bestows on those with needs; it is also a quality God expects His people to display. Jesus thus called the merciful "blessed" (Matt. 5:7); and He exhorted His disciples, "Be merciful, just as your Father is merciful" (Luke 6:36). He charged that the religious leaders "neglected the more important matters of the law—justice, mercy and faithfulness" (Matt. 23:23). By contrast, the good Samaritan showed mercy to a man who was beaten and robbed (Luke 10:36–37). In teaching the need for showing mercy to others, the Lord was confirming the commands of the Old Testament to be merciful, especially to the poor, the needy, widows, and orphans (Prov. 14:21, 31; 19:17, NKJV; Mic. 6:8).

In the Epistles the most typical use of mercy is found in God's provision of salvation for helpless sinners. Thus God "who is rich in mercy, made us alive with Christ even when we were dead in transgressions" (Eph. 2:4–5). "In His great mercy he has given us new birth into a living hope" (1 Pet. 1:3). "He saved us, not because of righteous things we had done, but because of his mercy" (Titus 3:5). Paul affirmed that God's mercy is sovereignly bestowed (Rom. 9:15–16, 18, 23) and reaches out to the disobedient (11:32). Divine mercy is the basis of special ministries (2 Cor. 4:1; 1 Tim. 1:16). Of great encouragement also to believers is the fact that we are exhorted to "approach the throne of grace with confidence, so that we may receive mercy and find grace to help us in our time of need" (Heb. 4:16).

Contemplation of God's abundant mercies bestowed on people with deep needs leads to Paul's urgent plea to believers, "I urge you, brothers, in view of God's mercy, to offer your bodies as living sacrifices, holy and pleasing to God—which is your spiritual act of worship" (Rom. 12:1).

—DKC

As you are conscious of God's mercy to you,
delight in showing mercy to others.

Messiah

THE WORD *messiah* comes from the Hebrew *māšîaḥ*, which means "anointed one." The related verb *māšaḥ* means "to anoint with oil." Each priest was consecrated to God by anointing with oil (Exod. 29:7), so that he was called "the anointed priest" (Lev. 4:3, 5, 16). Kings, too, were called the Lord's "anointed" (1 Sam. 2:10, 35; Pss. 20:6; 28:8), including Saul (1 Sam. 12:3, 5; 26:9, 11, 23; 2 Sam. 1:14, 16), David (19:21; Pss. 2:2; 18:50), and even Cyrus, king of Persia (Isa. 45:1). Even prophets were God's "anointed ones" (1 Chron. 16:22; Ps. 105:15). While the "Anointed

One" in Psalm 2:2 is a king of Judah, the verse refers ultimately to Jesus Christ, as Peter and John noted in Acts 4:26.

Twice Daniel spoke of "the Anointed One," that is, the Messiah, Jesus Christ (Dan. 9:25–26). *Christ* comes from *christos,* the Greek equivalent of the Hebrew for *Messiah.* When Andrew told his brother Peter about Jesus, he said, "We have found the Messiah" (John 1:41). The Samaritan woman told Jesus that she knew that the Messiah would come (4:25). Obviously people were anticipating the Messiah, whose coming had been predicted in the Old Testament.

As Peter stated in his sermon in Jerusalem on the Day of Pentecost, God the Father made Jesus "both Lord and Christ" (Acts 2:36), that is, both the Sovereign and the Messiah. Later Peter said again that God had sent Jesus as Israel's Messiah (3:20). Other apostles too proclaimed "the good news that Jesus is the Christ" (5:42). Soon after his conversion Saul presented arguments to the Jews to demonstrate that Jesus was the Messiah whom the people were anticipating. Saul even "baffled" the Jews by his reasoning "that Jesus is the Christ" (9:22). Also in Thessalonica and Corinth, Paul reasoned with Jews that Jesus is the Messiah (17:3; 18:5). Though a number of Jews believed, many others could not accept the idea that the Messiah would die an ignominious death by crucifixion. Most of the Jews who heard Jesus teach had also refused to receive Him as their Messiah and so they rejected Him. He Himself said that He must "be rejected by this generation" (Luke 17:25), and the apostle John wrote that "his own did not receive him" (John 1:11). But at His second coming the nation Israel will turn to the Lord and will welcome Jesus as their Messiah. He will reign over the world from Jerusalem as the King of kings and Lord of lords and also as Israel's Messiah.　　—JFW

Be faithful in sharing with others the good news that
Jesus is God's Anointed One and the only way of eternal salvation.

Millennium

THE WORD *Millennium* comes from a Latin word meaning "one thousand years." Six times Revelation 20:2–7 refers to the future reign of Christ on earth as being one thousand years in length.

After an angel binds and imprisons Satan (20:1–3), believers who will be martyred in the Tribulation will be resurrected (20:4–6) to reign with Christ for one thousand years. Clearly the thousand years will follow the Second Coming. At the end of the Millennium Satan will be loosed and will organize a rebellion against Christ, which will result in destruction of the rebels (20:9). Satan will then be cast into the lake of fire (20:10), the present earth will be destroyed, and new heavens and a new earth will be created (2 Pet. 3:10–13; Rev. 21–22).

A variety of opinions have arisen concerning these thousand years. Premillenarians believe that Christ will reign on the earth for a literal thousand years, in fulfillment of promises in the Old Testament that Christ will reign on David's throne in Jerusalem. Amillenarians deny a future reign of Christ on this earth and interpret the thousand years symbolically as referring to a long, indefinite period of time. Most amillenarians say the thousand years are being fulfilled in the spiritual kingdom of Christ in the present age, whereas others say they refer to the believers' present condition in heaven. Still others suggest that the thousand years speak of the new heavens and the new earth. The postmillennial idea that Christ will come after Christianity triumphs around the world (in a literal thousand years or a figurative long period of time) is held by only a few today. Contemporary liberals do not take these prophecies seriously and are almost always amillennial.

Though the interpretation of the Millennium has particular application to Revelation 20, it affects major sections of the Old Testament that speak of a kingdom on earth (Ps. 72) and of Israel's possession of her land (Gen. 12:7; 15:18–21; Ezek. 39:25–29; 47:13–23). Those who do not believe a future Millennium is in God's plan usually disregard these passages or treat them nonliterally.

In Christ's millennial reign He will rule over Israel, who will be restored to her land and for the first time will possess all the land God promised in the Abrahamic Covenant (Gen. 15:18–21). He will fulfill all aspects, both physical and spiritual, of the New Covenant with Israel (Jer. 31:31–34; Ezek. 36:24–38), and He will fulfill the Davidic Covenant as He rules from David's throne in Jerusalem (2 Sam. 7:12–16; Ps. 89:3–4, 28–29). Ruling over the entire world, He will bring universal peace. He will rule with supreme justice (Ps. 2:9; Isa. 11:3–5; 32:1). Satan will be bound "to keep him from deceiving the nations" (Rev. 20:3). The land will be unusually productive (Isa. 27:6; 35:1–7), and people will live long lives (65:20).

Believers look forward to that remarkable time, for they will reign with Christ as His coregents (2 Tim. 2:12; Rev. 3:21; 20:4), judging the world (1 Cor. 6:2). —JFW

Think about all God has planned for His children
when we will reign with Christ for one thousand years.

Mind

INDIVIDUALS HAVE THE INNATE CAPACITY to think, meditate, plan, desire, and the ability to express these functions in various ways. All these things relate to the innermost part of a human being. Even though there is no specific Hebrew word for "mind," functions that relate to the mind are discussed in the Old Testament. At least sixty-six times the New International Version uses the word "mind" to describe these actions. In passages where an activity of the mind is ascribed to God, one must realize that this is to accommodate human understanding. God works according to His sovereign plan, and no circumstance or human action can alter His purposes (1 Sam. 15:29; Ps. 110:4).

Limited references are made to the mind in the teachings of Jesus. The Lord did explain that the mind is a vital component of one's inner being. When asked about the greatest of the commandments, Jesus expanded on Deuteromony 6:5, which speaks of the love of one's heart, affirming that a person is to love the Lord with all his or her heart, soul, and mind (Matt. 22:37; Mark 12:30; Luke 10:27). This points to the fact that the mind, the intellectual part of a person, is closely associated with the actions of the heart and soul.

On another occasion Jesus explained the importance of understanding and perceiving truth. He rebuked Peter for not understanding about His death and resurrection (Matt. 16:23). Peter's mind was being influenced by the thinking of those who did not believe in Christ. A major problem with the disciples was their inability to comprehend Jesus' teachings (16:8–11). After His resurrection Jesus opened the minds of the disciples so they could understand the Scriptures more adequately (Luke 24:25). Apart from supernatural enlightenment people are not able to discern the things of God (1 Cor. 2:14).

Of supreme importance is the fact that the mind of Christ is the source and pattern for all believers. It is a mind in perfect harmony and submission to the Father, which was expressed in His incarnation and subsequent sacrificial death (Phil. 2:5). It is a mark of maturity when Christians possess the mind and attitude of Christ (3:15; 1 Cor. 2:16).

The apostle Paul used a variety of terms to describe the function of the mind. It is important to understand that when the mind or any aspect of the immaterial part of man is examined, it ultimately must be viewed in relation to the whole person.

The minds of unregenerate people, Paul noted, are hostile to God. Their minds are focused on human desires and stand in stark contrast to the mind controlled by the Spirit of God (Rom. 8:5–7). This kind of mind results in futility, separation from God, lack of restraint, and insensitivity to things that are pure and wholesome (Eph. 4:14–19). People who oppose the truth have depraved minds (Rom. 1:28; 2 Tim. 3:8). Those whose minds were resistant to the grace of God were called enemies of the cross of Christ and are headed for destruction (Phil. 3:18; Col. 1:21).

In contrast to the unregenerate mind, the minds of believers are focused on the desires of the Spirit (Rom. 8:6). Because the Spirit controls the mind, the Christian is able to discern all things and has the mind of Christ (1 Cor. 2:15–16). The mind of believers is at the center of spiritual activity and is renewed as individuals give themselves wholeheartedly to the Holy Spirit (Rom. 12:2; Eph. 4:22–23). As Christians put off the things related to the former way of life and live as children of light, they will comprehend the mind of the Lord and do the will of God (Eph. 5:8–17). Through prayer the peace of God guards the mind and the heart of believers and prevents anxiety (Phil. 4:6–7). When a believer's mind is under the control of the Holy Spirit and sensitive to the mind of Christ, he or she brings glory to God.

James encouraged believers to be single-minded and to trust the Lord in the midst of difficult circumstances, since a double-minded person is unstable and unworthy of God's assistance (James 1:5–8; 4:8). Writing to believers who were facing pressure to conform to evil desires, Peter said they needed their minds prepared for holy living (1 Pet. 1:13). Peter wrote of Christ as One who suffered in the flesh and resisted Satan's temptations. He exhorted his readers, "Arm yourselves also with the same attitude" (4:1). The word "attitude" is *ennoia,* one of several words rendered "mind," which conveys the idea of "thought." Having Jesus' attitude toward suffering enables believers to reject evil desires and to do God's will (4:2). The apostle John reminded believers that Christ has given them insight *(dianoia)* to know the true God (1 John 5:20).

—WGJ

Guard your mind and heart from the ever-present influences of the world, and center your attention on the Lord and the promises of His Word.

Ministry

SERVING GOD HAS ALWAYS BEEN the privilege and responsibility of human beings. Before sin came on the earth, Adam served God by working the ground (Gen. 2:15). In this verse the Hebrew word for "work" is *'ābad,* the same word translated "worship" in Exodus 3:12. Ministry in the Old Testament was service performed in obedience to God, and when the tabernacle and the temple were erected ministry was primarily the responsibility of the priests and Levites. The prophets spoke for God, and in that sense they served the Lord, though the term *ministry* was not normally used to explain their calling.

A much broader concept of ministry is found in the New Testament since all Christians are priests, and are to worship and serve the Lord (1 Pet. 2:5, 9; Rev. 1:6). When Christ died at Calvary, a new priesthood came into being, and the Levitical priesthood instituted by Moses was set aside. Jesus established a new and permanent priesthood (Heb. 7:24). Through the finished work of Christ's sacrifice, believers have obtained eternal redemption, and this enables them to serve the Lord (10:11–14).

Ministry takes on new dimensions under the priesthood and lordship of Christ. Jesus revealed to His disciples that the way of greatness was to be a servant (Mark 10:45). It was on that occasion that Jesus said His purpose in coming to the earth was to serve *(diakoneō).* Peter, who followed Jesus closely, described His ministry as "doing good" (Acts 10:38). Peter learned firsthand about the servant ministry of Jesus when He washed his feet and exhorted him to serve others (John 13:14–17; see also 1 Pet. 5:5). The character of ministry was suggested by Jesus in one of His last encounters with the apostle when He requested Peter to feed and care for His sheep (John 21:15–17). Effective ministry, modeled by Jesus, concerns quality as well as action and stems from a pure and humble heart (Ps. 101:6).

Ministry is a recurring theme in the Epistles. Paul's personal experience of serving the Lord in ministry began during the year he spent with Barnabas in Antioch (Acts 11:25–26). In the process of ministering to the church, Paul and Barnabas were deployed for an itinerant ministry (13:2–3). Though he was burdened for the people of Israel, Paul's ministry was primarily to the Gentiles (21:19; Rom. 11:13). When Paul spoke about his ministry to the Ephesian elders, Paul used the verb *douleuō*, "to serve as a bondservant" (Acts 20:19). His ministry was noted for humility and compassion. Teaching the Word of God played a major role in his ministry (20:21, 24, 27). Having been a shepherd to them, he exhorted them to follow his example and to pastor (literally, shepherd) the congregation (20:28).

Paul emphasized the significance of the Holy Spirit in one's ministry (2 Cor. 3:3–6). The ministry of reconciliation, he said, has been committed to all believers (5:18–19). Since ministry can be discredited, believers should not be a stumbling block to others (6:3). For some, like Paul, ministry may involve many hardships (6:4–10).

Paul also emphasized the importance of spiritual gifts in ministry (1 Cor. 12:4–11). In Ephesians 4:11–12, He taught that gifted people are given to the church "to prepare God's people for works of service." Christian ministry is not something people do in their own strength; they are dependent on the enablement of the Spirit of God.

Paul's letters to Timothy and Titus give evidence that the apostle believed in organized leadership for ministry within the church (1 Tim. 3:1–13; Titus 1:5–9). Good ministers are those who believe the truth, are living examples of God's grace, and faithfully teach this truth to others (1 Tim. 4:6). In his last letter Paul exhorted Timothy to fulfill all the responsibilities of the ministry God had entrusted to him (2 Tim. 4:5).

Peter added an important concept concerning ministry: All Christian service, besides benefiting others, is ultimately to bring praise and glory to God (1 Pet. 4:11).

—WGJ

Pursue opportunities to serve the Lord each day, and
write down specific ways you can minister to people in the body of Christ.

Miracles

A MIRACLE IS AN EVENT in which God reveals His divine power for the purpose of drawing people to Himself. Miracles not only inspire awe and wonder; they also have revelatory significance. Philosopher David Hume asserted that a miracle is "a violation of the laws of nature," but the Bible does not teach that natural law is something independent or separate from God as if He created the universe and then left it to operate by itself. To the contrary, natural law is to be understood as God's *ordinary* way of operating in the natural world (Ps. 19:1–3; 104; Heb. 1:3), and a miracle is therefore God's *extraordinary* manner of operating in the natural world. Sometimes people use the word *miracle* too loosely. Some occurrences may be unusual in their nature or their timing, but that does not mean they are miracles in the strict biblical sense.

Several Old Testament terms are translated "sign" and "wonder," both indicating God's intervention in history to affirm His presence and His control over events. The New Testament uses eight different Greek words in association with miracles. Four of these are the most prominent. *Dynamis* ("power") describes a miracle as an expression of divine power. *Sēmeion* ("sign") affirms that the miracle attests to God's presence. *Teras* ("wonder") portrays the effect of the miracle on the observer. These three terms occur together in Acts 2:22; Romans 15:19–20; 2 Thessalonians 2:9; and Hebrews 2:4. The fourth is *erga* ("works"). What men considered a "wonder," Christ regarded simply as a work of His hands.

Miracles are not scattered haphazardly throughout Scripture, but rather they appear in four specific periods of biblical history: the time of Moses and Joshua, of Elijah and Elisha, of Daniel, and of Christ and the early church.

In the Old Testament, miracles took place during critical periods of Israel's history. They served to accredit God's message and messenger. When Moses responded to God's call to return to Egypt to lead the

Hebrews out of bondage, miraculous signs were needed to convince the people that he had been sent by God and to convince Pharaoh to release the enslaved Israelites. The ten miraculous plagues in Egypt demonstrated to Israel that God was exercising His power on their behalf (Exod. 6:6–7). In addition, since each one of the plagues was directed at one of the gods of Egypt, God declared, "The Egyptians will know that I am the LORD when I stretch out my hand against Egypt" (7:5, see 17; 8:6, 17; 9:15, 29; 12:12). This truth applied also to the great miracle of the crossing of the Red Sea. God also performed numerous miracles on Israel's behalf when they were in the wilderness and as they invaded and conquered Canaan under Joshua's leadership.

In the period of the united monarchy (the reigns of Saul, David, and Solomon) miracles are conspicuously absent. God worked through the rulers, even with their frailties, and accomplished His purposes. When the kingdom was divided after Solomon's reign, it was a different story. Apostasy took hold in the Northern Kingdom through calf worship introduced by Jeroboam and Baal worship promoted by Ahab and Jezebel. Miracles performed by Elijah and Elisha demonstrated the powerlessness of Baal (for example, the contest on Mount Carmel, 1 Kings 18) and the omnipotence of the one true God.

During the Babylonian captivity Daniel and his friends stood out as godly leaders who reassured the exiles that their God was still alive, that He had greater prowess than the false gods of Babylon and Persia, and that He could still protect His people even though they were away from their homeland. The miracles performed in Babylon validated these truths (see Dan. 3, 5, 6).

The New Testament abounds in miracles because of the advent of Jesus Christ. In Old Testament times God acted in history, but with Christ's coming He entered history. Christ performed miracles during His earthly ministry to attest His deity, to demonstrate His messiahship, to show compassion to those in need, and to prepare the disciples for their future ministry. In addition, the miracles of Jesus' incarnation, resurrection, and ascension, though in a class by themselves, are intrinsic to God's provision of salvation for lost humanity. Of the miracles performed by Christ, only thirty-five are recorded in the Gospels. That the Gospel writers selected only those miracles that fit their purposes is apparent from numerous references to Christ's doing numerous miraculous works (Matt. 4:23–24; 8:16; 9:35; 11:4–5, 20–24; 12:15; 14:14, 36; 15:30; 19:2; 21:14).

Miracles continued in the early church (Acts 3, 5, 8, 9, 12, 13, 14, 16, 19, 20, 28). On some occasions they were direct divine interventions, as with the opening of the prison doors for the apostles (Acts 5, 12), but more often the miracles were performed by the apostles themselves in the power of the Holy Spirit. Paul spoke of signs, wonders, and miracles as "the things that mark an apostle" (2 Cor. 12:12; see also Rom. 15:18–19). The author of the letter to the Hebrews said that with signs, wonders, and miracles God bore witness to salvation (Heb. 2:4). Thus it is apparent that the miracles performed in the apostolic age were signs that authenticated the Christian message as well as the messenger. With the Christian faith established and the canon of Scripture completed, the need for authenticating signs no longer exists. As has been seen, not every generation was given miraculous signs. They appeared only in critical periods in biblical history, fulfilled their purpose, and then passed off the scene.

On the other hand, it is unwise to say God never performs miracles today. It can be affirmed, however, that it is not God's normal way of working, as it seemed to be in Jesus' ministry. Further, when God does heal someone miraculously, He does so sovereignly. Believers should follow the example of Jesus in Gethsemane when He prayed, "Not my will but yours be done" (Luke 22:42).

As the end of history approaches and the return of Christ to establish His kingdom on earth draws near, there will be another burst of miracles. Christ warned of this future day when "false Christs and false prophets will appear and perform great signs and miracles" (Matt. 24:24). Paul, too, spoke of "the lawless one," whose coming "will be in accordance with the work of Satan displayed in all kinds of counterfeit miracles, signs and wonders" (2 Thess. 2:9). In the Tribulation the Antichrist will perform miraculous works to convince people to worship him (Rev. 13:14; 19:20). At Christ's glorious appearance the beast will be defeated, and he will be "thrown alive into the fiery lake of burning sulfur" (19:20).   **—DKC**

*Learn significant truths about Christ
by studying the seven miracles of John's Gospel.*

Mystery

THIS ENGLISH WORD transliterates the Greek word *mystērion*. It is used with some frequency in the New Testament, primarily by the apostle Paul. The Bible does not use the word in the contemporary sense of something difficult to understand or something incomprehensible. (That meaning, however, may be involved when Paul wrote that when a person "speaks in a tongue . . . no one understands him; he utters mysteries with his spirit," 1 Cor. 14:2. That meaning may also be in view when Paul said that a person possessing the gift of prophecy was able to "fathom all mysteries and all knowledge," 13:2.)

In the pagan religions of Egypt, Persia, Greece, and Rome, mystery cults developed. In these groups secret rites and teachings were shared only with those initiated into the group and then sometimes only progressively. These mystery religions developed before the Christian era, but continued into it and later impacted the church to some degree. Paul's hometown of Tarsus was a center for one such mystery religion. This may have influenced his use of the word, but not the meaning given to it, for Paul's meaning is uniquely biblical.

One of the clearest uses of "mystery" in the Bible is Paul's reference to "the mystery that has been kept hidden for ages and generations, but is now disclosed to the saints" (Col. 1:26). Elsewhere he wrote that his ministry was "to make plain to everyone the administration of this mystery, which for ages past was hidden in God" (Eph. 3:9). Just before this he explained that "the mystery [was] made known to me by revelation" (3:3) and that it "was not made known to men in other generations as it has now been revealed by the Spirit of God's holy apostles and prophets" (3:5; see also Rom. 16:26).

Biblically a mystery is divine truth that God had not disclosed in Old Testament times but did reveal to the New Testament apostles and prophets to proclaim freely to everyone who will listen. The free, open sharing of the truth is what distinguishes a biblical mystery from one in a mystery religion. In the latter, sharing the mystery was limited to initiates, and sharing it with noninitiates was forbidden and punishable even by death.

The content of the biblical mystery is variously described, but it is summarized as "the mystery of Christ" (Eph. 3:4; Col. 4:3) and "the mystery of

God, namely, Christ" (2:2). More specifically it is called "this mystery, which is Christ in you, the hope of glory" (1:27), a truth never revealed in the Old Testament. Still more specifically it is identified as "that through the gospel the Gentiles are heirs together with Israel, members together of one body, and sharers together in the promise in Christ Jesus" (Eph. 3:6; see also Col. 1:26–27). This truth of the equal standing of gentile believers with Jewish believers in the church, the body of Christ, also was never revealed in the Old Testament. This was Paul's gospel (Rom. 16:25–27). Paul asked the Colossian Christians to pray that he "may proclaim the mystery of Christ . . . clearly" (Col. 4:3–4).   —JAW

Remember that the gospel of Christ remains a mystery
only when it is not proclaimed.

Nn

Natural Man

CHRISTIANS EXHIBIT certain characteristics that distinguish them from the general populace. The litmus test, according to the apostle Paul, is how a person responds to the things of God (1 Cor. 2:14–15). Individuals who welcome the things of God possess the Holy Spirit and are controlled and led by Him (Rom. 8:9, 14). The person who has never received Christ by faith does not have the Spirit (8:8–9) and is unable to understand the thoughts of God (1 Cor. 2:11, 14).

The Greek words Paul used to describe the person without Christ are *psychikos* and *anthrōpos* (2:14), which the New American Standard Bible translates "natural man" and the New International Version loosely renders "the man without the Spirit." This is the only place in the New Testament where this exact Greek phrase is used. The "natural man," that is, the unregenerate person, can know what other human beings can know because of the human spirit within him. But he is not capable of comprehending what God has revealed because this is possible only by the Spirit of God (2:13). Unsaved people may be brilliant, talented, prosperous, and even moral and good. However, their human wisdom is natural and unspiritual, not supernatural and from heaven (James 3:15).

The "natural man" is simply one who is born into the world, unrelated to God because of sin (Jude 19). He is "in Adam" (1 Cor. 15:22) in contrast to the saved, who are "in Christ." Believers, those who are "in Christ," are a new creation, possessing a unique relationship to God (2 Cor. 5:17).   —WGJ

Be sensitive to the fact that a person without Christ is incapable of understanding spiritual truth, and pray for the enlightenment of the Spirit that brings salvation.

Oo

Obedience

OBEDIENCE TO GOD AND HIS WORD is never an option for believers. The term *obedience* and related terms occur more than 250 times in the New International Version. The majority of these occurrences are in the Old Testament. The predominant Hebrew word is *šāmâ*, which means "to hear intelligently and attentively and respond appropriately." The corresponding words in the New Testament, *akouō* and *hypakouō*, are closely related to the Old Testament meaning.

In the Old Testament, the concept of obedience is built on the premise that God has spoken and that He expects His people to hear and to do as He commanded. Obedience was the main issue when God created Adam and Eve and placed them in the Garden of Eden. Because they failed to obey, their sin brought condemnation on the entire human race and they became separated from God (Rom. 5:12). God expected Adam and Eve to hear His warning and to obey His instructions.

When God selected Israel to be His people and then rescued them from Egypt, He expected obedience to the covenant He established with them through Moses (Exod. 19:5). The people responded by affirming their willingness to obey everything the Lord said (19:8). Obedience to God's Law would bring about a variety of blessings. God would defeat their enemies (23:22–23), He would take away sickness from among them (23:25), and they could expect a full life span (23:26). The land would be fruitful, and they would dwell in the land in safety (Lev. 25:18–19; 26:6–8).

When the Law was restated after Israel had wandered in the wilderness for forty years, the demands for obedience were once again highlighted. Possession of the land was based on Israel's obedience to the Lord's commands (Deut. 4:1–2). This would show the nations that the people of Israel were wise (4:6). The ultimate issue for them was life or death, and obedience to God and His commands would bring life (30:15–20).

The capstone of Old Testament teaching on obedience is in

Deuteronomy 6:4–5. Because God revealed His true character, the people were expected to love Him totally. Obedience is to come from the heart, so that a person's actions are an integral part of his life. God's commands were to be the first thing they thought about in the morning and the last thing at night (6:7).

Obedience is always a spiritual issue. It begins in the heart (30:1–2) and is an act of faith. The people were to obey God with all their heart (30:2). God said this was not too difficult for them to comprehend nor was it beyond their reach, for He had made His commands known and they had access to them (30:11–14). Paul referred to this in Romans 10:1–11. Obedience was more than executing specific requirements. This could be done superficially, which sadly was true of Israel (10:3). Thus ultimate obedience in the Old Testament was based on faith in God.

Abraham is an example of an obedient believer. God told him to go to a place he would later receive as his inheritance, and he obeyed and went. His obedience was because of His faith in God. Without faith, it is impossible to please God (Heb. 11:6–10).

Almost all the prophets spoke about how important it was for the Israelites to obey. Tragically Israel had already rejected her God, and her lack of obedience was a major reason for impending judgment. Jeremiah provided a ray of hope for the people as he prophesied of the New Covenant, in which God said He will put His Law in their minds and write it on their hearts so that they will obey (Jer. 31:33).

The New Testament includes certain new emphases in the teaching on obedience. In the Sermon on the Mount Jesus made it clear that the Mosaic Law could not be fulfilled by following the narrow interpretations given by the Pharisees (Matt. 5:20); obedience to God is required. Those who were obedient were the ones who heard the words of Christ and put them into practice (7:24). In the New Testament, obedience is a matter of following Christ, that is, believing in Him and doing what He commanded.

The significance of obedience was explained by Jesus at the close of His earthly ministry when He met with His disciples in the Upper Room. He explained that faith in Him is an absolute necessity (John 14:1), and that if they loved Him, they would obey His commands (14:15; 15:23). He taught that abiding or remaining in Him requires obeying His Word (15:10).

Jesus Himself is the model of obedience for all believers (15:10). Jesus became a servant and died on the cross in obedience to the will of the Father (Phil. 2:6–9). This illustrates the true nature of obedience. It is a responsive attitude to please God and should always characterize believers.

John, who was present when Christ addressed the disciples in the Upper Room, also stated that obedience is a necessary characteristic in a believer's life. It evidences one's salvation to others (1 John 2:3); the love of God is perfected through obedience (2:5); it has a positive effect on the believer's prayer life (3:22); and obedience demonstrates that a believer is abiding in fellowship with Christ (3:24). John also indicated that salvation does not come because a set of rules are obeyed; rather, it stems from one's faith being rooted in Christ. Obedience then is the visible evidence of such faith (3:23–24; 5:1–4). Christ is "the source of eternal salvation for all who obey him" (Heb. 5:9). Here obedience is a synonym for believing in Christ, which is true in several other passages as well, including Acts 5:32; Romans 16:26; and 2 Thessalonians 1:8.

Christians demonstrate to others that we belong to Christ when we believe in Him, obey His word, and demonstrate this obedience by loving others and doing His will.

The Bible also teaches that children are to obey their parents (Eph. 6:1), and citizens are to obey their political leaders (Rom. 13:1, 5) so long as doing so does not involve disobeying God (Acts 5:29). **—WGJ**

Trust in the Lord and live in obedience to His Word,
which is the pathway of happiness for every believer.

Oil

IN BIBLICAL TIMES OIL WAS MADE from a variety of natural sources, including almonds and castor beans, but primarily from olives. In fact, the English word "oil" is derived from the Latin *oleum*, which translates the Greek *elaian*, "olive oil." From ancient times olive oil has been used as food and in cooking, for illumination, as a medicine, as a cosmetic, in religious rites, for consecrating political and religious leaders, and showing hospitality. As a result olive oil was highly valued commercially.

Although olive trees are now cultivated all over the Mediterranean Basin as well as in other climatically favorable areas, in biblical times Palestine especially was known as "a land with . . . olive oil" (Deut. 8:8), along with other agricultural products. Its production was basic to Israel's economy both domestically and for export (2 Chron. 2:8–10, 15–16). When Elisha miraculously multiplied the "little oil" for the widow whose creditors were threatening to take her two boys as slaves, he directed her to "sell the oil and pay your debts. You and your sons can live on what is left" (2 Kings 4:1–7).

Olive oil is produced primarily from ripe, black olives, although some oil is produced from green olives. The harvest season for olives runs from September through November. The olives are allowed to fall from the trees and are gathered, or they are beaten from the trees with long rods. As with other crops, the poor people were allowed to glean what remained after the harvest was completed (Deut. 24:20).

A better grade of oil was produced by pressing the olives without crushing the kernels. Sometimes this was done by treading them underfoot like grapes (Mic. 6:15), or by crushing them with a pestle, producing what is called "clear oil" (Exod. 27:20). In later times mills were used to crush the kernels as well as the fruit, with the oil being extracted from the pulp in several stages of purity. The purer grades were used in cosmetics and religious ceremonies, and the less pure grades were used for cooking and lighting uses.

Because of the dry, hot climate in the eastern Mediterranean area, and in the deserts in particular, olive oil was rubbed on the skin to keep it soft. It was also applied to the head. As a result, it became customary to anoint the heads of visitors in one's home with olive oil, sometimes perfumed, as a token of hospitality (Ps. 23:5; Amos 6:6, NASB).

The Lord Jesus' experience in the home of Simon, the Pharisee, shows that anointing the head of a guest, especially one as honored as Jesus, was common courtesy. When Simon silently criticized Jesus for allowing "a woman who had lived a sinful life in that town" to anoint Him with perfumed oil and wash and kiss His feet, Jesus rebuked him for having omitted the normal courtesies of providing water to wash His feet, greeting Him with a kiss, and anointing His head with oil, the very things the woman had done in devotion and worship (Luke 7:36–50).

In a similar incident in Bethany of Judea, Mary, one of Lazarus's sisters, anointed Jesus with "a pint of pure nard, an expensive perfume." When Judas Iscariot and other disciples denounced her act of devotion and worship as a waste, Jesus rebuked them, saying that she had done it to prepare Him "for the day of [his] burial" (John 12:1–8; see also Matt. 26:6–13; Mark 14:3–9).

Oil was used medicinally in a variety of ways. Frequently it was one of the ingredients in medicines taken internally. It was also applied to open wounds as a healing, soothing ointment (Isa. 1:6) or together with wine as an antiseptic (Luke 10:34). Apparently it also was applied to the body externally as an ointment, perhaps to control fever (Mark 6:13), and sometimes it was accompanied with prayer (James 5:14). On the basis of these Scriptures, the Roman Catholic Church has developed the sacrament of extreme unction and the Greek Orthodox Church the rite called Euchelaion.

From ancient times until comparatively recently, olive oil was used in the Mediterranean area as fuel for illumination. The usual lamp was a small shallow clay bowl with the raised edge pinched almost together on one side to hold the wick extending outward. Such lamps are found in abundance in excavations and sold as souvenirs in the Near East. The average home had these lamps in several rooms (2 Kings 4:10). Because they were small, it was necessary to carry a supply of oil when using them outside at night, as Jesus' parable of the ten virgins shows (Matt. 25:1–10).

As noted above in the story of the sinful woman in the home of Simon, the Pharisee, and the story of Mary of Bethany anointing Jesus with "perfume" (Luke 7:37–38, 46; John 12:3, 5), olive oil was often combined with a scented substance such as myrrh, anise, cedar, cinnamon, ginger, peppermint, rose, or sandalwood. After the oil had become scented and the solid residue had settled, the oil was poured off and used as an ointment (Ruth 3:3; 2 Sam. 12:20; Esther 2:12).

The most significant use of olive oil, both ordinary and perfumed, in Scripture was for religious purposes. After God appeared to Jacob the night he left Beersheba for Haran, the next morning Jacob "took the stone he had placed under his head and set it up as a pillar and poured oil on top of it. He called that place Bethel" (Gen. 28:18–19), which means "God's house" (28:22; 35:14–15). Likewise, the tabernacle and all its furnishings and instruments were anointed with a special oil (Exod.

30:26–29; 40:9–11; Lev. 8:10–11; Num. 7:1) made to a specific formula (Exod. 30:22–24) to serve as "a holy anointing oil" (30:25; 37:29).

The same holy anointing oil was used for consecrating Aaron as the high priest and his sons as priests to serve God (Exod. 29:7; 30:30; 40:12–16; Lev. 8:12; 21:10, 12; Ps. 133:2). The care of the anointing oil was given to Aaron's son Eleazar (Num. 4:16) and later committed to some of the priests (1 Chron. 9:29–30). Although Moses laid his hands on Joshua and commissioned him as his successor (Deut. 34:9), apparently Joshua was not anointed with oil. Later, however, Samuel anointed Saul to be king over Israel (1 Sam. 10:1), as well as David (16:1, 12–13). After David designated Solomon to be his successor as king (1 Kings 1:30, 32–35), at David's direction Zadok the priest anointed Solomon as king over Israel (1:39). Also at Elisha's direction, one of his prophets anointed Jehu to kill "the whole house of Ahab" and serve as king of Israel (2 Kings 9:1–3, 6-7, 12–13).

In the Bible olive oil is symbolic of a number of things. A lack of oil signified famine (Joel 1:10; Hag. 1:11), while oil in abundance was evidence of God's blessing and prosperity (Job 29:6; Joel 2:19, 24). Olive oil was a symbol of joy (Ps. 45:7; Isa. 61:3; Heb. 1:9). Wasting oil is a sign of profligacy (Prov. 21:17), while using it carefully is evidence of prudence and wisdom (21:20). Supremely, however, anointing with oil is a symbol of the Holy Spirit's descent on and direction of the individual anointed (1 Sam. 10:1, 6–7, 9; 16:13). —JAW

*Since olive oil in the Bible is a symbol of gladness and joy,
become a "merchant" who dispenses joy freely.*

Pp

Paradise

PARADISE, the abode of the righteous dead, is a place of happiness and delight. The word itself is believed to be of Persian origin and appears as *pardēs* three times in the Old Testament: Song of Solomon 4:13 ("orchard"), Nehemiah 2:8 ("forest"), and Ecclesiastes 2:5 ("parks"). In the Septuagint, the Greek translation of the Old Testament, the word *paradeisos* is used for the Garden of Eden in Genesis 2 and 3. It is also found in Genesis 13:10 and Joel 2:3, where it again alludes to Eden.

Jewish tradition in New Testament times held the region of the dead to be in the heart of the earth, in hades, a place with two compartments. In one the wicked dead were in torment, and in the other the righteous dead were in bliss, that is, in paradise.

Christ used the word *paradeisos* only once. This was when He addressed the thief on the cross, "I tell you the truth, today you will be with me in paradise" (Luke 23:43). This is no doubt to be equated with the expression "Abraham's bosom" in the story of the rich man and Lazarus (16:22, NKJV). Some theologians hold the view that paradise was originally a portion of hades but that since the resurrection and ascension of Christ, paradise has been removed from hades and is now in the third heaven. This is in keeping with the fact that elsewhere the New Testament equates paradise with heaven. The change in location is believed by some to be described in Ephesians 4:8–10. Others feel that Scripture does not support any distinction between paradise and heaven, and that they together describe where Christ is (Luke 23:43; Phil. 1:23; 2 Cor. 5:8). When Jesus promised the thief the bliss of heaven on that very day, He affirmed a prospect that belongs to all believing Christians.

A second New Testament mention of paradise is in 2 Corinthians 12:4, in connection with Paul's reference to his "visions and revelations from the Lord" (12:1). The apostle's goal was to counter his opponents' boasts regarding their spiritual experiences with reference to one of his own, an experience that would silence his critics. The event Paul described here took place fourteen years before he wrote this epistle. While the date is not precise enough to identify the event with certainty, some suggest it took place when Paul was stoned at Lystra (Acts 14:19). Others date it sometime in the years A.D. 42–44 when Paul was at Tarsus before he began his missionary journeys. The important point, of course, is the event itself, in which the apostle was "caught up" (*harpazō*, the same verb used in 1 Thess. 4:17 of saints at the Rapture). Paul was transported to the third heaven (2 Cor. 12:2), that is, paradise (12:4). The "third heaven" is the abode of God as distinguished from the first heaven, the clouds or atmosphere, and the second heaven, the stars and planets. Paul was not permitted to disclose the glorious things he saw and heard in paradise. The heavenly experience nonetheless did enable him to write knowledgeably, "I desire to depart and be with Christ, which is better by far" (Phil. 1:23).

The third New Testament reference to paradise is in the promise to the church in Ephesus, "To him who overcomes, I will give the right to eat from the tree of life, which is in the paradise of God" (Rev. 2:7). Though the tree of life was originally in the Garden of Eden (Gen. 3:22), the Old Testament prophets predicted a restoration of the Edenic paradise (Isa. 51:3; Ezek. 36:35). While these prophecies will be fulfilled in the Millennium, the tree of life itself will reappear in the New Jerusalem in the eternal state (Rev. 22:2). To eat of its fruit symbolizes the partaking of the fullness of eternal life. **—DKC**

Thank God that because of Jesus' sacrifice on the cross paradise is the believer's certain hope.

Passover

PASSOVER WAS ONE OF THREE GREAT ANNUAL FESTIVALS at which all the men of Israel were commanded to appear before the Lord at the sanctuary (Exod. 23:14–17). It marked one of the most significant acts of divine intervention in Israel's history, the beginning of the nation's deliverance from its bondage in Egypt.

The institution of the Passover is related to the tenth plague, which brought death to the firstborn in Egyptian families. The Israelites were instructed to smear the blood of a lamb on the lintels and doorposts of their homes. When the Lord visited the land, He "passed over" (*pāsaḥ*) the blood-marked homes of the Israelites (Exod. 12:13), but the first-born sons of the Egyptians died. That night Hebrew families ate the roasted lamb with bitter herbs and unleavened bread, reminiscent of their bitter Egyptian bondage. They were also told to have their cloaks tucked into their belts, their sandals on their feet, and their staffs in their hands, showing their readiness for a hasty departure from Egypt.

Subsequent directions prescribed that when Israel entered Canaan the Passover rite was to be immediately followed by a seven-day period during which nothing leavened was to be eaten. This was called the Feast of Unleavened Bread, marking the beginning of the barley harvest (13:3–10).

The Passover celebration was intended to be repeated each year as a memorial of Israel's deliverance from Egypt and as a means of instruction to future generations (12:24–27; Lev. 23:5–8; Num. 28:16–25; Deut. 16:1–8). But Israel often neglected this observance as well as many other divine instructions and laws. After its institution (Exod. 12:28), the Passover was observed a year later at Sinai (Num. 9:1–5) and not again until the Israelites entered Canaan (Josh. 5:10). Only three observances are recorded between the nation's entrance into the Promised Land and their removal from it at the time of the Babylonian captivity, namely, during the reigns of Solomon (2 Chron. 8:13), Hezekiah (30:15), and Josiah (2 Kings 23:21; 2 Chron. 35:1–19). After the return of the Jews from captivity, a noteworthy Passover was celebrated after the second temple was dedicated (Ezra 6:19–22).

The New Testament includes many references to the Passover. Hebrews 11, in a retrospective view of many Old Testament heroes of faith, reviews Moses' life and states, "By faith he kept the Passover and the sprinkling of blood, so that the destroyer of the firstborn would not touch the firstborn of Israel" (Heb. 11:28). During the life and ministry of Christ on earth the Passover and the Feast of Unleavened Bread were of special significance. As a boy Jesus accompanied His parents as they went to Jerusalem each year for the Feast of the Passover (Luke 2:41). John's Gospel records at least three Passovers during Christ's ministry (John 2:13, 23; 6:4; 12:1; 18:28, 39; 19:14). Some believe the feast mentioned in

John 5:1 was a fourth Passover. When Jesus met with His disciples in the Upper Room He ate the Passover meal with them (Matt. 26:17–19; Mark 14:12–18; Luke 22:14–20). The breaking of the bread and the drinking of the wine symbolized Christ's forthcoming death on the cross. This event was to be memorialized by all His followers observing this rite until Christ's return (1 Cor. 11:24–26). It is probable that Christ was actually hanging on the cross when the Passover lambs were being killed (these animals were slain between 2:30 P.M. and 5:30 P.M. in the temple court). Thus Jesus is graphically portrayed as the "Lamb of God, who takes away the sin of the world" (John 1:29).

An estimated 120,000 to 180,000 Jews were present in Jerusalem at that time to celebrate the Passover, most of them having come from surrounding countries where they lived. Many of them, no doubt, were a part of the crowd at the cross, as Jesus, God's Lamb, died between two thieves. After A.D. 70 and the destruction of the temple there remained no altar for animal sacrifices; therefore from then until now the Jewish Passover became only a family observance with no shedding of blood.

Today, Samaritans make an annual pilgrimage from their homes in Nablus, Israel, up nearby Mount Gerizim. There they celebrate the Passover feast after seven lambs are slain and roasted. Thus two groups continue to observe a feast that had its complete fulfillment two thousand years ago on Mount Calvary outside Jerusalem.

For the church the Passover and the Feast of Unleavened Bread have a typological significance. Paul declared that Christ is "our Passover lamb" (1 Cor. 5:7). Believers must therefore put away the "old leaven" of malice and wickedness and in its place embrace "the unleavened bread of sincerity and truth" (5:8, NKJV).　　　　　　　　　　　**—DKC**

Meditate on the significance to you of Christ, the Passover Lamb.

Peace

IN THE BIBLE the word *peace* has a wide range of meanings. Basically it includes the ideas of wholeness, well-being, prosperity, and security, all associated with God's presence with His people.

The Hebrew word *šālôm* is translated "peace" over two hundred times. Sometimes it is simply a form of greeting (Gen. 29:6; 2 Kings 4:26), but more often it describes relationships—individual to individual (Gen. 34:21, NKJV; Josh. 9:15), nation to nation (Deut. 2:26; Josh. 10:21, NKJV; 1 Kings 4:24; 5:12), or God to humans (Ps. 85:8; Jer. 16:5, NKJV).

One of the Old Testament offerings was called the peace offering ("fellowship offering," NIV). Inasmuch as the Hebrew concept of peace embraces health, prosperity, security, and peace with God, the rendering "peace offering" is preferable. (R. K. Harrison suggests the translation "sacrifice of well-being.") The unique feature of this offering was the communal meal in which the worshipers, their families, and a Levite partook of a major portion of the sacrifice after it was offered. Brought as an act of thanksgiving, a vow, or a freewill offering, the peace offering was designed to give the worshiper an opportunity to express gratitude to God for His blessings (Lev. 3; 7:11–36).

In the psalms peace is a cherished possession for God's people, both nationally and individually. God declared He will bless "his people with peace" (Ps. 29:11). David felt deep anxiety when he was pursued by Saul and betrayed by friends and family, yet he could declare with confidence, "I will lie down and sleep in peace, for you alone, O LORD, make me dwell in safety" (4:8). The psalms repeatedly contrast the wicked and the righteous (for example, 1:3–5; 37:35–37), calling the latter a "man of peace" (37:37). Further, the psalmist declared that those who love God's Law possess "great peace" (119:165).

The prophets emphasized the same themes of the bestowment of peace on those who are rightly related to God (Isa. 26:3), but an absence of peace on the part of the wicked (57:20–21). The prophets also expected that peace will come someday to the nations. That peace will only come with the second advent of the Messiah, the "Prince of Peace" (Isa. 9:6–7). Redeemed Israel will enjoy this peace, but it will also extend throughout the whole earth. Zechariah predicted, "He will proclaim peace to the nations. His rule will extend from sea to sea and from the River to the ends of the earth" (Zech. 9:10). In that day God will be present with His people and will confirm to them His "covenant of peace" (Ezek. 34:22–25).

In the New Testament the Greek word *eirēnē*, "peace," occurs ninety times. In classical Greek this word described a time of rest when there was no war and people lived orderly, tranquil lives. Later the concept of an inner, personal peace was added. In the New Testament the meaning of peace was expanded to include the Old Testament concept of *šālôm*. Spiritual peace or well-being is based on a person's relationship with God (Rom. 5:1).

The birth of Christ was announced by angels who said, "Glory to God in the highest, and on earth peace to men on whom his favor rests" (Luke 2:14). The death of Christ removed the barrier between God and humankind. Paul declared that God reconciled all things to Himself, "by making peace through his blood, shed on the cross" (Col. 1:20; see also Eph. 2:14–18). Christ's resurrection appearances brought greetings and benedictions of peace to the disciples (John 20:19, 21, 26). The gospel itself is defined as "the good news of peace through Jesus Christ" (Acts 10:36; see also Eph. 6:15). Christ left a legacy of peace to His followers (John 14:27; 16:33) and assured them it was their inalienable privilege and possession (Phil. 4:6–7). Paul's common greeting "grace and peace," in each of his thirteen epistles (for example, Rom. 1:7; 1 Cor. 1:3) is not simply a wish; it is also a reminder of the gifts Christ grants to believers.

Those who are at peace with God are responsible to pursue peace in their relationships with others as an important aspect of growth in sanctification (Heb. 12:14; Col. 3:15; 1 Pet. 3:11). The presence of the indwelling Holy Spirit makes this possible (Rom. 8:6; 15:13), for "the fruit of the Spirit is . . . peace" (Gal. 5:22).

Christians are urged to pray for rulers and work for peace in their communities so that they may enjoy peaceful and quiet lives and be unhindered in proclaiming the gospel of peace (1 Tim. 2:1–2).

—**DKC**

Be thankful today that because of Christ we can be at peace with God.

Perfection

EVERY BELIEVER SHOULD HAVE the goal of being perfect (Matt. 5:48). However, this is not attainable if perfection is understood as sin-lessness or as reaching a position in life where there is no longer the capacity to sin. Perfection in the sense of sinlessness is true only of God. Teaching that promotes the possibility of becoming sinless in this life must either redefine the nature of sin or reject the clear teaching of Scripture in 1 John 1:8, 10.

No one who has ever lived on this earth has claimed to be sinless, except Jesus Christ (John 8:46; 1 Pet. 2:21–22). When the Scriptures state that Jesus was made perfect through suffering (Heb. 2:10, 5:8), it does not mean that anything was added to His divine/human nature. The writer meant that Christ was fully prepared for His role as our High Priest. His suffering enabled Him to sympathize with our weaknesses, yet without sin (4:15). As believers we ultimately will be like Christ (1 John 3:2; Heb. 11:40), but that will not take place until He comes back for us. This hope should have a purifying effect on us, but until He returns we must face the reality of sin in our lives.

The Hebrew word for "perfect" is *tām* or *tāmîm*. It can refer to a complete day (Josh. 10:13), something whole or healthy (Ezek. 15:5), or something ethically sound or upright (Ps. 19:13). Job was "perfect" in the sense that he was morally upright (Job 1:1, 8; 2:3). The Hebrew word is also used of animal sacrifices that were without blemish (Lev. 22:21–22).

The corresponding Greek word, *teleios*, "whole or complete," is used of believers who are mature (1 Cor. 14:20; Phil 3:15; Heb. 5:14; 6:1; James 1:4). Paul also used the word in connection with the perfect (that is, complete) will of God (Rom. 12:1–2).

When Jesus exhorted His disciples to be perfect *(teleios)* as God the Father is perfect (Matt. 5:48), He meant that God is the standard against which everything else should be measured. Every commendable quality and characteristic finds its highest expression in Him. He is not deficient in anything; He is the epitome of completeness. We are exhorted to be perfect in the sense of striving, by the Holy Spirit, to be like Him. We will never reach this ultimate goal in this life, but we are to pursue it.

In Matthew 19:16–24 Jesus told a rich young ruler, "If you want to be perfect, go, sell your possessions and give to the poor, and you will have treasure in heaven. Then come and follow me." What deficiency did this man have? Matthew answered this question. Because of his great wealth, the man was not willing to follow Christ (19:22). To him, money was more important than God. In a sense, money was his god, and so he lacked genuine faith in the Lord. He preferred to cling to his riches rather than humble himself before the Lord and by faith receive eternal life. Nowhere does the Bible teach that eternal life can be attained by keeping the Ten Commandments.

Paul's teaching on spiritual maturity is crystallized in Philippians 3:12–16. His stated goal was to know Christ and to be like Him. Even though his credentials were impeccable, he claimed he had not yet attained the goal: he had not "been made perfect." The ultimate goal was still before him. Yet from another standpoint Paul claimed he and others were perfect *(teleios)*, that is, mature. There is no contradiction here, since perfection or absolute maturity was not something he could attain, but growth and development did mark his life as one who was devoted to the Savior. This passage points out the balance between absolute and relative perfection, especially as it relates to maturity. One of the reasons Paul was so committed to preaching and teaching was to see every believer perfect (mature) in Christ (Col. 1:28). What was true for the individual was also applicable to the church (Eph. 4:12–13).

The writer of Hebrews adds another ingredient to the concept of spiritual maturity. He equates it with growth in doctrine or the solid food of the Word of God (Heb. 5:12–14). Since there is no possibility of repeating the conversion experience, Christians should be concerned with growth (6:1–6). The Scriptures are a key component in promoting spiritual maturity (2 Tim. 3:16–17).

When believers face various trials and testings in life, God's purpose is to foster their maturity *(teleios;* James 1:4). James wrote that maturity is exemplified by the person who not only listens to the perfect law (the Word of God) but also continues to do what it says (1:25). James also declared that the person who can control his tongue is perfect, that is, mature (3:2).

To the apostle John, love was a critical factor in perfection. He wrote that God's love is perfected in anyone who obeys the Word of God (1 John 2:5). Our love for one another is evidence that God dwells within us and that His love is made perfect (complete) in us (4:12). In fact, perfect love casts out fear (4:18).

Every believer looks forward to the time when Christ will come again and he or she will stand complete in Him. Yet in another sense there is the undeniable fact that because Christ died, every believer is already complete in Him (Heb. 10:12), that is, His death is sufficient to pay the penalty for all their sins. —WGJ

Ask the Spirit of God to teach you how to grow in your Christian life
so you can reach a consistent level of maturity in your walk with the Lord.

Position

THIS WORD REFERS to the believer's position or standing in the Lord Jesus Christ. It relates to the biblical truth of the security of the believer, because when a person receives the Lord Jesus as his or her Savior by faith and is born again, that one moves from a position outside of Christ to a new position "in Christ" (Eph. 1:3, 9, 13) and is identified with Him. Although the daily condition of the Christian's life may fluctuate, his position remains constant. Paul wrote that nothing "in all creation, will be able to separate us from the love of God that is in Christ Jesus our Lord" (Rom. 8:39).

In order to understand and appreciate the believer's position in Christ, it is necessary to understand one's position apart from Christ. The unbeliever is "dead in . . . transgressions and sins" (Eph. 2:1, 5; see Col. 2:13), which refers to spiritual, not physical, deadness. As a human being, each unsaved person is identified with Adam, the first man (Gen. 2:7) and progenitor of the human race. With his disobedience to God's command (2:16–17; 3:6–7), Adam immediately died spiritually (3:8–12) and became subject to physical death (3:17–19; 5:5). The human race is seen as being in Adam (1 Cor. 15:45–49) and therefore as participating in his sin (Rom. 5:12) and subject to his condemnation (5:15–19; 1 Cor. 15:21–22).

The unbeliever also lives in a world of spiritual darkness (Acts 26:18; Eph. 5:8; 6:12; Col. 1:13) and is spiritually blind (2 Cor. 4:4; 3:14–16). He is unknowingly energized by "the prince of the power of the air" (Eph. 2:2, NKJV), also called "the prince of this world" (John 12:31; 14:30; 16:11), "the god of this age" (2 Cor. 4:4), "the evil one" (John 17:15; 1 John 2:13, 14; 5:18–19), "the devil" (Matt. 4:8–9; Luke 4:5–7; John 8:44; Acts 13:10; 1 Tim. 3:6; James 3:15; 1 John 3:8, 10), and "that ancient serpent . . . Satan" (Rev. 12:9; 20:2). As a result of being empowered by Satan all unbelievers are "alienated from God" (Col. 1:21; see also Eph. 2:12) and are "God's enemies" (Rom. 5:10), subject to His wrath (2:5; Eph. 2:3; 5:6; Col. 3:6).

When a person receives Jesus Christ as his or her Savior by faith and is regenerated, the individual is identified with Christ and is "in Christ" (Rom. 16:7, 10; 2 Cor. 5:17; 12:2; Gal. 1:22). Christ in turn takes up residence in the believer (John 14:20; 17:23; Gal. 2:20; Eph. 3:17 Col. 1:27) by means of the indwelling Holy Spirit (John 14:17; Rom. 8:9, 11; 1 Cor. 3:16; 6:19; 2 Tim. 1:14). By the baptizing work of the Holy Spirit the believer is joined to Christ as a member of His spiritual body (1 Cor. 12:12–14, 20; Eph. 4:4, 11–16), the church (1:22–23; 5:22–30, 32).

Another aspect of the position of the Christian is that by his faith in Christ he is born into the family of God, thereby becoming a child of God (John 1:12–13; Rom. 8:14–17; see also Gal. 3:26; 4:5–7). As Paul wrote, "Now if [literally, 'since'] we are children, then we are heirs—heirs of God and co-heirs with Christ" (Rom. 8:17; see also Gal. 3:29; 4:7; 1 Pet. 3:7). God the Father has appointed the Lord Jesus, "his Son . . . heir of all things" (Heb. 1:2), and believers share in that future inheritance (1 Pet. 1:3–5), "the hope of eternal life" (Titus 3:7). The entire creation "waits in eager expectation for the sons of God to be revealed" (Rom. 8:19) and to "be liberated from its bondage to decay and brought into the glorious freedom of the children of God" (8:21). This is the believers' final "adoption as sons, the redemption of our bodies" (8:23). This sure hope of believers is to spend eternity "blameless and holy in the presence of our God and Father" (1 Thess. 3:13), "conformed to the likeness of his Son" (Rom. 8:29).

The position of believers is described in several other ways as well. Before receiving Jesus Christ as Savior, gentile believers were "excluded from citizenship in Israel and foreigners to the covenants of promise, without hope and without God in the world" (Eph. 2:12); but as a result of trusting Christ, they "are no longer foreigners and aliens, but fellow citizens with God's people and members of God's household" (2:19). As a result their "citizenship is in heaven. And [they] eagerly await a Savior from there, the Lord Jesus Christ" (Phil. 3:20).

Believers are also described as "living stones" that are being "built into a spiritual house" (1 Pet. 2:5). The individual believer is "a temple of the Holy Spirit" (1 Cor. 6:19), who is indwelling him (Rom. 8:9, 11; 2 Tim. 1:14), and believers collectively are called "a holy temple in the Lord" (Eph. 2:21) built on "the foundation of the apostles and prophets, with Christ Jesus himself as the chief cornerstone" (2:20; see also 1 Cor. 3:10–17; 2 Cor. 6:16).

By his baptizing work the Holy Spirit identifies each believer with Jesus Christ as a member of His body and gives him a spiritual gift to function appropriately (1 Cor. 12:4–11). This is illustrated by various parts of the physical body and their functions (12:14–26). As Paul concluded, "Now you are the body of Christ, and each one of you is a part of it" (12:27), with Christ the directing head (Eph. 1:22–23; 4:15; 5:23, 29–30; Col. 1:18; 2:19).

Although believers sin, confession will bring forgiveness and purification (1 John 1:8-10). The sinning believer has "one who speaks to the Father in our defense—Jesus Christ, the Righteous One" (2:1–2). That provision is not a license to sin (Rom. 6:1–14) but a guarantee of the security of the believer's position in Christ.   **—JAW**

Constantly bear in mind that, although your fellowship with Christ is affected by sin, your position in Christ remains secure.

Poverty

THE BIBLE OFTEN SPEAKS OF PEOPLE being poor, either economically (Prov. 10:15) or spiritually (Matt. 5:3; "poor in spirit" means to be humble). Those in economic poverty are of special concern to God (Deut. 15:7–11; 24:14–15; 1 Sam. 2:8; Ps. 12:5), especially orphans and widows (Exod. 22:22; Deut. 10:17–19; Ps. 146:9; Isa. 1:17; Jer. 22:3; Zech. 7:10; James 1:27). God made special regulations for their provision among His people Israel, such as allowing them to glean in the harvest fields each year (Lev. 19:9–10; 23:22; Deut. 24:19–21; Ruth 2:2–9, 17).

In the final analysis "the LORD sends poverty and wealth; he humbles and he exalts" (1 Sam. 2:7). He permitted Satan to do this to Job (Job 1:12–21), and He promised to do this to Israel for their failure to serve Him (Deut. 28:47–48). On the other hand, as the Book of Proverbs states, poverty sometimes results from laziness (Prov. 6:9–11; 24:30–34), from engaging in mere talk (14:23), entertaining fantasies (28:19), acting with haste (21:5), ignoring discipline (13:18), and being stingy (11:24; 28:22).

An example of generous giving in the midst of personal poverty is the "poor widow" who dropped into the temple treasury "two very small copper coins, worth only a fraction of a penny" (Mark 12:42; see Luke 21:2). Another example is the Macedonian churches, who "out of the most severe trial, their overflowing joy and their extreme poverty welled up in rich generosity. For I testify that they gave as much as they were able, and even beyond their ability.... They urgently pleaded with us for the privilege of sharing in this service to the saints" (2 Cor. 8:2–4). Their secret—and that of all Christian generosity—was that "they gave themselves first to the Lord and then to us in keeping with God's will" (8:5).

The supreme example of one who experienced poverty is, of course, Jesus Christ, who "did not consider equality with God something to be grasped, but made himself nothing, taking the very nature of a servant [literally, 'slave'], being made in human likeness. And being found in appearance as a man, he humbled himself and became obedient to death—even death on a cross" (Phil. 2:6–8; see also 2 Cor. 8:9). He was born to Mary, espoused to Joseph, a poor carpenter (Matt. 1:18–25; Luke 1:26–38), and lived His life as a poor, itinerant preacher, who lacked the funds to pay the temple tax (Matt. 17:24–27) and who had to be given a denarius, the poll tax, to be shown Caesar's picture on it (Matt. 22:18–21; Mark 12:15–17; Luke 20:24–25). After His death He was buried in a borrowed tomb (Matt. 27:57–60).

The spiritual condition of humanity is one of extreme poverty. People must recognize that their "righteous acts are like filthy rags" (Isa. 64:6). Recognizing this condition, David wrote, "I am poor and needy; may the Lord think of me" (Ps. 40:17; see also 70:5; 86:1; 109:22). When a person turns by faith to Jesus Christ, he then becomes spiritually wealthy (2 Cor. 8:9).   —JAW

Give to help meet the needs of the poor,
remembering that it stores up riches in heaven.

Praise

PRAISE CAN BE DEFINED as an expression of approval, esteem, or commendation. Synonyms are "laud," "acclaim," "extol," and "eulogize."

Scripture notes that praise is sometimes directed toward men and women (Prov. 31:28–31; 1 Pet. 2:14, NKJV), but the predominant biblical emphasis is on praise rendered to God. The angels continually praise God in heaven (Pss. 103:20; 148:2; Rev. 7:11–12). They praised God also when Jesus was born (Luke 2:13–14). Psalm 148 says angels, elements of nature, and animate and inanimate creation praise God together. Heaven and earth are said to be involved in praising God (Pss. 89:5; 96:11; 98:4). God's chosen people were obliged to praise Him, and it was intended that their praise would lead gentile nations to know and praise the Lord (67:2–3). The song of Moses (Exod. 15), in which God is praised for His redemptive acts, is an early example of Israelite homage; but the highest expression of their worship is found in the Book of Psalms, which in the Hebrew Bible carries the title "Book of Praises." Almost all the psalms contain some note of praise. According to this treasured book God is to be praised for His goodness and mercy to Israel and all peoples, for His vindication of the righteous in times of persecution, for His rulership over all mankind, and for His might as the Creator and Sovereign of the universe. Subjects of praise are also the Scriptures, Zion as God's earthly dwelling place, and the Davidic dynasty destined to occupy the throne of Israel.

Special times of praise in the Old Testament period included the Sabbaths, new moons, and various festivals. For example, Psalms 113–118, called collectively the *Hallēl*, were sung at Israel's great festivals —Passover, Pentecost, and Tabernacles—and also on other holy days. At the Passover Feast Psalms 113 and 114 were sung before the meal and Psalms 115–118 afterward. In addition, the psalms make clear that the godly were to be marked by continually praising God: "Seven times a day I praise you for your righteous laws" (119:164); "From the rising of the sun to the place where it sets, the name of the LORD is to be praised" (113:3); "I will praise the LORD all my life; I will sing praise to my God as long as I live" (146:2).

The advent of the Savior, Jesus Christ, brought a fresh outburst of praise (Luke 2:10–13). Paul, in a series of quotations from the Old Testament, emphasized that the fulfillment of divine prophecies to the Jews evoked praise to God from believing Gentiles, who along with believing Jews, are included in the family of God (Rom. 15:7–12). In a remarkable doxology the apostle praised God the Father for choosing us for salvation (Eph. 1:6); he praised God the Son for redeeming us through His sacrificial death (1:12); and he praised God the Holy Spirit for sealing us as God's own children (1:14).

Peter declared, "But you are a chosen people, a royal priesthood, a holy nation, a people belonging to God, that you may declare the praises of him who called you out of darkness into his wonderful light" (1 Pet. 2:9). Likewise, the author of Hebrews exhorted his readers, "Let us continually offer to God a sacrifice of praise—the fruit of lips that confess his name" (Heb. 13:15).

In the Book of Revelation the apostle John recorded a triumphant song of praise, a mighty hymn of thanksgiving in heaven that "sounded like the roar of a great multitude" (Rev. 19:1). Four times the great chorus sang "Hallelujah!"—a word (occurring only here in the New Testament) that transliterates a Hebrew expression meaning "Praise Yah," that is, "Praise God." The singing throng, looking back, praised God for His judgments, particularly His judgment on Babylon (19:2–3). This judgment will occur toward the end of the Great Tribulation. John then noted that the chorus will praise God for Christ's imminent coming and reign on earth (19:6). This passage contains the true "Hallelujah Chorus." It sets the stage for eternity when God's redeemed people will fulfill the admonition of the psalmist, "Let everything that has breath praise the LORD" (Ps. 150:6).   —DKC

> Praise God, from whom all blessings flow;
> Praise Him all creatures here below;
> Praise Him above, ye heavenly host;
> Praise Father, Son, and Holy Ghost.

Strive to praise God consistently for His blessings.

Prayer

HYMN WRITER JAMES MONTGOMERY penned some of the most meaningful words about prayer: "Prayer," he said, "is the soul's sincere desire, uttered or unexpressed, the motion of a hidden fire that trembles in the breast." In its simplest form prayer is talking to God. Often it takes the form of a request, while other times it is an expression of praise and gratitude to God. Prayer can be for ourselves or for others, and we can talk to God in private or with others. The Scriptures, particularly the Book of Psalms, are filled with examples of prayers. The New Testament also records many prayers and also gives instruction on how and why to pray.

The Old Testament uses a variety of words relating to prayer. A survey of these words helps us understand the scope of prayer. Intercession (Num. 21:7), entreaty (Exod. 32:11), confession (Ezra 10:1), supplication (1 Kings 8:30), call for help (Gen. 32:9–11), request (30:22), thanksgiving (Deut. 26:10–11), praise (Ps. 103), protection and deliverance (2 Chron. 32:20), judgment (1 Kings 17:1–2), healing (Isa. 38:1–5), cleansing (2 Chron. 30:18–20)—all these are included in Old Testament prayers.

People in the Old Testament who prayed believed in God and considered Him approachable. They sensed He cared for them and would respond to their petitions. Prayers were not limited to places of public worship, nor to certain times. For many, calling on the name of the Lord was as natural as any human communication they enjoyed. Some prayers were spontaneous, and others give evidence of careful thought and expression.

Principles about prayer can be gleaned from the prayers recorded in the Old Testament. Abraham's intercession for the people of Sodom and Gomorrah was based on the righteousness of God (Gen. 18:22–33). Abraham's servant sought God's guidance in selecting a bride for Isaac, demonstrating our need to pray according to the will of God (24:12–14, 26–27). The struggle that often occurs in prayer is illustrated by Jacob's encounter with God (32:24–32). When Moses sensed the anger of the Lord against the Israelites, he sought the Lord on their behalf, based on His promises (Exod. 32:9–14). Through Moses' prayers on behalf of the Israelites we learn that nothing is impossible with God (Num. 11:1–2, 10–23).

God's response to Joshua's prayer after the defeat by Ai shows how sin can affect the answer to our prayers (Josh. 7:8–12). David's prayer in 2 Samuel 7:18–29 teaches that God works on behalf of His great name. Solomon's prayer after his kingdom was established highlights the importance of humility in talking to God (2 Chron. 1:7–12). God's response to humility is also seen in Manasseh's prayer (33:12–13).

Disobedience to the Word of God can also affect the outcome of our prayers (Ezra 9:1–15). God told Jeremiah not to pray for Israel, because He would not respond when they were disobedient (Jer. 7:16, 23–26). Jonah's prayer is a good illustration of how God responds to those whose hearts are open before Him (Jon. 2:1–9).

Just as a variety of terms were used in the Old Testament to describe prayer, so the New Testament has a rich selection of words for prayer. One of the most common terms used, primarily in the Gospels and Acts, is *aiteō*, "to ask something of someone." Interestingly Christ never used this word when He prayed to the Father. The word Jesus used most of the time was *erōtaō*, "to request or ask a question" (for example, Matt. 16:13; John 14:16; 17:20). Another basic word is *deomai*, "to request, beseech, or beg," based on a need. The most common term for prayer is *proseuchomai*, used of voicing a request to a deity.

Paul and the other New Testament writers provided instruction on prayer, but the seed thoughts on prayer can be traced to Christ. In light of the many references to Christ's own prayer life, it seems strange that little is recorded about the disciples' prayer life. Even when they accompanied Jesus during His times of prayer, they seem to have been observers rather than participants (Matt. 26:36–45; Luke 22:39–46). His presence may have made prayer seem unnecessary or redundant, because after His ascension their prayer life was intensified (Acts 1:14).

Jesus' prayer life gave the disciples many opportunities to learn the importance of prayer, and it gives all believers a model for praying. Luke's Gospel gives the most comprehensive picture of Christ's commitment to prayer. Luke stated that Jesus was praying when His baptism occurred (Luke 3:21). Prayer was an essential part of His daily life (5:16). He spent a whole night in prayer before choosing His disciples (6:12). Before He performed the miracle of multiplying the loaves and fish, He looked up to the Father in prayer (9:16). When He was transfigured, He was praying (9:29). Praise to the Father broke from His lips as He received the seventy-two who returned from their appointed mission (10:21). On another occasion, at the disciples' request, He provided a model for prayer (11:1–4). He spoke parables that exhorted them to pray (18:1). His personal concern for His disciples kept Him praying for them (22:31–32). The night before He was crucified He spent a significant period of time in prayer to the Father (22:39–44). Those who stood by the cross and watched Him die heard His last words which were spoken to God (23:46). After the resurrection He prayed before eating with two of His friends (24:30).

Two main sources for the Lord's teaching on prayer are the Sermon on the Mount (Matt. 5–7) and the Upper Room Discourse (John 13–17). From these passages the following concepts about prayer may be gleaned: Our attitude in prayer is crucial (Matt. 6:5–6, 14–15), quality is more important than length (6:7), God's will should always be paramount (6:10), nothing is too mundane for prayer (6:11), we must be sensitive to sin and confess it (6:12), believers must be aware of the adversary (6:13), God answers prayer (6:7–8), God gives us the best in answer to prayer (6:9–12), prayer should be in the name of Christ, that is, in accord with His character (John 14:13–14), prayer must be for the glory of the Father (14:13), prayer is to be based on the most intimate relationship with the Lord (15:1–7), and prayer should be according to His Word (15:7).

Other passages in the Gospels give additional instruction. Prayer must be made in faith (Matt. 21:22; Mark 11:24), it must be genuine (9:29), persistent prayer is welcomed (Luke 11:5–10), God will not hold back what is best for His own (11:9–13), believers should not give up in voicing their requests to God (18:1–5), and they should pray in accord with the will of God (22:42).

The Book of Acts presents a revealing picture of the role of prayer in the early church. From the very beginning of the church at Pentecost, prayer was at the heart of the believers' daily life (Acts 2:42; 4:24, 31; 6:4). When the gospel went to Samaria, the role of prayer was significant (8:15). Peter's ministry was carried on through prayer (9:40; 10:9, 31). The corporate prayer of the church was instrumental in Peter's escape from prison (12:5, 12). Barnabas and Saul were sent out as missionaries by the church at Antioch after a time of prayer (13:3). Leaders for churches were selected with prayer and fasting (14:23). Some churches, like the one at Philippi, began as a result of faithful prayer (16:13). Prayer sustained Paul and Silas during their imprisonment (16:25). The closing chapters of Acts show how prayer marked the life and ministry of Paul as he struggled to preach the gospel in the midst of great opposition.

Paul's letters to the churches show how prayer was to be conducted in these congregations. The spread of the gospel depended on the prayers of

God's people (Rom. 15:30–31; Eph. 6:19–20; Col. 4:4; 2 Thess. 3:1). Group prayer allowed many to be involved in ministry (2 Cor. 1:11). Paul was concerned about the decorum of men and women in their practice of prayer (1 Cor. 11:3–16; 1 Tim. 2:8). His prayers for the Ephesian and Colossian believers, with their strong theological content, give insight into his pattern of praying (Eph. 1:15–23; 3:14–21; Phil. 1:9–11; Col. 1:10–12). Prayer is essential in standing against Satan (Eph. 6:18), and prayer is to be continual (1 Thess. 5:17). Paul exhorted Christians to pray for those in places of authority (1 Tim. 2:1–2). His letters also provide an example of his personal prayer life, especially his burden for the nation Israel (Rom. 10:1). Paul said that not all his prayers were answered in the affirmative, and that God had reasons for saying no (2 Cor. 12:7–10).

The remainder of the New Testament focuses on specific issues relating to prayer. James and Peter discussed hindrances to prayer and the significance of a godly life (James 4:1–3, 5:13–18; 1 Pet. 3:7, 4:7). John emphasized praying according to God's will (1 John 5:13–15) and in obedience to His commands (3:22). Jude reminded believers to pray in the Holy Spirit (Jude 20). The writer of Hebrews described the ministry of the risen Christ as our Great High Priest, who intercedes for us (Heb. 4:14, 7:24–25). Probably no teaching in Scripture is more pertinent to the Christian life and the progress of Christianity than that on prayer.

—WGJ

Take every opportunity to talk with the Lord,
and keep an updated list of requests that you can pray about daily.

Predestination

PREDESTINATION MEANS THAT EVENTS and situations in the plan of God are made certain in advance. It is part of God's work in eternity past in adopting a complete plan for the universe, including all that would eventuate.

Four verses in the New International Version have the verb *predestine,* which translates the Greek *proorizō* (Rom. 8:29–30; Eph. 1:5, 11). The same Greek verb also occurs in Acts 4:28, where it is translated "to determine beforehand," and in 1 Corinthians 2:7, where the word "destined" is used. Romans 8:29–30 spells out what is involved in predestination. Scripture links predestination to God's plan for believers to be transformed into the image of Christ. "For those God foreknew he also predestined to be conformed to the likeness of his Son, that he might be the firstborn among many brothers" (8:29). Paul then detailed the process: "And those he predestined, he also called; those he called, he also justified; those he justified, he also glorified" (8:30). In the verses that follow, Paul pointed out how this makes impossible the bringing of any charge against those who have been justified or declared righteous in God's sight (8:30–34), concluding that nothing can separate a believer from the love of Christ (8:35–39).

Like the doctrine of election, the doctrine of predestination is not fatalism, even though all events have been rendered certain by the intelligent act of God. In eternity past God chose (elected) some individuals, predestining them to receive salvation and to be conformed to His Son, Jesus Christ. He also determined the method by which they would be brought to the knowledge of the gospel, believe in Christ, and be saved. God's election does not force anyone to believe, but election does insure the fact that they will certainly believe. Certainty differs from coercion. While the full issue is perhaps beyond human understanding, it is clear from the Scriptures that this is what is revealed. Those who are saved can rejoice in the fact that they were included in the plan of God from eternity past. —JFW

If you are a believer, enjoy the certainty of salvation in Christ.

Priesthood

SCRIPTURE PRESENTS THE PRIESTHOOD as an institution of critical importance. In Old Testament times the work of the priesthood symbolized achieving and retaining acceptance by and fellowship with God. In the New Testament it provides the basis for understanding the redemptive work of Jesus Christ.

In patriarchal times priestly functions were performed by heads of families, as exemplified by Abraham and Job. Noah, after the Flood, built an altar and sacrificed burnt offerings (Gen. 8:20–21). Abraham built altars at Bethel, Mamre, and Moriah (12:7; 13:4; 22:1–13). Job offered sacrifices on behalf of his children (Job 1:5). The Bible refers also to the priesthood of Melchizedek (Gen. 14:18), of the Egyptians (41:50; 46:20; 47:22), and of the Midianites (Exod. 2:16; 3:1; 18:1). Moses apparently appointed priests prior to the Levitical priesthood (19:22, 24; 24:5). After the institution of the Hebrew priesthood, some who were not priests sometimes performed priestly duties, such as Gideon (Judg. 6:24–26), the men of Bethshemesh (1 Sam. 6:14–15), Samuel (7:9), David (2 Sam. 6:13–17), Solomon (1 Kings 8:22–24), and Elijah (1 Kings 18:23). These actions were not disapproved; but they must be viewed as exceptional cases.

Moses, following divine instruction, appointed Aaron and his sons as priests (Exod. 28:1) to serve as mediators between God and Israel, and to minister in holy things on behalf of the people. Aaron and his sons were consecrated in a seven-day ceremony that was elaborate, solemn, and meaningful (Exod. 29; Lev. 8). They also wore special priestly garments, Aaron's as high priest being more elaborate than those worn by the other priests (Exod. 28:2–39). The main task of the high priest was to officiate at the ceremonies of the Day of Atonement (Lev. 16). The ordinary priests were assigned to officiate at the specified Levitical sacrifices and offerings (Lev. 1–6) and to declare clean those who had been made ceremonially unclean by certain infectious diseases (Lev. 13–14). They also performed certain other less significant duties (23:24; 25:10; Num. 10:10). The Levites functioned as servants to the priests. They were charged with the physical care of the tabernacle and were responsible to move it from place to place in the wilderness (1:47–53; 3:1–38; Deut. 11:8–9). The Chronicles record that the Levites were musicians and treasurers (1 Chron. 6:31–32; 9:19; 16:4–5, 7; 25:1–7; 26:1, 20; 2 Chron. 8:14).

The priests and Levites did not receive a tribal portion of the land as an inheritance; instead, they were supported by the tithes, firstfruits, and parts of various sacrifices (Num. 18). The Levites, however, were given forty-eight cities and surrounding pasture lands to live in, thirteen of which were for Aaron's sons, the priests (Num. 35; Josh. 21).

The Old Testament records numerous failures with respect to the priesthood. In the period of the judges, Micah established an apostate shrine and an unlawful priesthood (Judg. 17). At the time of the division of the united kingdom, Jeroboam I appointed priests who were not from the tribe of Levi (1 Kings 12:31) and also served as a priest himself (12:32–33). Ahaz offered sacrifices on an altar modeled after one he had seen in Damascus (2 Kings 16:10–16). Uzziah was smitten with leprosy because he usurped the priest's office (2 Chron. 26:16–20). Because of the gross sins of the sons of Eli the high priest, it was predicted that his descendants would lose the priestly office (1 Sam. 2:27–36). This prophecy was fulfilled in the days of Solomon when the priestly line passed to the Zadokites, descendants of Aaron through his son Eleazar (1 Kings 2:27; 1 Chron. 6:4–8; 24:3).

By New Testament times the high priesthood was no longer held for life even though that is what Jewish law prescribed. The Romans did not approve of such a concentration of power in one person so they changed high priests frequently. Annas, for example, was appointed high priest by Quirinius, governor of Syria in A.D. 6 but was deposed in A.D. 15. He was succeeded by five of his sons and his son-in-law Caiaphas (Luke 3:2; John 18:12–13).

When Jesus healed lepers, He sent them to the priests at the temple in keeping with the Mosaic regulation (Mark 1:44; Luke 5:14; 17:14). By acknowledging these miracles the priests would be forced to give testimony to Jesus' mighty works. At the close of Jesus' ministry the priesthood was closely involved in His death (Matt. 26:3, 14, 57–65; 27:1). They were also major antagonists of the leaders of the early church (Acts 4:1–6; 9:1–2). Yet Luke recorded that during these days "a large number of priests became obedient to the faith" (6:7).

When the Romans destroyed the temple and Jewish state in A.D. 70, the Old Testament Jewish priesthood disappeared from history. While the Jews subsequently made some attempts to continue the priestly order and the sacrificial system, they were not successful and soon abandoned the institution entirely.

The letter to the Hebrews declares that the Old Testament priesthood was fulfilled in Jesus Christ. Aaron and Melchizedek form the connection between the Testaments in that both typify or foreshadow Christ's priesthood. Christ's priestly *duties* are after Aaron's priesthood in that He offered Himself as a sacrifice for sin (Heb. 7:27), He entered heaven, the Most Holy Place, by virtue of His blood (9:7, 12, 24), thereby securing our eternal redemption (9:12) and giving us free access to the throne of grace (4:16). As to the priestly *order*, Jesus' priesthood is patterned after that of Melchizedek. The New Scofield Reference Bible notes several ways in which the Melchizedekian high priesthood is greater than the Aaronic: Aaron in Abraham paid tithes to Melchizedek (7:4–10); the Aaronic priesthood made nothing perfect (7:11–22); the Aaronic priests died whereas Christ lives (7:23–28); the Aaronic priests served as shadows of Christ, the reality (8:1–5); and Christ mediates a superior covenant (8:6–10:18). It is therefore evident that Jesus Christ, as both High Priest and atoning Sacrifice, fulfilled everything the Old Testament priesthood pictured.

While the term *priest* is never used in the New Testament of a minister in the church, believers are described as a "holy priesthood, offering spiritual sacrifices acceptable to God through Jesus Christ" (1 Pet. 2:5); "a kingdom and priests to serve his God and Father" (Rev. 1:6; see also 5:10); "and priests of God and of Christ and will reign with him for a thousand years" (20:6). From the time of Martin Luther these verses have been viewed as the basis for the universal priesthood of all believers over against any claims by a priestly caste to mediate between God and individual believers.

The priesthood of Christians involves, above all else, sacrificial obedience to God. Paul wrote, "I urge you, brothers, in view of God's mercy, to offer your bodies as living sacrifices, holy and pleasing to God—which is your spiritual worship" (Rom. 12:1). The author of Hebrews exhorted, "Through Jesus, therefore, let us continually offer to God a sacrifice of praise—the fruit of lips that confess his name. And do not forget to do good and to share with others, for with such sacrifices God is pleased" (Heb. 13:15–16).　　　　　**—DKC**

List several spiritual sacrifices that believers
as New Testament priests are exhorted to offer to God.

Prophecy

PROPHECY ASSUMES THE REALITY of supernatural revelation from God. To deny the possibility that God can predict what lies ahead inevitably denies that the Bible is supernaturally inspired and that the prophets who spoke had genuine messages from God. Not all prophets were writers of Scripture, but many were. The term *prophet* describes one who received supernatural messages from God and was commissioned to pass these messages on to God's people. A true prophet had the supernatural experience of being a channel of God's truth. What God revealed through His prophets covered a wide gamut of truth, some of it moral and some of it predictive, but in every case the prophets' messages carried God's authority. About one-fourth of Scripture was predictive when it was first revealed. Many books of the Old and New Testaments are largely prophetic, including Daniel, Ezekiel, Jeremiah, significant portions of the Gospels and the Epistles, and the Book of Revelation. Major areas of prophecy include Israel, the nations, and the church.

While prophecy was often given in symbols, the Bible itself usually explains the meaning of the symbol so that the prophecy presents a factual statement. The popular idea that prophecy is not literal is not supported by Scripture. About half of the Bible's prophecies have already been fulfilled literally, which shows that when God speaks He expects to be understood in the normal meaning of the words.

Prophets conveyed their messages from God both orally and in written form. Written prophecy is often a record of oral transmission. The process by which truth was received by the prophets varies; God sometimes spoke directly and sometimes He spoke in dreams and visions. But the result was that God communicated truth about the present and the future through the prophets, His spokesmen. In the last four hundred years before Christ no prophet appeared except Anna, a prophetess (Luke 2:36), and John the Baptist (Matt. 21:26), both of whom immediately preceded Jesus. Then came Christ, the greatest of all prophets (Deut. 18:15; Matt. 21:11; Acts 3:22; 7:37). In the first century God spoke through both men and women prophets. Once the Scriptures were completed, however, the gift of prophecy seems to have ceased (1 Cor. 13:8).

The Holy Spirit, however, illuminates the Scriptures to make them understandable to believers. As some prophecies have been fulfilled, readers have a renewed appreciation of what the Bible predicted.

False prophets were distinguished from true prophets by several factors, including whether the prophecies were fulfilled (Deut. 18:21–22). Usually there was some evidence that the message of a prophet of God was true; sometimes the prophets were verified by a miraculous sign.

Attacks on the inspiration of the Bible, especially by higher critics in recent centuries, have tended to reduce confidence in the Scriptures as the inspired, inerrant Word of God. Obviously any low view of Scripture results in a low view of prophecy.

In interpreting prophecy properly, it is necessary to assume that the Scriptures are inerrant and thus reliable, that prophecy is expressed in terms in which the natural meaning is the intended meaning, and that the details of the prophecy are very important and, if ignored, lead to false doctrines. Also in some cases there is multiple fulfillment, that is, the prophecy was partially fulfilled and then was or will be completely fulfilled at some later time.

The fundamental purpose of prophecy is to give believers the necessary facts to plan wisely for future events that will eventually take place. However, prophecy is intended not only to be informative but also to be challenging—a rebuke for sin and a message of hope. (See, for example, 1 Cor. 15:58; 1 Thess. 3:13; 4:18; Titus 2:11–13; James 5:7–9; 2 Pet. 3:11, 13; 1 John 3:2.)   —JFW

Write down the specific promises God has for the future,
knowing that these will certainly be fulfilled as written.

Propitiation

SINCE THE WRATH OF GOD is an integral aspect of His nature, His holy and righteous character must be upheld and His wrath averted if a sinner is to experience salvation and the forgiveness of sins. The biblical meaning of propitiation is that God's wrath has been turned away from the sinner because of the supreme sacrifice of the Lord Jesus Christ on the cross. The doctrine of propitiation does as much to enhance the concept of the grace of God as any other truth. The light of God's impeccable holiness never shines brighter than when it is contrasted to the sinfulness of humankind. God's love was most clearly displayed when God Himself provided the sacrifice of His Son to avert His wrath and satisfy His holiness. God's grace was supremely evident when Christ's sacrifice on the cross was received by the Father as the total payment for the sins of the world (1 John 2:2).

The meaning of propitiation is based on several closely related Greek words, each of which is used twice in the New Testament: *hilaskomai,* "to propitiate" (Luke 18:13; Heb. 2:17), *hilasmos,* "propitiation" (1 John 2:2; 4:10), and *hilastērion* (Rom. 3:25; Heb. 9:5). These words are translated in slightly different ways in the New International Version. In Luke 18:13 (NKJV), the tax collector recognized his unrighteousness in the sight of God and asked the Lord to "be merciful" to him, and in Hebrews 2:17 the word is rendered to "make atonement." In Romans 3:25 the word is translated by the phrase "a sacrifice of atonement." The two occurrences of *hilasmos* in 1 John are both translated "atoning sacrifice." The New American Standard Bible translates these passages (except Luke 18:13) with the term "propitiate." The meaning of the Greek word for propitiation has been questioned by those who deny the concept of satisfying God's wrath in salvation. They have suggested that *expiate,* "to atone," better describes what the word means. However, that translation does not adequately address the issue of God's wrath.

In using these terms Paul emphasized the substitutionary death of Christ (Rom. 3:25); the writer of Hebrews described Jesus as the faithful High Priest atoning for sin (Heb. 2:17); and John declared that Christ is the Righteous One, worthy to be the Sacrifice for the sins of the whole world (1 John 2:2). Romans 3:25 and 1 John 4:10 clearly show that God Himself is the Provider of the all-sufficient sacrifice, thus establishing the depth of God's love in the process of propitiation.

—WGJ

Rejoice in the fact that God is satisfied with Christ's death as the payment for your sins and that you will never be condemned for these sins.

Providence

WHILE THE WORD *providence* does not occur in Scripture, it does represent a true biblical doctrine. The Westminster Confession of Faith states, "God, the great Creator of all things, doth uphold, direct, dispose, and govern all creatures, actions and things, from the greatest even to the least, by His most wise and holy providence" (5.1). Scripture declares that the world in which we live continues because "the Son is the radiance of God's glory and the exact representation of his being, sustaining all things by his powerful word" (Heb. 1:3). Further, "He [Christ] is before all things, and in him all things hold together" (Col. 1:17).

Providence contradicts deism, which likens God to a watchmaker who wound up a watch and left it running. So God supposedly created the world and its natural laws but takes no part in its functioning. Also eliminated by a biblical view of providence are such concepts as dualism, which sees two equal powers of good and evil in the universe; chance, which sees all things happening by accident; and fatalism, which sees events as uncontrollable and without any good purpose. Psalm 33:12–15 and Acts 17:24–28 counter these false views and clearly describe how God personally sustains and governs the world and humankind.

Israel experienced God's special love and care in Old Testament times (Amos 3:1; Mal. 1:2). Moreover, after the period of gentile visitation God's unbroken love for Israel is to be manifested in her future restoration (Acts 15:14–16; Rom. 11:1–27). And in the present dispensation the church, the body of Christ, is the object of God's providential love (Eph. 3:14–19).

Providence may be defined as "God's timely provision for the needs of humans." Biblical examples of such divine actions are numerous. A vivid case is found in the story of Abraham when he was instructed to sacrifice his son Isaac. In response to Isaac's question Abraham affirmed, "God himself will provide the lamb for the burnt offering" (Gen. 22:8). The divine provision of the ram moved Abraham to name the mountain where they stood with a new name that celebrated God's providence (22:14). Joseph's experiences in Egypt, in which he saw the tragedies of his youth changed into the triumphs of his adulthood, are properly seen as evidences of God's providence. In fact, the record of these events is a classical statement in Scripture on divine providence. Joseph himself said to his fearful brothers, "Don't be afraid. Am I in the place of God? You intended to harm me, but God intended it for good to accomplish what is now being done, the saving of many lives" (50:19–20).

Jonah's life, too, was touched by divine intervention when the Lord providentially used a great fish and a small worm to direct the prophet's course. The entire Book of Esther portrays the amazing workings of providence that lead to the preservation of the Jewish people in a foreign land. The small Book of Philemon tells the interesting story of how the slave Onesimus was providentially directed to the apostle Paul hundreds of miles away in Rome.

Believers are constantly under God's providential watchcare. The psalmist declared, "You hem me in—behind and before; you have laid your hand upon me" (Ps. 139:5), and, "For he will command his angels concerning you to guard you in all your ways" (91:11). In the New Testament we have affirmations of divine providence by Jesus (Matt. 6:26) and Paul (Rom. 8:28–39).

God's timely interventions in our lives are always recognizable by the eye of faith. Thanksgiving to such a personal and loving God is the only proper response believers should have to God's wonderful providential care. **—DKC**

In a journal or diary write daily examples of God's providence.
Look back at the end of the year and you will be greatly encouraged!

Rr

Rapture

WHILE THE OLD TESTAMENT REVEALED the first and second comings of Christ, it nowhere prophesied a rapture of the church. In fact, by misunderstanding the Old Testament prophecies, Israel expected that at Christ's first coming he would establish His millennial reign on earth. They overlooked or ignored the Old Testament predictions about His sufferings and death in His first advent. This is why the disciples who were following Christ were hoping to have a part in His glorious kingdom. Toward the end of His public ministry He told them He would suffer and die and then be raised the third day. They had difficulty believing this because it did not fit into their understanding of prophecy.

The Rapture refers to a whole generation of believers being caught up into heaven without dying. Jesus first introduced this truth in the Upper Room when He promised, "And if I go and prepare a place for you, I will come back and take you to be with me that you also may be with me where I am" (John 14:3). He added that He would be in His Father's house, a reference to heaven. He did not discuss His return further at that time because they were confused on the first and second comings of Christ. They would not have been able to comprehend fuller teaching about an additional coming when He will take His own out of the earth. Later the apostle Paul explained the doctrine of the Rapture more fully (1 Thess. 4:13–18). Forced to leave Thessalonica because of opposition, Paul sent Timothy back to inquire on their condition (3:2–5). Timothy found them standing true to the faith (3:6–8), but they were puzzled by the question as to what would happen to some of their loved ones who had died since Paul left. In answering their questions Paul detailed what will happen at the Rapture.

The Rapture gives hope to Christians whose believing loved ones die, assuring them that they will see their loved ones again. The truth of the Rapture, Paul said, is just as certain as the death and resurrection of

Christ (4:14). When living believers in the church age are caught up to be with the Lord, their dead loved ones will be resurrected immediately before them. Both the believers who have died and those who are still living will at that moment be given bodies suited for heaven. "For the Lord Himself will come down from heaven with a loud command, with the voice of the archangel, and with the trumpet call of God, and the dead in Christ shall rise first. After that we who are still alive and are left will be caught up together with them in the clouds to meet the Lord in the air. And so we will be with the Lord forever" (4:16–17). The expression "will be caught up together," which presents the doctrine of the Rapture, could have been translated "will be raptured together," in other words, snatched from the earth and taken to heaven. When Christ comes in the clouds to take us to Himself, our being caught up or raptured to be with Him will occur in an instant, "in a flash, in the twinkling of an eye" (1 Cor. 15:52).

Dead church-age believers are said to be "asleep" now, that is, at death their bodies look like people who are sleeping (1 Cor. 15:6, 18, 20, 51; 1 Thess. 4:13–15; see also Mark 5:39; John 11:11, 13). But in the Rapture their bodies will come out of the graves, will be joined with their souls, and will be given resurrected bodies like Jesus' glorified body. Living saints will also be given resurrection bodies the moment they are caught up. "When he appears, we shall be like him, for we shall see him as he is" (1 John 3:2). The corruptible (dead bodies) will become incorrupt, and the mortal (living saints whose bodies are decaying) will become immortal (1 Cor. 15:42, 52–54). Paul called this "the redemption of our bodies" (Rom. 8:23).

In 1 Thessalonians 5:1–11 Paul discussed when this will occur. He wrote that after the Rapture, the period known as the Day of the Lord—a time of tribulation that will embrace the whole world—will begin. Some people teach that the Rapture will occur after the seven-year Tribulation. But passages that discuss the Rapture give no hint of any intervening events such as the Tribulation that must occur before the Lord comes for His church. This contrasts with passages on Christ's second coming to set up His kingdom on earth, which will be preceded by many events prophesied in Revelation 6–18. Many arguments support pretribulationalism, the view that the Rapture will occur before the Tribulation, and several passages clearly support it.

Matthew 25:31–46 depicts an event that will occur soon after the Second Coming. Christ will assemble the gentile believers who will be living then. Described as sheep and goats, the sheep represent the saved and the goats represent the lost. If the Rapture occurred at the time of the Second Coming, the sheep would have been taken out in the Rapture, leaving only the goats. Thus no further separation would be necessary.

Another passage that supports the view that the church will be raptured before, not after, the Tribulation is Revelation 3:10. Jesus Christ promised that believers will be kept out of, not kept through, "the hour of trial that is going to come upon the whole world." They will be kept from the Tribulation by being raptured before it begins.

Also the Tribulation will be a time of God's wrath (6:16), and Jesus has rescued us "from the coming wrath" (1 Thess. 1:10; see also 5:9).

Posttribulationalists—those who say that the church will go through the Tribulation and that the Rapture will occur at the end of the Tribulation—seek to support their view by pointing to Jesus' words in John 16:33, "In the world you will have tribulation" (NKJV). However, this statement refers to troubles or difficulties believers face in this life. Posttribulationalists also suggest that the Scriptures make no clear statement about the Rapture preceding the Tribulation or that there are two aspects to Jesus' second coming (the Rapture, and later His return to the earth). The facts is, however, that posttribulationists cannot point to any Scripture that says the Rapture will occur at Jesus' second coming. However, as noted earlier, on the whole, the biblical evidence suggests that the Rapture of the church will precede the Tribulation.

The Rapture gives believers hope (it is called "the blessed hope," Titus 2:13); it encourages them to lead pure lives (1 Thess. 3:13; James 5:8–9; 1 John 3:3); and it is a source of comfort to those whose believing loved ones have died before the Rapture (1 Thess. 4:18). Anticipating the possibility of this event occurring soon, believers "eagerly wait for our Lord Jesus" to come (2 Cor. 1:7). "We eagerly await a Savior from [heaven], the Lord Jesus Christ" (Phil. 3:20; see also 1 Thess. 1:10).   —JFW

*Conduct your life in a manner that reflects the hope
of Christ's soon coming for His church.*

Reconciliation

THE BRINGING TOGETHER of two or more parties into unity, harmony, or agreement by removing the cause of disharmony is called reconciliation. This biblical doctrine brings into focus human alienation from God because of sin and God's provision through the cross of Christ for restoring individuals to God's favor.

A major passage that presents this doctrine is Romans 5:6–11, in which unsaved people are said to be "powerless," "ungodly," "sinners," and "God's enemies." Sin has created a barrier between God and humanity, placing us in a position of hostility toward our Creator. The remedy for such a tragic plight is reconciliation, the removal of the enmity that stands between people and God, and that remedy is accomplished through the death of Jesus Christ. "When we were God's enemies, we were reconciled to him through the death of his Son" (5:10). "He has reconciled you by Christ's physical body through death to present you holy in his sight, without blemish and free from accusation" (Col. 1:22).

Paul declared in 2 Corinthians 5:19 that God reconciled "the world to himself." That is, because of the death of Christ for lost humanity, the whole world was changed in its relation to God. By this change, people were rendered savable. Yet individuals must respond by faith in the finished work of Christ on the cross. And when they do, at that moment they become reconciled to God. The moving appeal of the apostle is therefore, "We implore you on Christ's behalf: Be reconciled to God" (5:20).

The fact that Scripture speaks only of humans being reconciled to God and not of God being reconciled to humans does not minimize the truth of God's hatred for sin. People have come under God's righteous judgment because of sin. God in His holiness cannot look on sin. His righteous demands against the sinner must be satisfied, and this satisfaction (propitiation) is also fully provided by the perfect sacrifice of Jesus Christ.

In Ephesians 2:11–12, Paul wrote about an inveterate hostility that divided Jews and Gentiles. There was between them a wall of hatred and contempt. Jews considered Gentiles "dogs," that is, ceremonially unclean, who were to be avoided if at all possible. Gentiles treated Jews in a similar fashion, considering them enemies. Yet Christ Jesus, the Peacemaker, broke down this barrier of hostility so that believing Jews and believing Gentiles can live together in unity and harmony (2:14). Further, Paul spoke not only about reconciliation between Jewish and gentile believers but also about the reconciliation of both groups to God "through the cross" (2:16). The basic message of this passage is timely and relevant for a world divided by ongoing hatred and hostilities. When angry sinners have been brought into harmony with God at the cross, they can be truly reconciled to each other.

Paul declared that God "has committed to us the message of reconciliation" (2 Cor. 5:19). That message is summarized in the words that immediately follow: "God made him who had no sin to be sin for us, so that in him we might become the righteousness of God" (5:21). The apostle himself exemplified for all of Christ's followers in succeeding generations what it means to be His ambassador, faithfully proclaiming "the message of reconciliation."   **—DKC**

Pray that God will lead you to someone with whom you can share
"the message of reconciliation."

Redemption

THE CONCEPT OF DELIVERANCE from some type of bondage on the basis of the payment of a ransom is called redemption. Redemption describes the means by which salvation is achieved.

In the Old Testament both property and life could be redeemed by a fitting payment. The firstborn in Israel had to be redeemed by money since they were spared in the final plague which fell on Egypt (Exod. 13:13–15). If an Israelite lost his estate or was forced to sell himself into slavery, both he and his property could be redeemed if a kinsman provided the redemption price (Lev. 25:25–27, 47–54; Ruth 4:1–12).

God is called Israel's Redeemer (Ps. 78:35). In stating His plan to deliver Israel from bondage in Egypt, He declared, "I will redeem you with an outstretched arm" (Exod. 6:6). When Israel was once again in captivity, in Babylon, God promised to be its Redeemer (Jer. 31:11; 50:33–34). Thus, while it appears that the majority of Old Testament references to God's redemptive activity are physical rather than spiritual in nature, Israel's deliverance from Babylon did come about because God forgave the sins that occasioned that calamity. Spiritual redemption, that is, redemption from sin, is clearly stated in Psalm 130:7–8: "O Israel, put your hope in the LORD, for with the LORD is unfailing love and with him is full redemption. He himself will redeem Israel from all their sins."

In the New Testament, redemption is strictly a work of God accomplished by and through Jesus Christ. The mission of Christ as Redeemer is declared in His own words, "For even the Son of Man did not come to be served, but to serve, and to give his life a ransom for many" (Mark 10:45). His earthly life, He said, would conclude in a self-sacrifice that would serve as a spiritual ransom of sinners from their bondage to sin. In the early church the idea arose that Christ redeemed lost sinners by paying a ransom to the devil. Anselm (1033–1109), archbishop of Canterbury, refuted this theory in his *Cur Deus Homo* (Why God Became Man). The Scriptures are silent as to whom the ransom was paid, though certainly it would have been to God Himself if to anyone. The emphasis, in any case, is not on the recipient of the ransom but on the sufficiency of the payment made by Christ.

The most extensive development of the doctrine of redemption is found in the writings of Paul. He declared that Christ "gave himself for us to redeem us from all wickedness" (Titus 2:14); that Christ "redeemed us from the curse of the law by becoming a curse for us" (Gal. 3:13); that "He redeemed us in order that the blessing given to Abraham might come to the Gentiles through Christ Jesus, so that by faith we might receive the promise of the Spirit" (3:14). The apostle sometimes coupled redemption with justification and propitiation (Rom. 3:24; 1 Cor. 1:30). He also stressed the *present* benefits of redemption: "In him we have redemption through his blood, the forgiveness of sins" (Eph. 1:7), as well as the *future* blessing of the deliverance of the body from its present debility: "We wait eagerly for our adoption as sons, the redemption of our bodies" (Rom. 8:23; see also Eph. 4:30).

Peter too, emphasized that redemption was purchased at great price, namely, by "the precious blood of Christ, a lamb without blemish or defect" (1 Pet. 1:19). The author of Hebrews stressed the perfection of the redemptive work of Christ (Heb. 9:25–27).

In the vocabulary of the Christian no word can be considered more precious or treasured than "Redeemer," because it reminds us that our salvation, while free, was paid for by the One who gave Himself for our sins. Fanny J. Crosby expressed this truth beautifully in one of her many hymns.

—**DKC**

Redeemed—How I love to proclaim it!
Redeemed by the blood of the Lamb;
Redeemed by His infinite mercy,
His child, and forever, I am.

Praise God for the past, present, and future benefits of redemption.

Regeneration

TO OVEREMPHASIZE THE IMPORTANCE of this doctrine is impossible, because regeneration or the new birth is the dividing line between heaven and hell. From God's perspective every individual is either spiritually dead and destined for eternal perdition, or spiritually alive because of His regenerating power and destined for eternal glory.

The word *regeneration* occurs only in Matthew 19:28 and Titus 3:5 (NKJV). In the former passage the word refers to the future time of Christ's reign when the earth will be renewed and the nation of Israel will be reborn. In Titus the word is used in the spiritual sense of individual renewal or rebirth.

In the early church numerous theologians, including Justin Martyr, Irenaeus, Clement of Alexandria, Tertullian, Cyprian, Athanasius, and others, taught that water baptism was the means through which the Holy Spirit brought regeneration to the individual. They also failed to distinguish between regeneration and justification. Theologians of the Reformation period affirmed the biblical truth that regeneration is solely a work of God accomplished by the Holy Spirit. In modern-day liberal theology regeneration is viewed as primarily an ethical issue, a matter of personal conduct and not a divine work. Evangelicals agree that regeneration is a work of God for believers separate from ecclesiastical rites. It involves simply the instantaneous change from spiritual death to spiritual life through the impartation of eternal life. In His conversation with Nicodemus Jesus affirmed the need for regeneration. Three times He said the new birth is an absolute necessity (John 3:3, 5, 7). Four reasons underlie Christ's strong declaration: the state of total depravity, the state of spiritual death, the nature of heaven, and the character of God. In their natural condition every human being is totally (that is, in every part) depraved or corrupt and without any merit in God's sight (Job 15:14–16; Rom. 3:9–18). The only remedy for such a condition is a re-creation by God (Gal. 6:15).

Apart from salvation people are spiritually dead (Eph. 2:1–3; 4:17–19), alienated from God, and thus insensible to the realities of the spiritual world. As a stone could not grow without entering the organic world, so a spiritually dead person cannot be transformed by self-reformation but only by the impartation of divine life.

The nature of heaven also argues for the need for regeneration. As the abode of God, heaven will have no sin or defilement (Rev. 21:27; 22:15). Enjoyment of such a spiritual or heavenly kingdom demands a spiritual or heavenly nature, a nature that can be obtained only through regeneration, God's work whereby believers become "partakers of the divine nature" (2 Pet. 1:4, NASB). God's holiness, considered against the dark background of man's depravity, underscores the significance of Jesus' words, "You must be born again." God in His holiness cannot look on sin (Ezra 9:15; Isa. 59:1–2). Only the regenerated person, one whose sin is viewed through the blood of Christ and whose unrighteousness is covered by His righteousness, is qualified "to share in the inheritance of the saints in the kingdom of light" (Col. 1:12).

Who can accomplish this work to meet man's desperate need for regeneration? Unfortunately, in spite of the clear testimony of Scripture, unclear or inaccurate answers have been given to this question. Close attention to the biblical teaching on the subject reveals several facts: (1) The human will is not the cause of regeneration (John 1:13; 6:44; Rom. 9:16). (2) The divine will is the cause (Ezek. 36:23–38; John 3:5; 1 Cor. 3:6–7; James 1:18; 1 Pet. 1:3). (3) The Holy Spirit is the Agent of regeneration (John 3:5–8; Titus 3:5). The work of regeneration has its inception and conclusion with God; it is His work.

The *means* by which God accomplishes regeneration is the

Scriptures. "He chose to give us birth through the word of truth" (James 1:18). "For you have been born again . . . through the living and enduring word of God" (1 Pet. 1:23). Other passages that state that the Word of God is an instrument in regeneration are John 5:24–25; Romans 1:16; 10:17; Philippians 2:16; and 1:23). Of course, not everyone who reads the Scriptures is regenerated. But the Bible is an instrument in regeneration when it is used by the Holy Spirit.

The divine work of regeneration is pictured as a new birth, a spiritual resurrection, a new creation, and a spiritual transformation. The most familiar and perhaps most significant descriptive term is "new birth." In John 3:3–7 birth of body and birth of soul are compared. The life imparted at physical birth is the same kind of life possessed by the parents; the life imparted by spiritual birth is in reality God's life and is therefore eternal. To be born physically is to be brought into a human family, and to be born again spiritually is to be made forever a part of God's family. Spiritual resurrection is another metaphor of regeneration, mentioned often in the New Testament (John 5:21, 24–25; Rom. 6:13; Eph. 2:1, 5; Col. 2:12; 3:1–2). Since believers have been resurrected spiritually (that is, have new life in Christ), they are exhorted to live as resurrected people.

The change accomplished by regeneration is also described as a new creation (2 Cor. 5:17; see also Eph. 2:10; 4:24). Referring to the future regeneration of Israel, Ezekiel said, "I will give you a new heart and put a new spirit in you" (Ezek. 36:26). And similarly, in this church age God imparts a new heart or a new nature to everyone—whether Jew or Gentile—who believes. This new nature includes new capacities to glorify God. Of course, it is in conflict with the "old" or sinful nature, which remains (Rom. 7:14–25).

Regeneration is also a spiritual translation. Paul wrote, "He has delivered us from the power of darkness and conveyed us into the kingdom of the Son of His love" (Col. 1:13, NKJV). God has delivered (literally, "rescued") the believer from the rebel kingdom of the tyrant Satan and translated (literally, "lifted over") the believer into the domain or kingdom of Christ, God's beloved Son. While this kingdom will be visibly manifested on earth in the age to come, it is today a spiritual kingdom composed of those who have received Christ by faith and who possess "righteousness, peace and joy in the Holy Spirit" (Rom. 14:17).

Regeneration is the source or fountain of all Christian experience. The eternal life so imparted and the new nature so created bring at once new desires, new capabilities, and new realities, which combine to introduce the regenerated person to new experiences: a new love for God, for prayer, for the Bible, for God's people, for godliness, and for lost humanity.

—**DKC**

Recall the persons and circumstances in your life that led to your new birth.

Remnant

A REMNANT IS THE RESIDUE of something that is left after the majority of it is taken away. This is true in general parlance, as in, for example, a remnant of a bolt of cloth, as well as in the more theological sense. The Bible often speaks of a remnant in the general sense. Joseph told his brothers in Egypt, "God sent me ahead of you to preserve for you a remnant on earth" (Gen. 45:7). Similarly, after reporting that God had given Israel in victory "the whole region of Argob, Og's kingdom of Bashan" (Deut. 3:4), Moses wrote, "Only Og king of Bashan was left of the remnant of the Rephaites" (3:11). Also God promised concerning Judah's idolatry, "I will cut off from this place every remnant of Baal" (Zeph. 1:4).

As with Og, the concept of a remnant is applied to the survivors of a conquered kingdom. This is true of Gibeon (2 Sam. 21:2), Babylon (Isa. 14:22), Philistia (14:30), and Moab (16:14). In this sense a remnant of the northern kingdom of Israel is mentioned after its conquest by Assyria (2 Chron. 34:9, 21), and after the conquest of the southern kingdom of Judah by Babylon (36:20). Later Ezra spoke of the group that returned to Judah from Babylon with him as a remnant (Ezra 9:8, 13–15).

The idea of a remnant is also applied by the prophets to the Jewish people in a spiritual sense. Isaiah, for example, in connection with his prophecy of God's judgment on Assyria (10:5, 12), wrote, "In that day the remnant of Israel . . . will truly rely on the LORD" (10:20), and "A remnant will return . . . to the Mighty God" (10:21). This refers to the remnant's return from Babylon, as described by Ezra (Ezra 9:8–15). However, that remnant, as Ezra confessed, hardly relied on the Lord.

Furthermore, Isaiah wrote of a coming day when "the Lord will reach out his hand a second time to reclaim the remnant that is left of his people ... from the four quarters of the earth" (Isa. 11:11–12). Jeremiah wrote that God promised, "I myself will gather the remnant of my flock out of all the countries where I have driven them" (Jer. 23:3–8; 31:7–8).

After the Romans destroyed Jerusalem in A.D. 70, the Jewish people were scattered worldwide. Micah prophesied that the "remnant of Jacob will be in the midst of many peoples like dew from the LORD" (Mic. 5:7) and "like a lion among the beasts of the forest" (5:8). Although Israel has now been established as a nation and the Jewish people are slowly returning to their land, God has promised to restore them "from all the nations where he scattered" them when they "return to the LORD [their] God" (Deut. 30:2). At that time, the Lord said, He "will circumcise your hearts and the hearts of your descendants, so that you may love him with all your heart and with all your soul, and live" (30:6; see also Jer. 31:33–34).

The apostle Paul made it clear that a remnant of Israel, including himself, was "chosen by grace" (Rom. 11:5) to be saved as part of the church. The church, however, is not the remnant of Israel, nor has God abandoned His plan for His people Israel (Jer. 31:35–37). In God's plans, however, only a remnant of Israel (Isa. 10:21–22; Rom. 9:27) as well as of all humanity (Acts 15:16–18) will be saved.　　**—JAW**

Seek to win all you can for Christ,
but recognize that all believers will be only a remnant of humankind.

Repentance

JOHN THE BAPTIST CAPTURED THE ATTENTION of the people of Israel when he appeared in the wilderness of Judea and commanded them to repent (Matt. 3:1–2; Luke 3:3; see also Acts 13:24). The startling reason for this message was that the kingdom of heaven was close at hand. John was considered a prophet and his message attracted loyal and believing Israelites who had been praying for a spiritual awakening (Luke 1:8–17; 2:25–26, 36–38). The call to repentance by John the Baptist was repeated by Jesus as He began His ministry in Jerusalem (Matt. 4:17).

The primary New Testament word for repentance is *metanoia*, "to change one's mind." The context determines the purpose for the change. One other word, *metamelomai*, "to regret, to be sorry" (2 Cor. 7:8–10), adds little to the understanding of the doctrine of repentance. As stated above, the early occurrences of the term *repentance* pertained to the approaching kingdom (Matt. 3:2) and the forgiveness of sins (Luke 3:3). "Forgiveness" and "kingdom" were well-known subjects to the Israelites, but with the coming of Christ some distinctions became apparent and the people needed to change their thinking about these issues.

The King James Version translates two Old Testament words by the word "repentance." *Nāḥam*, "to regret, to be sorry, to be comforted," reflects the emotions involved in change. Normally this Hebrew word was used when the Scriptures described God's attitude about change (Exod. 32:14; Num. 23:19; 1 Sam. 15:11). In each of these verses the New International Version translators selected different English words to express the meaning of the word. The primary Hebrew word that describes change, and which is translated "repentance" in some instances, is, "to turn, return," used well over a thousand times. The Septuagint (the Greek translation of the Hebrew Old Testament) usually translated *šûb* by the Greek word *epistrephō*, "to turn about." This means that the Greek term *metanoia*, normally rendered "repentance," was not identical with either of the two Hebrew words. Thus the use of *metanoia* in the New Testament signaled an emphasis not integral to the Hebrew words. In addition, the English word *repentance* derives from the Latin and does not express the exact meaning of *metanoia*. With the presence of Christ in the world people needed to understand who He was and why He had come and this demanded a change in their thinking. So the word *metanoia* accurately expresses how Israel was to respond to Christ and His message.

Jesus spoke about repentance in relation to several subjects: the kingdom (Matt. 4:17; Mark 1:15); judgment (Matt. 11:20–21; 12:41; Luke 10:13; 11:32; 13:3, 5); faith (Mark 1:15); forgiveness of sins by unbelievers (Luke 5:32; 24:47); and forgiveness of believers' sins (17:3–4). The context of each of these verses shows why a change was necessary. In some cases the context mentions the consequences for those who do not repent (Matt. 11:20–24; Luke 13:3, 5; 15:7, 10). Repentance and faith are closely related concepts, as seen in Acts 20:21.

From the teachings of Christ in the above passages, in the Gospels, it appears that when the term *repentance* was used in relation to salvation it was almost an interchangeable synonym for faith, rather than an action distinct from faith.

In their preaching of the gospel the apostles often mentioned repentance (Acts 2:38; 3:19; 5:31; 8:22; 17:30; 20:21; 26:20). Peter related human repentance to God's forgiveness of sins (2:38; 3:19; 5:31; 8:22). In Paul's defense before King Agrippa he declared that the message God gave him to preach included "repentance" and "turning to God" (implying faith in God). He also stated that the way believers lived should give evidence of their repentance (26:20).

In the conversion experiences recorded in Acts—the Ethiopian eunuch (8:26–39); Saul of Tarsus (9:1–18; 22:6–16; 26:12–18); Cornelius (10:1–43); Sergius Paulus (13:6–12); Lydia (16:13–15); and the Philippian jailer (16:25–34)—repentance is not mentioned. In fact, the details for each one differs, but a pattern is observable. Each conversion record includes the convicting work of the Holy Spirit, followed by faith in Christ, who made salvation possible through His death and resurrection. And then the believer was baptized. The order was never changed, though each experience differed in some ways. These experiences support the proposition that faith and repentance are not separate steps in the salvation process. Whereas *repentance* was used in the Gospels to represent the conversion experience, the term *faith* served that same function in the Book of Acts. In Acts 20:21 *repentance* and *faith* are used in such a way in the Greek that they are seen together like two sides of a coin.

In Romans 2:4 and 2 Corinthians 7:10 the apostle wrote of God's work in bringing people to repentance. Paul expressed concern that believers in the Corinthian church might become insensitive to sin and not repent (12:21). He also urged Christians to exercise patience in dealing with unbelievers in the hope that they might repent and come to salvation (2 Tim. 2:25). Hebrews 6:6 taught that "repentance" (or salvation) cannot be repeated because Christ cannot be crucified a second time. And Peter declared that God wants everyone to come to repentance (2 Pet. 3:9).

The apostle John did not use the word *repentance* in his Gospel or in his Epistles, but he used it eleven times in the Book of Revelation. Since Revelation 2–3 include the messages of the risen Christ to seven local churches, they emphasize not salvation but rebukes to the churches with calls for changed behavior (2:5 [twice], 16, 21–22; 3:3, 19). The four other uses (9:20–21; 16:9, 11) pertain to unbelievers who will be on the earth during the time of Tribulation, people who will refuse to repent and thus will suffer judgment at the hand of God.　　　**—WGJ**

Follow the admonition of the risen Christ and cling to your first love;
be quick to change your mind and your affections if your love wanes.

Rest

THE SOVEREIGN GOD HIMSELF set the pattern for taking rest when "on the seventh day . . . he rested from all the work of creating that he had done" (Gen. 2:2–3). Since God is omnipotent (17:1; 35:11), this rest was not from His being tired; it was a rest that came from satisfaction with a completed task. God's rest is presented as the basis, however, for humankind's need for physical rest every seventh day (Exod. 16:23–26; 20:8–11; Lev. 23:3; Deut. 5:12–15). God has also created the cycle of light and darkness to provide daily rest for humans and all creation (Gen. 1:14–19).

Jesus Christ experienced the need for physical rest. He rested by the well at Sychar in Samaria while His disciples went to buy food (John 4:4–6), and He fell asleep in a boat crossing the Sea of Galilee (Mark 4:38; Luke 8:22–23). When Jesus and His disciples were pressured by the crowds, He told them, "Come with me by yourselves to a quiet place and get some rest" (Mark 6:31). Adequate physical rest is a divinely ordained physical human need.

In Scripture the word *rest* is also used to speak of physical death. Jacob instructed Joseph not to bury him in Egypt: "When I rest with my fathers, carry me out of Egypt and bury me where they are buried" (Gen. 47:30). God told Moses on the east side of the Jordan River, "You are going to rest with your fathers" (Deut. 31:16). David's death was similarly described (2 Sam. 7:12; 1 Kings 1:21), and Job spoke of death as a rest (Job 3:13, 17).

The word *rest* is also used in Scripture to speak of peace, freedom from turmoil and warfare. Moses told the Israelites that when they crossed the Jordan River and settled in Canaan, God "will give you rest from all your enemies" (Deut. 12:10; see 25:19; Josh. 1:13). When Joshua "took the entire land" and "gave it as an inheritance to Israel according to their tribal divisions . . . the land had rest from war" (11:23–24; see 23:1). David was the warrior king, but God gave him "rest from all his enemies around him" (2 Sam. 7:1), and He gave Solomon rest as well (1 Kings 5:4; 8:56). The same was true of Asa (2 Chron. 14:6–7; 15:15), Jehoshaphat (20:30), and Nehemiah (Neh. 9:28).

Rest is also used to speak of peace in the personal sense—emotional, mental, and physical. In Job's perplexity about his difficult experiences, he wrote, "I have no peace, no quietness; I have no rest, but only turmoil" (Job 3:26). After Ruth reported to Naomi on Boaz's gift and words in the field, Naomi said that Boaz would not rest (in the sense of being at peace) "until the matter is settled today" (Ruth 3:18). David wrote, "My soul finds rest in God alone" (Ps. 62:1, see 62:5). And other psalms read, "He who dwells in the shelter of the Most High will rest in the shadow of the Almighty" (91:1), and "Be at rest once more, O my soul, for the LORD has been good to you" (116:7). Such statements express spiritual as well as psychological peace.

Such spiritual peace as a result of faith in Jesus Christ and God the Father is what the Lord Jesus was offering when He said, "Come unto me, all you who are weary and burdened, and I will give you rest. Take my yoke upon you and learn from me . . . and you will find rest for your souls" (Matt. 11:28–29). Through Isaiah God said that rest is, in effect, the same as faith: "In repentance and rest is your salvation, in quietness and trust is your strength" (Isa. 30:15; see also Jer. 6:16; 31:25).

If Israel faithfully worshiped and served the Lord, then they would experience His peace and security in a physical sense. However, because of their persistent unbelief, rebellion, and sin, God did not allow the adult generation that came out of Egypt to enter Canaan. He said, "I declared on oath in my anger, 'They shall never enter my rest'" (Ps. 95:11).

That physical rest in Canaan, however, was illustrative and symbolic of spiritual salvation. This is the point the author of the Epistle to the Hebrews made to the wavering professing Jewish Christians when he quoted Psalm 95:7–11 in Hebrews 3:7–11, 15; 4:3, 5, 7. In this age of grace in which we are living, the only way any individual, Jew or Gentile, can find spiritual rest and salvation is through receiving Jesus Christ as his or her Savior, thereby becoming a member of His body, the church. Following the rapture of the church, however, Jesus Christ will return to minister once again to His chosen nation, Israel. He will give the nation physical and spiritual rest during the Millennium, for as the Lord said through Jeremiah, "I will come to give rest to Israel" (Jer. 31:2).

—JAW

As you labor for Christ and the glory of God,
learn to rest in Christ and the grace of God.

Resurrection

EVIDENCE FROM THE OLD TESTAMENT supports the New Testament assertion that those who believed God looked for life beyond their present circumstances (Heb. 11:10). Abraham faced the reality that he would lose his son Isaac when God instructed the patriarch to offer him as a sacrifice (Gen. 22:2). But Abraham believed that somehow Isaac would return with him, and he told this to his servants (22:5). Commenting on Abraham's faith, the writer of Hebrews stated that Abraham believed that God could raise the dead, and that "figuratively speaking, he did receive Isaac back from death" (Heb. 11:19).

In the midst of a broken spirit Job affirmed emphatically his belief in the resurrection (Job 19:25–27). David's belief in the hope of resurrection, expressed in Psalm 16:8–11, was used by Peter to explain Christ's resurrection (Acts 2:24–28). Isaiah brought hope to believing Israelites, when he declared that the dead will live and bodies will rise (Isa. 26:19). The prophet Daniel spoke of resurrection, some to everlasting life and some to everlasting contempt (Dan. 12:1–3). Many who lived during the time of Christ and had studied the Old Testament believed in the resurrection (Acts 23:8).

The teaching of a literal bodily resurrection has its basis in the resurrection of Christ. Early in His earthly ministry Jesus spoke of His resurrection, but people didn't understand it until after the event occurred (John 2:20–22). On at least three occasions He predicted His death and resurrection (Matt. 16:21; 17:22–23; 20:18–19). During His earthly ministry He demonstrated His own power to raise individuals from the dead (9:24–25; Luke 7:14–15; John 11:43–44), though they were not raised, as He was, with glorified bodies.

Several times Jesus spoke of the Resurrection. In John 5:28–29, He said everyone will be resurrected: those who had done good (exhibiting the kind of action based on faith in Christ) and those who had done evil (revealing their unbelief). After Lazarus died, Jesus told Martha that He Himself is the Resurrection and the Life and that those who believe in Him will never die (11:25–26).

Jesus' resurrection was a major theme in the preaching of the apostles. Because Christ had risen, the Holy Spirit was poured out on believers (Acts 2:32–33). The power of the risen Christ brought healing to an invalid by the temple gate (4:10). Because of the Resurrection Peter and others faced severe opposition with amazing courage (5:29–32). Saul's conversion came from the fact that he saw the risen Christ and responded in faith (9:4–5; 22:6–10; 26:15–19). The truth of Jesus' resurrection was a significant part of the message that went to the Gentiles (10:39–43; 13:30–38). When Paul preached in the synagogues, he included the fact of Jesus' resurrection (17:2–4). The resurrection of Christ, Paul affirmed, is proof that God will judge the world (17:31). Paul implied that the Jews in Jerusalem rejected him because of his belief in the doctrine of the Resurrection (23:6; 24:15, 21; 26:8). Peter affirmed that people can experience the new birth because Jesus Christ has been raised from the dead (1 Pet. 1:3).

Paul made a significant contribution to the doctrine of the Resurrection in 1 Corinthians 15. He stated that Jesus' resurrection is one of the two essential tenets of the gospel (1 Cor. 15:4). The resurrection of Christ assures that everyone who has believed in Him will be raised from the dead (15:52).

Paul also wrote of a time sequence and order in the future Resurrection. First is Christ's own resurrection (15:23). Second will be the resurrection of believers (15:23), that is, those who have died during the church age will be raised at the Rapture (15:51–56; 1 Thess. 4:16). Old Testament saints (Dan. 12:2) and those martyred during the Tribulation (Rev. 20:4) will be raised at the Second Coming. All these believers raised just before the millennial kingdom will be part of the first resurrection (20:6). At the end of the Millennium all the dead who have not put their faith in God will be raised to stand before the Great White Throne judgment (Rev. 20:11–15). The Scriptures are silent as to how the Lord will handle the resurrection of saints who will have died in the Millennium.

Paul's other contribution to the teaching of the resurrection in 1 Corinthians 15 concerns the nature of the resurrection body. It will be similar to the natural body but with some significant differences. The term *imperishable* was used by Paul to describe the qualities that give it power and glory (1 Cor. 15:43, 50, 53–54). In contrast to the natural body the resurrected body will be a spiritual body (15:44), that is, it will be like the body Christ possesses now in heaven (15:45–49). Thus it is to be recognizable, endurable, glorious, and fully adapted to the eternal life believers will enjoy with the Lord.

One dynamic of the teaching on the Resurrection concerns its relationship to the practical life of the believer. The apostle Paul stated that God's power seen in Jesus' resurrection can be appropriated by believers (2 Cor. 13:4). Power means strength or ability to overcome obstacles. One of Paul's goals was to experience more fully the enabling of the risen Christ in his own daily life (Phil. 3:10). Paul's final words to Timothy included the exhortation to remember that because Jesus Christ is risen from the dead, He could assist him in his life and ministry (2 Tim. 2:8). **—WGJ**

The Resurrection allows each believer to enjoy the presence of Christ every day and assures us of our hope for the future.

Revelation

REVELATION IS THE PROCESS by which God communicates to humans by various means. Apart from His revelation human intelligence could not discover the truths revealed.

Revelation is "God's secret wisdom, a wisdom that has been hidden and that God destined for our glory before time began" (1 Cor. 2:7). The truths revealed are called "the deep things of God" and "the thoughts of

God" (2:10–11). "No eye has seen, no ear has heard, no mind has conceived" these truths, "but God has revealed it to us by his Spirit" (2:9–10). God's truth is revealed "in words taught by the Spirit, expressing spiritual truth in spiritual words" (2:13).

Revelation can be in many forms, including natural revelation in the physical world, which demonstrates the knowledge, power, and love of God (Ps. 19:1–4; Acts 14:17; Rom. 1:20). In Bible times God sometimes revealed truths through dreams and visions. Other times His revelation was direct, as when He communicated with Adam or Moses. On many occasions angels were God's agents of communication. In one sense the entire Bible is a revelation of God because every word in Scripture has been inspired by God (2 Tim. 3:16), and the Bible teaches spiritual truth (John 17:17). Writing under the inspiration of the Holy Spirit, the human authors of the Bible expressed exactly what God wanted recorded, so that the Bible is truth from God Himself. Believers in Christ are indwelt by the Holy Spirit, "the Spirit of truth," who teaches them and helps them understand the things of God (John 14:26; 16:13).

—JFW

Each day carefully read the Bible, God's primary means of revelation today.

Rewards

SCRIPTURE REVEALS that there are many rewards or compensations for Christians who serve God faithfully, even though believers face persecution or even martyrdom. Some rewards are immediate for the Christian who walks in the will of God. He experiences what is called the fruit of the Spirit, which is "love, joy, peace, patience, kindness, goodness, faithfulness, gentleness, and self-control" (Gal. 5:22–23). Christians can never enjoy life and find meaning apart from yielding themselves to God and depending on the Spirit (Rom. 12:1–2; Gal. 5:16).

Some rewards will not be given until the Rapture. At that moment Christians will receive a new, immortal body, and they will be without sin. After the rapture of the church, Christians will be judged at the judgment seat of Christ. "For we must all appear before the judgment seat of Christ, that each one may receive what is due him for the things done while in the body, whether good or bad" (2 Cor. 5:10; see also Rom. 14:10). This judgment in heaven is not a judgment on sin but one of reward, because believers have been justified by faith (5:1) and stand before God with no condemnation (8:1, 33–34). Several times Jesus said rewards will be given to believers in heaven (see Matt. 5:12; 6:1, 4, 6, 18). As recorded in the last chapter of the Bible, Jesus said, "Behold, I am coming soon! My reward is with me" (Rev. 22:12).

The nature of the judgment at the judgment seat of Christ is illustrated by a building being tested by fire (1 Cor. 3:10–15). Some believers will receive rewards, whereas others, who have not been faithful, will experience loss of rewards. Paul also said our receiving rewards will be like a runner receiving a prize after a race (9:24–27). He wrote that he desired to serve God faithfully so that he would receive "a crown that will last forever" (9:25). At this judgment each believer will have to "give an account of himself to God" (Rom. 14:12), that is, to report how he or she lived. Those who long for Jesus' return will receive "the crown of righteousness" (2 Tim. 4:8). The believers' rewards may consist of positions of privileged service as they serve throughout eternity.

—JFW

To receive reward from God, live with heavenly values in mind.

Righteousness

THE HEBREW AND GREEK WORDS for "righteousness" mean action in conformity with an accepted and approved standard. In its biblical usage it means action in conformity with *God's* standard, which is God Himself. By nature God is infinitely holy (Isa. 6:3; Rev. 4:8). Therefore righteousness is an attribute of His nature (Ezra 9:15; Pss. 116:5; 119:137; 129:4; 145:17; Jer. 12:1; Lam. 1:18; Dan. 9:7, 14) and is expressed in all His actions. God loves righteousness (Pss. 11:7; 33:5) and has established a standard of righteousness for His creatures (Deut. 6:24–25), a standard human beings are unable to meet.

God wants people to learn that, in comparison with His righteousness, "all our righteous acts are like filthy rags" (Isa. 64:6). People also need to learn that meeting God's standard of righteousness involves inward thoughts as well as outward actions. Jesus explained that "anyone who is angry with his brother will be subject to judgment" (Matt. 5:22) and "anyone who looks at a woman lustfully has already committed adultery with her in his heart" (5:28).

When a young man responded to Jesus' listing of the social commandments (19:18–19) by saying "All these I have kept" (19:20), Jesus told him to sell all his possessions, give it to the poor, and become His disciple (19:21). The young man went away sad, because wealth was his god (19:22). Regarding his own reasons for having "confidence in the flesh," Paul said that "as for legalistic righteousness, [he was] faultless" (Phil. 3:4–6). But then he wrote, "But whatever was to my profit I now consider loss . . . I consider them rubbish, that I may gain Christ and be found in him, not having a righteousness of my own that comes from the law, but that which is through faith in Christ—the righteousness that comes from God and is by faith" (3:7–9).

Although they fell woefully short of God's standard, the rich young ruler (Luke 18:18–23), Paul before his conversion (Phil. 3:4–6), and even the Pharisees (Matt. 5:20; 23:28) did demonstrate a human righteousness in comparison with others. They conformed outwardly to the Ten Commandments. Many unregenerate men and women do carry out commendable deeds, but yet apart from Christ they will be judged by God for their unrighteousness. In God's sight the so-called righteous acts of the unsaved "are like filthy rags," that is, they are useless to provide salvation (Isa. 64:6). However, degrees of punishment in hell may be based on unsaved individuals' deeds (Luke 12:47–48; Rom. 2:6; Rev. 20:11–13). In similar fashion the righteous actions of Christians will be rewarded according to their motives and their conformity to the will of God (1 Cor. 3:10, 12–15). When Jesus returns, He "will reward each person according to what he has done" (Matt. 16:27; see also Rev. 22:12).

God cannot accept human beings into His presence on the basis of their human righteousness, but He has carried out a plan that enables Him by His grace to provide a righteous standing to each person who by faith accepts the redemptive death of the Lord Jesus Christ, the sacrificial Substitute (Rom. 3:21–26). In the Ten Commandments God provided His righteous standard to demonstrate to men their inability to fulfill it and to lead them to faith in Christ (Gal. 3:21–24).

As the eternal Son of God incarnate in human form, the Lord Jesus Christ is the only human being to live a totally righteous life. He was "the Holy and Righteous One" (Acts 3:14; see also 7:52; 22:14; 1 John 2:1), who alone of all men could say that "the prince of this world is coming. He has no hold on me" (John 14:30) and "Can any of you prove me guilty of sin?" (8:46). God's acceptance of Jesus' sacrifice of Himself as the perfect "Lamb of God" (John 1:29, 36; see also 1 Pet. 1:19), bearing the Father's judgment on the sin of the world, enables God to apply His righteousness to each person who receives Jesus Christ as his or her Savior.

Although perfect righteousness is the *position* of each person identified with Jesus Christ by faith, it is not his *possession*. That awaits his entrance into the presence of God at either death or the rapture of the church (Eph. 2:4–7; Col. 3:1–4). Meanwhile in this life the believer in Christ is among "those who hunger and thirst for righteousness" (Matt. 5:6). The Christian can pray with David, "Lead me, O LORD, in your righteousness" (Ps. 5:8).   **—JAW**

As a Christian, transform your righteous standing before God into righteous living for God through the Word of God and the power of the Holy Spirit.

Ss

Sabbath

THE JEWISH DAY OF REST and worship was called the Sabbath (from the Hebrew verb *šābbat*, meaning "to cease" or "to desist from work." The Sabbath originated when God rested on the seventh day after completing His work of creating the universe (Gen. 2:2–3). He declared the seventh day to be holy, thus setting a pattern for the human race to follow. The next mention of the Sabbath is in connection with the giving of manna (Exod. 16:23–30). Later the command to keep the Sabbath was included in the Decalogue at Sinai (20:8–11; Deut. 5:12–15). The latter action, according to these passages, was based not only on God's resting after creation but also on His deliverance of Israel from Egypt.

The Mosaic Law decreed that the Israelites were to keep the Sabbath by not doing any work that day. This included such minor things as gathering wood (Num. 15:32–36) and starting a fire for cooking (Exod. 35:3). Also forbidden were carrying heavy loads (Jer. 17:21), traveling (Exod. 16:29), and trading (Amos 8:5, Neh. 10:31; 13:15, 19). The Sabbath was to be observed by a sacred assembly (Lev. 23:3), by doubling the required sacrificial lambs with their drink and grain offerings (Num. 28:9), and by the priests providing new bread in the holy place (Lev. 24:8).

The Sabbath symbolized Israel's covenant relationship with God. "The Israelites are to observe the Sabbath, celebrating it for the generations to come as a lasting covenant" (Exod. 31:16). Thus Sabbath-keeping became the sign of the Mosaic Covenant, much as circumcision was the sign of the Abrahamic Covenant (Gen. 17:11).

In addition to the weekly Sabbath, three feast days were observed with a Sabbath rest, all in the seventh month (September/October): the Feast of Trumpets on the first day, the Day of Atonement on the fifteenth day, and the Feast of Tabernacles on the twenty-third day (Lev. 23:24, 32, 39). The seventh year was a sabbatical year (25:2–7), indicating that the Hebrews calculated years more by sevens than by decades. After seven "sabbatical years" the fiftieth year was to be celebrated as a year of jubilee. On that occasion land reverted to its original owner (25:8–31), and Israelites in bondage recovered their freedom if they had not been previously released (25:32–54; compare Deut. 15:12). The prophets emphasized to Israel the importance of keeping the Sabbath (Isa. 58:13–14). But the nation failed to do so and was removed from the land so that it might have its Sabbath rest (Lev. 26:32–35; 2 Chron. 36:20–21; Ezek. 20:10–24).

During the intertestamental period Jewish scribes created a complicated code of regulations governing Sabbath observance. These regulations led to the formulation of thirty-nine articles, which forbade various kinds of ordinary work on the Sabbath. These petty, legalistic regulations brought Jesus into conflict, not with the Mosaic Law regarding the Sabbath, but with the rabbis' additions to the Law. The Gospels report that on six occasions Jesus collided with Jewish prejudices regarding the Sabbath. The scribes were more concerned about the strict observance of a day than about the needs of people. Jesus insisted, "The Sabbath was made for man, not man for the Sabbath" (Mark 2:27). He also asserted that He was Lord of the Sabbath (2:28).

The early Christians worshiped on the first day of the week (Acts 20:7), although Christian Jews apparently also attended synagogue services and continued for a time to observe the Sabbath. The Council of Jerusalem, however, made no mention of Sabbath-keeping for gentile Christians who had come into the church. Paul considered the Mosaic Law a yoke of bondage from which Christians are freed (Gal. 5:1). He made no distinction between the moral and ceremonial law since the old covenant in its entirety had been abolished at the Cross (2 Cor. 3:14). Further, Paul affirmed that God canceled the written code with its regulations, "nailing it to the cross" (Col. 2:14). Since Christians are free from the burden of the Law, of which the Jewish Sabbath was a part, there are no biblical grounds for imposing Sabbath-keeping on believers in the present church age (Col. 2:16). The author of Hebrews used the Hebrew Sabbath to illustrate "God's rest" into which a believer enters when he "rests from his own work" (Heb. 4:9–10). Rather than challenging his readers to keep the Sabbath, he exhorted them to "make every effort to enter that [spiritual] rest" (4:11), that is, to enjoy the peace and rest Christ gives each believer at salvation.

—DKC

Thank God for a Sabbath rest from human effort for salvation.

Sacrifice

SACRIFICES AND OFFERINGS are mentioned frequently in Scripture. These terms are often used interchangeably, though the word *offerings* connotes the fact that everything brought to God in a worship ceremony was viewed as being offered to Him. Some scholars hold that Israel adopted the religious practices of surrounding nations when their system of sacrifice was inaugurated. While it is true that remains of temples, including bones of sacrificial animals, have been found in Mesopotamia, Syria, Palestine, Egypt, Anatolia, and the Aegean region, it is clear from Scripture that Israel's Old Testament sacrifices were inaugurated in response to a revelation from God.

Another clear point of distinction is the fact that in pagan cultures the sacrifice was regarded as food for the gods. While Israel's sacrifices pleased God, they were not His food. The emphasis, rather, was on the blood. The Lord declared, "The life of a creature is in the blood, and I have given it to you to make atonement for yourselves on the altar; it is the blood that makes atonement for one's life" (Lev. 17:11). Thus, though the worshiper deserved death because of his sin, God allowed him to provide a substitute, a living animal, which was slain as sin's penalty.

Before the Mosaic Law, sacrifices were offered by various individuals. The first animal to be killed on behalf of humans was when God Himself killed an animal to provide skins to cover Adam and Eve's nakedness after the Fall (Gen. 3:21). The Cain and Abel story (Gen. 4) reveals that God had made clear to the first family the proper way to approach Him. Abel responded with faith to that revelation and offered "a better sacrifice" than Cain. Faith is always the right response to revelation (Heb. 11:4). In addition, long before the Mosaic Law was given, sacrifices were offered by Noah, Abraham, Isaac, Jacob, and Job (Gen. 8:20; 12:7–8; 13:18; 15:9–17; 22:2–14; 26:25; 33:20; 35:3; Job 1:5; 42:7–9).

With the giving of the Law at Mount Sinai a complex and well-defined system of sacrifice was established. Both the material of the sacrifices and the ceremonies connected with offering them were minutely prescribed.

The major description of the Mosaic sacrificial ritual is found in Leviticus 1–7. Five offerings are described, which fall into two categories: those of "an aroma pleasing to the LORD," namely, burnt offerings (1:3–17), cereal offerings (2:1–16), and fellowship or peace offerings (3:1–17); and the expiatory sacrifices, which included sin offerings (4:1–5:13) and guilt or trespass offerings (5:14–6:7).

The relative frequency of these offerings is described in a kind of sacred calendar for Israel, recorded in Numbers 28–29. Each day, morning and evening sacrifices were required (28:3–8), and on the Sabbath the daily offerings were doubled (28:9). At the time of the new moon, more sacrifices were prescribed (28:11–15). In addition, Israel's year featured seven religious assemblies during which numerous sacrifices and offerings were presented to the Lord. These convocations were the Passover, symbolizing Israel's redemption from Egypt (Exod. 12; Lev. 23:5; Num. 28:16); the Feast of Unleavened Bread, symbolizing the removal of sin (Exod. 12:15–20; Lev. 23:6–8; Num. 28:17–25); the Feast of Firstfruits, expressing thanksgiving to God for the barley harvest (Lev. 23:10–14); the Feast of Weeks, celebrating the wheat harvest (23:15–21); the Feast of Trumpets, a solemn gathering to prepare for the Day of Atonement (23:23–25); the Day of Atonement, an annual assembly for national repentance and atonement for sins (Lev. 16; 23:26–32); and the Feast of Tabernacles, giving thanksgiving to God for the harvest of fruit, olive oil, and wine, plus a memorial of Israel's wilderness experience (23:33–44).

Besides having special meaning for Israel, the sacrifices and offerings also had typical significance, that is, they foreshadowed the person and work of Christ. The Passover lamb prefigured "Christ, our Passover lamb" (1 Cor. 5:7). The burnt offering typified Christ's offering Himself to God in a vicarious death for sinners (Eph. 5:2; Heb. 9:14; 10:5–7). The cereal or grain offering typified Christ's offering to God a perfect life (Matt. 3:15; John 17:4). The peace offering foreshadowed Christ "making peace through his blood, shed on the cross" (Col. 1:20). The sin offering pictured Christ's suffering "outside the camp" to provide redemption for sinners (Heb. 13:12). He was made "sin for us," that is, He became our sin offering (2 Cor. 5:21). The guilt or trespass offering typified Christ, who in His death atoned not only for sin's guilt but also for the damage or injury of sin (Ps. 51:4; Isa. 53:10).

The efficacy of the Levitical sacrifices has been seriously debated. Was the forgiveness achieved by the Old Testament sacrifices full and complete or was it only partial and temporary? Various answers have been given: (1) Ceremonial impurity was cleansed but the guilt remained until the sacrifice of Christ. This has been referred to as "the law with its incomplete atonement." (2) The Levitical sacrifices only covered the sin; there is no real forgiveness. (3) Sin was not removed once for all by an animal sacrifice but only for a period of time, such as from one sin offering to another or from one Day of Atonement to another. (4) Preferable is the view that an Old Testament sacrifice, when brought in faith, provided a covering for unintentional transgressions (Lev. 4:1–2, 13, 22, 27; 5:14–15, 17–18) and a temporary stay of divine wrath in anticipation of the Cross.

The Gospels record that in Jesus' day the sacrificial system continued in effect. Jesus did not call for its abolition (Matt. 5:23–24). In fact He told lepers whom He had cleansed that they were to make the offerings required by the Mosaic Law (8:4; Luke 17:14). However, in conversation with a teacher of the Law Jesus agreed that to love God and one's neighbor is more important than burnt offerings and sacrifices (Mark 12:33–34). Jesus also spoke of His imminent death as a sacrifice (Mark 10:45 and Matt. 20:28; Mark 14:24 and Luke 22:20; Matt. 26:28).

In the Pauline Epistles the apostle emphasized that Christ's death on the cross was an expiatory sacrifice (Rom. 3:25; 5:9; 1 Cor. 10:16; Eph. 1:7; 2:13; Col. 1:20). Paul also spoke of the "pleasing-aroma" sacrifices, especially the burnt offering, as the basis for his appeal to believers to offer their bodies "as living sacrifices, holy and pleasing to God" (Rom. 12:1).

Peter affirmed that believers are redeemed by the blood of Christ (1 Pet. 1:18–19; see also 1:2; 3:18). John wrote that Christ's death provided cleansing and propitiation (1 John 1:7; 2:2; 5:6, 8; Rev. 1:5). Hebrews 8–10 shows how the Old Testament sanctuary and sacrifices were shadows or types, all pointing to Christ and all fulfilled in Him.

Ezekiel prophesied that animal sacrifices will be offered in the millennial kingdom (Ezek. 43:13–27). The prophet described the prominent place the altar will occupy in the millennial temple as well as the animal sacrifices to be made there. It seems difficult to reconcile these facts with the statement in Hebrews that Christ "offered one sacrifice for sins forever" (Heb. 10:12, NKJV). But there is no contradiction, since just as the Old Testament sacrifices looked forward to the death of Christ, the millennial sacrifices will look back to the Cross. They will serve as memorials of His death, as the Lord's Supper does today. No animal sacrifice, past or future, can take away sin (10:4).   —**DKC**

Give thanks to God the Father, Son, and Holy Spirit
for the sacrifice of Christ on the cross.

Salvation

THE MAGNITUDE OF GOD'S LOVE and grace is most evident when sinful people consider it in relation to salvation. In describing this subject Paul used such phrases as God's "incomparably great power" (Eph. 1:19), "the riches of God's grace that he lavished on us" (1:7–8), "his glorious inheritance" (1:18), "his great love for us" (2:4), and "the incomparable riches of his grace" (2:7). The writer of the Book of Hebrews called it "a great salvation," with a warning not to ignore this truth (Heb. 2:3). Jude ascribed "glory, majesty, power, and authority" to the Savior (Jude 25). In fact, this subject occupies the attention of the angelic world (1 Pet. 1:12).

John wrote that someday all heaven will resound with praise to the Savior for His great salvation (Rev. 5:9–14; 19:1). To this day salvation has caused people to rejoice in song. Moses and the people of Israel sang about God's salvation when they were rescued from Egypt (Exod. 15:1–18). Later the Lord gave Moses another song about deliverance to teach the people so they could sing it after they were in the land He promised them (Deut. 31:19; 32:1–43). David and others sang songs of God's deliverance for the nation and for themselves (1 Chron. 16:23; Pss. 32:7; 95:1; 96:2; 98:1). Isaiah and Jonah were among the prophets who put their thoughts about God's salvation into song (Isa.12:2; Jon. 2:9). The Book of Revelation reveals that songs of redemption will be sung throughout all eternity (Rev. 5:9; 14:3; 15:3–4).

Salvation is the work of God in which He has provided a way for humans to be delivered from their sinful condition, by means of the sacrificial death of Christ and His resurrection from the dead. This salvation and new life can be received only by faith and is apart from any merit or work of the believing individual (Eph. 2:8–9). The primary Old Testament verb for salvation is the Hebrew verb *yāšaʿ*, "to save, deliver, rescue." In the New Testament the Greek words are *sōzō*, "to save, preserve, rescue," and *sotēria*, "salvation, deliverance."

The deliverance of the Israelites from Egypt was one of the most powerful demonstrations of God's ability to deliver (Exod. 14:13–14). From this event the people acknowledged that God is the Source of salvation and that what was impossible from a human perspective was an opportunity for God to display His grace and power for those He loved. Throughout Israel's history God fought for their deliverance, beginning with the initial entrance into the Promised Land (Josh. 5:14; 10:14). In the future God will again fight for Israel (Zech. 14:3), and the whole nation will experience salvation as prophesied by Isaiah (Isa. 59:20) and Paul (Rom. 11:26).

God's salvation in the Old Testament was more than national; it also included individuals who put their faith in Him. Hebrews 11:1–40 highlights a number of people in the Old Testament who trusted in God and experienced personal salvation. The psalms record the personal testimony of those who enjoyed salvation from the Lord (for example, Pss. 18:2; 37:39–40; 62:1; 118:14). Also the prophets spoke of personal salvation (Isa. 12:2; Jon. 2:9).

When the Lord Jesus came to earth, angels announced that a Savior had been born (Luke 2:11). John the Baptist declared that Jesus is the "Lamb of God, who takes away the sin of the world" (John 1:29). Jesus Himself stated that He came to give His life as a ransom for sin (Matt. 20:28; Mark 10:45), and that He came to seek and save the lost (Luke 19:10). The way of salvation, clearly stated in John's Gospel, is by faith in Christ (John 3:16; 10:9–10). The night before His crucifixion Jesus explained to His disciples that His death was for the forgiveness of sin (Matt. 26:28), but it wasn't until after His resurrection that they fully understood this truth (Luke 24:45–47).

Many facts about our salvation are presented in the Epistles. Viewing this multifaceted doctrine is like looking into a kaleidoscope of theological terms. Each word brings new facets of information, depending on the perspective or viewpoint. Some of these are "redemption" (Rom. 3:24; 1 Cor. 1:30; Heb. 9:12), "reconciliation" (2 Cor. 5:18–19; Rom. 5:11), "propitiation" (1 John 2:2, NASB), "regeneration" (Titus 3:5, NASB), "eternal life" (Rom. 5:21; 1 Tim. 1:16; 1 John 2:25), "delivered" (2 Cor. 1:10), "freedom" (Gal. 5:1; Eph. 3:12), "justification" (Rom. 4:25; 5:16), "grace" (3:24; Eph. 1:7; 2 Tim. 1:9), "victory" (1 Cor. 15:54, 57) "peace" (Eph. 2:15, 17; Col. 1:20, "forgiveness" (Eph. 1:7; Col. 1:14), "hope" (Rom. 5:2; Col. 1:23; 1 Pet. 1:3), "chosen" (Eph. 1:11; 1 Pet. 1:2), "adoption" (Rom. 8:15, NASB; 8:23), "sanctified" (1 Cor. 1:2; 6:11; Heb. 10:29), "glorified" (Rom. 8:30), "fellowship" (1 Cor. 1:9; 1 John 1:7), "inheritance" (Col. 1:12; 1 Pet. 1:4), and "blessed" (Rom. 4:7–8; Eph. 1:3).

The grace of God that brings salvation will continue to be manifested even after the church has been raptured. During the Great Tribulation, multitudes from every nation on the face of the earth will be saved (Rev. 7:9–17). Though the Bible does not explicitly reveal the details of salvation during the Millennium, it can be assumed that people will be saved in the same way since children will be born (Isa. 65:20, 23), and the only way of salvation will remain through faith in Christ. Perhaps one of the reasons for the reinstitution of the sacrifices according to Ezekiel's prophecy (Ezek. 40:38–47) is to remind everyone graphically that even in an idyllic environment, salvation is possible only through faith in Christ who offered Himself as the Sacrifice for sins. Throughout eternity salvation will never lose its significance because the Lamb who was slain will always be present (Rev. 22:3).

—WGJ

Each day think at least one aspect of salvation
that is meaningful to you and share it with a friend.

Sanctification

SANCTIFICATION REFERS to either the process or the result of being set apart for a specific person or purpose. The noun itself does not occur in the New International Version, but variations of the verb "to sanctify" occur in the New Testament with some frequency, and variations of the verb "to consecrate" occur in the Old Testament numerous times. Since these words are used in relation to persons and things set apart to God, who is "the Holy One of Israel" (Ps. 71:22; Isa. 10:20; see Prov. 9:10), they are usually translated "sanctify" (John 17:17) or "to make holy" (Gen. 2:2–3).

The basic idea of being set apart to God is seen when God directed the people of Israel through Moses, "Consecrate to me every firstborn male . . . whether man or animal" (Exod. 13:2; see also 13:12–13, 15; 22:29–30). Later God directed that the Levites be set apart to His service in place of the firstborn sons (Num. 3:12–13, 45–48; 8:14–18). Inanimate objects, such as the tabernacle, the altar of sacrifice, the ark of the testimony, and all the articles of furniture in the tabernacle (Exod. 29:44; 30:26–29) were consecrated, showing that the idea of being holy in a moral sense is a derived, not a basic, concept (Gen. 2:3).

The Lord sanctified Israel in the sense of separating them to Himself as His people. When he said to Abram, "Leave your country, your people and your father's household and go to the land I will show you" (12:1), He promised to bless him and his descendants. After God brought Israel out of Egypt, He told them, "You will be for me a kingdom of priests and a holy nation" (Exod. 19:6; see also 22:31), and, "You are a people holy to the LORD your God" (Deut. 7:6; 14:2, 21; see 26:19;and 28:9). Since God is infinitely holy in the moral sense (Lev. 11:44, 45; 19:2; 20:7; Isa. 6:3; 1 Pet. 1:15–16; Rev. 4:8), His call to Israel and to believers today to be holy involves moral sanctification as well as separation to Him (2 Cor. 6:17).

Moral sanctification is applied to individuals in a threefold sense. First, there is positional sanctification, received by each person the moment he or she trusts Jesus Christ for salvation. Since Jesus Christ lived a completely sinless life and provided a perfect, sinless sacrifice for sin in His death on the cross, each individual identified with Him by faith is viewed by God the Father as standing in Christ's moral sanctification. For this reason God's people, whether in the Old or New Testament, are "called saints" (Rom. 1:7, literal translation; Eph. 1:1; Phil. 1:1), because that is their standing in Christ. This is true even of the believers at Corinth, whom Paul addressed as "sanctified in Christ Jesus and called saints" (1 Cor. 1:2, literal translation), even though his two epistles to them show that they fell short of being saintly in their activities.

Second, God directs believers to "be holy in all you do" (1 Pet. 1:15;

see also 2 Cor. 7:1; 1 John 3:3). Each believer is "a temple of the Holy Spirit" (1 Cor. 6:19), and the Holy Spirit seeks increasingly to express His holy nature in the daily life of each person He indwells (Rom. 8:4–5, 14; Gal. 5:16, 25). Even though the process is subject to advances and retreats and will never reach its consummation in this earthly life, the day-by-day lives of Christians are subject to "the sanctifying work of the Spirit" (1 Pet. 1:2; see also 1 Thess. 4:7; 2 Thess. 2:13). This is the aspect of progressive sanctification, which is achieved by the individual believer's submission to and active cooperation with the indwelling Holy Spirit.

The third aspect of sanctification is final, or complete, sanctification. This step, which brings a believer into full conformity with one's position or standing before God, will be achieved either at the death of the individual Christian or at the rapture of the church. Jesus "loved the church and gave himself up for her to make her holy, cleansing her by the washing with water through the word, and to present her to himself as a radiant church, without stain or wrinkle or any other blemish, but holy and blameless" (Eph. 5:25–27). Christians are promised that "when he appears, we shall be like him, for we shall see him as he is" (1 John 3:2). Therefore "everyone who has this hope in him purifies himself, just as he is pure" (3:3). —JAW

Strive to manifest your position in Christ as a saint
in your daily life, to God's glory.

Satan

DESCRIBED AS A FALLEN ANGEL and head of the demon world, Satan has various titles in the Bible, including devil, serpent (2 Cor. 11:3), dragon (Rev. 12:9), angel of the abyss (9:11), ruler of this world (John 12:31; 16:11, NASB), prince of the power of the air (Eph. 2:2, NASB), god of this world (2 Cor. 4:4, NASB), tempter (Matt. 4:3), Beelzebul (Matt. 12:24, NASB), and the evil one (Matt. 13:19; John 17:15; 1 John 5:18–19). Old Testament passages (Isa. 14:12–17; Ezek. 28:11–19) reveal that Satan was originally created as a holy angel along with the other angels; he sinned against God and became the head of the fallen angels who joined with him and who form the demonic world. Described as "O morning star, son of the dawn!" (Isa. 14:12), Satan aspired to become like God, "I will make myself like the Most High" (14:14). Ezekiel 28 speaks of a king of Tyre, but the description of this wicked person goes beyond that of any human being. Before his fall Satan was "the model of perfection, full of perfection and perfect in beauty" (28:12). He was "in Eden, the garden of God," and he was "anointed as a guardian cherub" (28:13–14). Also he was on the holy mountain of God "blameless in [his] ways from the day [he was] created till wickedness was found" in him (28:14–15).

The first specific mention of Satan is found in the Book of Job (Job 1:6–12; 2:1–7), assuming the Book of Job was the first book of the Bible to be written. Accusing believers in heaven, he also accused Job of serving from impure motives, because God had been good to him. Many times the Scriptures refer to Satan opposing the work of God and seeking to do all he can to thwart God's purpose. Like a lion he seeks to pull believers away from God (1 Pet. 5:8), to hinder them (1 Thess. 2:18), and to deceive them (Gen. 3:13; 2 Cor. 11:3). In the Garden of Eden he appeared in the form of a serpent through whose form he tempted Eve (Gen. 3:1–5; see Rev. 12:9). Jesus called Satan a murderer (John 8:44). The devil denies the Word of God (Matt. 13:19, 39), put treason in the heart of Judas (John 13:2), blinds unbelievers to the gospel (2 Cor. 4:4), and hates Jesus Christ (John 13:27; see also 6:70; Luke 22:53). Satan is said to be already judged (John 16:11), but nonetheless he is still very active up to the time God will cast him out of heaven (Rev. 12). Satan will be bound during the millennial kingdom; he and the demonic world will be rendered inactive while Christ is reigning on the earth. But he will be loosed at the close of the Millennium, judged, and cast into the lake of fire (20:1–3; 7–10). —JFW

Be sensitive to the reality of the adversary's desire to thwart God's purpose
for your life and submit to the Lord's guidance through His Spirit.

Scripture

THE WORD *scripture* means "a writing," and "the holy Scriptures" (2 Tim. 3:15) are the sixty-six books of the Bible, which are inspired by

God. "All Scripture is God-breathed and useful for teaching, rebuking, correcting and training in righteousness, so that the man of God may be thoroughly equipped for every good work" (3:16–17). In 2 Chronicles 30:5 the words "what was written" refer to the holy Scriptures. And the two tablets of stone with the Ten Commandments are called "the writing of God" (Exod. 32:16).

Some portions of the Bible were dictated directly by God, but most were not. Regardless of how it was written, the Bible claims to have the authority of God, even though its truths are expressed through fallible men. Christ stated that the written Scriptures would be fulfilled down to the smallest letter (the Hebrew *yôd*) and the smallest part of a letter (Matt. 5:18).

The original writings have been lost, so that what we have are copies of them. Yet the hundreds of manuscripts of the Old and New Testaments, even though copies, are in remarkable agreement, and variations, though numerous, are seldom important theologically. Even where theological truth is not clear in some manuscripts, usually a clear passage can be found that clarifies the issue.

The science known as lower criticism seeks to determine from existing copies what the original said. The science has been so refined that for all practical purposes the Bible as we have it can be accepted as if it were the original.

A graphic illustration of this is the Book of Daniel, which in our Bibles is a translation of a copy dating from about A.D. 900. In the Dead Sea Scrolls, however, a manuscript was found dating from 100 B.C., about one thousand years earlier than the previous existing manuscripts. And yet the two manuscripts are practically identical with no important differences.

Usually correct readings can be determined from the antiquity of the manuscripts and the number of copies that agree. The science of lower criticism is a complicated process, dealing with hundreds of manuscripts, but the findings of careful scholars support the authenticity of the Bible as we have it. —JFW

Consistently memorize passages from the Bible
that will assist you in living the Christian life.

Security

WHEN PAUL WROTE, "For I am convinced that neither death nor life, neither angels nor demons, neither the present nor the future, nor any powers, neither height nor depth, nor anything else in all creation, will be able to separate us from the love of God that is in Christ Jesus our Lord" (Rom. 8:38–39), the message is clear: He believed his salvation was secure. "Security" is the belief that when God grants salvation through faith in Christ, it can never be lost because it is eternal.

From the beginning of His earthly ministry Jesus stated that those who believe in Him have eternal life (John 3:15, 36; 5:24; 6:47). On one occasion He explained that it was the Father's will that no believer be lost (6:38–40). Jesus told the Jewish leaders that those who believe in Him will never perish and no one can pluck them out of His hand (10:28). He strengthened His argument by emphasizing the fact that believers are in the hands of His Father who is "greater than all," and that "no one can snatch them out of my Father's hand" (10:29). The subject of security was one of the major themes in His extended prayer to the Father the night before He was crucified. He prayed specifically that God the Father would protect believers from the evil one (17:11, 15), just as Jesus had protected them during His earthly ministry (17:12). He prayed for the Father's protection on those who would believe down through the ages (17:20). In His prayer He stated that believers have a union with Him like the one He has with the Father (17:21). He also prayed that believers would be with Him to behold His glory (17:24). There is no reason to believe that this prayer of the Lord has been left unanswered.

The doctrine of security was taught by the apostle Paul in his writings. He proclaimed that through the death of Christ, believers have been justified and saved from God's wrath (Rom. 5:9). Added to that is the reality of the Resurrection; because Christ is alive, those who belong to Him will continue as long as He lives (5:10). Because Christ was raised to life and is at the right hand of God interceding for us, no one can separate Christians from Christ's love (8:34–35). Paul also taught that God has sealed the believer with His Holy Spirit until the day of redemption (Eph. 1:13–14; 4:30). Since all believers are indwelt and sealed with the Holy Spirit, they are in the body of Christ forever.

The Book of Hebrews was written to remind us of the present ministry of Christ as our Great High Priest. Because His priesthood is permanent, He is able to save completely (forever) since He continues to live and intercede for those He saves (Heb. 7:24–25). Because of His ministry on behalf of God's children, those who trust Him can have confidence and assurance that their salvation is secure (10:19–23).

To some people the concept of eternal security may seem arrogant; however, it must be seen as the result of God's grace. Since salvation is the supernatural work of God, the entire process from the beginning to the end is from Him. Security is based on the character of God and the nature of salvation. Some New Testament verses may seem to say that salvation is conditional and dependent on the believer's faithfulness (for example, 2 Tim. 2:12; Heb. 6:4–8). But this stems from taking these verses out of their immediate context in isolation from the rest of Scripture. Of course the Christian life has challenges, and no one in this life ever reaches a position of freedom from the presence of sin (Phil. 3:12; 1 John 1:8). The goal for every Christian is to be like Christ and not allow sin to be the master. If Christ's death was not sufficient to pay for every sin, there is no way He can be crucified again (Heb. 6:6). The biblical evidence is strong in affirming that His death is completely adequate and the believer is absolutely secure.   **—WGJ**

Praise the Lord daily for the certainty of your salvation
and the security you have in Christ.

Servant

BEING A SERVANT seems like a degrading or inferior role, but God used that word in describing those whom He held in highest esteem, including His Son, who is called the servant of the Lord (Isa. 42:1). In the Bible the word *servant* identifies those who were bondslaves as well as those who were in positions of distinction. Prominent people who were called servants include Abraham (Gen. 26:24), Moses (Num. 12:7), David (Isa. 37:35), and Daniel (Dan. 6:20).

A servant is one who obediently carries out his responsibilities for his master, seeks no recognition for himself (Luke 17:7–10), and cares for others. This service may be menial, or it may involve serving in official capacities such as Old Testament priests or church deacons. Sometimes people served others not by their own choice but because they were in bondage to others as slaves (Gen. 47:18–21).

The Israelites had servants in their households. If those serving were Israelites, specific laws were in effect to protect them. They were to be treated as hired workers and not as slaves (Lev. 25:39–43). Even when those serving were from other nations, they were to be treated with respect and dignity and often became part of the family. Every seven years all servants would be given freedom (Deut. 15:12). God commanded masters to treat their servants generously because God had redeemed the nation out of slavery from the hands of the Egyptians (15:13–15, 18). Often servants would opt to stay with their masters because of the loving care they had received, and then these people would become servants for life (15:16–17).

Israel as a nation had a unique calling from the Lord to be His servant (Isa. 41:8–9), witnessing to the power and greatness of God to all the nations of the world (43:10–13). In return the Israelites could expect the Lord to protect and care for them in every way (44:1–5). How tragic, though, that the nation as God's servant was spiritually blind to the Lord (42:19–20).

The prophet Isaiah wrote about another servant who was totally distinct from all others, the Messiah or the Servant of the Lord. Isaiah pictured Him as gentle, one who would not raise His voice on the streets or bruise a reed (42:2–3); yet the power of the Spirit would be on Him and ultimately He would establish peace on the earth (11:2–5). Through Him the gentile world will have opportunity for salvation, and the light of His salvation will shine to the ends of the earth (49:6). In the following chapter the obedience of Messiah to do the will of the Father was graphically portrayed (50:5–7). The climax of Isaiah's prophecies about the Servant of the Lord was a stunning description of His bearing the sins of the world in His death, being stricken for the transgressions of Israel (53:4–8). This was God's purpose, even though Israel rejected the message of salvation (53:1–3).

Matthew indicated that the miraculous ministry of Jesus was a fulfillment of Isaiah's words about the Servant of the Lord (Matt. 12:17–21;

see Isa. 42:1–4). Jesus referred to His role as a servant when He spoke to the disciples about who would be considered great in the kingdom. He stated that the Son of Man came to serve and not to be served (Mark 10:45). In the hours before His crucifixion Jesus stated (in Luke 22:37) that He was fulfilling the words of Isaiah 53:12, which referred to the suffering Servant. The apostle John recorded the dramatic scene in the Upper Room when Jesus took a towel and washed the feet of His disciples, something only servants did (John 13:1–15). Years later Paul reflected on the crucifixion of Christ and highlighted the servant attitude of Jesus, who was obedient to the will of the Father, even to death (Phil. 2:6–11).

Since the apostles were followers of Christ, it is not surprising that they identified themselves as servants of the Lord (Rom. 1:1; James 1:1; 2 Pet. 1:1; Jude 1; Rev. 1:1). To be a servant was the pathway of blessing, according to the words of Jesus (John 13:15–17). When Paul wrote in Romans 6:15–23 about the power of the death and resurrection of Christ, he emphasized the reality of the bondage of sin and the need for believers to be servants of righteousness rather than slaves to sin.

One other concept of servanthood in the Epistles concerns ministry and is expressed by the Greek word *diakonos*, someone who carries out an appointed task. This is the term used for the work of a deacon (1 Tim. 3:10, 13). Christians are servants of the New Covenant (2 Cor. 3:6), of righteousness (11:15), of Christ (1 Tim. 4:6), and of the gospel (Eph. 3:7). Although there are different kinds of spiritual gifts and different ways of serving, there is only one Holy Spirit, one Lord, and one God who enables believers to serve (1 Cor. 12:4–6). Since all believers are servants, they stand equally before the Lord. No matter what task God has assigned to us as servants, we are totally dependent on Him for growth and development so that all glory and honor belongs to Him (3:5–9).
　　　　　　　　　　　　　　　　　　　　　　　　　　　　　　　—WGJ

Exemplify the qualities of the Lord Jesus, especially a servant's heart like His, and always consider the needs of others.

Sin

ONE OF THE MORE INTRIGUING ISSUES in theology is the study of sin and its effect on every individual. The Bible records the entrance of sin into the world, the devastating results of sin, God's grace that provides forgiveness of sin, and the fact that one day God will terminate all sin in the universe forever.

The story of Adam and Eve sheds light on the entrance of sin into the human race. "The serpent," who appears in Genesis 3:1 without any explanation, is identified in the Book of the Revelation as the devil (Rev. 12:9). In his adversarial position Satan placed himself in opposition to God and His word. From Satan's encounter with Adam and Eve the meaning of sin became apparent. Because the integrity of the Lord was challenged, it is clear that sin is something that is contrary to God's character (Gen. 3:5). God had told Adam and Eve not to eat from the tree of the knowledge of good and evil, and they disobeyed His command (2:17; 3:6). Thus anything said or done contrary to God's Word is sin.

Other truths about sin are learned from Cain's experience (4:3–6). The term for "sin" in that passage means "to miss the mark." Sin is anything that comes short of God's perfection. Of even greater consequence was the fact that Cain's action was against God. This was also David's testimony after his sinful affair with Bathsheba. In Psalm 51:4 he acknowledged that his sin was against God. The ramifications of sin are certainly widespread, but what makes sin so detestable is that it is directed against the holy, righteous, loving God.

The sacrificial requirements of the Law, detailed in the Book of Leviticus, augment the truth that sin is essentially wrongdoing directed toward God. Thus people are guilty, and redemption and restoration are mandatory. Sin drives people from God and excludes them from fellowship with Him (Lev. 1:4).

The prophets spoke repeatedly about sin as transgression or rebellion against God and His Law (for example, Isa. 1:2; 43:27; Jer. 2:29; Ezek. 2:3–4). Amos indicted the nations around Israel for their transgressions (Amos 1:3–2:4) and then included Judah and Israel in his list (2:4–3:15). Because of those transgressions God's judgment was imminent. Another term the prophets used to describe sin was "going astray" (see Isa. 53:6; Ezek. 44:10). Many had been led astray by false prophets (Jer. 23:32; Ezek. 13:10).

From these examples a composite view of sin can be seen. It is a going astray from God, missing the mark, rebellion, transgression, opposing God, and nonconformity to God's character and/or laws.

The New Testament teaching on sin built on what was revealed in the Old Testament. Certainly the Jews had an awareness of the meaning of sin and its consequences. That is why the announcement by John the Baptist was both timely and significant. John identified Jesus as "the Lamb of God who takes away the sin of the world" (John 1:29). The singular word *sin* emphasizes the inherent sin of humankind rather than sinful acts. Jesus came to deliver people from their sinful state and to give them eternal life (3:16).

Much can be learned about sin from the teachings of Jesus, not only by what He said but also by the way He dealt with sinners. Jesus taught that sin is "missing the mark" (Matt. 5:30; 26:28; John 8:21, 24); "evil," usually related to moral corruption (Matt. 5:11; Luke 6:45; John 5:29); unrighteousness (Matt. 5:45); "lawlessness" or hostility toward God (1 John 3:4; and "transgression" or deviation from the truth (Mark 11:25, NASB; Matt. 6:14–15). The Bible leaves no doubt about the universality of sin (Eccles. 7:20; Rom. 3:23; 5:12). This is also affirmed by His statement that sin comes from within and resides in the heart (Matt. 15:19; Mark 7:20–23). Sin results in condemnation (John 5:29; 3:18) and death (8:24; Rom. 6:23). Before He was crucified He explained that His death would be for the forgiveness of sins (Matt. 26:28).

The Epistles amplify the teachings of Christ and the Old Testament on sin. In Romans 1–3 Paul skillfully developed the fact that both Gentiles and Jews are all under sin, and he cited Old Testament passages to substantiate his charges (3:9–18). Because sin has enslaved people, Paul explained how the death and resurrection of Christ makes sin powerless in the believer, so that it no longer has the right to control him or her (6:5–14). Christians have been set free from the penalty and power of sin (6:18). The Law had no power to deliver a person from sin; in fact, the Law only made individuals more aware of sin (7:7–8, 13).

Paul was convinced that the presence of sin in the life of Christians was destructive and could keep them from living for Christ. Most of his Epistles address this issue in some detail. Sin affects the way believers treat each other (Rom. 12:17, 21; 14:6, 23); it is the reason people have a wrong attitude toward governing authorities (13:4); it can divert attention from the real purpose of the Christian life (15:11–14). Sin within the church is displeasing to the Lord and needs to be removed (1 Cor. 5:13). One's attitude in worship can result in personal discipline from God (11:27–32). Sin can destroy the believer's freedom in Christ (Gal. 5:13); it affects the unity of the church (Eph. 4:1–6); one's walk with the Lord is hindered by sinful practices (Col. 3:5–10); the purity of believers is in jeopardy because of sin (1 Thess. 4:3–8); and sin causes greed and improper desires for power (1 Tim. 6:10).

In light of all the problems sin can inflict on the church and believers in the church, Paul issued certain exhortations: Flee from and put off every form of evil and pursue righteousness (Col. 3:5–11; 1 Tim. 6:11; 2 Tim. 2:22); study and apply the Scriptures, which provide training in righteousness (3:16); put on the total armor God has provided (Eph. 6:11–18; 1 Thess. 5:8); be controlled by the Spirit and put on all the gracious qualities of the Spirit (Rom. 8:9; Gal. 5:16, 22–23; Col. 3:12); follow the example of godly leaders (Phil. 3:17–19); consider yourself dead to sin but alive to God (Rom. 6:11); and yield your body to the Lord as an instrument of righteousness (6:13).

Echoing the Lord's teaching about sin, James explained how the sins of the tongue can corrupt the whole person (James 3:6); bring disunity to the church (4:1–2); cause Christians to slander one another (4:11–12); and even bring physical sickness (5:14–16). Peter's contribution to the theology of sin was his exposé of the sinful practices of false teachers and their devastating effect on the church (2 Pet. 2:1–22). The apostle John explained how sin affected the fellowship of believers with God, who is holy and righteous (1 John 1:5–6). Specific sins should be confessed because forgiveness is available when confession is made (1:9). John declared that a genuine believer is not characterized by sin, and this distinguishes the righteous from the unrighteous (3:7–10). The apostle also stated that sin is lawlessness, and because believers are indwelt by Christ they should not continue to sin in a lawless manner (3:4–6). When Christ returns to the earth, He will triumph over sin, Satan, and death (Rev. 20:1–15). God has promised that in the city of God there will be no more death or evil or anything impure (21:4, 8, 27). **—WGJ**

*Keep in mind that sin does not have to enslave Christians
because of the many God–given provisions and promises.*

Sleep

THE SCRIPTURES OFTEN USE the imagery of sleep to convey the concept of death. This is not the same as so-called soul sleep, since the Bible clearly depicts the consciousness of those who die (Luke 23:43; 2 Cor. 5:8; Phil. 1:23). Instead the term *sleep* graphically portrays the fact that in the resurrection there will be an "awakening" of the body. When King David died, he "slept with his fathers" (1 Kings 2:10, NASB). The same was said of Solomon (11:43, NASB) and other kings. Job used the word *sleep* when he talked about death (Job 14:12). David called out to God for deliverance; otherwise, he said, he would "sleep in death" (Ps. 13:3). Moses stated the same concept when he declared that God would "sweep men away in the sleep of death" (90:5), and Jeremiah described the wicked as sleeping (Jer. 51:39, 57).

The New Testament uses the same metaphor of sleep to describe death. Jesus said that Jarius's daughter, who had died, was asleep (Matt. 9:24), and the Lord told His disciples that Lazarus, who had died, had fallen asleep (John 11:11). Luke wrote that Stephen, the first Christian martyr, "fell asleep" (Acts 7:60). In portraying death Paul stated that some Christians had "fallen asleep" (1 Cor. 11:30), and Peter referred to scoffers who spoke of their ancestors who had fallen asleep (2 Pet. 3:4, NASB).

In explaining the significance of the resurrection, Paul used the term *sleep* to describe those who have died in Christ and whose bodies will be resurrected (1 Cor. 15:18, 20, 51). Those who have fallen asleep (1 Thess. 4:13–15) are called "the dead in Christ" (4:16). One other aspect of the resurrection is the apostle's teaching that not everyone will sleep (die), for believers who are alive when Christ returns will be changed along with those who are asleep in Christ (1 Cor. 15:51–52). This event, called in 1 Thessalonians 4:13–18 a "catching up" (the Rapture) of believers, includes both those who had fallen asleep in Christ and those who will be alive at that time. No teaching in the Bible has provided greater hope to Christians, especially those bereaved of loved ones.

In tracing this term throughout Scripture other uses can be found. Sometimes God forced sleep on individuals so they appeared to be anesthetized. Those people fell into a "deep sleep." This was true of Adam (Gen. 2:21), Abraham (15:12), Jacob (28:12), and others. God's special purposes were brought about when this took place.

Sleep was also a term used for sexual relations (16:2; 30:3, 15; 38:16). Solomon also used the word in describing those who were lazy and unwilling to work (Prov. 6:9–11). On one occasion the psalmist felt God was asleep because it seemed to him that the Lord had hidden His face from him (Ps. 44:23–24).

Paul used this graphic word when exhorting believers to be spiritually alert (Rom. 13:11), putting off sin (13:12–14). He also spoke of spiritually insensitive believers as "asleep" (1 Thess. 5:6–7), unaware of the darkness surrounding them (5:4–5).

Most passages where "sleep" occurs, however, refer to natural sleep. The context makes clear whether the term is used in a normal or a metaphorical sense. **—WGJ**

Rejoice in the hope that all who have died in Christ are asleep in Jesus and will be awakened to take part in the Resurrection.

Soul and Spirit

THESE TWO WORDS ARE CONSIDERED TOGETHER because of the difficulty in determining biblically whether they are separate elements of the immaterial nature of man or are interchangeable terms for the immaterial nature. The word *soul* translates *nepeš* (Hebrew) and *psychē* (Greek), and the word *spirit* translates *rûaḥ* (Hebrew) and *pneuma* (Greek). The words translated "spirit" are also translated at times "air," "breath," and "wind."

That each human is a bipartite being—material and immaterial—is obvious: "The LORD God formed man from the dust of the ground and breathed into his nostrils the breath of life, and the man became a living being [literally, 'a living soul']" (Gen. 2:7). Each person is conscious of his physical nature (his body) and of his immaterial nature (his conscience, mind, and will), but he is not aware of the distinction between his soul and his spirit. That inability does not mean that a definite distinction between soul and spirit does not exist, however.

Scripture sometimes attributes the same qualities and the same actions to both soul and spirit. Job spoke of "the anguish of my spirit" and "the bitterness of my soul" (Job 7:11), while David wrote, "My soul is in anguish" (Ps. 6:3) and Asaph described his spirit as "embittered" (73:21). The pharaoh's "mind [literally, 'spirit'] was troubled" (Gen. 41:8), while the psalmist wrote, "My soul is downcast within me" (Ps. 42:6). Jesus said that He came "to give his life [literally, 'soul'] as a ransom for many" (Matt. 20:28), and yet Matthew wrote that Jesus "gave up his spirit" (27:50; see also Luke 23:46; John 19:30). Jesus said, "Now my heart [literally, 'soul'] is troubled" (John 12:27), and John reported that "Jesus was troubled in spirit" (13:21). These and other references suggest that the words *soul* and *spirit* are used interchangeably and refer to the same immaterial nature of man.

Other Scripture verses, particularly in the Pauline Epistles, seem to draw a distinction between one's soul and spirit. Paul prayed for the Thessalonian believers, "May your whole spirit, soul and body be kept blameless at the coming of our Lord Jesus Christ" (1 Thess. 5:23). In 1 Corinthians 2:14–3:3 he wrote of the fleshly man, the soulish man, and the spiritual man, with apparent distinctions between them. Similarly in 15:44–47, he drew a distinction between "a natural [literally, 'soulish'] body" and "a spiritual body." Hebrews 4:12 states that "the word of God is living and active. Sharper than any double-edged sword, it penetrates even to dividing soul and spirit." Such passages seem to make a distinction between soul and spirit.

On the basis of such passages many Bible students accept a tripartite division of human beings (body, soul, and spirit), known as trichotomy. Others, however, point out that the Scriptures also speak of the human heart (Gen. 6:5; 1 Sam. 1:13; Ps. 111:1, Matt. 5:8), conscience (Gen. 20:6; Job 27:6; 1 Cor. 4:4; 1 Pet. 3:16), and mind (Deut. 28:28, 65; Ps. 26:2; Matt. 22:37; 2 Cor. 2:13).

No one, however, suggests that the immaterial part of humans consists of five parts—soul, spirit, heart, conscience, and mind—as if they were all distinguishable. As a result many Bible students accept the twofold division (material and immaterial), known as dichotomy.

At the same time most theologians probably also recognize some kind of distinction between the soul and spirit. In general, when speaking of humanity's immaterial nature in relation to creation (Job 33:22; Ps. 63:5; Prov. 2:10; 19:8) and other people (Job 30:25; Prov. 22:5), the word *soul* is used. On the other hand the word *spirit* is generally used when speaking of a person's immaterial nature in relation to God (Ps. 51:10; Prov. 20:27; John 4:23) and to spiritual things (Ps. 31:5; Rom. 8:10; 1 Cor. 5:5). It may be significant that the word *soul* occurs more frequently in the Old Testament, while the word *spirit* is used more frequently in the New Testament. As a result it seems best to consider each person as being basically dichotomous, but also to recognize a minor distinction between soul and spirit in one's immaterial nature. —JAW

Determine to serve God with your whole being,
whether or not you can distinguish between your soul and spirit.

Spiritual Gifts

ON THE DAY OF PENTECOST a movement began that has grown from a small insignificant group to a powerful body of believers that includes millions of people around the world. This has been accomplished through the risen Christ, who ascended to heaven and gave gifts and gifted people for the growth and development of His church. These gifts played a major role in God's strategy to call out a people for Himself and to glorify His name (1 Pet. 2:9–10).

The spiritual gifts of the New Testament are distinct from the gifts God gave people in earlier times. In Old Testament times the Lord selected certain individuals and gave them wisdom and abilities in preparing garments for the priests (Exod. 28:3). He gave Bezalel and Oholiab wisdom and ability in all kinds of crafts that could be taught to others so that the work on the tabernacle could be completed according to God's standards (31:3–6; 35:30–35; 36:1–2). In the church, however, every believer has been given a spiritual gift (a supernatural enabling or ability) so that everyone in the body of Christ can participate in the Lord's work in a particular way (1 Cor. 12:7, 11).

Several New Testament passages discuss the gifts of the Spirit: Romans 12:3–8; 1 Corinthians 12–14; Ephesians 4:7–13; and 1 Peter 4:10–11. In 1 Corinthians 12–14 Paul was correcting what he considered the misuse of gifts by providing guidelines the Christians needed to follow in using their gifts effectively. In Romans 12:3–8 Paul explained the manner in which the gifts are to be exercised; Ephesians 4:7–13 focuses on the people who received gifts; and 1 Peter 4:10–11 gives exhortations to speak and to serve in a manner that glorifies God.

These four Scripture passages do not describe in detail what is entailed in each gift, nor is there a definition of the term *spiritual gift*. But it is clear that spiritual gifts refer to abilities that go beyond one's natural capacities.

Spiritual gifts were given to build up and serve the church, the body of Christ (Eph. 4:12; 1 Pet. 4:10). These gifts are given sovereignly (1 Cor. 12:4–6). The diversity of gifts is illustrated by the human body (12:12–27), suggesting that every believer has a primary function in the body of Christ (12:27). Of course, each believer might also have other talents apart from his or her spiritual gifts.

Since gifts are given sovereignly by God at salvation (12:11), individual desires are not the reason a person receives a particular gift. Paul did say, "but eagerly desire the greater gifts" (12:31), but this may well be a declarative statement ("you are eagerly desiring the greater gifts") rather than a command. In that case Paul was saying that the Corinthians were wanting the more significant spiritual gifts but should not have been doing so.

Paul's statement about praying for the interpretation of tongues was not the same as praying to possess the "gift" of interpretation (14:13), unless the congregation was asking the Lord to bring a believer into the church who possessed that gift. Praying for God's assistance in preaching, teaching, witnessing, or giving is something every believer can do, but praying to receive a particular gift has no biblical support. Paul's exhortation to the church in 1 Corinthians 14 was to correct an attitude among some believers who were exalting the more spectacular gifts. Paul did prioritize the gifts in 1 Corinthians 12:27–28, particularly to correct the Corinthian error of elevating one gift above all others.

Some gifts were foundational, such as the gifts of apostles and prophets (Eph. 2:20), especially those who received direct revelation from the Lord. Certainly there is no need now to reproduce the foundation of the church; instead believers are to build on that foundation. Such foundational gifts were no longer needed after the church was established.

The four lists of spiritual gifts in the New Testament are not identical, which suggests that these are representative gifts and not exhaustive statements on all possible gifts. If there were particular gifts necessary for the founding of the church, could possibly other specific gifts be needed at various times in the history of the church? God's sovereignty may dictate that some gifts have ceased, and new gifts are given in accord with His purposes and plans for His church.

Some gifts were misused, copied, or counterfeited (1 Cor. 12:1–3). That's why Paul wrote extensively about the gift of tongues in the Corinthian church. Understandably the gift of tongues might be exhilarating to the one who exercised such a gift. However, the gifts were to edify the whole congregation and not just the individual (14:4, 12, 13–17, 19). Since the gift of tongues was to bring "some revelation or knowledge or prophecy or word of instruction" (14:6), there is serious question whether this gift existed beyond the first century, since all biblical revelation ceased when the last book of the New Testament was written. Paul's personal illustration about his own childhood and growth to manhood suggests that some gifts would not be necessary once the church passed its infancy (13:8–11) and reached "perfection" (13:10), that is, maturity. Elsewhere Paul used the word *perfect* (Greek, *teleion*) to mean "mature" (Eph. 4:13; Phil. 3:12, 15).

Because spiritual gifts are important to the church, Christians need to serve others and to glorify the Lord by exercising their gift(s). One characteristic that distinguishes a church from other groups is the gifted people who by God's grace can carry out the functions and responsibilities of a local congregation (1 Cor. 1:7). Leadership within a congregation can assist members in discerning their gifts. Timothy is a good example. The elders and Paul recognized that Timothy had the gift of a pastor and so they ordained him for the work of the Lord (1 Tim. 4:14; 2 Tim. 1:6). Even when a believer is not sure what his or her spiritual gift might be, that person can engage in various church ministries, and often in that process will discover his or her spiritual gift.

—WGJ

Realize God has graciously gifted you, and seek opportunities to serve Him.

Spirituality

BEING A CHRISTIAN is not the same as possessing true spirituality, although both have the same starting point. The basis of any relationship with God begins with salvation, or what the Bible calls the new birth (John 3:3). Even in the Old Testament those who believed God and were considered saints had a relationship with the Holy Spirit. Whether or not individuals were indwelt by the Spirit in the days before Pentecost, the presence of the Spirit was deemed essential for a close walk with the Lord (Ps. 51:10–12).

Much can be learned by examining how the apostle Paul developed the concept of a spiritual person in 1 Corinthians 2:11–16. Paul taught that no one can understand the things of God unless he or she possesses the Spirit of God. In fact, such truths are foolishness to an unregenerate person (2:14). This means that true spirituality is based on salvation through faith in Christ and the indwelling of the Holy Spirit. There is a distinct difference between people who are Christians and those who have not believed.

Since every believer has a relationship with the Spirit through salvation, does this mean that everyone is spiritual? The answer is no, for as Paul explained, some Christians are not spiritual (3:1). Spirituality, or being a spiritual person, involves having other characteristics.

Discernment is a major attribute of spirituality (2:15–16). This comes because of the Holy Spirit's work within the believer. The Spirit's ministry of controlling believers is called the filling of the Holy Spirit (Eph. 5:18). And because Christ dwells in believers, they can know the mind of Christ (1 Cor. 2:16), that is, spiritual persons will reflect the mind and heart of the Lord by wise decisions.

Once an individual has received Christ as his or her Savior and is indwelt by the Holy Spirit, that person is capable of making decisions that please the Lord. This does not happen automatically, nor does it mean that every decision or judgment will always be what the Spirit desires. But when the Holy Spirit is controlling thoughts and actions, the results will be proper discernment and good decisions. Then the fruit of the Spirit will characterize the believer's life (Gal. 5:22–23).

When Christians fail to allow the Spirit to guide their thoughts, either because of neglect or disregard for His presence, they act like people who are without Christ. This was the problem in the church in Corinth. Christians were not reflecting the qualities of the Spirit; rather, they were acting in a "worldly" manner, that is, as infant Christians, not mature believers (1 Cor. 3:1). The result was fragmentation and division in the body of Christ (3:4).

The fact that Paul used the figure of an infant to describe the Christians at Corinth helps us understand that spirituality is also a process, a matter of growth and development under the influence and control of the Holy Spirit. New believers can make proper decisions and often do because they yield to the Spirit's control. However, the experiences of new believers, like those of infants, are limited. Time is needed for growth and development to face the challenges of the Christian life. Spirituality is a result of growth. Peter exhorted believers to rid themselves of actions that characterize unbelievers and to grow up in their salvation (1 Pet. 2:1–2). In this passage he emphasized the role of the Word of God, which he called "spiritual milk" (2:2). The Scriptures provide the foundation for one's walk with the Lord.

Living like Christ can be realized only as individuals meet the challenges of everyday life as He did and became the example for believers to follow (2:21). Paul stated emphatically that the Christian life is a journey and that he had not obtained all that was available in knowing Christ (Phil. 3:12). His concern was to keep pressing on toward the goal of being like Him (3:14). The "spiritual" Christian seeks to follow the Lord's leading and to be like Christ in every way.

Since the standard for spirituality is Christ, spirituality means being characterized by the qualities that are true of Him; and that can be produced in the lives of believers only by the indwelling Holy Spirit. How these qualities are expressed in everyday life is an important aspect of spirituality. People who are spiritual do certain things as well as refrain from some things. They will express love to God without reservation and will love others in the body of Christ. They will even show love and graciousness to their enemies (Rom. 12:9, 20–21). Spiritual people seek to live according to the principles set forth in Scripture and desire to study the Word of God and put into practice what it says (2 Tim. 2:15; 3:14–17; Heb. 4:12; 5:11–14; 1 Pet. 2:2). They will seek to worship God individually and with other believers (Heb. 10:22–25). Spirituality will be expressed by proper conduct in the home (Eph. 5:22–6:4; 1 Pet. 3:3–7), and people who are spiritual will lead Christlike lives in society and will respect civil authority (1 Pet. 2:13–17). They will live godly lives even in a hostile environment (3:13–17).

Although the emphasis concerning spirituality is positive, the Bible does warn that there are things that should not characterize the spiritual individual. Living under the control of the Spirit stands in direct opposition to sinful desires (Gal. 5:16–21). This is why Paul exhorted believers to put off certain desires that characterize life apart from the Spirit (Eph. 4:22) and to put to death whatever relates to evil desires and sexual immorality (Col. 3:5; see also 1 Pet. 4:2–3). Sometimes believers are to flee certain things, including the love of money (1 Tim. 6:11). They are to reject ungodliness emphatically (Titus 2:11).

Usually with every list of negatives there is a corresponding list of positive actions. It is important to notice that no list of prohibitions is complete and there is no attempt on the part of Paul and other New Testament writers to use only the negatives to define spirituality.

—WGJ

*Ask the Spirit of God to reproduce in you the beautiful qualities
of Christ that will make you a truly spiritual person.*

Stewardship

RESPONSIBILITY AND ACCOUNTABILITY have been an integral part of life since the beginning of creation. God gave human beings authority to subdue the earth and rule over it (Gen. 1:28). He gave Adam and Eve and all their descendants responsibility for the physical resources of the earth. This authority stems from the fact that God made man and woman in His image. Since everything belongs to God (Ps. 24:1), individuals are not owners but rather are stewards accountable to God.

In a parable Jesus taught several principles of stewardship (Luke

16:1–13). He said believers are to use worldly wealth (money) to accomplish eternal results (16:9). The quantity of one's possessions is not so important as the quality of one's character. The faithful person can be trusted with little or much (16:10; 19:11–27). For this reason Jesus said later that the widow who had put two small copper coins in the temple treasury had given more than all the others, because she gave out of her poverty and from her heart (21:1–4). The wise use of material possessions often determines spiritual responsibilities (16:11). Everyone is accountable to the Lord for using his resources (16:13).

Paul emphasized that faithfulness is to be the hallmark of a steward. The New International Version translates the word *steward* by the phrase "those who have been given a trust" (1 Cor. 4:1–2). Stewardship is not restricted to material possessions. Paul said the message of the gospel was a trust committed to him, and he felt compelled to proclaim it (9:15–18). Stewardship extended to the revelation God gave him about the development of the church, the body of Christ (Eph. 3:2–6). Elsewhere he said he was responsible as a steward to preach the Word of God in its fullness (Col. 1:25). The stewardship of giving is prominent in Paul's second letter to the Corinthian church. He wrote that God's gracious provisions make it possible for believers, as stewards, to be generous givers (2 Cor. 9:11).

Peter contributed to this topic by saying that Christians are stewards of spiritual gifts (1 Pet. 4:10, NASB). God gives gifts to all believers and expects them to exercise these gifts to serve others (4:11).

In today's society the emphasis on stewardship seems to focus on the use of earthly possessions, but the New Testament emphasizes spiritual responsibilities. 　　　　　　　　　　　　　　　　　　　**—WGJ**

Make a covenant with the Lord to give generously of the resources He has given you; plan to spend time each week in some ministry for Christ.

Substitution

WHEN JESUS CHRIST was nailed to the cross at Calvary, a transaction took place that cannot be totally captured with one word or phrase. The death of Christ is unique in history since He did not deserve to die, because He had no sin of His own (2 Cor. 5:21). His death was planned by God in eternity past (Isa. 53:10; Eph. 1:8–9; 1 Pet. 1:18–20, NASB). He died in the place of every person in the world and thus He was a substitute. Because He died for every sinner, everyone who believes He took his or her place on the cross receives eternal salvation and will not come under condemnation (Rom. 8:1).

The substitutionary death of Christ is well documented in the Bible. Jesus Himself taught that His death was substitutional, for He said He gave His life "a ransom for many" (Matt. 20:28; Mark 10:45). In both verses the Greek preposition *anti*, translated "for," means "in the place of." When Caiaphas, the high priest, referred to one man dying "for the people" (John 11:50), he unknowingly spoke of Jesus' death (11:51).

Paul's writings support the teaching that Christ's death was substitutional. When he wrote that Christ "died for all" (2 Cor. 5:14–15), he used the preposition *hyper*, which conveys not only the idea of "on behalf of" but also the meaning "in place of." In Galatians 3:13 Paul stated that believers have been redeemed from the curse of the Law because Christ became a curse "for" *(hyper)* them. Paul made a strong statement about Jesus' substitutionary death when he wrote that Jesus "gave himself as a ransom [*antilytron*, literally, 'a ransom in place of'] for [*hyper*] all men" (1 Tim. 2:6). The writer of Hebrews wrote that Jesus experienced "death for [*hyper*] everyone" (Heb. 2:9). Peter also taught the substitutionary atonement of Christ, for he wrote that "Christ died for sins once for all, the righteous for the unrighteous" (1 Pet. 3:18).

The teaching of a substitutionary death is supported by the Old Testament. The sacrificial system under the law of Moses required the slaying of an animal when an Israelite had sinned unintentionally (Lev. 4:4–5). The slain animal took the place of the offender. Though these substitutionary deaths were not adequate to remove sin permanently, they did satisfy the demands of the holy God until Christ offered Himself as the once-for-all Sacrifice for the sins of the world (Heb. 10:11–14).

—WGJ

Accept the truth that Jesus Christ died in your place, and rejoice in the realization that God is pleased with the sacrifice of His Son.

Suffering

IN EVERY SENSE OF THE WORD—physical, emotional, mental, psychological, spiritual—suffering entered human experience with the sin of Adam and Eve in the Garden of Eden. God had commanded Adam not to "eat from the tree of the knowledge of good and evil," warning him that if he ate he would "surely die" (Gen. 2:17). God's judgment on Eve and all women was that their pain in childbearing would be greatly increased (3:16). And for Adam and all his descendants the ground was cursed so that "painful toil" is required to cultivate the land (3:17). This labor to produce crops would involve "the sweat of your brow" (3:19). In the final analysis all suffering, even the suffering of Jesus Christ, springs from this sin and its punishment.

Like Adam and Eve many people bring suffering on themselves, either as the natural consequence of their actions or as God's judgment on them. Solomon warned his son against drunkenness and gluttony, saying, "Drunkards and gluttons become poor, and drowsiness clothes them in rags" (Prov. 23:21, see also 23:29–30). He also observed that "a companion of fools suffers harm" (13:20) and that "the simple keep going" in the face of danger "and suffer for it" (22:3; 27:12). Likewise, "Laziness brings on deep sleep, and the shiftless man goes hungry" (19:15); and the selfish and greedy person, who "withholds unduly . . . comes to poverty" (11:24).

Suffering is also a punishment from God for refusing to trust Him and for rebelling against Him. This is the story of Israel in the wilderness (Num. 14:34–35) and their descendants (14:33) during the times of the judges (Judg. 2:10–19). Eventually both the Northern Kingdom of Israel and the Southern Kingdom of Judah were conquered and led into captivity (Lam. 1:12, 18). Concerning those who break His commandments, God said, "I will punish their sin with the rod" (Ps. 89:32), and Paul wrote, after warning against sexual immorality, "The Lord will punish men for all such sins" (1 Thess. 4:6).

Through the ages many people have drawn the conclusion that all suffering is punishment from God for sin. This was the conclusion of Job's friends about his suffering (Job 4:7–8, 17; 8:3–4) and the conclusion of the disciples about the "man blind from birth" (John 9:1–2). Job was delivered into Satan's hands, however, to demonstrate that Job was not serving the Lord simply for the blessings he received (Job 1:8–12; 2:3–6). And Jesus explained that the man had been born blind "so that the work of God might be displayed in his life" (John 9:3).

Because of our relationship to Adam, everyone, as Eliphaz said, is "born to trouble as surely as sparks fly upward" (Job 5:7), and the Christian is not exempt. Suffering, however, has many other causes. It can be punishment for sin, or God's attempt to get a person's attention and response. It can be part of God's spiritual child-training program (Heb. 12:4–12), or preparation for special spiritual service. It can be an attack of Satan or of his human agents permitted by God. In any case it can be the means of bringing greater glory to God as the Christian endures it faithfully and successfully.

The supreme example of faithfully enduring suffering to the glory of God is the Lord Jesus Christ. He "endured . . . opposition from sinful men" (Heb. 12:3). Jesus told the disciples that "he must go to Jerusalem and suffer many things . . . and that he must be killed" (Matt. 16:21; see also 17:12). His physical suffering was climaxed by His death on the cross of Calvary (27:33–44).

Excruciating as it was, Jesus' physical suffering on the cross did not compare to His spiritual suffering, for "God made him who had no sin to be sin for us" (2 Cor. 5:21; see also Rom. 4:25; 8:3; Gal. 3:13), and He became the substitutionary Sacrifice for human sin. The anticipation of this spiritual suffering is seen in Jesus' prayer in the Garden of Gethsemane (Matt. 26:37–39, 42), and it is reflected in the darkness "from the sixth hour until the ninth hour . . . over all the land" (27:45) and in Jesus' cry "in a loud voice, *Eloi, Eloi, lama sabachthani?*—which means, 'My God, my God, why have you forsaken me?'" (27:46).

The believer in the Lord Jesus is called on to share in the sufferings of Christ. Paul wrote, "I fill up . . . what is still lacking in regard to Christ's afflictions, for the sake of his body, which is the church" (Col. 1:24). Since all believers are members of Christ's body, the church (Rom. 12:5; 1 Cor. 12:12–13, 27), when "one part suffers, every part suffers with it" (12:26). Paul also wrote that "the sufferings of Christ flow over into our lives . . . which produces in you patient endurance of the same sufferings we suffer" (2 Cor. 1:5–6).

Peter pointed out that there is nothing particularly commendable about enduring punishment that is deserved. But he also wrote, "If you suffer for doing good and you endure it, this is commendable before God. To this you were called, because Christ suffered for you, leaving you an example, that you should follow in his steps" (1 Pet. 2:20–23). Later he wrote, "But even if you should suffer for what is right, you are blessed. . . . It is better, if it is God's will, to suffer for doing good than for doing evil" (3:14, 17).   —JAW

Through prayer and self-examination seek God's purpose
in any suffering you experience.

Tt

Tabernacle

THE TABERNACLE WAS THE PLACE where God met with the Israelites after the Exodus from Egypt. In Egypt there were many sanctuaries or temples; their remains can be seen at Karnak, Luxor, and other places. But Israel was to have only one worship center, the tabernacle, and later the temple. Scripture clearly reveals four purposes for the tabernacle: (1) It provided a way for God to dwell in the midst of His people (Exod. 25:8). (2) It provided a way whereby God could reveal His glory (40:34–35). (3) It made it possible for a sinful people to approach a holy God. (4) It provided a picture of our redemption in Christ. According to Hebrews 8–10 the tabernacle foreshadows the earthly and heavenly spheres of Christ's ministry. Christ therefore is the antitype of the tabernacle—its furniture, priests, altar, and sacrifices.

The Old Testament refers to three tabernacles: (1) the provisional tabernacle erected by Moses outside the camp after the sin of the golden calf. It was called the "tabernacle of meeting" (Exod. 33:7, NKJV) and was the place where God met and talked with Moses. (2) The Sinaitic tabernacle built according to minute instructions the Lord gave Moses (Exod. 25–27; 30–31; 35–40; Num. 3–4; 7). (3) The Davidic tabernacle (2 Sam. 6:17, NKJV) erected by David in Jerusalem to house the ark of the covenant (6:12) until the temple was built.

The ground plan of the Mosaic tabernacle consisted of the outer court and the tabernacle itself. The court was formed by curtains hung from pillars which were secured in bronze bases. The altar of burnt offering stood in the court inside the entrance gate (Exod. 27:1–8) and reminded the worshiper that sacrifice was an absolute requirement by which to approach God. Also in the court was the bronze laver (30:13–21). Here the priests washed their hands and feet after offering sacrifices and before entering the holy place. As the psalmist later declared, clean hands and a pure heart are essential to draw near to God (Ps. 24:3–4).

The tabernacle proper also stood within the court and consisted of curtains draped over a framework (Exod. 26). The building thus created was divided into two compartments, the Holy Place and the Most Holy Place. These in turn were separated by a veil, which symbolized the barrier that separates or comes between sinners and God.

The Holy Place, which could be entered only by the priests, contained three objects of furniture. First was the altar of incense, which stood before the veil (Exod. 30:1–7). Incense was offered every morning and evening, symbolizing prayer ascending to God at the beginning and end of each day. The second piece of furniture in the Holy Place was a table on which was placed the twelve loaves or cakes of showbread, called also "bread of the Presence" (25:23–30). The bread was eaten by the priests once a week as an act of thanksgiving for the sustenance of life. The third piece of furniture in the holy place was the golden lampstand (25:31–40), which provided light for the priests to serve in the darkened room. It represented Israel as God's channel of light in the world (Zech. 4).

The only piece of furniture in the Most Holy Place was the boxlike ark of the covenant (Exod. 25:10–15). The ark contained the Decalogue (25:16) representing God's demands on His people. A lid of solid gold, called the atonement cover, the mercy seat, or the propitiatory, covered the ark and its contents. On the Day of Atonement blood was sprinkled on the mercy seat by the high priest, the only person in Israel who was allowed, once a year, to enter the Most Holy Place (Lev. 16:11–17). God's Shekinah glory rested between two crafted cherubim on the ends of the blood-sprinkled lid (Exod. 25:22; 40:34–35; Lev. 16:2). The Lord's essential presence could dwell with His people in this earthly seat of His glory only because of the expiatory blood of sacrifice.

The tabernacle was set up at Sinai on the first anniversary of the Exodus (Exod. 40:2, 17). When Israel left Sinai and journeyed toward Canaan, the ark of the covenant preceded the people when they were marching (Num. 10:33–36). For nearly thirty-eight years they wandered in the wilderness, but their headquarters were at Kadesh. After Israel crossed the Jordan River into Canaan, the tabernacle was set up at Gilgal, a temporary site (Josh. 4:19; 5:10; 9:6; 10:6, 43). In time a more permanent location was located at Shiloh in Ephraim, a site convenient for the men to attend the three annual pilgrimage feasts (18:1). During the time of the judges, the Philistines captured the ark in battle and then destroyed Shiloh (1 Sam. 4). The ark was soon returned to Israel and stayed at Kiriath Jearim for several years (6:21–7:1). Later the tabernacle was located at Nob (21:1–6) and Gibeon (1 Chron. 16:39; 21:29). When David captured Jerusalem, he erected a tabernacle and brought the ark from Kiriath Jearim (2 Sam. 6:17; 1 Chron. 16:1). So for a time there were two tabernacles, one in Gibeon and one in Jerusalem. The original tabernacle and altar were ultimately transported six miles from Gibeon to Jerusalem and kept in the temple as a relic (1 Kings 8:4). The tabernacle, according to 1 Kings 6:1, spanned a period of nearly five hundred years of Israel's history.

As noted, the tabernacle in both its furnishings and priestly ritual served as Israel's worship center and also foreshadowed Christ in both His earthly and heavenly spheres of ministry. The brazen altar typifies the cross of Christ on which He offered Himself without spot to God (Eph. 5:2). The laver pictures Christ cleansing the believer from sin's defilement (John 13:2–10). The golden lampstand typifies Christ as our Light, the One who enlightens our hearts and enables us to carry His light to a dark world (1:9; 8:12; Eph. 5:8). The showbread or bread of presence is a type of Christ who nourishes and sustains the believer-priest (1 Pet. 2:9; Rev. 1:6). The manna pictures the life-giving Christ; the showbread, the life-sustaining Christ. The altar of incense typifies Christ as the believer's Intercessor (John 17; Heb. 7:25). The veil that separated the Holy Place from the Most Holy Place is a type of the human body of Christ given in sacrifice to provide an unobstructed way to God (Matt. 26:26; 27:50; Heb. 10:20). At the Crucifixion the veil was supernaturally torn in two, symbolizing that there was now instant and open access to God. The ark of the covenant with its blood-sprinkled lid, or mercy seat, portrays the transformation of the divine throne from a throne of judgment to a throne of grace, all because of the shed blood of Christ (Heb. 4:14–16; 9:24–26; 10:19–22).

In the biblical account of the tabernacle everything begins with the description of the ark of the covenant in the Most Holy Place. This teaches us that God in grace is the Initiator of salvation. He is the One who reaches out to the lost on the basis of His sacrifice. The human approach to God, on the other hand, begins from without. Sinful humans must begin at the brazen altar, that is, at the Cross, where atonement for sin was made. —DKC

Study with care the Old Testament tabernacle,
since it gives us a picture book of our redemption.

Temple

ONE OF THE MASTER STROKES of history was David's capture of Jerusalem, which became the political and religious capital of Israel (2 Sam. 6). Further, it was David's desire to build an adequate dwelling place for Israel's God, a permanent building of stone to supplant the tabernacle. Because David had shed blood in battle, he was forbidden to build the temple, but he purchased the site for it (24:18–24), collected most of the necessary finances and materials, and even drew the plans for the structure (1 Chron. 22:3–5, 14; 28:2, 11–19). David acknowledged that the Spirit of the Lord guided him in all these matters. Yet the task of building was committed to his son, Solomon.

Although the general plan for the temple was similar to that of the tabernacle, the dimensions were doubled, except for the height, which was tripled. The walls were of stone and were covered with gold (1 Kings 6:22). The veil between the Most Holy Place and the Holy Place was replaced with a double door of gold-covered olive wood (6:16, 20). The ark of the covenant resided in the Most Holy Place. No idol stood in the sanctuary, which made the temple (and before that, the tabernacle) distinct among the pagan temples of the ancient world. In the Holy Place were ten golden lampstands, five on each side, and ten tables for utensils and accessories, five on each side (2 Chron. 4:8). Also in this room was a table for the "bread of the Presence." On a porch on the front of the building stood two hollow bronze pillars, named Jakin and Boaz (1 Kings 7:15–22). Freestanding columns of this sort were characteristic of ancient Near Eastern temples.

Two courts ran around the temple, the inner one exclusively for the priests and the outer one, called the "large court," intended for the use of the people (2 Chron. 4:9). The most striking object in the inner court was the molten sea, a huge, round tank of bronze provided for priestly ablutions (4:2–5). In addition, there were ten tables and ten lavers for the flaying and washing of the sacrifices (4:6). The altar of burnt offering, made after the pattern of the one in the tabernacle, also stood in the inner court (1 Kings 8:64).

Construction of the temple took seven years and six months (6:37–38; 2 Chron. 3:1). It was dedicated in a weeklong ceremony, which was climaxed by fire falling from heaven to consume the burnt offering (6:13–7:1). The temple was filled with the Shekinah glory of God, signifying His approval and acceptance of the temple.

In addition to being Israel's worship center, the temple served as a depository of national wealth, and thus was a target of foreign attack. It also was plundered by Israel's kings to buy off oppressors (1 Kings 14:25–28; 15:16–19; 2 Kings 12:17–18; 14:8–14; 16:7–9). Temple worship sometimes fell into disuse but was restored by such reforming kings as Joash (2 Kings 12; 2 Chron. 24:1–16), Hezekiah (2 Kings 18:1–6), and Josiah (2 Kings 22–23; 2 Chron. 34). Judah's last king, Zedekiah, rebelled against Nebuchednezzar, who attacked Jerusalem, took the king captive, and burned the city and temple to the ground (586 B.C.). Thus the 380 years of the temple came to an end, fulfilling Jeremiah's somber prophecies regarding the destruction of Jerusalem, the temple, and the people on account of their sins (Jer. 25).

When the Jews returned from captivity (538 B.C.), they erected what has been called Zerubbabel's temple or the second temple. They first rebuilt the sacrificial altar and reestablished the prescribed pattern of worship (Ezra 3:1–6). But the initial enthusiasm died, and it was not until 520 B.C., with the prodding of the prophets Haggai and Zechariah, that actual construction began. The restored temple was completed and dedicated four years later (6:15). While some dimensions are given in Scripture, they are incomplete, and no details are stated regarding the temple's appearance. It can be assumed that it occupied the same location and followed the same general plan as the Solomonic temple, though without its splendor. According to the Jewish Talmud, the rebuilt temple lacked five items that were a part of Solomon's temple: the ark of the covenant, the fire that consumed the initial sacrifices, the Shekinah glory, the Holy Spirit, and the Urim and Thummim. Josephus, a first-century A. D. Jewish historian, stated that the Most Holy Place was empty except for a stone where the atoning blood was sprinkled on the Day of Atonement. In the Holy Place there were one golden lampstand, one table of showbread, and the altar of incense. In front of the temple building stood an altar of unhewn stones the same size as Solomon's bronze altar (2 Chron. 4:1). In the intertestamental period the temple was plundered and defiled by the Syrian ruler Antiochus Epiphanes (175–164 B.C.), but it was restored and cleansed by Judas Maccabeus. The latter events set the stage for the annual Jewish Feast of Dedication (John 10:22), known today as Hanukkah.

In 37 B.C. Herod gained control of Jerusalem with Roman help, and in about 21 B.C. he began to dismantle the second temple in preparation for the construction of a grand structure that would subsequently be known as Herod's temple. The Bible gives little information about this temple, the main source being Josephus, a contemporary. Herod's motive for building his temple was to placate his Jewish subjects by building a sanctuary as magnificent as Solomon's. The new structure had the same dimensions as the first temple and was filled with the same furniture except that the Most Holy Place was left empty. Surrounding the temple were the four courts of the priests, of Israel, of the women, and the outer court of the Gentiles.

Jesus showed respect for the temple and frequently visited it. At the age of twelve He conversed with the rabbis in the temple courts and called the temple His Father's house (Luke 2:41–50). Twice He cleansed it in righteous indignation (Matt. 21:12–13; John 2:13–16). Jesus wept over the impending destruction of Jerusalem (Luke 19:41–44) and predicted the razing of the temple (Matt. 24:1–2). These prophecies were fulfilled at the hands of the Romans in A.D. 70. Before this, the early church used the temple courts after Pentecost as its meeting place (Acts 5:12, 21, 42).

After the crucifixion, resurrection, and ascension of Christ, the physical temple was rendered obsolete. The believer, indwelt by the Holy Spirit, is in this age the true temple (1 Cor. 3:16–17; 6:19; 2 Cor. 6:16). The same is true of the aggregate of believers, the church (1 Pet. 2:5; Eph. 2:22).

In the end times, following the rapture of the church, the Jews will build a temple in Jerusalem and restore their ancient sacrifices. The Antichrist, however, will disrupt the Jewish worship and take control of this temple, arrogantly exalting himself as God (Dan. 9:27; 2 Thess. 2:4).

Another temple will be erected in Jerusalem after Christ's return to earth, and during His millennial kingdom this temple will be the center for worship. The millennial temple is described in detail in Ezekiel 40:2–47:2. (See also Isa. 11:1–16; 35:1–10; 60:1–22; Zech. 14:8–20.)

The Bible closes with a glorious description of heaven. John had a vision of the "Holy City, the New Jerusalem, coming down out of heaven from God" (Rev. 21:2). He looked in vain for a temple in the New Jerusalem, "because the Lord God Almighty and the Lamb are its temple."

—DKC

Realize how important it is to treat your body with care,
since it is the temple of the Holy Spirit.

Temptation

THE HEBREW AND GREEK WORDS for *tempt* and *temptation* are used to indicate both enticement to sin and God's testing of a person's worth and character.

Both the Old and New Testaments make it clear that the ultimate source of temptation to sin is Satan. His role in connection with the Fall (Gen. 3) and the affliction of Job (1:6–2:10) is transparent. Satan's part as the tempter in the Christian's life is noted in various New Testament passages (1 Cor. 7:5; 1 Thess. 3:5; 1 Pet. 5:8–9; Rev. 2:10). Temptation may also arise from a love of the world. This includes "the cravings of sinful man, the lust of his eyes and the boasting of what he has and does" (1 John 2:16). Even the best of persons have been seduced by sensuality, covetousness, and pride. Paul warned, "So, if you think you are standing firm, be careful that you don't fall" (1 Cor. 10:12). A third source of temptation springs from people themselves, as James made clear: "Each one is tempted when, by his own evil desire, he is dragged away and enticed" (James 1:14). However, James emphatically declared, temptation to sin never comes from God: "When tempted, no one should say, 'God is tempting me.' For God cannot be tempted by evil, nor does he tempt anyone" (1:13).

While God never tempts, He does test the reality of His people's trust in Him. This was true in the case of Abraham (Gen. 22:1), Israel (Exod. 15:25; 16:4), the tribe of Levi (Deut. 33:8), Hezekiah (2 Chron. 32:31),

David (Ps. 26:2), Philip (John 6:5–6), and His children (1 Pet. 1:7). Exemption from testing is not promised to believers, but God does provide grace and strength to endure it (1 Cor. 10:13; 2 Cor. 12:7–8; 1 Pet. 4:12–16; 2 Pet. 2:9).

The Old Testament refers to God being tested by Israel in the wilderness (Exod. 17:7; Num. 14:22; Ps. 95:8–9). The New Testament records the fact that the Pharisees and Sadducees tested Jesus with the hope that He would make self-incriminating statements (Matt. 16:1; 19:3; 22:35; Mark 8:11; 10:2; Luke 20:23). Ananias and Sapphira tested the Holy Spirit by lying (Acts 5:9). Paul admonished the Corinthian believers not to "test the Lord" as Israel had done (1 Cor. 10:9; see Num. 21:4–9). Christ's temptation by Satan in the wilderness of Judea after His baptism demands special attention. No doubt Jesus was subject to temptation throughout His ministry (Luke 4:13), but the crucial temptation is the one described in Matthew 4, Mark 1, and Luke 4. This temptation presents some probing questions: (1) Could Jesus Christ have sinned? (2) If not, could He be tempted? (3) If He couldn't sin, what was the purpose of the temptation?

Theologians have debated whether Christ had the ability to sin. Some have argued that Christ *could have sinned* but did not. Others have held that Christ was able *not* to sin. Still others declared that Christ was *not able* to sin. Essential to solving this apparent dilemma is the recognition that Christ possessed (and possesses) both a human and a divine nature. The human nature by itself was peccable or able to sin even though Christ did not possess a fallen, sin nature (Heb. 4:15). But Christ's human nature was never separated from His divine nature. He was, however, not a man to whom a divine nature was added. Rather, He was God who took on a human nature by the Incarnation. He became thereafter an indivisible person, the totally and forever unique God-Man. As such, Christ, the divine-human person, could not sin. A wire is bendable or flexible when it stands alone, but it is absolutely unbendable when welded to a bar of steel.

But if it is granted, on the basis of the above facts, that Christ could not sin, could He be tempted? Even though human logic may fail us at this point, the question is answered by the narrative accounts of Christ's temptation in the Synoptic Gospels, and by the clear declaration by the author of Hebrews, "We have one who has been tempted in every way, just as we are—yet was without sin" (Heb. 4:15).

God's purpose in allowing Christ to be tempted was not to see if He would sin but to demonstrate His sinlessness. In addition, enduring temptation enabled Him to become "a merciful and faithful high priest." As the writer of Hebrews explained, "Because he himself suffered when he was tempted, he is able to help those who are being tempted" (Heb. 2:17–18).

The question remains as to how believers should deal with temptation. The following seven principles can serve as guidelines in connection with this important, but often neglected, area of Christian living. (1) The reality of temptation from the world, the flesh, or the devil must be recognized (1 John 2:15–17). Paul declared that temptation is "common to man" (1 Cor. 10:13). (2) Temptation, though real, is not constant but rather periodic. This principle is clearly illustrated in the lives of Joseph (Gen. 39), David (2 Sam. 11), and Jesus (Luke 4:13). (3) Scripture is a sure defense against satanic temptation. Jesus defeated the devil by quoting three times from the Book of Deuteronomy. John stated, "I write to you, young men, because you are strong, and the word of God lives in you, and you have overcome the evil one" (1 John 2:14).

(4) A corollary of the above is found in Peter's exhortation to resist the devil, "standing firm in the faith" (1 Pet. 5:9). The action urged is defensive, not offensive, and is explained by Paul's description of the Christian's armor (Eph. 6:11–17). (5) When tempted, Christians should take the "way out" God has promised to provide (1 Cor. 10:13). Joseph did (Gen. 39:12), whereas David did not (2 Sam. 11:1–4). (6) In Gethsemane Jesus strongly cautioned His disciples to be alert: "Watch and pray so that you will not fall into temptation" (Matt. 26:41). Christians should not allow themselves to get into situations where they have the freedom or privacy to yield to temptation. (7) God has provided rich resources for believers to use when they are tempted. These are the Word of God (1 John 2:14), the indwelling Holy Spirit (4:4), and the interceding Son of God (Luke 22:32). With God's help the Christian can be a victor and not a victim of temptation. —**DKC**

"Yield not to temptation, for yielding is sin."

Theophany

THE WORD *theophany* IS FORMED from the Greek noun for God (*theos*) and the Greek verb "to appear" or "to manifest" (*phaneō*). A theophany is a temporary, visible appearance or manifestation of God. It is a form of revelation by which God makes His presence known to people in human or symbolic form. A theophany must be distinguished from the permanent revelation of God in Jesus Christ, which we call the Incarnation.

The most frequent appearance of God in human form is that of the Angel of the Lord. This extraordinary angel who represents Himself as deity appeared to Hagar (Gen. 16:7), Abraham (18; 22:11–12), Lot (19), Jacob (32:29–31; Hos. 12:4–5), Moses (Exod. 3:2–6), Balaam (Num. 22:22), Joshua (Josh. 5:14–15), Gideon (Judg. 6:11–14), Manoah and his wife (Judg. 13:1–21), and David (1 Chron. 21:15, 18, 27). The Angel of the Lord led the Hebrews out of Egypt (Exod. 13:21; 14:19), and He reproached the Israelites for their disobedience after they settled in Canaan (Judg. 2:1–4).

These verses clearly point to the deity of this angel because He is identified as God, called Himself God, received worship, and spoke with divine authority. Also these numerous appearances show that the Angel of the Lord is distinguished from God the Father. Such preincarnate appearances may be called Christophanies.

God also revealed Himself in symbolic form. When God made a covenant with Abraham, He appeared under the form of "a smoking fire-pot with a blazing torch" (Gen. 15:17). God spoke to Moses from a burning bush (Exod. 3:2–6). The pillar of cloud and fire were representations of God's presence with His people. The cloud guided them on their journey during the day, and the fire provided light and protection at night (13:21–22; 14:19, 24; Num. 14:14). God's presence was also made known at Sinai by thunder, lightning, fire, smoke, and a thick cloud (Exod. 19:16, 18; 24:15–18). The Lord manifested Himself to Israel in the form of a shining light called the Shekinah glory, that is, the glory of God that dwelt with His people. When the tabernacle was completed the glory of God descended. "Then the cloud covered the Tent of Meeting, and the glory of the LORD filled the tabernacle. Moses could not enter the Tent of Meeting because the cloud had settled upon it, and the glory of the LORD filled the tabernacle" (40:34–35). Centuries later, when Solomon's temple was finished, "the cloud filled the temple of the LORD. And the priests could not perform their service because of the cloud, for the glory of the LORD filled his temple" (1 Kings 8:10–11). At the time of the Babylonian exile Ezekiel watched in a vision as the Shekinah glory left God's earthly sanctuary, city, and people (Ezek. 11:22–23). This departure signaled that judgment would soon fall on Jerusalem. The city would then be devoid of God's blessing until a far distant time when God's kingdom will be established on earth, when His glory will once again fill the temple, and when He will dwell with His people forever (43:1–5).

Theologically, the theophanies attest to the Old Testament glimpses into the triune nature of the Godhead, and they anticipated the New Testament doctrine of the incarnation of Christ (John 1:14; 8:56).

—DKC

Read the Old Testament carefully, looking for theophanies, evidences that even before the Incarnation God pursued humanity, revealing Himself to people in human or symbolic form.

Times of the Gentiles

IN THE GENESIS 10 ACCOUNT of the origin of the races, a new departure in racial distinctions was made through the descendants of Shem, one of Noah's three sons. Of Shem's many descendants God selected Abram as the founder of a new racial line, later called Israel. Not all of Abram's descendants, however, are included in Israel, as demonstrated by the birth of Ishmael (16:15) and the children of Keturah (25:1–4). Only the descendants of Jacob's twelve sons are considered Israelites. All others are known as Gentiles.

Gentiles were prominent in Daniel's prophecies of the four world empires of Babylon, Medo-Persia, Greece, and Rome (Dan. 2; 7). In addition, there were the earlier gentile empires of Egypt and Assyria.

From the standpoint of prophecy it is important to note that God has a separate program for the twelve sons of Jacob and their descendants. Of interest, too, is the fact that most of the writers of Scripture, all the Old Testament prophets, all the New Testament apostles, and Jesus Christ were Israelites.

Ethnoi, the common Greek word for "nations," normally means "peoples" and thus refers to humankind (regardless of race) or the nations other than Israel. But *ethnos* is sometimes used in relation to a particular race such as Israel (for example, John 11:51–52).

The word *Greeks (hellēnoi)* referred to all Gentiles or non-Jews (as in Acts 21:28; Rom. 1:14; 1 Cor. 1:22). Thus it is important to distinguish between God's plan and prophecies for Israel and His plan and prophecies for Gentiles. This is especially important in the premillennial concept of the millennial kingdom in which Israel will be prominent and Christ will rule as her Messiah on David's throne in Jerusalem.

The expression "the times of the Gentiles" is a period of history in prophecy that began in 605 B.C. with Jerusalem being overrun by Gentiles. This gentile abomination will continue until the second coming of Christ. Luke 21:24 states, "They [Israel] will fall by the sword and will be taken as prisoners to all the nations. Jerusalem will be trampled on by the Gentiles until the times of the Gentiles are fulfilled." The times of the Gentiles thus includes the time of the four kingdoms predicted in Daniel 2 and 7. The fourth kingdom will be the restored Roman Empire, over which the Antichrist will rule for three and a half years just before the second coming of Christ.

The times of the Gentiles is not to be confused with the term "the fullness of the Gentiles," which refers to a more limited time during which Gentiles are saved. As stated in Romans 11:25, "I do not want you to be ignorant of this mystery, brothers, so that you may not be conceited: Israel has experienced a hardening in part until the full number of the Gentiles has come in." This refers to the present age of the church, which began on the Day of Pentecost, and in which God is calling out Gentiles to salvation as part of the body of Christ. The fullness of the Gentiles will end with the Rapture, but the times of the Gentiles will end when Christ returns to the earth. —JFW

Study the scriptural teachings about future events,
and pray that the coming of Christ will be soon.

Tongues

AFTER LISTING A DOZEN DIFFERENT COUNTRIES from which Jews had gone to Jerusalem on the Day of Pentecost, Luke recorded that the people said they heard the Galilean disciples "declaring the wonders of God in our own tongues!" (Acts 2:11). Here the word *tongues,* which originally means the instrument of the human body by which we speak, was applied to spoken languages. On the Day of Pentecost the disciples had the spiritual "ability to speak in different kinds of tongues" (1 Cor. 12:10, 28).

First, however, we must consider the tongue as an instrument of expression and communication. The apostle James observed that "the tongue is a small part of the body, but it makes great boasts" (3:5), and it is "a fire, a world of evil among the parts of the body" (3:6). He wrote, "With the tongue we praise our Lord and Father, and with it we curse men who have been made in God's likeness. Out of the same mouth come praise and cursing," and he concluded, "My brothers, this should not be" (3:9–10).

The need for a gift of speaking in different languages resulted from God's judgment on the human race at sometime following the Flood. At that time "the whole world had one language and a common speech" (Gen. 11:1). Men's desire to "make a name" for themselves (11:4) by building a city and tower led God to "go down and confuse their language" so that they did not understand each other (11:7). God also "scattered them over the face of the whole earth" (11:9).

The miracle on the Day of Pentecost, when the disciples "began to speak in other tongues as the Spirit enabled them" (Acts 2:4), was a miraculous, God-given ability to speak in the various languages of the foreigners attending Pentecost. Others say the disciples spoke in ecstatic utterances, and the foreigners somehow miraculously understood them as if they had spoken in their individual languages. However, Luke said the miracle was the Holy Spirit's working on the disciples who spoke (2:4), not on the listeners who heard. Also Luke wrote that the apostles spoke in the "languages" of the people (2:6, 8). Some accused the disciples of having had "too much wine" (2:13). But Peter replied, "These men are not drunk. . . . It's only nine in the morning" (2:15).

The next specific mention of "speaking in tongues" in conjunction with "the gift of the Holy Spirit" was in the house of Cornelius (10:45–46). This speaking in tongues could not have been ecstatic utterances because Peter said these Gentiles had "received the Holy Spirit just as we have" (10:47). If at Pentecost the disciples were speaking in actual languages the disciples had not learned, the believing Gentiles in Caesarea, too, must have spoken actual languages.

The same is true of Paul's experience in Ephesus with the disciples who had received "John's baptism" but did not know of the Holy Spirit (19:1–3). After being "baptized into the name of the Lord Jesus" and having Paul place "his hands on them, the Holy Spirit came on them, and they spoke in tongues and prophesied" (19:5–6). On each of these three occasions in Acts, the speaking in tongues accompanied or followed the descent of the Holy Spirit and validated the message and ministry concerning Jesus Christ to a group where unbelief of some sort was involved.

In his lengthy discussion about tongues-speaking Paul said that "the ability to speak in different kinds of tongues" and "the interpretation of tongues" (1 Cor. 12:10, 28, 30) were gifts and manifestations of the Holy Spirit (12:4, 7). He seems to have identified speaking in tongues with languages known to the speaker (14:6–13). Paul wrote, "I speak in tongues more than all of you" (14:18), a claim undoubtedly true in light of his extensive missionary travels.

On one hand Paul explained, "Tongues, then, are a sign, not for believers but for unbelievers" (14:21–22), and he quoted Isaiah 28:11–12, a statement illustrated by the incidents in Acts. As a sign to unbelievers tongues-speaking would authenticate the reality of the apostles' message (see 2 Cor. 12:12; Heb. 2:3). On the other hand, if "everyone [in the church] is speaking in tongues" (1 Cor. 14:23, literal translation), apparently without interpretation, unlearned and unbelievers in the church assembly would say, "you are out of your mind" (14:23).

As a result Paul set forth these regulations for speaking in a tongue in church: "two—or at the most three—should speak, one at a time, and someone must interpret. If there is no interpreter, the speaker should keep quiet in the church and speak to himself and to God" (14:27–28). He concluded, however, "do not forbid speaking in tongues. But everything should be done in a fitting and orderly way" (14:39–40).

Apparently the Christians in Corinth were speaking repeatedly in tongues without interpretation, mimicking the Grecian pagan oracles of the time. Such pagan speech, also frequently without interpretation or other regulations, characterizes the speaking-in-tongues movement that has gained widespread acceptance and attention in this century. If Paul's regulations were observed, much of the current movement would disappear. —JAW

Avoid the excesses of emotionalism so common in many churches today, seeking instead to "live by the Spirit" (Gal. 5:16).

Transfiguration

THE TRANSFIGURATION OF CHRIST is recorded in each of the Synoptic Gospels (Matt. 17:1–8; Mark 9:2–8; Luke 9:28–36). This significant event took place on a "high mountain" only days after Peter's confession at Caesarea Philippi. Various locations have been suggested, such as the Mount of Olives, Mount Carmel, Mount Tabor, and Mount Hermon. Because of its elevation (over nine thousand feet) and its proximity to Caesarea Philippi (twelve miles northeast), a southern ridge of Mount Hermon seems to be the best choice.

Three things took place at the Transfiguration. First, "his face shone like the sun, and his clothes became as white as the light" (Matt. 17:2). This was not merely a change in outward appearance; it was a transformation caused by His divine glory shining through His body. The glory the Son of God rightly owned returned for a brief time (see John 17:5). Thus Peter, James, and John saw Christ as He is in His present ascended glory (Rev. 1:14–16) and as He will be when He returns at His second coming in power and glory (Matt. 24:30).

Second, Moses and Elijah appeared and spoke with Jesus about His death (literally, His "exodus"; Luke 9:31). These two figures represented the Law and the Prophets of the Old Testament. Their discussion with Christ about His forthcoming death, burial, and resurrection demonstrated that His passion would provide a redemption from sin, much as the Old Testament Exodus provided release from the bondage in Egypt. It is noteworthy that Moses and Elijah both had a vision of God on a mountain (Exod. 24; 1 Kings 19); both are mentioned in the last verses of Malachi (Mal. 4:4–6); and, according to some, both will appear on earth during the Tribulation (Rev. 11).

Third, a heavenly voice said, "This is my Son, whom I love. Listen to him!" (Mark 9:7; see also Matt. 17:5; Luke 9:35). These words came in response to Peter's impulsive suggestion that he build three booths or shelters, one each for Jesus, Moses, and Elijah. No doubt Peter wanted to prolong this grand experience. In addition, he may have thought the kingdom had come and that it would therefore be appropriate to build booths for the Feast of Tabernacles (Lev. 23:33–43; Zech. 14:16). At any rate, God's message was a rebuke for placing Jesus on the same level as Moses and Elijah. God's words also identified Jesus as the Prophet of Deuteronomy 18:15–18, and as the Messiah who must suffer death as He had recently announced in Caesarea Philippi (Matt. 16:21). This is what the disciples must hear and accept. Jesus' teaching about the Cross was correct and was in accord with the will of God.

Each of the Gospel accounts of the Transfiguration is preceded by Jesus' cryptic words, "I tell you the truth, some who are standing here will not taste death before they see the Son of Man coming in his kingdom" (Matt. 16:28). These words can be understood correctly only in the light of the fact that Jesus' preaching about the kingdom was coming to an end because of the nation's rejection of Christ and the imminent death of the King. The disciples therefore needed confirmation that the messianic kingdom will indeed be established in fulfillment of promises made to Israel, later if not immediately. The Transfiguration provided this assurance. Later Peter associated Jesus' glory at the Transfiguration with the glory of Christ at His second coming to establish His earthly kingdom (2 Pet. 1:16–18).

The word "transfigure" *(metamorpheō)* is also used twice in the New Testament in appeals to believers. In Romans 12:2 Paul exhorted, "Do not conform any longer to the pattern of this world, but be transformed by the renewing of your mind." The behavioral modification enjoined will come about only by a "metamorphosis," that is, a total change from inside out. The key to this change is the mind which can be made new by practicing the spiritual disciplines of prayer, Scripture reading, Christian fellowship, and others. The apostle described the nature of the sought-after change in 2 Corinthians 3:18, "And we, who with unveiled faces all reflect the Lord's glory, are being transformed into his likeness with ever-increasing glory, which comes from the Lord, who is the Spirit." As believers yield themselves to the Holy Spirit, He will enable them to manifest the fruit of the Spirit (Gal. 5:22–23). The result will be a gradual transformation into Christlikeness, the ultimate goal of the Christian life.

—**DKC**

Imagine what it was like to look on the glorious Christ on the Mount of Transfiguration, and then remember that when He returns we too will behold His glory.

Tribulation

THE SCRIPTURES OFTEN MENTION trouble or tribulation as a universal experience. Everyone faces trouble in one way or another. As Jesus said, "In this world you will have trouble" (John 16:33). And Eliphaz told Job, "Man is born to trouble as surely as sparks fly upward" (Job 5:7). James wrote that we face "trials of many kinds" (James 1:2). While troubles are inevitable, God always enables believers to endure them.

Revelation 7:14 refers to "the great tribulation." This is a particular period of trouble of three and a half years leading up to the second coming of Christ. Daniel 12:1 refers to it as "a time of distress such as has not happened from the beginning of nations until then." And Jesus said it will be a time of "great distress, unequaled from the beginning of the world" and will "never . . . be equaled again" (Matt. 24:21). Obviously this special period of time differs from trouble in general.

This period of great tribulation, in which God's wrath will be poured out on the unbelieving world in an unprecedented way, will begin when the Antichrist will desecrate the Jewish temple (which is yet to be built) and will establish the temple as the place where he is to be worshiped (2 Thess. 2:4). He will perform "counterfeit miracles" (2:9). This will occur forty-two months (three and a half years) before Christ's second coming. It will happen in the middle of the seven-year period of Daniel 9:24–27, what is commonly called "the seventieth week of Daniel." (Each "seven" or "week" refers to seven years.)

This is confirmed by Revelation 13:5, which states that the world ruler ("the beast," that is, the Antichrist) will exercise authority over the world for forty-two months. This three-and-a-half-year period is also confirmed by the expression "time, times and half a time" (Dan. 7:25; 12:7; Rev. 12:14), and 1,260 days (12:6), that is, forty-two months of thirty days each. Jeremiah 30:7 predicted that this period will be a terrible "time of trouble for Jacob," but that he (that is, the nation Israel) will be saved out of it (30:10–11), when Christ returns in His second coming. Many people will come to Christ in the seven-year period after the Rapture, and many of them will be martyred for their faith. Revelation 7:9–17 speaks of them as a great multitude "who have come out of the great tribulation" (7:14), that is, they will be delivered from the rigors of the Great Tribulation by death and will be safe in heaven.

According to 20:4–6, their bodies will be resurrected after the second coming of Christ and they, along with church-age believers, will reign with Christ for a thousand years. In the Great Tribulation the world ruler, the Antichrist (1 John 2:18, 4:3), will reign over the entire world (Rev. 13:7) for three and a half years prior to the Second Coming. At Christ's return to earth the beast will be captured and cast into the lake of fire (19:20; 20:10). This is the one whom "Jesus will overthrow with the breath of his mouth and destroy by the splendor of his coming" (2 Thess. 2:8).

In the terrible time of tribulation before Christ's coming to earth God will pour out His wrath on unbelieving Gentiles and Jews. This will include seven "seal" judgments (Rev. 6), seven "trumpet" judgments (Rev. 8–9), and seven "bowl" judgments (Rev. 15–16).   —JFW

Be grateful to the Lord that the church will be raptured
before the terrible "seventieth week of Daniel."

Trinity

ALTHOUGH THE WORD *Trinity* does not occur in the Bible and the doctrine is not explicitly stated in a single passage of Scripture, it is a biblical truth. The Christian belief that the one God subsists in a triunity of coequal, coeternal, coextensive persons—Father, Son, and Holy Spirit—is constructed from abundant evidence in God's Word. The doctrine is logically developed from the biblical testimony, but it is the product of revelation, not logic.

The closest that any single passage of Scripture comes to providing the evidence for the doctrine of the Trinity is the baptismal formula, "baptizing them in the name of the Father and of the Son and of the Holy Spirit" (Matt. 28:19). The fact that baptism is to be in the "name," not "names," indicates that the God revealed in Scripture is one God, not three gods. At the same time that name is that "of the Father and of the Son and of the Holy Spirit," indicating that three persons, which are more than modes of manifestation, comprise the one God.

Evidence for the doctrine of the Trinity is seen in the incarnation of the eternal Word of God (John 1:1–2), the Son of God (1:14, 18), who is Jesus Christ (Matt. 1:20–25; Luke 1:30–38). Also in conjunction with the incarnation and ministry of Jesus Christ and especially subsequent to His sacrificial death, burial, resurrection, and ascension to heaven, the Holy Spirit has come and ministered in a special way in the formation of the church as the body of Christ (1 Cor. 12:13). As a result the evidence is more complete and stronger in the New Testament than in the Old.

The Old Testament, however, is not devoid of evidence for God's existence as a Trinity of persons; it is simply that the evidence is not as clear and specific. The revelational emphasis for Israel in the Old Testament in the ancient world of polytheistic idolatry was on the one true God. "The LORD our God, the LORD is one" (Deut. 6:4), and He alone is to be worshiped and served (4:35, 39). Clear Trinitarian evidence was not necessary until the second person of the Trinity became incarnate as Jesus Christ.

The Old Testament evidence for the Trinity is somewhat analogous to an article of furniture in a darkened room; it is there, but it cannot be seen until the door is opened or the light is turned on. Even the statement "The LORD is one," allows for a plurality of persons. The Hebrew word rendered "one" is not the word that means absolute singularity (*yaḥîd*, Gen. 22:2, "your only son"), but the word that suggests plurality in unity (*ʾeḥād*, as in 2:24, "they will become one flesh"). The plural noun translated "God" (*ʾĕlōhîm*) is a plural of majesty because it is used many times with singular verbs (for example, "created," 1:1). But it is also used with plural verbs and plural pronouns—"let us make man in our image, in our likeness" (1:26). In addition, the Hebrew of Ecclesiastes 12:1 reads, literally, "Remember your Creators in the days of your youth." Recognition of an allusion to God as a Trinity in such references cannot be ruled out.

Other possible allusions to the Trinity in the Old Testament are the threefold benediction of Numbers 6:24–26 and the threefold ascription of holiness to "the LORD Almighty" by the seraphs in Isaiah 6:3 (see also Rev. 4:8). On occasion God seems to be distinguished from God (Pss. 45:6–7; 110:1; Hos. 1:6–7). And the Word of God (Pss. 33:6; 107:20; 147:15–18), and the Spirit of God (Gen. 1:2; Isa. 63:10; Ezek. 2:2; 8:3; Zech. 7:12) are personified.

The clearest evidence of plurality in God in the Old Testament, however, is the identification of the Angel of the Lord with the Lord Himself (Gen. 16:7–13; 22:11–18; 31:11–13; Exod. 3:2–10; Judg. 6:11–26; 13:3–23), especially in view of the declaration, "I am the LORD, that is my name! I will not give my glory to another or my praise to idols" (Isa. 42:8).

In the New Testament the Trinity is seen at the baptism of Jesus, when "the Holy Spirit descended on him in bodily form like a dove. And a voice came from heaven: 'You are my Son, whom I love; with you I am well pleased'" (Luke 3:22; see also Matt. 3:16–17; Mark 1:10–11; John 1:32–34). The three persons of the Godhead are also closely associated in Ephesians 4:3–6 and in the Lord Jesus' explanation that when He would depart, the Holy Spirit would come from God the Father (John 14:16–20, 23, 26; 15:26; 16:7, 12–15).

When Jesus Christ claimed, "I and the Father are one" (John 10:30; see also 5:16–18), the Jews recognized this as a claim of equality with God in person, not just in purpose (10:33). The writers of the New Testament also recognized the Lord Jesus as God, calling Him "the image of the invisible God" (Col. 1:15; see also 2 Cor. 4:4) and "the radiance of God's glory and the exact representation of his being" (Heb. 1:3). Paul also wrote that "God was pleased to have all his fullness dwell in him" (Col. 1:19), and "being in very nature God, did not consider equality with God something to be grasped" (Phil. 2:6).

The evidence concerning the Holy Spirit is not as clear or as complete as the evidence concerning Jesus Christ. This is understandable since His ministry, as Jesus told the disciples, is to "testify about me" (John 15:26) and to "bring glory to me by taking from what is mine and making it known to you" (16:14). Jesus also implied the deity of the

Holy Spirit by stating that "blasphemy against the Spirit will not be for-given" (Matt. 12:31–32). Peter told Ananias that "you have lied to the Holy Spirit" (Acts 5:3) and "not lied to men but to God" (5:4).

The three persons of the Godhead—Father, Son, and Spirit—work cooperatively in their various works. This is true of creation in which God the Father (James 1:17; Gen. 1:14), Jesus Christ (John 1:3; Col. 1:16; Heb. 1:2, 10–12), and the Holy Spirit (Gen. 1:2; Job 33:4; Ps. 104:30) were all involved. Also all three were involved in the Incarnation—Father (Luke 1:28, 32), Jesus Christ (Matt. 1:21, 23), Holy Spirit (1:20; Luke 1:35). All three persons are involved in the salvation of a believer, who is chosen by God the Father (Eph. 1:3–6), redeemed by Jesus the Son (1:7–12), and indwelt and sealed by the Holy Spirit (1:13–14). This work of the triune God is also stated in Ephesians 2:18; 3:2–5; and Titus 3:4–7. Also the persons of the Trinity cooperate in equipping believers with spiritual gifts for the building up of the church, the body of Christ (1 Cor. 12:4–6).

In carrying out the work of the triune God, is an administrative order is maintained: The Father is the first person, the Son is the second person, and the Holy Spirit is the third person. This is not a chronological order or an order of importance, but simply an administrative order. As a result, the Father initiates all the work of God such as sending the Son (John 3:17; Rom. 8:3). Jesus Christ, the Son, in turn, came to do the will of God the Father (John 4:34) and does "only what he sees his Father doing" (5:19; compare 5:30; 8:28; 12:49; 14:10). The Holy Spirit in turn seeks to glorify Jesus Christ and God the Father (16:14–15) by testifying concern-ing them (14:26; 15:26; 16:7, 13). The work of the triune God is from the Father, through the Son, and by or in the power of the Holy Spirit. In this age of grace the purpose of God is that the Lord Jesus Christ should be exalted and glorified (Eph. 1:20–23; Phil. 2:9–11; 2 Thess. 1:12; 1 Pet. 1:21). In the end, however, after all things have been subjected to Christ, "then the Son himself will be made subject to him who put everything under him, so that God may be all in all" (1 Cor. 15:28).   —JAW

Focus your eyes of faith on Jesus, for in seeing Him you see
God the Father and God the Holy Spirit (John 14:9–10).

Truth

AS THE SELF-EXISTENT One, who is the Creator of all that exists, God is truth and all truth is God's truth. He is called "the God of truth" (Ps. 31:5; Isa. 65:16), and God declared, "I, the LORD, speak the truth; I declare what is right" (Isa. 45:19). In accord with this is the further statement that the One "who came from the Father" was "full of grace and truth" (John 1:14), and that "grace and truth came through Jesus Christ" (1:17). Jesus claimed, "I am the way and the truth and the life" (14:6), and in His earthly ministry He often said, "I tell you the truth" (for example, Matt. 5:18, 26). Also the Holy Spirit is called "the Spirit of truth" (John 14:17; 15:26; 16:13; 1 John 4:6). And John also wrote that "the Spirit is the truth" (5:6).

Because truth resides in God, His message and revelation to humankind is called "the truth" (John 17:17; see also Pss. 19:7–11; 119:89–92). The angel who appeared to Daniel called the Scriptures "the Book of Truth" (Dan. 10:21). Jesus told Pilate, "For this reason I was born, and for this I came into the world, to testify to the truth. Everyone on the side of truth listens to me" (John 18:37). These statements led Pilate to ask, "What is truth?" (18:38). When God in the person of Christ returns to Jerusalem, it "will be called the City of Truth" (Zech. 8:3).

In the Bible truth is identified with the gospel message concerning Jesus Christ (Gal. 2:5, 14; Col. 1:5), especially as this is proclaimed by the apostles (2 Cor. 4:1–4; Eph. 1:13; 4:15–16, 20–21; 5:8–10; 3 John 1:8). "The church of the living God" is "the pillar and foundation of the truth" (1 Tim. 3:15). Each believer is commanded, "Stand firm then, with the belt of truth buckled around your waist" (Eph. 6:14).

In the final analysis truth corresponds to reality, to what actually is. That is why truth is found in God, His being, and His work of salvation provided through Jesus Christ. The philosophical search for truth finds its solution in theology—in God Himself. **—JAW**

Pray with David, "Guide me in your truth and teach me, for you are God my Savior" (Ps. 25:5).

Types

THE ENGLISH WORD *type* translates the Greek word *typos,* rendered variously as "print" (John 20:25, NKJV), "pattern" (Heb. 8:5), "form" (Rom. 6:17), and "example" (1 Cor. 10:6, 11, Titus 2:7). Other Greek words found in the New Testament related to typology are *skia* ("shadow," Heb. 8:4–5); *parabolē* ("figure" or "symbol," 9:9, KJV); *hypodeigma* ("copy" or "pattern," 9:23); and *antitypos* ("antitype").

A type is an Old Testament institution, event, person, object, or ceremony which has reality and purpose in biblical history, but which also by divine design foreshadows something yet future. The term *antitype* describes that future fulfillment.

A type is similar to, but not the same as, prophecy. Both point to the future, but prophecy is more specific and teaches a doctrine, whereas a type only illustrates a doctrine taught elsewhere. A type differs from a symbol in that a symbol is a timeless sign pointing to the past, present, or future. A type, on the other hand, always points to the future.

A clear distinction must be made between allegorical and typological interpretation. Allegorical interpretation introduces something foreign or hidden into the meaning of the text, giving it a supposed deeper meaning. Origen (around A.D. 185–254) and others in the early church carried this method to exaggerated lengths. Typological interpretation of the Old Testament is based on the unity of the two Testaments and the established fact that something in the Old prefigures or foreshadows something in the New.

The question as to how much of the Old Testament is typical is not answered easily. The early church fathers were mostly unrestrained and fanciful in their typology. The same was true of many scholastics in the Middle Ages. The Reformers were more conservative in their typology, though they gave little attention to the subject. Subsequently Bishop Herbert Marsh of England (1757–1839) enunciated what came to be known as Marsh's Principle, namely, that nothing in the Old Testament is to be considered typical unless the New Testament declares it to be so. This principle appealed to many students of Scripture because of its simplicity and authoritative nature. Others objected and felt Marsh's Principle was an unwarranted restriction on the field of typology. They argued that it assumes that the types of the Old Testament were exhausted by the New Testament writer, whose choices would seem to be quite arbitrary. It seems rather that the types affirmed in the New Testament are only samples taken from a storehouse where still others are to be found. But the question remains, How can types be identified? Since "only God can make types," how can the interpreter determine what is divinely designed? First, a type is indicated when Scripture expressly designates something as a type. For example, Adam is said to be a type of Christ (Rom. 5:14, NKJV). Second, a type can be identified by an interchange of names, as in Christ being called the "Passover lamb" (1 Cor. 5:7). Third, where there is a clear analogy, it is safe to say a type is present. Joseph may therefore be considered a type of Christ because there are many clear analogies between his life and Christ's earthly life.

Certain guiding principles should be followed in interpreting types. (1) The historical purpose of the event, person, or institution should be discussed before typical elements are presented. If the historical element is ignored, the interpreter in effect is allegorizing the biblical text. (2) Unity must exist between a type and its antitype, that is, a common principle must bind them together. One writer, for example, made the stone Jacob used for a pillow at Bethel a type of Christ, the foundation stone of the church. Obviously, however, no common principle binds these two "stones" together. (3) Nothing of a forbidden or sinful nature should be considered a type of what is inherently good. For example, Jacob receiving the blessing of his father, Isaac, while dressed in the garments of Esau has wrongfully been made typical of the believer receiving the blessing of God while dressed in the garments of Christ. Even more objectionable is the suggestion that Samson and the harlot of Gaza typify Christ and Israel in the Tribulation. (4) A type should not be pressed in all of its details. The interpreter should distinguish between what is essential in a type and what is peripheral. Moses was a type of Christ as a deliverer, a prophet, an advocate, and a Lawgiver. It would be wrong, however, to insist that all the details of Moses' life and ministry are typical of Christ. Also the Book of Hebrews finds the typical meaning of the tabernacle in the functions of the furnishings and in the priests and their sacred ministries, not in the boards and bars, nor in the tent pins and tarpaulins.

A disciplined and enlightened typology can enrich the study of

Scripture and enable the interpreter to be one "who correctly handles the word of truth" (2 Tim. 2:15). **—DKC**

Do not neglect the study of Old Testament types,
because they provide wonderful illustrations of New Testament truths.

Uu

Unbelief

PEOPLE WHO DENY OR REFUSE TO BELIEVE what God has revealed about Himself and eternal life are in a state of unbelief. In describing unbelief the New Testament writers looked back to Old Testament events. Though no specific word for unbelief is used in the Old Testament, there are many illustrations of it. The people in Noah's day were in unbelief and rebellion (Gen. 6:5–7), and so God destroyed them by the Flood. Peter said these people in unbelief were "ungodly" (2 Pet. 2:5). Unbelief was attributed to the Israelites, whom God had delivered out of Egypt, when they hardened their hearts and rebelled against God (Heb. 3:19). They had failed to respond to what they had seen God do on their behalf (3:9; Ps. 95:9). Jude stated that God took the lives of those Israelites who did not believe (Jude 5). At the root of their problem was an unbelieving heart (Heb. 3:12).

Unbelief is the condition of all those who are without Christ, those who have not believed in the salvation provided by Christ through His death on the cross (John 3:36). As unbelievers they are blinded to the light of the gospel (2 Cor. 4:4). This unbelief need not be permanent, as illustrated in the life of Paul. This was not something he overcame by his own efforts. Instead, through God's grace and mercy his heart was opened to receive the message about Christ (1 Tim. 1:13–16). Later Paul reminded believers that the unbelief of Israel is not permanent (Rom. 11:20–23).

Unbelief was also the reason people rejected Christ's miracles during His earthly ministry (Matt. 13:58; Mark 6:6). The word *unbelief* was used by a father whose son was possessed by a demon. The man asked the Lord to help him overcome his unbelief (9:24). His request did not come because of a rebellious spirit, for he was humbled in the presence of the Lord. But he did sense his need for divine assistance to believe, possibly because of the power of Satan that had been so evident in his son's life for such a long time. Christians may face difficult challenges in life, but God promises victory because of our faith in Christ (1 John 5:4–5). —WGJ

Don't doubt the ability of the Lord to help you in the most difficult circumstances because your faith is "the victory that overcomes the world."

Union with Christ

ONENESS WITH CHRIST is intimated in the fact that the church is the bride of Christ. Their unity is also indicated in the fact that they have eternal life, which they share. Also by the baptism of the Spirit believers are placed at the moment of salvation in the body of Christ, the church, of which He is the Head, and thus they are joined to each other by virtue of their being members of His body. Being justified by faith (Rom. 5:1), believers are seen by God as being clothed in the righteousness of Christ, and so they are united in faith (Eph. 4:13).

Salvation so unites a believer to Christ that it is as if he or she died with Christ, was buried with Him, and was raised with Him (Rom. 6:3–5). The believer's union with Christ is part of his salvation in which he passed from death to life (John 5:24) and from being in Adam to being in Christ. The phrase "in Christ," used repeatedly by Paul, depicts an indestructible relationship to Christ. And besides each believer being in Christ, Christ indwells each believer. As Paul wrote, He is "Christ in you, the hope of glory" (Col. 1:27). —JFW

Thank the Lord regularly because of the wonderful personal relationship Christians have with the risen Christ.

Vv

Vine

THE ABUNDANCE OF VINEYARDS in the Middle East makes the vine an excellent symbol for conveying several abstract truths in the Bible. The Old Testament speaks of vines in a variety of ways. Jacob told Joseph his inheritance would be abundant like "a fruitful vine" (Gen. 49:22). If Israel obeyed God's laws, then He would enable them to enjoy abundant grape harvests (Lev. 26:3–5). Moses enabled the people to visualize the fertility of the Promised Land by describing it as a land of "vines and fig trees" along with other fruits and grains (Deut. 8:8). The vine symbolized national wealth and a satisfying life (1 Kings 4:25). The psalmist used the imagery of a vine in describing a godly wife in a home that honored the Lord (Ps. 128:3). To sit under one's own vine pictured the blessing, safety, and enjoyment of Israel in the future (Mic. 4:4; Zech. 3:10). When a vine failed to produce fruit, it was a sign of God's judgment (Jer. 8:13). Amos reminded the Israelites that it was the Lord who struck their gardens and vineyards because of their neglect of Him (Amos 4:9). When people planted vineyards, others assumed they planned to establish a residence at that place. That is because of the length of time and attention needed to maintain grapevines (Jer. 29:5).

The Old Testament writers often spoke of Israel as a vine. The psalmist said Israel, as a vine out of Egypt, grew and flourished (Ps. 80:8–11). In Isaiah's song of the vineyard (Isa. 5:1–7), Israel is portrayed as God's choice vine planted in a fertile hillside. God Himself cared for the vineyard and expected the nation to be fruitful. The results were not what He wanted, and because of this the nation experienced His judgment. In explaining Israel's future the prophet described the nation as a vine planted in her own land never to be uprooted again (65:21–22; Amos 9:14–15).

The most significant use of the vine concerned the Lord's teaching about Himself and His relationship to His disciples (John 15:1–17). He taught them that He is the true Vine, God the Father is the Gardener

(15:1), and His followers are the branches. Their work for the Lord is called fruit (15:5). The vine is an apt figure to portray the intimate relationship Jesus would have with His disciples. This unique relationship assures believers of a productive and meaningful life.   —WGJ

Stay in constant fellowship with Christ, since He is the Vine and since you as a branch cannot bear fruit without Him.

Vows

A VOW IN SCRIPTURE is a voluntary promise made by a person to God, usually in expectation of some divine favor. Sometimes, however, a vow was made simply as an act of devotion to God. Vows are found most frequently in the Old Testament, especially in Psalms, but are occasionally mentioned in the New Testament as well.

In several cases vows were taken as a type of bargain with God. Jacob at Bethel vowed to make that place a shrine and give God a tithe if He would protect him on his journey and provide for his physical needs (Gen. 28:20–22). Jephthah vowed to sacrifice to God whatever first came out of his house to meet him if he came home victorious over the Ammonites (Judg. 11:30–31). Hannah vowed that if God would give her a son, she would return the child to Him for a lifetime of service. Absalom, while living in exile in Geshur, vowed to worship the Lord in Hebron if He enabled him to return to Jerusalem (2 Sam. 15:7–8).

Vows that are primarily expressions of thanks to God abound in the psalms (Pss. 22:25; 50:14; 56:12; 61:8; 65:1–2; 76:11; 116:14, 18).

Vows made to express dedication of one's self to the Lord find their major example in the Nazirite vow (Num. 6:1–8). A person desiring to serve God for a certain period of time or for life pledged to refuse to eat of the fruit of the vine, to leave his or her hair uncut, and to refrain from any contact with dead bodies. While this vow was normally made voluntarily, on occasion parents dedicated a child to be a Nazirite for life, as with Samson (Judg. 13), Samuel (1 Sam. 1:9–11), and John the Baptist (Luke 1:15, 80).

Vows in the Old Testament were not commanded and it was not

considered a sin to refrain from making a vow (Deut. 23:22). However, once a vow was made it must be kept (23:21, 23; Num. 30:2; Eccles. 5:4). Warnings were given against rash vows (Prov. 20:25; Eccles. 5:5–6). A father could disaffirm a rash or irresponsible vow made by an unmarried daughter (Num. 30:5), and a husband could do the same regarding a vow made by his wife (30:8).

The term *vow* occurs only twice in the New Testament, both times in connection with the apostle Paul. Apparently at the beginning of his ministry in Corinth, Paul had taken a Nazirite vow, allowing his hair to grow for about eighteen months. Leaving Corinth, he had his hair cut since the time of the vow was over (Acts 18:18). Later, in Jerusalem Paul joined in the purification rites of four men involving the payment of vows in the temple. The four men seem to have taken a Nazirite vow that required some costly sacrifices at the conclusion. Since they could not afford to pay for them, Paul underwrote the expense, no doubt for the purpose of placating Jewish believers (21:22–24). While Paul has been criticized for his actions in this situation, he later said he did not violate his own conscience (23:1). Further, the apostle here only confirmed a settled principle of his ministry to become like a Jew to win the Jews and to become like one under the Law so as to win those under the Law (1 Cor. 9:20). Regarding the sacrifices he made, Paul no doubt looked on them as memorials of Christ's sacrifice.

In the days of Jesus the Pharisees and teachers of the Law seriously misused vows (Matt. 15:3–6; Mark 7:9–11). Jesus charged them with substituting their own traditions for God's commands, citing as an illustration their violation of the fifth commandment regarding the honoring of one's parents. To escape from their obligations to care for aged parents they took a vow declaring that their resources were "Corban," that is, gifts devoted to God. Such a formula uttered over money and property donated to the temple supposedly exempted the person from obeying the commandment to meet the needs of elderly parents. Jesus sharply denounced such hypocrisy: "Thus you nullify the word of God by your tradition that you have handed down. And you do many things like that" (7:13).

The absence of frequent references to vows in the New Testament stands in contrast to the frequent mention of vows in the Old Testament, where they are expressions of piety. Nonetheless New

Testament believers are often urged to demonstrate devotion to the Lord because of the richness of our spiritual blessings in Christ. Paul declared, "For you were bought at a price; therefore glorify God in your body" (1 Cor. 6:20, NKJV; see also Rom. 12:1–2).   **—DKC**

Be careful to keep any vow or commitment you made
to the Lord or to any person.

Ww

Walk

WALK, A COMMON WORD IN SCRIPTURE, is used in both a literal and a figurative sense. Examples of the former are in Mark 1:16 ("As Jesus walked beside the Sea of Galilee, he saw Simon and his brother Andrew casting a net into the lake"); Luke 4:30 ("But he [Jesus] walked right through the crowd and went on his way"); and John 5:9 ("At once the man was cured; he picked up his mat and walked"). Figuratively the word describes a believer's conduct or spiritual state. For example, Enoch and Noah both "walked with God" (Gen. 5:24; 6:9), and God charged Abraham to "walk before me and be blameless" (17:1). Before crossing the Jordan River into Canaan Moses exhorted the Israelites, "Observe the commands of the LORD your God, walking in his ways and revering him" (Deut. 8:6).

In the New Testament, John told his readers that they were lying if they claimed to be in fellowship with God and yet walked in "the darkness" (1 John 1:6). On the other hand, "if we walk in the light, as he is in the light, we have fellowship with one another" (1:7). Christians are also exhorted to walk by faith (2 Cor. 5:7), "to walk in obedience to his commands" (2 John 6), "to walk worthy of the calling with which you were called" (Eph. 4:1, NKJV), to "walk in love" (5:2, NKJV), and to "walk as Jesus did" (1 John 2:6).

The most significant of these New Testament admonitions is found in Galatians 5:16, "I say then: Walk in the Spirit, and you shall not fulfill the lust of the flesh" (NKJV). The Greek term for "walk" in this verse is *peripateō*, a compound word meaning "to walk around." The English equivalent "peripatetic" describes a person who walks from place to place. In ancient Greece the Peripatetic School of Philosophy was named after Aristotle, who walked about in the Lyceum of Athens as he taught his students. In the New Testament, while the Greek word is sometimes used in a strictly literal sense, more often it is used in the figurative sense to describe a person's lifestyle. Thus in Galatians 5:16 the word *peripateō* refers to one's general tenor of life, that is, pursuing one's daily course of duty, accomplishing one's usual tasks, meeting the inevitable temptations, victories, defeats, joys, and sorrows of life. In brief, the entire life of the believer is to be lived under the guidance and direction of the Holy Spirit. J. B. Phillips paraphrases the command in Galatians 5:16, "Live your whole life in the Spirit."

Paul declared that if Christians do walk in or by the Spirit, that is, if we depend on the Holy Spirit to give us the desire and power to do the will of God, we will not carry out the evil impulses of our fallen nature. Instead, we will be able to resist and conquer them. While that doesn't mean we will be sinless, it does mean we will sin less! It is important to note that Paul was issuing a command to believers, who are responsible to refuse to obey the promptings of the evil nature, the flesh, by obeying the promptings of the Holy Spirit. In short, we must say no to sin and simultaneously trust the Holy Spirit to give us spiritual victory.

The remaining verses in Galatians 5 flow out of the command and promise of verse 16. First, from a negative standpoint, if we do not "walk in the Spirit" but rather "walk according to the flesh" (Rom. 8:4, NKJV), our lives will display the "works of the flesh," a startling catalog of sins (Gal. 5:19–21). On the other hand, if we do depend on God's help by living in dependence on His Spirit, our lives will exhibit the fruit of the Spirit (5:22–23), a catalog of graces supremely manifested in Jesus Christ and potentially found in us.

A recent development in care for senior citizens is called "assisted living." In the spiritual realm this is a familiar biblical concept. Jesus said to His disciples, "Apart from me you can do nothing" (John 15:5). Paul reinforces this truth by insisting that life can be lived in only one of two styles: We can "walk by the Spirit" relying on His power and enablement, or we can attempt to go it on our own, producing the works of the flesh, the dreary picture of what happens when people reject God's resources. What a comfort and encouragement that the Holy Spirit wants to produce His fruit in us. In essence He wants to make us Christlike, God's ultimate purpose for His children (Rom. 8:29). **—DKC**

Strive with God's help to walk in a manner worthy of your Christian calling.

War

WITH WARS HAVING REACHED GLOBAL PROPORTIONS in the twentieth century and with the development of nuclear weapons of mass destruction, the need to eliminate wars seems more urgent than ever. At the same time, smaller conflicts and so-called police actions of peacekeeping agencies seem to have become more prevalent. Perhaps these are in fulfillment of the Lord Jesus' predictions of the approaching "end of the age" (Matt. 24:3): "You will hear of wars and rumors of wars. . . . Nation will rise against nation, and kingdom against kingdom" (24:6–7; see also Mark 13:7–8; Luke 21:9–10). As long as sinful human beings remain on earth, war will continue. Whether conflicts between individuals or nations, they arise from "desires that battle within you" (James 4:1–2).

Building on the Lord Jesus' statement, "Blessed are the peacemakers, for they will be called sons of God" (Matt. 5:9), some of the early church fathers were pacifists. With the Christianization of the Roman Empire under Constantine, however, and then the invasion of the empire from the north, defensive wars were considered justified. Now most church leaders recognize the need for governments to maintain standing armies for protection and to engage in just wars as necessary, although the number of strict pacifists has also increased.

In the Bible, particularly in the Old Testament, God appeared in support of His people Israel in warfare. In most cases these were just wars, such as Abram's rescue of his nephew Lot from Kedorlaomer and his allies (Gen. 14:1–16). Others were "holy wars," such as those in which Israel was to drive out the inhabitants of Canaan because of their idolatry and wickedness (Gen. 15:16; Exod. 23:20–24, 27–33; Lev. 18:24–28). Many of them were defensive wars, such as those against Assyria (2 Kings 15:29; 17:3–6) and Babylon (25:1–11).

Because of her location in Canaan, a land corridor between Egypt to the south, Assyria to the north, and Babylon to the northeast, Israel faced constant warfare, in which God desired to help. In Moses' song of victory after the defeat of the Egyptian army in the Red Sea God is called a warrior (Exod. 15:3), and Jeremiah claimed, "The LORD is with me like a mighty warrior" (Jer. 20:11). During the time of the judges God used surrounding nations to invade and conquer Israel as a means of punishing His people for their rebellion and to restore her to Himself (Judg.

3:10; 11:4). Only during the reign of Solomon was Israel free of war (1 Kings 4:25), perhaps as a result of his large and effective army (1:26; 10:26; 2 Chron. 1:14).

It is important to notice that in the Bible military service was not a career to be put aside. Naaman, the "commander of the army of the king of Aram" (2 Kings 5:1) was healed of his leprosy by Elisha (5:9–15) without being rebuked for his military service. The same was true of the centurion who asked Jesus for healing for his servant (Matt. 8:5–13; Luke 7:1–10), and of Cornelius, who received Jesus Christ as his Savior under the ministry of Peter (Acts 10:3–48).

When Jesus Christ establishes His millennial kingdom of righteousness and peace, "He will judge between the nations and will settle disputes for many peoples" (Isa. 2:4). At that time, "they will beat their swords into plowshares and their spears into pruning hooks. Nation will not take up sword against nation, nor will they train for war anymore" (Mic. 4:3). Unfortunately until that time war will continue.　　　　**—JAW**

In personal as well as national matters, remember that
"wisdom is better than weapons of war" (Eccles. 9:18)
and "a gentle answer turns away wrath" (Prov. 15:1).

Wealth

THE BIBLE EMPHASIZES THE FACT that God is the Creator, Owner, and Distributor of wealth. Possession of riches is not condemned by Scripture. In fact, some of the great stalwarts of the faith were men of wealth, such as Abraham, Isaac, Job, Solomon, Joseph of Arimathea, Barnabas, and Philemon.

In the Old Testament, riches were considered an indication of God's blessing (1 Sam. 2:7; Eccles. 5:19). He promised material prosperity to Israel so long as they obeyed His laws (Deut. 7:12–15). This pledge is repeated and expanded in Deuteronomy 28. Moses declared to the people, "If you fully obey the LORD your God and carefully follow all his commands I give you today, the LORD your God will set you high above all the nations on earth. . . . The LORD will grant you abundant prosperity—in the fruit of your womb, the young of your livestock and the crops of your ground. . . . However, if you do not obey the LORD your God and do not carefully follow all his commands and decrees I am giving you today, all these curses will come upon you and overtake you. . . . The LORD will send on you curses, confusion and rebuke in everything you put your hand to, until you are destroyed and come to sudden ruin because of the evil you have done in forsaking him" (28:1, 11, 15, 20). God also promised material blessing to individual Israelites who obeyed the Lord's commands. The psalmist declared, "Blessed is the man who fears the LORD, who finds great delight in his commands. . . . Wealth and riches are in his house, and his righteousness endures forever" (Ps. 112:1, 3).

The Old Testament also emphasizes that wealth has its dangers in that it can war against the soul. It can cause a person to trust in his riches rather than in God. Biblical warnings about this sin are numerous (Deut. 8:13–14; Pss. 49:6–7; 52:7; 62:10; Prov. 18:11).

Jesus said much about wealth. Basic to His teaching was the important principle that "a man's life does not consist in the abundance of his possessions" (Luke 12:15). Jesus warned believers not to amass riches on earth but rather in heaven, because "where your treasure is, there your heart will be also" (Matt. 6:21). He said that the deceitfulness of wealth stifles the Word of God and makes it unfruitful in the heart (13:22). After His conversation with a wealthy young man whose heart was focused on his wealth rather than on God, Jesus said, "It is hard for a rich man to enter the kingdom of heaven" (19:23). Wealth can even imperil one's salvation! After giving the parable of the shrewd manager, Jesus warned, "No servant can serve two masters. Either he will hate the one and love the other, or he will be devoted to the one and despise the other. You cannot serve both God and Money" (Luke 16:13).

The Book of Acts records positive and negative illustrations of the use of wealth in the early church in Jerusalem. To meet the material needs of poor believers, others, including Barnabas, sold their lands or houses and gave the money to the apostles to distribute to the needy (Acts 4:32–37). Ananias and Sapphira, however, lied to God and the apostles about the amount of money they brought, and that deceit led to their deaths (5:1–11).

The Epistles have less to say about money than the Gospels; however, Paul and James did address the subject. Paul sharply warned that people who pursue wealth may fall into a trap that leads to destruction because "the love of money is a root of all kinds of evil. Some people, eager for money, have wandered from the faith and pierced themselves with many griefs" (1 Tim. 6:10). The apostle further charged the wealthy to be generous, sharing their riches and thus laying up "treasure for themselves as a firm foundation for the coming age" (6:18–19). James admonished believers not to show favoritism to the rich when they met together (James 2:1–13). He also denounced the unsaved wealthy of his day who had accumulated their riches by defrauding the innocent and the poor (5:1–6).

Scripture also refers metaphorically to spiritual wealth or riches. Paul spoke of "the riches of his [God's] kindness, tolerance and patience" (Rom. 2:4); the "riches of his glory" (9:23); the great spiritual riches to be enjoyed by Gentiles after the conversion of Israel at Christ's second coming (11:12); "the depth of the riches of the wisdom and knowledge of God!" (11:33); "the riches of God's grace that he lavished on us with all wisdom and understanding" (Eph. 1:7–8); "the incomparable riches of his grace, expressed in his kindness to us in Christ Jesus" (2:7); and "the glorious riches of this mystery, which is Christ in you, the hope of glory" (Col. 1:27). The spiritual wealth of the believer is well summarized in 2 Corinthians 8:9, "For you know the grace of our Lord Jesus Christ, that though he was rich, yet for your sakes he became poor, so that you through his poverty might become rich."   **—DKC**

Determine not to allow your possessions to war against your soul.

Will of God

THE BIBLE FREQUENTLY SPEAKS of God's purposes and plans as His "will." His will usually refers to what He has decreed, but occasionally God's will refers to what He desires but has not decreed. For example, it is His will (desire) that no one perish (2 Pet. 3:9), but He has not decreed that everyone will be saved. Nor is it His desire that any children should be unsaved (Matt. 18:14).

Many acts of God, however, are His will in the sense that He has planned them and will carry (or has carried) them out. It was His will to create "all things" (Rev. 4:11), and even birds do not fall apart from His will or plan (Matt. 10:29). It was His plan that Christ be crucified. As Isaiah wrote, "It was the Lord's will to crush him [the Messiah] and cause him to suffer" (Isa. 53:10). When the people crucified Him, they did, as Peter said, what God's "power and will had decided beforehand should happen" (Acts 4:28). Jesus was handed over to them "by God's set purpose" (2:23).

Jesus said His ministry was "to do the will of him who sent me" (John 4:34; 6:38). In His praying in Gethsemane He said He was willing to go to the cross because He knew that was the Father's will (Luke 22:42). This was anticipated in Psalm 40:8, as explained in Hebrews 10:7, 9.

Jesus said that the Father's will or plan is that everyone who believes in Christ will have eternal life (John 6:40). Paul wrote that those who believe in Christ are saved "because of [God's] own purpose and grace" (2 Tim. 1:9), for they are "called according to his purpose" (Rom. 8:28). This plan also means that believers are adopted as God's children "in accordance with his pleasure and will" (Eph. 1:5).

By His will God also gives spiritual gifts to believers (Heb. 2:4). In five of his epistles Paul acknowledged that he was an apostle only because God willed it (1 Cor. 1:1; 2 Cor. 1:1; Eph. 1:1; Col. 1:1; 2 Tim. 1:1).

God also willed (planned) that believing Jews and Gentiles be united in the body of Christ (Eph. 2:15; 3:11).

Believers are to seek to know or understand God's will (Acts 22:14; Eph. 5:17; Col. 1:9), and are to "do" it, that is, to see that what He desires is carried out in their lives. As David prayed, "Teach me to do your will" (Ps. 143:10). While the Bible does not give a specific formula on how each believer should find God's will for his education or vocation, the Scriptures do present specific commands that express His will. It is God's will (desire) that believers be holy (1 Thess. 4:3), that they be grateful (5:18), dedicate themselves to the Lord (2 Cor. 8:5), do good (1 Pet. 2:15), and suffer, if necessary, for doing good (3:17; 4:19). They are to live not for human desires but for God's will (4:2).

God wants us to make wise decisions, taking into account circumstances, wise counsel, the leading of the Spirit, and biblical principles. When a Christian follows God's will, his or her relationship to Christ is made more intimate (Matt. 12:50), and he is assured of rewards in heaven (Heb. 10:36). Unlike the world, which will pass away, those who follow the will of God will live forever (1 John 2:17).

Therefore believers are to be equipped to do God's will (Heb. 13:21) and are to stand firm in it (Col. 4:12). God listens to the prayers of those who do His will (John 9:31), and He answers prayers that are voiced with the desire that His will be done (1 John 5:14; see also Rom. 1:10; 15:32; James 4:15).

We can rest in the fact that God's will is "righteous" (Deut. 33:21) and "good, pleasing, and perfect" (Rom. 12:2).   **—JFW**

Rejoice in the fact that God
"works out everything in conformity with the purpose of his will" (Eph. 1:11).

Wisdom

CONTRASTS OFTEN MAKE TRUTH more recognizable. This seems to be the method used in the Bible to enable us to understand true wisdom. In teaching about wisdom Solomon used the figure of two women (Prov. 8–9). One is a virtuous lady, called wisdom, who is concerned about others (8:1–5). She speaks words that are worthy, right, just, and true (8:6–9). What she has to offer is more precious than gold or rubies (8:10–11). Her ways will help people know and understand God (9:10), and those who follow her will enjoy many happy and long years (9:11). In stark contrast is the woman called Folly (9:13). She cares only for her own enjoyment. She is seductive, and what she says is untrue (9:17–18). Her ways do not lead to God; in fact, they lead to destruction. The Book of Proverbs makes numerous observations about the characteristics and actions of wise people in contrast to foolish people.

In Jesus' teaching ministry He often used contrasts to sharpen certain distinctions. In explaining the difference between a wise person and a foolish person, He contrasted the actions of a man who built his house on a rock and the one who built on sand. Jesus said the person who hears His word and puts it into practice is like the wise man, but a foolish person disregards His teaching (Matt. 7:24–27). As He said sometime later, "Wisdom is proved right by her actions" (11:19).

A striking contrast in Paul's teaching concerns wisdom. In explaining the gospel message to the Corinthian church, he contrasted the wisdom of humankind to the wisdom of God (1 Cor. 1:20–31). In God's wisdom He chooses the weak things of the world to confound the wisdom of the unsaved world. To Gentiles God's wisdom seems foolish because it involved Jesus, who was rejected by His people and crucified. The world's wisdom *seems* superior because of its eloquent words of knowledge and philosophy (1:20). It has the illusion of cleverness and is bold and persuasive (2:4). Because this thinking has no room for God, it will perish and be brought to nothing (2:6).

James drew a similar contrast about wisdom. He stated that true wisdom, which comes down from heaven (James 3:17), reflects the very characteristics of the Lord and is recognizable in the life of a believer. The world's so-called wisdom, however, is the exact opposite; it is "earthly, unspiritual, of the devil" (3:15). This, too, can be detected because its qualities result in evil practices (3:16).

In a general sense wisdom means to have understanding and good judgment. It also carries the thought of discernment and skill, knowing how to apply knowledge, whether to abstract matters or to things more tangible. The worldly wise may possess knowledge and expertise that make them successful in business, the professions, or the arts. Nebuchadnezzar, for example, was considered an outstanding national leader and had wise men in his cabinet, but they did not know God (Dan. 4:18). God in His grace has created people with the ability to think, learn, be creative, have skills in many areas, and be able to apply these successfully. Individuals who have no relationship with God can be wise in this one-dimensional way and can function well in this world system. But this wisdom lacks the quality of true wisdom, which can come only through a personal relationship with God (Prov. 1:7). Human wisdom, no matter how brilliant, will always fall short of the divine aspect of wisdom and is doomed for failure, with the end result of despair (Eccles. 1:18; Eph. 4:17–19).

In contrast to this natural wisdom is the wisdom that finds its source in God. Daniel's statement about "the God of heaven" emphasizes that all wisdom belongs to God. He gives wisdom to the wise, and only He can reveal things unknown to human understanding (Dan. 2:19–23). The Bible states that God gave wisdom to the craftsmen who built the tabernacle (Exod. 31:3–11) and workers who made the priestly garments (28:3–5). This indicates that what God granted went beyond normal skills.

Solomon was given unusual abilities to govern the people of Israel (1 Kings 4:29–31; 2 Chron. 1:11–12). Even other worldly leaders realized that his wisdom was superior (1 Kings 10:6–9). The wisdom from God is so distinct it can even be recognized by pagans (Dan. 5:14).

The New Testament expresses the ultimate fact about wisdom when Paul wrote that all the treasures of wisdom and knowledge reside in Christ (Col. 2:2–3). The apostle John was given the privilege of viewing heavenly scenes. In one scene he saw thousands of angels in heaven praising Jesus Christ, the Lamb of God, for His greatness, including His wisdom (Rev. 5:11–12). In the other scene he saw a great multitude of people from every nation, tribe, people, and language, who will participate with the angels in offering praise to God for His wisdom, power, and strength (7:9–12). —WGJ

Ask the Lord for wisdom to understand His Word and discern truth,
and then be consistent in applying what you know to be right.

Woman

THE CREATION OF THE HUMAN RACE was the capstone of God's creative work. The creation of both male and female was necessary to achieve the image of God (Gen. 1:26–27) in human beings. The Hebrew word ʾādām was the generic name for humanity, including both male and female, as well as the specific name for the male (2:20).

The detailed account of woman's creation, as well as man's, follows in Genesis 2. Adam was formed "from the dust of the ground" and "became a living being" when God "breathed into his nostrils the breath of life" (2:7). Then, after the man named all the animals and birds without finding a "suitable helper" for him (2:19–20), God anesthetized Adam, took one of his ribs, and "made a woman from the rib he had taken out of the man" (2:21–22). Adam said, "She shall be called 'woman,' for she was taken out of man" (2:23). "For this reason," God said, "a man will leave his father and mother and be united to his wife, and they will become one flesh" (2:24). These accounts reveal the basic equality of the male and the female as well as the order of relationship between them.

This order of relationship is stated by the apostle Paul when he wrote, "For Adam was formed first, then Eve" (1 Tim. 2:13), and, "For man did not come from woman, but woman from man; neither was man created for woman, but woman for man" (1 Cor. 11:8–9). As a result "the head of the woman is man" (11:3), and "in the Lord, however, woman is not independent of man, nor is man independent of woman. For as woman came from man, so also man is born of woman. But everything comes from God" (11:11–12).

Because "the husband is the head of the wife as Christ is the head of the church, his body" (Eph. 5:23), wives are to "submit to [their] husbands as to the Lord" (5:22) and "as the church submits to Christ, so also wives should submit to their husbands in everything" (5:24; compare Col. 3:18; Titus 2:5; 1 Pet. 3:1). This follows the command to all believers to "submit to one another out of reverence for Christ" (Eph. 5:21) and precedes the command to husbands to love their wives "just as Christ loved the church" (5:25) and "as their own bodies" (5:28).

To some degree this position of the woman in the family and in the church is the result of Eve's yielding to the temptation of the serpent in the Garden of Eden and her leading Adam into sin (Gen. 3:1–8). Man's headship is seen in the fact that sin entered the human race through Adam (Rom. 5:12, 14–18), but the fact remains that "Adam was not the one deceived; it was the woman who was deceived and became a sinner" (1 Tim. 2:14; see also 2 Cor. 11:3). As a result Paul wrote, "I do not permit a woman to teach or to have authority over a man; she must be silent" (1 Tim. 2:12). This silence is in the leadership and ministry of the congregation, because Paul gave directions for a woman when "praying or prophesying" (1 Cor. 11:5, 13).

The woman's position of importance together with the man is seen in the commandment, "Honor your father and your mother" (Exod. 20:12; Lev. 19:3; Deut. 5:16; 27:16; Matt. 15:5; 19:19; Mark 7:10; 10:19; Luke 18:20; Eph. 6:2). Furthermore some women held positions of importance in Israel in the Old Testament. Miriam, sister of Aaron and Moses (Num. 26:59), was a prophetess, who led the women in a song of victory after the defeat of the Egyptian army in the Red Sea (Exod. 15:20–21). She was a leader in Israel with her brothers (Mic. 6:4). Deborah, also a prophetess, was a judge in Israel (Judg. 4:4), who helped Barak deliver Israel from Sisera (4:6–24) and joined him in a song of deliverance and victory (5:2–31). Also Huldah (2 Kings 22:14–20; 2 Chron. 34:22–29) and Isaiah's wife (Isa. 8:3) were prophetesses. Also important in Israel's history were Rahab (Josh. 6:17–25; Heb. 11:31; James 2:25), Ruth (Ruth 1–4), Hannah (1 Sam. 1–2), and many others.

The woman's vital position of importance and significance, especially as a wife, is stated in the epilogue to the Book of Proverbs (31:10–31), which begins with the statement, "A wife of noble character . . . is worth far more than rubies," and ends with the admonition, "Give her the reward she has earned, and let her works bring her praise at the city gate." She is described as industrious, talented, generous, wise, and a good investor, manager, and merchant, and a source of benefit and blessing to her husband and her children. She epitomizes what God intended the woman and the wife to be when He created her to be "a helper suitable" for man (Gen. 2:18; see also 2:22).

Women also figured prominently in the life and ministry of the Lord Jesus Christ. Foremost, of course, was his mother, Mary, who is mentioned at various points in Jesus' ministry and stood by the cross as He died (John 19:25). Despite His anguish, Jesus committed her care to "the disciple whom he loved" (19:26–27). Mary also met with the believers in Jerusalem after the Lord's ascension (Acts 1:14).

Other women who figured prominently in Jesus' ministry were Martha and Mary, the sisters of Lazarus, in Bethany (Luke 10:38–42; John 11:1–45; 12:1–8), and "Mary (called Magdalene) . . . Joanna . . . Susanna; and many others" (Luke 8:2–3). As Luke explained, "These women were helping to support them [Jesus and the disciples] out of their own means" (8:3), and some of them witnessed Jesus' crucifixion (Matt. 27:55–56). "Mary Magdalene and the other Mary were sitting there opposite the tomb" (Matt. 27:61), intending to return after the Sabbath to prepare Jesus' body for proper burial (28:1). As a result Mary Magdalene was the first person to see the resurrected Christ (John 20:14–18). Still other women whom Jesus encountered in His ministry were the woman at the well at Sychar (4:4–42), the widow of Nain (Luke 7:11–17), and the woman "subject to bleeding for twelve years" (Mark 5:25–34).

Women also figured prominently in the apostolic church and the ministry of the apostles. Other women were with Jesus' mother in the Upper Room after Jesus' ascension (Acts 1:14). Peter restored Tabitha to life (9:36–42), and the disciples gathered in the house of "Mary the mother of John, also called Mark" to pray for Peter's release from prison (12:5, 12–17). Paul spoke highly of Lois and Eunice, Timothy's grandmother and mother (2 Tim. 1:5; 3:14–15), and Lydia was important in the establishment of the church at Philippi (Acts 16:13–15, 40).

Paul called Priscilla and her husband Aquila "my fellow workers in Christ Jesus" (Rom. 16:3). They met him and provided employment for him in Corinth (Acts 18:2–4), and on his way to Syria they accompanied him as far as Ephesus (18:18–19), where they led Apollos into a more accurate knowledge of the gospel (18:26). Apparently they remained and ministered in Ephesus (1 Cor. 16:19; 2 Tim. 4:19). Paul spoke highly of Phoebe (Rom. 16:1–2), Mary (16:6), Tryphena and Tryphosa (16:12), Persis (16:12), Rufus's mother (16:13), Julia, and the sister of Nereus (16:15). Paul's limitations on the ministry of women in church services did not minimize his acceptance of and appreciation for their faithful ministry for Christ.

In the apostolic church women were given ministries to fill, specifically that of prophetess (Acts 21:8–9) and deaconess (Rom. 16:1). Apparently widows in need were provided for (Acts 6:1). Widows over sixty years old were put on a list to receive help if they were not cared for by family members (1 Tim. 5:5–11).

In today's churches there are many opportunities for ministry by women that do not violate Paul's restrictions. The woman is still a helper suitable for the man, who shares in the human image of God.

—JAW

Respect and submit to each other, man and woman, out of reverence for Christ.

Word

IN THE BIBLE THE ENGLISH NOUN *word* translates the Hebrew noun *dābār* and the two Greek nouns *logos* and *rhēma*. These Hebrew and

Greek words refer to a rational utterance that conveys a concept or idea residing in one's mind. As a result the ultimate use of the word *word* is the apostle John's statement, "In the beginning was the Word, and the Word was with God, and the Word was God" (John 1:1). The inevitable result of that statement is that "the Word became flesh, and made his dwelling among us. We have seen his glory, the glory of the One and Only Son, who came from the Father, full of grace and truth" (1:14). This Word, who became incarnate as Jesus Christ, visibly expressed God in the Old Testament as the Angel of the Lord, who was recognized as God (Gen. 16:9–13; 22:11–18; Josh. 5:14–15; Judg. 6:11–27; 13:3–23; 1 Chron. 21:15, 18), and claimed to be God (Exod. 3:2–17).

In addition to the appearance of the Angel of the Lord, God spoke directly to the patriarchs (Gen. 3:9, 11, 13–14, 16–17; 4:6, 9–10, 15; 6:13; 7:1; 8:15; 9:1, 8, 12, 17; 12:1; 13:14) and appeared to them in visions (15:1; 26:2; 46:2; Num. 24:4, 16) or dreams (Gen. 15:12–13; 20:3; 28:12; 31:10–13, 24). God also used visions and dreams to communicate His messages to the prophets, as God explained to Aaron and Miriam (Num. 12:6) and as illustrated by Samuel (1 Sam. 3:1, 15), Solomon (1 Kings 3:5, 15), Isaiah (Isa. 1:1), Micah (Mic. 1:1), Nahum (Nah. 1:1), and Zechariah (Zech. 1:8).

In Abram's vision "the word of the LORD came to Abram" (Gen. 15:1, see also 15:4), indicating that it was an audible as well as visual communication. This also shows that "the word of the LORD" was a message from God, not just a single word or phrase. In His rebuke of Aaron and Miriam, God explained that with Moses, "I speak face to face, clearly and not in riddles" (Num. 12:8; see also Exod. 33:7–11, 18–23; Deut. 34:10). As a result Moses acted "as he was commanded by the word of the LORD" (Num. 3:16, 51).

The phrase "the word of God," therefore, became characteristic of the messages received by the prophets, whether for the present or the future. This began with Samuel (1 Sam. 15:10) and continued with Nathan (2 Sam. 7:4), Gad (24:11), Solomon (1 Kings 6:11), Shemaiah (12:22), Jehu (16:1), Elijah (17:2, 8), Elisha (2 Kings 7:1), and most of the writing prophets.

The phrase "the word of God" is used in connection with John the Baptist (Luke 3:2), who was a prophet in the Old Testament tradition (1:76; see also Matt. 11:9–15; Luke 7:24–27); but it was not used in connection with Jesus, who was the Word of God in person, nor was it used with any other spokesman for God in the New Testament. This is because, although "in the past God spoke to our forefathers through the prophets at many times and in various ways . . . in these last days he has spoken [literally, 'He spoke'] to us by his Son" (Heb. 1:1–2). The message of the apostles centered around the person and work of the Lord Jesus Christ, even when it included truth from the Old Testament.

As a result, the phrases "the word of God" and "the word of the Lord" are identified with the message of the gospel (Acts 8:14, 25; 11:1; 13:5, 44, 46, 49; 19:20; Phil. 1:14; 1 Thess. 2:13; 1 Pet. 1:23). Because the message of the gospel incorporated testimony from the Jewish Scriptures, the Old Testament, those phrases soon became identified with the Scriptures. Paul exhorted the Ephesians to take "the sword of the Spirit, which is the word of God" (6:17), whether spoken or written. Because "the word of God is living and active" (Heb. 4:12; see also 1 Pet. 1:23), Paul charged Timothy, "Preach [literally, 'proclaim as a herald'] the Word" (2 Tim. 4:2), in which case "Word" is capitalized because it applies both to Jesus Christ and to the Scriptures.

The word of God, whether personal, spoken, or written, is "perfect" and has many other admirable qualities (Ps. 19:7–9). Jesus declared, "Heaven and earth will pass away, but my words will never pass away" (Matt. 24:35; Mark 13:31; Luke 21:33), and Peter wrote, "The word of the Lord stands forever. And this is the word that was preached to you" (1 Pet. 1:25). **—JAW**

By life and witness fulfill Paul's charge to Timothy,
"Preach the Word; be prepared in season and out of season" (2 Tim. 4:2).

Work

THE PRIMARY HEBREW WORD translated "work" (*'āsâ*) means "to construct, make, produce," or it refers to the result of such activity. The primary Greek word (*ergon*) comes into English in the word *energy* and speaks of the force or power involved in work. The theme of work in the Bible cannot be considered apart from discussing the work of God involving all three persons—Father, Son, and Holy Spirit—as well as the work of human beings. This involves spiritual as well as physical work. The work of God began with the creation of "the heavens and the earth" (Gen. 1:1), all the plants (1:11–13) and animals on the earth (1:20–25), climaxing with man and woman (1:26–27). Involved in the work of creation were the Word of God, that is, the preincarnate Lord Jesus Christ (John 1:3; Col. 1:16; Heb. 1:2, 10), the Holy Spirit (Gen. 1:2; Ps. 104:30), and God the Father (James 1:17). With the completion of His creative work God "rested from all his work" (Gen. 2:2–3), not because of exhaustion but out of satisfaction.

Despite His being satisfied with His work in creation, God's continuing work is seen in the cohesive principle of the universe, not simply an abstract law of gravity but the active power of God (Rom. 11:36; Eph. 4:6). This is assigned at least in part to the eternal Word who became the incarnate Christ (Col. 1:17; Heb. 1:3). Whenever He so desires, God can suspend and transcend this principle in what we call miracles.

When sin entered the human race, God undertook a new work, a program of providing salvation for all human beings who would respond by faith to His offer and promise. The basis of this provision was the sacrificial substitutionary death of His Son, Jesus Christ, on the cross of Calvary, a provision eternally planned by God the Father (Eph. 1:11; 3:11) and administered through various dispensations (3:9; Rom. 16:25; Col. 1:26). This involved working with Israel as His "own possession among all the peoples . . . a kingdom of priests and a holy nation" (Exod. 19:5–6, NASB; see also Deut. 7:6). The people of Israel have been temporarily put aside because of their rebellion and sin, and so God has extended salvation to the Gentiles and has established the church, the body of Christ (Rom. 11:1–24). When Christ returns to the earth, Israel will be restored to God's favor and regenerated (Deut. 30:1–6, 8; Jer. 23:5–8). Meanwhile the work of the triune God is building the church.

The Lord Jesus Christ joined God the Father in His work of salvation, becoming incarnate, ministering on earth, providing the substitutionary sacrifice for sin, and serving as "head over everything for the church, which is his body" (Eph. 1:22; see also 5:23). As Jesus told His disciples, he came "to do the will of him who sent me and to finish his work" (John 4:34). He told the Jews, "My father is always at his work to this very day, and I, too, am working" (5:17), and, "The very work that the Father has given me to finish, and which I am doing, testifies that the Father has sent me" (5:36).

Jesus said a blind man's condition "happened so that the work of God might be displayed in his life. As long as it is day, we must do the work of him who sent me" (9:3–4). In the Upper Room Jesus told the apostles that "it is the Father, living in me, who is doing his work" (14:10). In anticipation of His impending sacrificial death as well as His earthly ministry, Jesus prayed to God the Father, "I have brought you glory on earth by completing the work you gave me to do" (17:4). On the cross His final words were, "It is finished" (19:30).

When we think of human work, God's judgment on Adam for his sin comes to mind: "Cursed is the ground because of you; through painful toil you will eat of it. . . . By the sweat of your brow you will eat your food" (Gen. 3:17, 19). This speaks of the arduous, disliked side of work. However, before the Fall, human work began on a much more pleasurable note in the Garden of Eden. "The LORD God took the man and put him in the Garden of Eden to work it and take care of it" (2:15). Although all work has a vexing side, the enjoyable, satisfying part has also remained.

In spiritual matters, work has two aspects. The first is man's unsuccessful efforts to earn God's acceptance and approval. Salvation, moreover, is not obtained through human "works." People are "justified by faith apart from observing the law [literally, 'works of the law'"] (Rom. 3:28). Salvation is "the gift of God, not by works, so that no one can boast" (Eph. 2:8–9; see also 2 Tim. 1:9; Titus 3:5).

Second, after receiving salvation by God's grace through faith, the believer is "created in Christ Jesus to do good works, which God prepared in advance for us to do" (Eph. 2:10; see Titus 2:14). The Holy Spirit instructed the church at Antioch, "Set apart for me Barnabas and Saul for the work to which I have called them" (Acts 13:2). Paul recognized his own spiritual work (1 Cor. 9:1; 16:9) and mentioned the spiritual work of Tryphena, Tryphosa, Persis (Rom. 16:12), Timothy (1 Cor. 16:16), and Epaphroditus (Phil. 2:25). He also challenged and encouraged Corinthian believers (1 Cor. 15:58; 2 Cor. 9:8), Archippus (Col. 4:17) and Timothy (2 Tim. 4:5), in the work for the Lord.

When Paul admonished the Philippian Christians to "continue to work out your salvation with fear and trembling" (Phil. 2:12), he was apparently concerned about their problem of discord and selfishness (2:2–5). So he urged them to live in accord with the salvation they already had through faith in Christ. Believers are to work *out* their salvation, that is, to put it into practice, not work *for* their salvation. The word "your" is plural, suggesting that the believers as a congregation were to be delivered from disunity and pride. **—JAW**

Through Bible study and prayer seek to discover and to carry out the work God has prepared for you to do (Eph. 2:10).

World

THE BIBLICAL CONCEPT of the world did not envision the vast universe discovered by modern astronomy. In fact, the primary Hebrew words translated "world" (*'ereṣ* and *tēbēl*) are both also frequently translated "earth" or "land" in referring to the physical ground in part (Exod. 3:8) or in total (Gen. 1:1; 2:1; Pss. 91:2; 93:1). The primary Greek word for "world" is *kosmos,* which identifies the world as an orderly system. A less frequently used word is *aiōn,* from which we get *aeon,* which describes the world in terms of time. Another Greek word is *oikoumenē,* from which comes the word *ecumenical,* which speaks of the inhabited world. Basically in biblical times the people thought and spoke of the world in terms of what they could see and know, much as the average person does today.

The first fact the Bible establishes about the world is that it is God's creation. The psalmist wrote, "The heavens are yours, and yours also the earth; you founded the world and all that is in it" (Ps. 89:11; see also Gen. 1:1; Pss. 24:1; 50:12; 90:2; John 1:3; Col. 1:16; Heb. 1:2). Furthermore the world was created according to a divine plan (Isa. 14:26–27), and God "founded the world by his wisdom" (Jer. 10:12; 51:15; see also Prov. 8:22–31). Therefore, as David wrote, "The heavens declare the glory of God; the skies proclaim the work of his hands. . . . Their voice goes out into all the earth, their words to the ends of the world" (Ps. 19:1–4; see also Job 12:7–10; Isa. 41:19–20; Rom. 1:20).

With the entrance of sin into human experience in the Garden of Eden (Gen. 3:1–8) Satan gained control of the unregenerate human race (Eph. 2:1–2) and the entire world system (1 John 5:19). As a result, the devil could validly offer the Lord Jesus "all the kingdoms of the world" if He would "bow down and worship" him (Matt. 4:8–9). Since the Fall, God has been working to let people know that He is the One to worship, doing this in the Old Testament through miracles, such as David's slaying of Goliath and the Philistines (1 Sam. 17:45–47) and Naaman's healing from leprosy (2 Kings 5:15), and through His choosing and dealing with the people of Israel (Exod. 34:10).

After the provision of salvation in the sacrificial death of His Son on the cross for the world of humanity (John 3:16), God has sought to get the message of the gospel to all the world. Jesus commanded the apostles, "Go into all the world and preach the good news to all creation" (Mark 16:15; see also Matt. 28:19; Acts 1:8). Called by God to be an apostle to the Gentiles (9:15; 22:21), Paul carried the gospel throughout Asia Minor, the Grecian peninsula, and as far as Rome (and possibly on to Spain).

Because the world has been usurped by Satan through deception, people lie under God's condemnation and will ultimately be judged. David wrote that God "will judge the world in righteousness" (Pss. 9:8; 98:9). When God's voice spoke from heaven in anticipation of the Lord's sacrificial death, Jesus explained, "Now is the time for judgment on this world; now the prince of this world will be driven out" (John 12:31). Part of the ministry of the Holy Spirit since His coming after Jesus' resurrection and ascension is to "convict the world of guilt in regard to . . . judgment, . . . because the prince of this world now stands condemned" (John 16:8, 11). Paul told the Athenians that God "has set a day when he will judge the world with justice by the man he has appointed" (Acts 17:31), the resurrected Jesus Christ.

Since the world in the sense of the world system is now controlled by Satan (1 John 5:19; see also 2 Cor. 4:4; Eph. 2:2), the apostle John commanded, "Do not love the world or anything in the world" (1 John 2:15). He added that "everything in the world . . . comes not from the Father" (2:16) and that "the world and its desires pass away" (2:17).

While God seems to be postponing judgment on the present world because He "desires all men to be saved and to come to the knowledge of the truth" (1 Tim. 2:4, NASB; see 2 Pet. 3:9), the Christian has to live and minister in the world (2 Cor. 10:3), face the hatred of the world (1 John 3:13), and do battle against the devil and "the powers of this dark world" (Eph. 6:12). Believers are to "use the things of the world" (1 Cor. 7:31), but they must constantly remember that "friendship with the world is hatred toward God" and that "anyone who chooses to be a friend of the world becomes an enemy of God" (James 4:4). When God's time of judgment comes, believers "will judge the world" (1 Cor. 6:2) and angels (6:3).   —JAW

While here on the earth we are to be a light in the world (Matt. 5:14)
and a witness for Christ as we look for His return.

Worship

WHEN GOD CREATED THE HUMAN RACE, it was His purpose to reveal Himself to His creatures so that they in turn would recognize Him and respond to Him in various ways. He placed within the heart of each individual the desire and need to worship. Even without a specific recorded command, Cain and Abel sensed the need to bring an offering to God. It was a matter of the heart, as indicated by God's conversation with Cain. If he did what was right, God would accept his sacrifice (Gen. 4:6–7). Noah built an altar (8:20), but who taught him to do so? Abraham built an altar to the Lord after God appeared to him (12:7). When Abraham was taking Isaac to offer him as a sacrifice in obedience to the Lord's command, he understood this event as an occasion for worship (22:5). Centuries later God gave Moses the Law, with its prescribed manner of worship for the nation Israel.

A partial understanding of the meaning of worship is derived from the words the Bible uses for worship. One Hebrew word means "to bow down or to prostrate oneself on the ground." This shows respect, adoration, and a recognition of someone considered superior, especially royalty. The corresponding Greek term is *proskyneō*, "to fall down and prostrate oneself." Another Hebrew word, *'ābad*, conveys the concept of serving, and its Greek counterpart, *latreuō*, expresses the same idea of serving. These words portray the outward form of worship, which is to be an expression of an inner attitude of humility and service toward the Lord. The Bible emphasizes that only worship from the heart pleases the Lord.

Since the psalms were personal expressions of worship, they provide insight into the meaning of individual worship during Old Testament times. Psalms show that worship stems from a personal heart relationship with God. These expressions of worship in the psalms were varied and manifold, including praise, petition, and thanksgiving. They included confession mingled with frustration and uncertainty. Also the psalmists wrote many beautiful descriptions of God and His greatness. In fact, every aspect of God's character can be seen in the psalms, thus revealing that worship centers around the Lord, extolling His virtues and expressing thanks for His salvation and watchful protection.

The Old Testament prophets often wrote of the danger of superficial worship—words and actions without meaning. Many prophets ministered during times when Israel was turning away from God. For example, Jeremiah called people in Israel to change their ways as their worship was empty words and phrases (Jer. 7:2–7). He was also aware that people were worshiping other gods, even being more wicked than their ancestors who had forsaken the Lord (16:11). Because they worshiped pagan gods, God brought great devastation on Jerusalem (22:9).

Yet there was hope for the nation and the people. The prophets spoke of the future when people from all nations will go to Jerusalem and worship the Lord (Isa. 66:22; Zech. 14:16). The nation Israel has a glorious future, and the worship of the Lord will be a central feature in that day.

Probably the most definitive passage concerning worship is John 4:4–26, which reveals Jesus' words about worship in His conversation with a Samaritan woman. When she spoke of the tension between the ways the Samaritans and the Jews worshiped, Jesus grasped the opportunity to teach an important lesson about true worship (4:23).

In this brief passage Jesus explained a number of things about worship. He confirmed the fact that God created man to worship Him (4:23). He affirmed that Israel's worship was significant because God had revealed Himself to the nation and had chosen them to be the channel of salvation to the world. Worship apart from God is not genuine

(4:22). A major change was coming (4:21, 23); in fact, Jesus said it "has now come" (4:23). God would remain the focus of worship, but a much more intimate relationship would be in effect. True worshipers would be able to go directly to God; in fact, He would be seeking them.

Jesus then emphasized two concepts about worship. Worship is to be "in spirit and in truth" (4:24), and these concepts are in keeping with the character of God. Since God is "spirit" the best way to reach Him is in the realm of the spirit, that is, in one's innermost being. This calls for believers to exercise faith in the Lord, because without faith it is impossible to please Him (Heb. 11:6). The second aspect, "in truth," is equally important, for worship is possible only if it conforms to what God has revealed. Jesus Himself is the truth (John 14:6). Later He reminded the disciples that when the Spirit of truth would come He would lead them into all truth (John 16:13). This was fulfilled with the writings of Paul, Peter, John, and the other New Testament authors.

Jerusalem had been the center of life and worship for the Jews. But because of the Lord's death, resurrection, and ascension, the place of worship is no longer important. Christ has become the Great High Priest in heaven, and His throne of grace is available to everyone who comes to Him in faith (Heb. 4:14–16). No longer are animal sacrifices needed, and no one now needs to approach God through an earthly priest.

Worship was a vital part of church life, as recorded in the Book of Acts. The earliest report in Acts 2:42–47 gives us a picture of a worshiping congregation. Paul's epistles give insight into worship as people prayed, sang, listened to the reading of Scripture, gave generously of their resources, and expressed praise to God. On the first day of the week believers gathered in worship to celebrate their faith in the Lord.

Interestingly the Book of Revelation has almost as many references to worship as all the other New Testament passages combined. The scene in heaven described by John in Revelation 4–5 is unparalleled in all of Scripture. Based on the qualities of God the Father and His Son, Jesus Christ, angels and all the redeemed in heaven fall down in worship. Revelation 21 records John's vision of the new heavens and the new earth, the eternal state when all the redeemed will worship the Lord continually. Worshiping and serving the Lord God will be the eternal privilege of all those who have been redeemed by the precious blood of the Savior.   —WGJ

*Take time every day to reflect on the majesty of the Lord
and allow your heart to respond in praise and adoration.*

Wrath

SINCE GOD IS HOLY and absolutely righteous, it should not be surprising that these attributes have a negative aspect. God is called a "consuming fire" (Heb. 12:29), that is, One who is to be feared (Isa. 8:13–14; Heb. 10:31). He is a God of wrath (Rev. 6:16–17). Wrath is not considered one of God's attributes, but it is a necessary response because of who He is. The prophet Habakkuk declared that the eyes of God are too pure to look on evil (Hab. 1:13); thus the very nature of His character demands His wrath. Those who failed to recognize God, even though the creation has clearly revealed Him, deserve His wrath (Rom. 1:32). When God's love is rejected, it is only right that His wrath be expressed (John 3:16, 36).

The wrath of God is against all ungodliness and wickedness, and the earliest recorded expression of His wrath can be traced to the rebellion of Satan and the angels who followed with Him (Luke 10:18; 2 Pet. 2:4). The Old Testament includes many illustrations of God's wrath. The Flood covered the entire world and wiped out every living creature except those in the ark because of the wickedness God could not tolerate (Gen. 6:7). He destroyed Sodom and Gomorrah because their sin was so grievous (18:20). The plagues of Egypt were God's judgment on Pharaoh and his nation and were targeted against the gods of Egypt (Exod. 12:12; 15:7). Before the Israelites ever stepped into the Promised Land, God warned them that disobedience to the Mosaic Law would bring His severe judgment on them (Deut. 28:58–63). The Assyrian Captivity was a result of God's wrath against Israel's sins (Isa. 9:18–21). Jeremiah warned the people of Judah that God's wrath would come on them unless they had a change of heart (Jer. 4:3–4). The Babylonian Captivity became a reality because of Judah's sin (7:20). Scores of times the prophets spoke of God's anger and wrath.

Warnings about God's wrath abound in various New Testament passages, reminding believers that an unprecedented time of judgment is coming on the world before the Lord returns to establish His millennial kingdom. Jesus taught this to His disciples (Matt. 24:15, 21), and Jeremiah and Daniel had prophesied it too (Jer. 30:7; Dan. 9:27; 11:31; 12:1). This devastating series of events in the seven-year Tribulation is recorded in Revelation 6–18. This period of time will unveil "the wrath of the Lamb" (6:16). During this time at least two-thirds of the people living on the earth will be wiped out (6:8; 8:11; 13:15; 16:18–21). People will seek death to try to escape God's wrath (6:16–17; 9:6). The coming of the Lord with His saints will mark the end of this terrible Tribulation period (19:11–16).

Only faith in the Lord Jesus Christ can save people from the wrath of God (John 3:36; Eph. 2:3–4). His death paid for the sins of the world, and believers are justified by His blood and "saved from God's wrath through him" (Rom. 5:9). Rejecting Christ will ultimately cause an individual to suffer the wrath of God and to be cast into the lake of fire (Rev. 20:14–15). Believers will be delivered from eternal wrath (John 3:16; Rom. 6:23). Also those who trust in Christ will be saved from the time of wrath known as the Tribulation (1 Thess. 1:10; 5:9; Rev. 3:10).

—WGJ

Be sensitive to those who are in danger of experiencing the wrath of God,
and pray fervently for their salvation.

Scripture Index

16:33	264, 288, 357	1:9	157	4:1–6	279
17	237, 343	1:9–11	23	4:2	20
17:1–26	56	1:10	14	4:4	113
17:2	127	1:10–11	157	4:5–12	113
17:4	311, 388	1:14	274, 383, 384	4:8	166
17:4–5	139	1:16	20	4:8–12	20
17:5	24, 139, 157, 355	1:20	20	4:10	302
17:11/12	320	1:21–22	20	4:12	108
17:15	267, 317, 320	1:24	155	4:18/19–20	146
17:17	304, 316, 362	1:24–26	20	4:24	275
17:20	274, 320	2	100	4:26	55, 163, 241
17:20–23	1	2:4	166, 353	4:27	163
17:21	320	2:6/8	353	4:28	90, 104, 378
17:23	20, 231, 268	2:11	353	4:30	163
17:24	320	2:13	353	4:31	166, 275
18:12–13	279	2:14–36	20	4:32	227
18:28	228, 261	2:15	353	4:32–37	376
18:31	78	2:17	101	4:35	20
18:37	362	2:20	84	4:37	20
18:38	149, 362	2:21	30	5	249
18:39	261	2:22	247	5:1–11	20, 98, 376
19:4/6	149	2:23	90, 104, 378	5:3	164, 361
19:10/11	145	2:24–28	301	5:3–4	164
19:14	261	2:27	163	5:4	361
19:30	77, 329, 388	2:30	135	5:9	348
19:38	95	2:31	55, 127	5:11	97
19:39	15	2:32–33	302	5:12	20, 346
20:17	23, 24, 117, 121, 157	2:36	55, 225, 241	5:12–14	113
		2:36–42	226	5:12–16	153
20:19/21	264	2:38	33, 298	5:16	90, 92
20:21–23	146	2:42	110, 227, 275	5:17	160
20:25	363	2:42–47	393	5:19	14
20:26	264	2:44	227	5:21	346
20:28	22	2:46	227	5:23–31	20
20:30–31	112	3	249	5:29	146, 255
21:15	208	3:1–10	153	5:29–32	302
21:15–17	246	3:11–26	20	5:30	81
		3:14	163, 307	5:31	298
Acts		3:14–15	72	5:32	255
1:2	104	3:16	113	5:37	19
1:3	20, 79	3:18	55	5:42	20, 241, 346
1:5	34, 165	3:18–19	79	6	217
1:6	205	3:19	298	6:1	216, 384
1:6–11	23	3:20	241	6:1–4	227
1:8	65, 108, 146, 165, 390	3:21	11, 30	6:1–5	214
		3:22	281	6:1–6	57

The
Swindoll Leadership Library

ANGELS, SATAN AND DEMONS
Dr. Robert Lightner

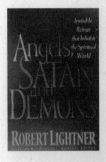

The supernatural world gets a lot of attention these days in books, movies, and television series, but what does the Bible say about these other-worldly beings? Dr. Robert Lightner answers these questions with an in-depth look at the world of the "invisible" as expressed in Scripture.

BIBLICAL COUNSELING FOR TODAY
Dr. Jeffrey Watson

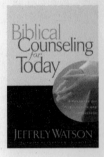

Written by veteran counselor Dr. Jeffrey Watson, this handbook explores counseling from a biblical perspective—how to use Scripture to help others work through issues, choose healthy goals, and work toward those goals for a healthier, more spiritually grounded life. In *Biblical Counseling for Today,* both professional and lay counselors will find insightful, relevant answers to strengthen their ministries.

COACHING MINISTRY TEAMS
Dr. Kenn Gangel

When it comes to effective discipleship, it takes a discipler, a coach, who is capable of not only leading by example, but also empowering his "players" to stay the course. In fifteen practical chapters, Christian education expert Kenn Gangel examines, among other topics, the attitudes in "The Heart of a Champion," leadership modeling in "Setting the Standard for the Team," and strategic planning in "Looking Down the Field."

THE CHURCH
Dr. Ed Hayes

In this indispensable guide, Dr. Ed Hayes explores the labyrinths of the church, delving into her history, doctrines, rituals, and resources to find out what it means to be the Body of Christ on earth. Both passionate and precise, this essential volume offers solid insights on worship, persecution, missions, and morality: a bold call to unity and renewal.

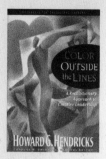

COLOR OUTSIDE THE LINES
Dr. Howard G. Hendricks

Just as the apostle Paul prodded early Christians "not to be conformed" to the world, Dr. Howard Hendricks vividly—and unexpectedly—extends that biblical theme and charges us to learn the art of living creatively, reflecting the image of the Creator rather than the culture.

EFFECTIVE CHURCH GROWTH STRATEGIES
Dr. Joseph Wall and Dr. Gene Getz

Effective Church Growth Strategies outlines the biblical foundations necessary for raising healthy churches. Wall and Getz examine the groundwork essential for church growth, qualities of biblically healthy churches, methods for planting a new church, and steps for numerical and spiritual growth. The authors' study of Scripture, history, and culture will spark a new vision for today's church leaders.

EFFECTIVE PASTORING
Dr. Bill Lawrence

In *Effective Pastoring*, Dr. Bill Lawrence examines what it means to be a pastor in the 21st century. Lawrence discusses often overlooked issues, writing transparently about the struggles of the pastor, the purpose and practice of servant leadership, and the roles and relationships crucial to pastoring. In doing so, he offers a revealing look beneath the "how to" to the "how to be" for pastors.

EMPOWERED LEADERS
Dr. Hans Finzel

What is leadership really about? The rewards, excitement, and exhilaration? Or the responsibilities, frustrations, and exhausting nights? Dr. Hans Finzel takes readers on a journey into the lives of the Bible's great leaders, unearthing powerful principles for effective leadership in any situation.

END TIMES
Dr. John F. Walvoord

Long regarded as one of the top prophecy experts, Dr. John F. Walvoord now explores world events in light of biblical prophecy. By examining all of the prophetic passages in the Bible, Walvoord clearly explains the mystery behind confusing verses and conflicting viewpoints. This is the definitive work on prophecy for Bible students.

THE FORGOTTEN BLESSING
Dr. Henry Holloman

For many Christians, the gift of God's grace is central to their faith. But another gift—sanctification—is often overlooked. *The Forgotten Blessing* clarifies this essential doctrine, showing us what it means to be set apart, and how the process of sanctification can forever change our relationship with God.

GOD
Dr. J. Carl Laney

With tenacity and clarity, Dr. J. Carl Laney makes it plain: it's not enough to know *about* God. We can know *God* better. This book presents a practical path to life-changing encounters with the goodness, greatness, and glory of our Creator.

THE HOLY SPIRIT
Dr. Robert Gromacki

In *The Holy Spirit*, Dr. Robert Gromacki examines the personality, deity, symbols, and gifts of the Holy Spirit, while recapping the ministry of the Spirit throughout the Old Testament, the Gospel Era, the life of Christ, the Book of Acts, and the lives of believers.

HUMANITY AND SIN
Dr. Robert A. Pyne

Sin may seem like an outdated concept these days, but its consequences remain as destructive as ever. Dr. Robert A. Pyne takes a close look at humankind through the pages of Scripture and the lens of modern culture. As never before, readers will understand sin's overarching effect on creation and our world today.

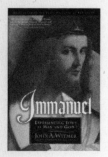

IMMANUEL
Dr. John A. Witmer

Dr. John A. Witmer presents the almighty Son of God as a living, breathing, incarnate man. He shows us a full picture of the Christ in four distinct phases: the Son of God before He became man, the divine suffering man on Earth, the glorified and ascended Christ, and the reigning King today.

A LIFE OF PRAYER
Dr. Paul Cedar

Dr. Paul Cedar explores prayer through three primary concepts, showing us how to consider, cultivate, and continue a lifestyle of prayer. This volume helps readers recognize the unlimited potential and the awesome purpose of prayer.

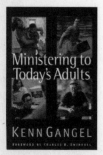

MINISTERING TO TODAY'S ADULTS
Dr. Kenn Gangel

After 40 years of research and experience, Dr. Kenn Gangel knows what it takes to reach adults. In an easy-to-grasp, easy-to-apply style, Gangel offers proven systematic strategies for building dynamic adult ministries.

MORAL DILEMMAS
J. Kerby Anderson

Should biblically informed Christians be for or against capital punishment? How should we as Christians view abortion, euthanasia, genetic engineering, divorce, and technology? In this comprehensive, cutting-edge book, J. Kerby Anderson challenges us to thoughtfully analyze the dividing issues facing our age, while equipping believers to maneuver through the ethical and moral land mines of our times.

THE NEW TESTAMENT EXPLORER
Mark Bailey and Tom Constable

The New Testament Explorer provides a concise, on-target map for traveling through the New Testament. Mark Bailey and Tom Constable guide the reader paragraph by paragraph through the New Testament, providing an up-close-and-to-the-point examination of the leaders behind the page and the theological implications of the truths revealed. A great tool for teachers and pastors alike, this exploration tool comes equipped with outlines for further study, narrative discussion, and applicable truths for teaching and for living.

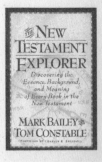

SALVATION
Earl D. Radmacher

God's ultimate gift to His children is salvation. In this volume, Earl Radmacher offers an in-depth look at the most fundamental element of the Christian faith. From defining the essentials of salvation to explaining the result of Christ's sacrifice, this book walks readers through the spiritual meaning, motives, application, and eternal result of God's work of salvation in our lives.

SPIRIT-FILLED TEACHING
Dr. Roy B. Zuck

Whether you teach a small Sunday school class or a standing-room-only crowd at a major university, the process of teaching can be demanding and draining. This lively book brings a new understanding of the Holy Spirit's essential role in teaching.

TALE OF THE TARDY OXCART AND 1501 OTHER STORIES
Dr. Charles R. Swindoll

In this rich volume, you'll have access to resourcing Dr. Charles Swindoll's favorite anecdotes on prayer or quotations for grief. In *The Tale of the Tardy Oxcart*, thousands of illustrations are arranged by subjects alphabetically for quick-and-easy access. A perfect resource for all pastors and speakers.

WOMEN AND THE CHURCH
Dr. Lucy Mabery-Foster

Women and the Church provides an overview of the historical, biblical, and cultural perspectives on the unique roles and gifts women bring to the church, while exploring what it takes to minister to women today. Important insight for any leader seeking to understand how to more effectively minister to women and build women's ministries in the local church.